SPIRITUAL ECOLOGY OF MONASTERIES AND GOMPAS

Himalya Past and Present Series

MOUNTAINS OF THE GOD

Spiritual Ecology of Himalaya Region

(In Two Volumes)

SPIRITUAL ECOLOGY OF MONASTERIES AND GOMPAS

(Volume 2)

Editor

K.S. Gulia

ISHA BOOKS

Delhi - 110009

Spiritual Ecology of Monasteries and Gompas

ISBN: 81-8205-420-6 (Set)

ISBN: 81-8205-422-2 (Vol. 2)

Published in 2007 in India by
ISHA Books
B-63, 1st Floor, New Gupta Colony,
Near DDA Market,
Delhi-110009
Phone: 9212142040
E-mail: ishabooks@hotmail.com

Laser Typesetting at: Best Computers, Delhi
Printed at: Salasar Imaging System, Delhi

Contents

Introduction

In this book, *Spiritual Ecology of Gompas and Monasteries,* we have discussed in detail topics like religious ecology, temples and monasteries, lamaism and the monks, monastic institutions and priesthood, monasteries and their economic structures, tantric Buddhism and spiritual, ecology.

In India, dense jungle and mountain ranges have always been the abodes of gods, goddesses, saints, rishis and hermits. This is so with the Himalayas, in the period that Buddhism was in ascendancy in India, it made great inroads in the Himalayan region. Later on when Buddhism and Hinduism converged, leaving a thin line to separate them, these were the two religions, which for seventeen hundred years dominated the region of Himalayas from Kashmir to Nepal and Sikkim. When Islam made inroads into India, it came to Kashmir also though it did not travel far in the Himalayas, and somehow stayed restricted to some areas of Himachal Pradesh. There are many temples in Jammu and Kashmir, in Himachal Pradesh, in Nepal and Bhutan and Sikkim. There are monasteries and gompas in Ladakh, Nepal, Bhutan and Sikkim. Month after month, week after week, day after day, devotees and pilgrims, from the length and breadth of the country come to these temples and shrines for *darshans* of their deities. In Jammu, there is Vaishno Devi temple, in Kashmir there is the Holy Cave of Amarnath. Every district of Jammu and Kashmir, Himachal Pradesh, Uttaranchal, Nepal, Bhutan and Sikkim has these famous temples, shrines, gompas and monasteries.

In Chapter 1 of the book, we discuss the temples and monasteries of Himalayan region. Hinduism and Buddhism are the main religions of people living in the Himalayas. These faiths have led to the establishment of hundreds of temples and monasteries in the Himalayan region. Some of these temples are a thousand years old.

The Ladakh region of Jammu and Kashmir is renowned all over the Buddhist world. Himachal Pradesh is famous as Dev Bhumi or land of the gods. Temples of Himachal Pradesh are known for their architectural grandeur. There are monasteries in Lahual and Spiti tracts of Himachal Pradesh where the Buddhism is the main religion.

The Second Chapter of the book is on Lamaism. Buddhism was introduced in Tibet after millennia of paganism (Bon religion) in the seventh century A.D. Scholars believe that philosophically and religionwise, Tibet is an ancient island floating on new ideas that pervade the world. Lamaism is a widely accepted nomenclature applied to Tibetan Buddhism.

Lamaism is predominantly a monastic religion. About a quarter of the Tibetan population takes to monastic way of life, temporarily or permanently, frequenting monasteries or shutting themselves up in them. The effect of such a way of life of the citizens has enormous social and domestic implications. Because of the Chinese occupation of Tibet, numerous Lamas of every hierarchical rank have shifted to Nepal. There is certainly a surplus of them in monasteries, gompas and in villages where they teach children. The Lamas perform their daily duties without so much as committing the smallest evil act. At every step they repeat prayers. During the four seasons, certain ceremonies are performed at fixed times. The village or the temple is the place where such festivals and ceremonies take place. They take on special importance when the Lama clergy along with a number of representatives participate.

In the Third Chapter we discuss Monastic Institutions and Priesthood. The monastery and its monks are forces of vital importance for Sherpa society and Sherpa culture. The village, with its inhabitants engrossed in the pursuit of husbandry and trade, represents only one side of Sherpa life. Monasteries and nunneries represent the other side. It is also represented by the lonely cave-dwellings of hermits and the small settlements of lamas within easy reach of the habitations of lay village-folk. The worship of local deities, foremost in the religious thought of layman is not excluded from the ritual performances of the monasteries. There is no cleavage between the Buddhist doctrine practiced in the monasteries and the religion of the ordinary villager. Both have their roots in Tibetan religious traditions.

Chapter Four discusses Lamaism. Lamaism or Tibetan Buddhism is the State religion of Sikkim. The majority of people profess it. As Lamaism is essentially priest craft, it has been dealt with mainly in priestly aspects, and do not touch much of ethics and metaphysics of which most of the lamas are wholly ignorant. It discusses the introduction of Buddhism in Tibet, the schism between northern and southern schools of Buddhism, its nature, its mythology and mysticism, tantricism, and image worship.

It also discusses introduction of Lamaism in Tibet. It was in connection with the building of a monastery that Padma Sambhava first came to Tibet. The King's endeavours to build a monastery had been frustrated by earthquakes. These quakes were attributed to devils. On the King's request Padma Sambhava arrived in Tibet. He overpowered all the demons with his powers and enlightenment. The King was able to establish the first community of lamas.

Chapter Five discusses Monasteries. It is their geographical study. A monastery has its own hierarchy of monastic grades. Both in Tibet and Bhutan the monastery played a dominating role during the period of unification under particular Buddhist sects - Gelugpa in Tibet and Drugpa in Bhutan. In the state of Sikkim it emerged under the guidance of three lamas from Tibet and Buddhism became the state religion. Even though Sikkim followed Buddhism and remained under Tibet's tutelage for long period the monasteries played a different though no less important role in the hereditary ruling system where the monks did exert considerable influence on the administration of the State. The establishment of monastic schools changed the old monastic education system. One of the main reasons for such a change is the declining number of monks for teaching as in the traditional system each student had to be assigned to one monk.

It may be said that the monastery is the first and foremost among all kinds of institutions in Sikkim. For a long period, they performed as the pivot of many functions, both religious and temporal. Why they never acted as a growth center for the neighbourhood has been a mystery.

Chapter Six discusses Monasteries of Sikkim with special reference to the economic structure of the land. The entire land of the kingdom belonged to the King. Over time, the King granted various landlords land. It was either in lieu of services or as special inducements. The King had appointed some officers who were called Kazis. The Kazis and other officers exercised limited civil and criminal jurisdiction within the lands and revenue of which they collected. This system was in vogue for hundreds of years till Sikkim merged with India. Since then the socio-political and economic character of the State has undergone many changes. The society is fast accruing a cosmopolitan character. Though agriculture still remains the main occupation in rural Sikkim, more industries are coming up in the semi-urban and areas Political adaptation to the new political and economic system has been quite fast.

Even when man was living in a cave or in a thatch, nature was a mystery to him. He would look in wonder when sun rose and couldn't understand where it went in the evening. Then would follow moon. Some time sun was there when moon would become visible in the east. He didn't understand what it was. Whenever he felt thirst, he would go and take water not knowing what it was nonetheless quenching his thirst. When rains would arrive, he would touch water, taste it and would know that he had been drinking it from the nearby stream. He then understood the other source from which water came, apart from the spring. He would go out when it was day, not daring to go out in the dark. Darkness was an unknown factor. When it was dark, he would hear all sorts of voices and sounds, some time emanating within his vision, some time he wouldn't know from where those voices were coming. He would imagine things beyond the tree that was visible to him; when light arrived, he would look again and find nothing. But something had been there, he knew. Religion evolved from his doubts and beliefs. That is what Chapter Seven is about.

Religion involves a set of beliefs and practices. It is a social system through which people seek mental and physical harmony with the powers of the universe, through which we attempt to influence the forces of nature. It is therefore considered to be the part of culture. As such, it has been an essential attribute of culture, which cannot be let out from the realms of humane.

The final development of Buddhism in India for that matter Sikkim - involves the growth of Tantric thought in both Buddhism and Hinduism. This has been discussed in the last chapter, Chapter Eight. Vedism had always based itself on magic and ritualistic magic in the fourth and fifth centuries BC, a new form of Hinduism, Tantrism, focussed primarily on magic. As applied to Buddhism, Tantrism focussed on the use of the physical world. The two Buddhists believed that all of physical reality was an illusion. The only thing that existed was Void or Emptiness. The tantras are revealed by the Lord in a transcendent sphere of existence and they differ from the sutras, old and new alike by telling of an entirely different kind of practice by means of which Buddhahood can be gained in this very life.

The Tantric Buddhists developed a methodology from the insight that the world is unreal. Just because the physical world doesn't exist doesn't mean that one should reject it. On the one hand, if the physical world doesn't exist, that means that one cannot commit right or wrong. One learned the teachings of Tantrism from a master, and then one joined a group of others who had been trained. There one would practice the rituals learned from the master.

It gives in detail the great divergence between the Buddhism of the early schools and the stage that Buddhism is at now. Nothing new has happened without first ensuring that it should accord with the doctrinal position. The doctrine itself still remained consciously Buddhist. What is more remarkable it continues to do so, even when feminine partners were introduced in the system. One should note also that Hindu divinities of first rank, Mahadev, Vishnu, Goddess Kali, Mahakal, Rahul were permitted entry only the capacity of defenders of the doctrine. Hence there has developed an enormous variety of mandalas to the bewilderment of anyone who attempts to gain a full acquaintance with the gods of Buddhism. Nevertheless the fundamental pattern and mental process remain the same.

1

Religious Centres, Customs and Festivals

Besides its high peaks, the Himalayan region is also famous as being the abode of gods, goddesses, saints, sages and hermits. This region has also been referred to as the Holy land. In fact the western Himalaya is the melting pot of three of the world's main religions, viz. Hinduism, Buddhism and Islam.

Hinduism and Buddhism are the main religions of people living in the Himalaya through there is a sizable muslim population also. These ancient religious faiths have led to the establishment of hundreds of temples and monasteries in the Himalayan region. Some of them are thousands of years old. Temples date back to the *Ramayana* and *Mahabharata* times. In 1996, the Tabo monastery in Spiti celebrated 1000 years of its existence.

In this chapter we shall deal with the important religious centres in various parts of the Himalayas as also the religious customs, fairs and festivals prevailing over there.

JAMMU AND KASHMIR

Temples

A large number of temples exist in the Jammu and Kashmir region. The important ones are:

1. *Vaishno Devi temple:* The famous Vaishno Devi temple, located in the Jammu hills near Katra, is one of the most revered temples in India. It is a temple dedicated to the goddess Vaishno Devi from all over India belonging to all religions. Lakhs of devotees visit this temple which is approached after an arduous foot trek from Katra. The shrine is inside a cave.
2. *Shankaracharya temple:* The Shankaracharya temple is

one of the most famous landmarks of Srinagar town, located atop the Shankaracharya hill near the Dal lake. This temple is dedicated to Lord Shiva.

3. *Sankat Mochan temple, Srinagar:* This Hanuman temple is situated on the banks of the Jhelum river in Srinagar town.
4. *Other temples:* Other important temples in this State are the Shiva and Lakshmi Narayan temples of Jammu town and the Durga temple at Katra. A number of temples are situated atop the Siwalik hills in the Jammu region.

Monasteries

The Ladakh region of J&K is home to many monasteries, which are renowned all over the Buddhist world. Each monastery or *gompa* is headed by a Kushok, while the title of Rimpoche is given to the heads of large monasteries. Most monasteries have an impressive structure which consists of various types of rooms and halls. A number of villages are attached with most gompas in Ladakh.

Main Monasteries of Ladakh are listed in the table below:

Monastery	*Number of Lamas*	*Number of Villages Attached to the Monastery*
Hemis	390	100
Thiksay	180	25
Likir	120	10
Phyang	115	14
Spituk	160	13
Lamayuru	198	16
Rizong	100	19
Stakna	70	12
Matho	75	5
Takthak	60	2

HIMACHAL PRADESH

Temples

The State of Himachal Pradesh is famous as *Dev Bhumi* or land of gods. There are thousands of temples in this State dedicated to numerous gods and goddesses. There exist many old and famous temples and each village has one or more temples. Villagers have a tendency to follow the directions of their local gods in all important matters. The blessings of gods is invoked even in case of illness and other mishaps. Thus, temples play an important role in the lives of the people of Himachal Pradesh.

Temples of Himachal Pradesh are known for their architectural splendour. These temples have different styles such as Shikhara, Pagoda, Mandap, flat-roofed and caves. Important temples in various parts of the State are:

1. *Kinnaur district:* Though Kinnaur is known for its monasteries, there are a number of temples in Nichar, Kalpa and Peo.
2. *Chamba district:* There are a number of old and famous Laxmi Narayan temples of the tenth century in Chamba. There are eighty-four or *chaurasi* temples in Bharmour. These stone temples are dedicated to Shiva and Narsingh under the name Mani Mahesh. The Mindhal temple is located near Sach.
3. *Lahaul and Spiti district:* A separate chapter describes many of monasteries in the region. The Triloknath temple in the Lahaul valley is worshipped both by the Hindus and Buddhists. The Shakti temple is located at Udaipur.
4. *Mandi district:* Mandi is known as the city with 81 temples. Amongst the famous temples of Mandi town are the Shiva, Shakti, Bhootnath and Tarna Devi temples. A temple is also situated on the banks of the holy Rewalsar lake. Many other temples are situated in this district, usually on the top of hills.
5. *Shimla district:* Many temples are located in Shimla district. These include the Bhima Kali temple at Sarahan, old Shakti temple at Hatkoti, Sankat Mochan at Sanjauli, Hanuman temple at Jakhu and Kali Bari temple in Shimla town.
6. *Kullu district:* Famous temples of Kullu district are the Hadimba devi, Manu and Durga temples at Manali, Vashisht Rishi and Rama temples at Vashisht, Gayatri temple at

Jagat Sukh, Tripura Sundri temple at Naggar and the Bijli Mahadev, Basheshwar and Raghunath temples at Kullu.

7. *Sirmaur district:* The Renuka and Parshu Ram temples situated on the banks of the Renuka lake are the major temples of this district. Other important temples are the Durga temples at Rajgarh, Sarahan and Poanta.
8. *Solan district:* Major temples of Solan district are the Durga temples at Solan, Kasauli, Subathu and Chail and the Shiva temples at Chail and Solan.
9. *Una and Hamirpur districts:* Many temples dedicated to various Hindu gods, mainly Shiva and goddess Durga, are located in Una and Hamirpur districts. There is a large temple of Durga in Dehra town.
10. *Bilaspur district:* The famous Naina Devi temple situated on the top of a hill near Bilaspur is the most revered temple in this district. It is dedicated to the goddess Naina Devi and is visited by lakhs of pilgrims each year. The Deot Sidh (Baba Balaknath) is a cave temple located near Bilaspur. Over the last two this temple has become very famous. An imposing temple dedicated to Shiva and Durga has come up in Bilaspur town.
11. *Kangra district:* Amongst all districts of Himachal Pradesh, Kangra is the called home of temples. Important temples of this district are the famous Chamunda Devi temple between Palampur and Dharamsala which is visited by lakhs of devotees each year. This temple, dedicated to the goddess Chamunda is situated on the banks of a small stream. The Jwalaji temple of the goddess of light is situated at Jwalaji. Other major temples are those of Brajeshwari Devi, Chintpurni, Baijnath and Bhagsunath.

Monasteries

There are many monasteries in the Lahaul, Spiti and Kinnaur tracts of Himachal Pradesh where Buddhism is the main religion. Several of these monasteries are these tracts, several of them being more than 500 years old. The Tabo monastery is over 1000 years old. In fact, monasteries are not isolated places of worship; they are centres known as monastic centres where worship and religious studies are done. Hundreds of lamas live in each monastery.

Monasteries have also come up outside Lahaul, Spiti and Kinnaur in the recent past. Important monasteries of this state are:

1. Lahaul Valley

(a) Shashur gompa was founded by Lama Dewa Gyasatsho at Keylong in the seventeenth century.

(b) Guru Ghantal gompa overlooking the confluence of the Chandra and Bhaga rivers is one of the most revered monasteries of Lahaul.

(c) Gumrang monastery is believed to have been established by Rinchen bZang-po.

(d) Tinno, Kolong and Khangsar monasterics.

(e) Tyul Gompa is associated with Padmasambhava.

(f) Gemur Gompa, which is one of the earliest lamaistic centres, is in the Lahaul valley.

(g) Darcha Dongma and Lapchang monasteries.

(h) Jholing monastery is believed to have been founded by Rinchen bZang-po.

(i) Khardang monastery, which was established several centuries back but was renovated by Lama Norbu.

(j) Othang gompa, which is the only monastery in Lahaul that belongs to the order Gelug Pa.

2. Spiti Valley

(a) Rangrik monastery was built at the site of an old monastery founded by Dromton.

(b) Ki monastery is very large and has a vast monastic complex attached with it.

(c) Kaza monastery is of the Sakya Pa order.

(d) Hikim monastery is also known as the Tangyu monastery. It is of the Sakya Pa order and was patronised by the Nonos of Spiti.

(e) Kibar monastery may be the ancient Lhablamahi dongpa monastery by built Rinchen bZang-po.

(f) Loasar, Hansa, Kaung, Komik, Langja, Lara, Lidang, Domal, Sanglung and Rama are village level monasteries.

(g) Lhalun monastery was founded in the eleventh century.

(h) Dhankar monastery was built in the twelfth century.

(i) Tabo monastery was founded in 996 by Rinchen bZang-po. It has recently celebrated 1000 years of its existence. The Tabo monastery is the only monastic complex with structural and cave types at one place.

(j) Tangti, Tiling, Mud, Sagnam, Todnam and Phar are village level monasteries of the Nyingmapa sect in the Pin valley.

(k) Gungri is the main monastery of the Nyingmapa sect in the Pin valley.

3. Kinnaur and Rampur

(a) Sumra monastery is the birthplace of Rinchen bZang-po.

(b) Leo, Hango, Nako and Chango monasteries in Hangrang area.

(c) Spillo or Pilu monastery.

(d) Namgia monastery.

(e) Riba, Rispa, Morang and Thangi monasteries.

(f) Tashigang monastery has a sandalwood image of Buddha.

(g) Chini, Telingi, Pangi, Purbani and Baring monasteries of Kalpa tehsil.

(h) Rampur monastery was built by Tikka Raghunath Singh.

4. Beas Valley

(a) Manali monastery was built by Gelug pa.

(b) Monastery at Macleodganj in Dharmsala.

(c) Rewalsar monastery is on the banks of the Rewalsar lake.

UTTARAKHAND

Garhwal

Some of the most revered shrines amongst Hindus are located in the Garhwal region, the most important one being Badrinath. There are only a few monasteries in Garhwal which have been constructed by the Tibetan refugee population. These are at Dehradun and Mussoorie. Important temples of Garhwal are:

1. Tehri District

(a) There are many temples dedicated to Shiva, Durga and other gods and goddesses in Tehri, Narendranagar and other towns of this district.

(b) The town of Deoparyag has many temples.

(c) The famous Surkhanda Devi temple is located atop a high peak near Kaddukhal.

2. Dehradun District

(a) The Tapkeshwar temple devoted to Lord Shiva is situated on the banks of a stream in Dehradun.

(b) Lakshman Sidh is a famous temple situated near Harrawala.

(c) There are a number of other temples in Dehradun town, which include the Hanuman temple and Panchayati mandir.

(d) The Dat temple of goddess Kali is located in the Siwalik range at the entrance to the Dehradun valley.

(e) The important temples in Mussoorie include the Laxmi Narayan and Durga temples.

(f) Rishikesh too has many temples including Bharat Mandir and Gita Bhawan.

3. Pauri District

(a) Important temples in Srinagar include the Kamleshwar temple of Lord Shiva, the Kalayaneshwar, Laxmi Narayan, Satyanarayan, Gorakhnath and Rajrajeshwari temples.

(b) The Kinkeoleshwar temple dedicated to Shiva is situated atop a hill near Pauri.

4. Chamoli District

(a) The temples of Narsingh, Vasudeo, Durga, Jyotirmath Mahadev and Bhakt Vatsal are important temples of Joshi Math.

(b) The famous temple dedicated to Lord Badri Vishal is situated at Badrinath. It is one of the four most holy places for Hindus. Lakhs of pilgrims come to visit this temple every year.

(c) The holy shrine of Kedarnath is dedicated to Lord Shiva. The Bhaironath temple is located near the main Kedarnath temple.

(d) Other important temples in Chamoli district are located at Hemkund, Tungnath, Rudranath, Gauchar, Agastmuni, Gaurikund, Rudraprayag, Karanprayag, Vishnuprayag, Hanuman Chatti, Nandprayag and Sonprayag.

5. Uttarkashi District

(a) Uttarkashi town has many important temples which include the Vishwanath, Shakti, Kulti Devi, Kali, Parshuram and Ekadash Rudra temples.

(b) The Yamuna temple is situated at Yamunotri.

(c) The temple dedicated to Ganga is located at Gangotri.

Kumaun

Various important temples of Kumaun are:

(1) Almora District

(a) Important temples in Almora town are the Shiva temple now known as the Nanda Devi temple, the Raghunath, Astha Bharav, Lakshmeshwar and Badrinath temples.

(b) The famous Kalika temple and Jhula temples are located in Ranikhet.

(c) A famous 900-year old Sun temple is located at Katarmal north-west of Almora.

(d) A cluster of 164 temples built by the Chand rulers are situated in and around Jageshwar.

(e) Baijnath has ancient temples belonging to the Pandava era.

(f) Dwarahat has a cluster of 55 temples of the Katyuri period.

(g) Someshwar has an ancient temple of Lord Shiva constructed by Raja Som Chand.

(h) There are many ancient temples in Bageshwar.

(2) Nainital District

(a) Hanuman Garhi is a religious complex near Nainital. It has a 4-mt high image of Lord Hanuman.

(b) The Naina Devi temple is located on the banks of the Nainital lake.

(c) The famous Kainchi temple dedicated to goddess Durga is located along the banks of a small stream near Bhowali.

(d) A Bhairav temple is located in the hamlet of Gorkhakhal.

(e) There are a number of temples in Haldwani and Kathgodam.

(3) Pithoragarh District

Various important temples in this district are located at Champawat, Devidhura, Chhota Kailash, Pithoragarh and Munisiari.

NEPAL

Hinduism is the official religion of Nepal. This is the only country in the world, which has Hinduism as its official religion. There are many temples and monasteries in Nepal with the latter being in the northern tracts of the country where Buddhism is prevalent.

Temples

There are hundreds of temples in Nepal dedicated to Shiva, Durga and many local gods and goddesses. Many of them are located atop mountains. There is a temple in each village and towns have several temples. Important temples in Nepal are:

1. *Pashupatinath temple:* This is a famous Hindu shrine situated in the outskirts of Kathmandu. It is dedicated to Lord Shiva. This temple is located on the banks of the Bagmati river. Thousands of pilgrims from Nepal and India visit this temple each year.

2. *Budha Nilkantha temple:* This temple is located north of Kathmandu. It has a reclining figure of Vishnu protected by snakes.
3. *Dakshin Kali temple:* This is another important temple situated near Kathmandu.
4. *Nyatapola temple:* This temple is situated in Bhadgaon. It has a five-storey pagoda with an impressive architecture.
5. *Kumari temple:* This temple is near the old royal palace in Kathmandu.
6. *Kashthamandap temple:* This is an ancient temple in Kathmandu believed to be the origin of the name Kathmandu. It was built from a single large tree in the sixteenth century.
7. *Temples of Patan:* Patan has several important temples which include the Krishna Mandir and Taleju temples built from stone.

Monasteries

Many Buddhist monasteries are located in the northern parts of Nepal where a sizeable population professing Buddhism lives. There are a number of important monasteries outside this tract also (Nakano, 1984).

1. *Swayambhunath monastery:* is the oldest monastery and lamasery believed to be more than 2000 years old. It stands atop a hill to the west of Kathmandu.
2. *Bodhnath:* is a monastery to the east of Kathmandu. The stupa here is considered to be the largest in the world.
3. *Lumbini:* There are many monasteries in Lumbini area which have great religious importance for Buddhists.

EASTERN HIMALAYA

1. The Ghoom monastery near Darjeeling is one of the largest monasteries in the eastern Himalaya.
2. There are large monasteries at Kalimpong, Gangtok, Phuntsoling, Punakha, Paro, Confluence and Thimpu.
3. The famous Lachung monastery is located at Lachung in northern Sikkim. It is a highly revered place for Buddhists.

4. The famous Tawang monastery lies in the Tawang valley of Arunachal Pradesh.

RELIGION AND CULTURE

The Himalayan region is inhabited by people belonging to different religions, faiths and having different social customs, festivals and fairs. This chapter deals with religious beliefs and culture of the people living in the Himalayas.

JAMMU AND KASHMIR

Religion

The people of Jammu and Kashmir primarily belong to three religious faiths or religions.

1. *Islam*—Islam is the main religion in the Kashmir valley, Kishtwar, some parts of the Jammu region and also in Kargil and Dras areas of Ladakh.
2. *Hinduism*—Hindus are in a majority in parts of the Jammu region though they also live in other regions of the State.
3. *Buddhism*—Buddhists dominate in most parts of Ladakh, except in Kargil. Buddhism came to Ladakh from the adjoining areas of Tibet. People of this religious faith also live in other parts of the State.
4. *Other religions*—People of other religious faiths living in Jammu and Kashmir are Sikhs, Christians and Jains.

Customs

As is everywhere in India, the culture and customs of people living in the three regions of the State differ. In the Jammu region, considerable importance is attached to the purity and cleanliness of food and drink by the people, particularly those belonging to the Rajput and Brahmin castes. One cannot enter into the kitchen or eating area with footwear on. Before a person begins eating, he must wash his hands and pray to the gods he believes in. This is considered essential for introducing solemnity to what one eats. As far as possible, the whole family eats together.

The staple food varies according to the type of agriculture practiced.

So also are the eating habits. In areas where rice is cultivated, it forms a part of their diet once or twice a day, usually accompanied by wheat or maize. Three meals a day are usually taken. In the urban areas, the food habits of the people vary considerably.

Muslims in the Valley and adjoining areas follow strict Islamic practices. People are highly religious and follow the holy Quran. Marriages are arranged by families and when a relationship is settled, the parents of the girl and boy arrange an informal meeting and settle a day for the bethrothal which is known as *nishani*. Then the father of the groom visits the home of the bride taking presents with him. The marriage is completed in the *nikah* ceremony when a Mullah obtains signatures of both parties on written documents.

Rice is the staple food of the people both in the rural and urban areas. It is widely cultivated in the Kashmir valley. Over all the foods habits of Muslims as well as Hindus are simple.

The customs of the Buddhists of Ladakh are based on religion. They may marry Muslims of the same region. By nature, the Ladakhis are active and are usually occupied in work. They have evolved a way of life suited to the harsh environmental conditions they live in. The people of Ladakh work according to the rhythm of nature. In the rural areas, they till the land in spring and summer. In autumn, the Ladakhis prepare for the approaching winter by collecting firewood, dry vegetables and meat and repairing their homes. The harsh and long winter season is spent in making household items such as carpets, ropes, pashmina shawls and baskets. There is not much outdoor during winter. In spring, once it begins to get warmer, the people prepare the field for crops.

Festivals

In the Jammu region, the Hindus and Sikhs celebrate their traditional festivals like Lohri, Baisakhi, Holi and Diwali with great enthusiasm and gaiety. The festivals depend on the religious beliefs. The festivals of Hindus and Sikhs are common is the region.

Amongst the Muslims of Kashmir, besides the traditional festivals of Id, a number of other festivals are celebrated. These are:

Festivals of Kashmir

1. *Urs—Dastgir*—This is a festival celebrated in honour of Syed Abudul Qadir Gillani, a top ranking Muslim saint of Baghdad, whose

spiritual attainments are renowned all over *Muslim Asia*. This festival falls on the eleventh day of the fourth lunar month of the Hijra year. On this day, a hair of the saint is displayed from the balcony of the Khangah at Khanyar, Srinagar, where it has been deposited after being brought from Kabul in 1802. On this occasion, people gather and recite holy verses from the Quran.

2. *Urs Shah Hamdan*—This is the oldest Muslim festival of Kashmir, celebrated on the sixth day of the last lunar month. It falls on the death anniversary of Mir Sayid Ali Hamdani, a patron saint of Kashmir. On this day, a large number of people assemble and recite verses from the holy Quran.

3. *Urs Naqshband Saheb*—A religious festival celebrated in honour of Khawaja Sayyed Baba ud-Din Naqshband, a well known saint from Central Asia.

4. *Urs Aisham Saheb*—This festival is celebrated on the death anniversary of Sheikh Yaqub Safri, a poet, scholar and mystic on the twelfth day of the eleventh lunar month.

5. *Urs Batamallo Saheb*—This festival is celebrated on the death anniversary of Shaikh Dawood, popularly known as Batamalloo or the father who feeds others with cooked rice. His shrine is situated in the south-west of Srinagar city. The pandits of Kashmir though Hindus, also have faith in this saint.

6. *Urs Misa Saheb*—This festival is celebrated in the month of Poh in honour of the saint Abdul Rehman who is revered by both Muslims and Hindus.

7. *Urs Khawaja Habibullah Nowsheri*—The shrine of Khawaja Habibullah, a great saint of Kashmir is situated at Nowshera to the north of Srinagar. This festival is held on his death anniversary.

8. *Urs Syed Qamar Saheb*—The shrine of Syed Qamar Saheb is situated near Srinagar. This festival is held at Ganderbal each year on the second Thursday and Friday of August. The festivities go on for two or three days and thousands of people visit the shrine.

9. *Urs Mirzakamal Saheb*—This festival is held on the last two days of the twelfth month of the lunar year. Thousands of people assemble and recite holy verses from the Quran.

10. *Urs of Zain-ud-din*—This is the most important Muslim festival of Anantnag district. On this day the urs of Zain-ud-din is celebrated in the village of Asishmuqum. The Sheikh is understood to have been a prince of Kishtwar known as Zai Singh, before his conversion to Islam. This urs is celebrated by both Muslims and Hindus.

11. *Eid or Id*—This is the most important festival of the Muslims of Jammu and Kashmir which is celebrated with great pomp and show. The people wear new clothes on this day and offer mass prayers. They greet each other and exchange gifts and presents.

Festivals of Ladakh

Culture of any region is on view fully when there are festivals. This is true of Ladakh too. This is on display in the many festivals which are held in Ladakh.

1. *Losar mela*—Losar is the most famous festival of Ladakh, celebrated in the eleventh month of the Buddhist calendar (in December). According to historians, the king of Ladakh, Jamyang Namgyal gave a countrywide call to the people for war with the king of Skardu during the fifteenth century. Losar pertains to the new year and it was decided that the new year should be celebrated before the battle as many would not survive. The battle was won and since then the new year is celebrated early.

During this festival, illuminations and prayers are held in the monastery in the evening. A huge fire is lit to consume the evil spirits of the year that is ending. There is a traditional dinner at night in which people from all communities dine together. On the next day, people pay homage to the king.

2. *Shubla mela*—This festival is celebrated at Mulbek of Kargil tehsil in July. Thousands of people participate in this festival and fair.

3. *Gustor mela*—This festival is celebrated in January every year at Karzab village of Zanskar tehsil. It is held for two days.

4. *Sani mela*—Celebrated in July every year at Sani village in Zanskar tehsil, this festival is attended by thousands of people from all over Ladakh.

5. *Padam mela*—The Buddhists of Zanskar tehsil celebrate this festival at Padam in November every year. It lasts for two days.

6. *Chheshu mela*—This festival is popular in Leh tehsil, which is celebrated for two days in June-July at Hemis, to commemorate the birthday of Padmasambhava. On the first day of the festival, the image of Drukpa Rimpoche is suspended from thc main gate of the gompa. People sing and dance around the effigy of a devil in human form made from butter and maize floor. It is cut to pieces with swords.

The Kushok suspends the image of Gial Share from the gate of the gompa and it is worshipped by the devotees. Dances by masked men take place on the last day and offerings are made. Thousands of people from all over the world participate in these festivities.

7. *Tsemo mela*—This festival is held at the Tsemo monastery in the middle of February every year. On the first two days of this festival which usually begins on the fifteenth day of February, the lamas worship and dance. They dance before the former ruling family of Ladakh on the third and fourth day. A procession is taken out on the fifth day and wooden effigy known as Dosmochhey devil is made.

Six funeral pyres are lit on which different effigies are placed. The musicians play tunes of mourning. An effigy is cut and people rush to take a part of it as the belief prevails that it brings wealth and happiness to the family. The Tsemo festival is very popular in Leh district with thousands of people taking part in the festivities.

8. *Fertility festival*—This festival is held on the occasion of harvesting the crop, which is a time for joy and rejoicing, particularly if the crop has been a good one. The festivities continue for about a week. This is an occasion for drinking, eating good food and making marry. In some tribal areas of Ladakh where the survivors of the Aryan immigrants maintain a distinct lifestyle, the villagers indulge in sex, believing that as the land, the womenfolk too would bear them good children. This festival may be held once in every three years and is one of the brightest events in the lives of the tribal population of the region.

In Ladakh, communal dances are a traditional part of festivities. The various dances of Ladakh are:

1. *Ladakhi or social dance*—The Ladakhi or social has been an important part of cultural and social occasions. This is a slow dance and monotonous in action. It consists of small steps with the variation between different steps being so less and some time emperceptible that

they appear to be inconsequential. This form of dance is a living tradition and people perform it even in the fast moving world of today.

2. *Devil dance*—This dance is a fascinating display of body rhythm and musical skill. It has deep temporal and spiritual themes. The main object of this dance is to depict the victory of Buddhism over the Bon religion which was practised in Ladakh during the early ages. It is performed by lamas in the gompas on the occasion of various festivals. Different divinities are portrayed by the dancers wearing masks. They depict good and evil by gestures and movements. The colourful costumes and masks of dancers and their movements make this dance extremely attractive. The spectators usually know the symbols and meanings of various gestures and movements and hence are able to understand it properly.

Attractive costumes made of brocade silk in bright red, blue, pink, green and other colours are worn by the dancers. They also have elaborate headgear. Swords and knives are wielded by them during the dance. The figures usually portrayed in these dances are Padmasambhava and the god of wealth, and Yama the lord of death and his dhoop.

HIMACHAL PRADESH

Religion and Customs

Hinduism is the main religion in Himachal Pradesh. Customs reflect the true picture of the moral consciousness of a community or people. The main customs of the people of this hill state are outlined below:

1. *Birth*—Birth ceremonies in Himachal Pradesh are very peculiar. During the wife's pregnancy a non-vegetarian does not kill any husband animal with his own hands though he may eat meat. A pregnant woman must not go near a burning place or stream. She is also prohibited from looking at a lunar or solar eclipse. It has been proved that if a pregnant woman goes out in the open during any of eclipses, her child has a distinct eclipse mark on his/her body.

Villages in Himachal don't have modern health case facilities Primary health care centres are also scattered. Therefore most of time child birth takes place at home or in the nearby primary health centre if there is one. Mostly midwives assist the mother in delivery. The mother is given special diet immediately after delivery.

The birth of a son is announced by distributing sugar lumps or parched grains amongst friends and relatives soon after the event. Musicians play music at the door of the blessed family in eastern parts of the State. Young girls and children are fed to celebrate the event. The maternal uncle of the new-born baby sends gifts and clothes for him.

2. *Mundan*—This is the first occasion on which the hairs of the child are cut. It may take place in the first, third, or fifth year of his life. All the hair growing on the child's head are removed and offered at the shrine of a deity or thrown in a river or stream. In this ceremony too, there is feasting of relatives and friends who give presents to the child. The most important for Mundan ceremony is the holy temple of Godess Jwalaji.

3. *Naming or Namkaran*—This is an important rite that is performed when the child is about two years old. He is given a specific name by his parents. This is accompanied by chanting of religious hymns and feasting. In some areas the *namkaran* ceremony takes place when the child is one, three, six or nine months old. The parents may leave the choice of name to the priest. In Lahaul valley a child is named within the first year and the ceremonial day is observed as a festive occasion with the sacrificing of a goat whose meat is eaten by all.

People of the upper castes or classes have a first name, second name and surname. They may use the suffix Ram, Lal, Das, Chand or Singh. Surnames used in various parts of the State are Thakur, Verma, Sharma, Gupta, Rathore, Chauhan, Tomar, Tekta and Negi.

4. *Marriage*—Betrothal is the first step in a marriage ceremony in Himachal. The boy's male relatives usually takes the initiative in this matter. The father, uncle or elder brother of the boy to be married usually settles the marriage. This custom in however undergoing change. Modernisation is leaving its marks. Those Himachal who go to metros for work same time arrange inter-caste marriages.

Dowry is usually not paid though this system has now become a part of the marriage ceremony many cities and small towns of the state. In some parts (e.g. Shimla and Sirmaur districts) a reverse system is in vogue. The groom's father pays a certain amount to the bride's father for meeting the expenses of marriage. This is known as *dhari.*

Polyandry and polygamy were in vogue in some parts of the State in the past. However, at present such cases are very rare and found in very remote and inaccessible areas.

Festivals

As everywhere else in the country, festivals are an important part of the cultural life of the people of Himachal Pradesh. They have a distinct cultural, religious, social and educational identity. Many of these festivals are derived from the sectarian Hinduism of the period after the migration of the Rajput people from the plains to these hills (7th to 15th century). This led to the introduction of festivals like Holi, Dussehra and Diwali. A number of festivals are associated with the worship of Shiva and Shakti, while others are associated with places of pilgrimage sacred to a deity, like Chentpurni, Jwalaji, Kangra or Baba Balaknath.

Climatic needs and other characteristics of the season influence ceremonies and celebration of the region. There is a festival for every such occasion. In Himachal Pradesh, festivals play an important role in the lives of the people. This has been outlined in the following points.

(a) Festivals form their main holidays.

(b) On the occasion of festivals, men, women and children put on their best clothes and converge on a common place usually the village square.

(c) Festivals are occasion, for worshipping gods and deities, usually collectively.

(d) This is also an occasion for mass feasting, drinking and dancing.

Important festivals celebrated in different parts of the State have been discussed in the following text.

1. *Chet*—Chet is the first month of the Hindu year. The first day of the month of Chet is celebrated as a festival with the belief that the entire year will bring them happiness and joy. In Bharmour this festival is known as Dholru. The entire village rejoices on the occasion of this festival.

2. *Navratras*—Navratras are observed in most parts of the State. The eighth day of the Navratras is called Durga Ashtami. The people keep fast on this day and the entire family visits the Durga temple. Some people eat once in a day on all days of the Navratras.

3. *Baisakhi*—This festival is generally celebrated on the first day of the Baisakh month (13th April) or one or two days earlier. It is known as Bissu or Bisha in the Shimla hills; Beesh or Bisowa in Kinnaur and Bishoo in Pangi.

4. *Haryali*—This is a festival of the rainy season which is celebrated on the first day of the month of Sawan (usually on 16th July). It marks the onset of the rainy season each year. In the plains, i.e., this is celebrated as Teej. This festival is known as Haryali in Kangra and Sirmaur; Rhyali in the upper hills of Shimla district; Dakhram in Kinnaur and Jubbal, and Shegtsum in the Lahaul valley.

5. *Rakhpunya or Rakhi*—Like amongst Hindus all over India. This is the festival of the first full moon in the month of Sawan. It is also known as Rakhri or Salonoo or Salunu. A sacred thread is tied to the brother's wrist by his sister or by the Brahmin around the wrist of different people in the village. The former system is more prevalent in the urban and semi-urban centres. The tying of a sacred thread around the brother's wrist signifies the affection between brother and sister.

6. *Chrewal*—This is a festival of fire which is celebrated on the first day of the month of Bhadon (middle of August). It continues for about a month.

7. *Jagra*—This is a festival held towards the close of the month of Bhadon (first half of September) in which prayers are offered to a village deity. Either the deity is invited to one's house or the prayers are performed at his temple on a fixed day. Villagers from the neighbourhood also attend this ceremony.

The festival takes place on the fourth day of the bright phase of the moon. Fast is kept by one member of each household. After this, the procession goes back to the temple with the deity. After dark, worshippers carry splints of wood in their hands and dance and sing on this occasion.

8. *Phulech*—This is a festival of flowers celebrated only in Kinnaur. It is also known as U-Khyang. In September, the villagers go to the high hills and collect flowers. On the day of the festival the whole village gathers and offers garlands of beautiful flowers to the local deity.

9. *Sair*—This festival is celebrated in the Kangra valley and some parts of Shimla hills usually on the first day of the month of Ashad

(middle of September). Sair is an important day for these people. This day marks the departure of the rainy season and the people thank God because the rains have gone, leaving their homes and crops undamaged.

10. *Dussehra and Diwali*—Both these festivals are celebrated with great pomp and gaiety. They are in no way different from that of the plains. In Kullu, Dussehra is an occasion for the gathering of gods and goddesses from the surrounding countryside. Lakhs of people collect on this occasion. Ramlila is staged in every part of the State on the days preceding Dussehra. The goddess Durga is widely worshipped for ten days before Dussehra. These days are known as Navratrey.

Diwali or the festival of lights is celebrated on Kartika Amavasya. The local deity is worshipped and people light their homes with small earthen lamps and candles. They burst crackers in the evening.

11. *Lohri*—Also known as Maghi, this festival is widely celebrated with gaiety by the people of the lower hills. It falls, on the first day of the month of Magh (or middle of January). The people greet and call on each other. In the evening a bonfire is lit in the village courtyard and there is dancing and feasting.

12. *Shivratri*—This is an important religious festival celebrated in most parts of the state. It falls in the month of Phagun (February). The God Shiva is widely worshipped on this day. There is great reverence for Shiva in these hills. The festival is celebrated individually and collectively. Many people keep fast on this day. Food is taken in the evening after the day long prayers are over.

13. *Nawala*—This is a festival of the Gaddi tribes living in Kangra, Chamba and Mandi districts. There is no particular day on which Nawala is celebrated though each family must celebrate it once in a year. Lord Shiva is worshipped and thanked for his blessings in the year that has gone by.

Fairs

In Himachal Pradesh, fairs are community events in which all people errespective of religion.

Important fairs held in different parts of the State have been discussed in the following text.

1. *Minjar*—This fair is held in Chamba and parts of Kangra. Harvest season starts around the end of August. Once the haroesting starts everybody becomes busy. Before the season starts is the time when one can relax. It starts on the second Sunday of the month of Sawan (August). The Minjar fair serves as a source of leisure and recreation to thousands of people before the onset of the harvest season.

The main functions are held on the banks of the Ravi river below Chamba town. Prior to the merger of Chamba state the ruler used to organise this fair. Now this is done by the district administration. On the last day of the fair, thousands of people dressed in colourful clothes gather one the banks of Ravi river to make offerings to Varuna, the god of rain. This is done by floating minjars (maize flowers and coconuts) in the Ravi river. A procession is also taken out on this occasion.

2. *Naina Devi Fair*—This fair is held in August at the famous Naina Devi temple in Bilaspur district. Thousands of pilgrims come to have a *darshan* of the goddess during this period.

3. *Kullu Dussehra*—This is one of the most famous fairs of the State. It begins on Vijayadashmi day and continues for seven days. On the first day of the fair, the idol of Raghunath is carried in a chariot to a fixed place in Kullu maidan by pulling ropes which is considered to be sacred act. Village deities from the surrounding areas are brought to Kullu. They also accompany this colourful procession.

Thereafter all gods of Kullu come to the maidan to pay homage to Lord Raghunath. On the following days the gods are worshipped and paraded both in the mornings and evenings. The famous idol of Raghunath was brought from Ayodhya in 1657. Thousands of pilgrims and tourists visit the fair each year. This is the time for festivities. A big fair is held on all the days of the festival. This is the time for doing purchase for Diwali. The fair automatically turns into a market.

4. *Lavi*—This is an ancient trade fair held in early November each year at Rampur which is the gateway to Kinnaur. The fair is held in a special level ground which has been set aside for this purpose. It is situated on the banks of the Satluj river. The fair is held for three days.

Though Lavi has been organised on regular basis for the past 300 years or more, it has a much older history. The fair has served as a meeting ground for traders from Kinnaur (earlier also Tibet), Shimla, Kullu, Mandi, Kangra, Solan, Sirmaur, Lahaul-Spiti and from the plains.

5. *Renuka Fair*—This is a colourful religious and trade fair held on the banks of the Renuka lake in Sirmaur district. It is celebrated for three days starting on the eleventh day of the waxing moon of the month of Kartik.

According to the legend, goddess Renuka lived near the lake with her husband Rishi Jamdagni. Their son Parshuram visited her every year. This fair is held to commemorate the annual meeting of Renuka and Parshuram who is believed to be an incarnation of Vishnu. At the beginning of the fair, idols of Parshuram are bathed in the lake and taken in a procession to the Parshuram temple situated atop a hill. Thereafter the idols are installed there. This fair is held at a time when the local people have harvested their kharif crops and are in a position to sell the extra foodgrains. Winter is round the corner and supplied are required to staked. Thus, the Renuka fair is also a trade fair in the sense that it is an opportunity for trading. People from upper reaches like Harepurduar and Lahul and Spiti come to the fair for trading goods.

Many religious ceremonies are performed during this fair. The people dance, sing and eat. There is recreation for all members of the society.

6. *Shivratri Fair*—Another famous fair is the Shivratri fair of Mandi. This is a week-long religious fair which is renowned for the worship of Lord Shiva. It is held in Mandi town along the banks of the Beas river. The main functions held in this fair are:

(a) Gods and goddesses from the surrounding hills are brought on *raths* on the shoulders of their devotees to Mandi on Shivratri day. The town is tastefully decorated for receiving these revered deities.

(b) They first go to the Madho Rai temple and then proceed to pay their celestial homage to Lord Shiva at the Bhutnath temple.

(c) A week-long fair of folk dances, skits and other forms of amusements begins.

(d) At the conclusion of the festivities a night vigil is kept by the gods and their devotees. The main events in the coming year are forecast.

(e) A prayer is held on the last day and the gods depart after paying homage once again to Lord Shiva. They are offered *chadars.*

7. *Nalwari Fair*—Basically this is a cattle fair which is held in Bilaspur. In this fair cattle are traded on a large scale. On the occasion of this fair, races, wrestling bouts and other forms of rural entertainment are also held.

8. *Jwalamukhi Fair*—This is a religious fair held during the *navaratras* at the Jwalamukhi temple. Similar fairs are held during this period at the temples of Chamunda Devi, Kangra, Chintpurni and Bajreshwari and every other temple in the State.

9. *Natwar Fair*—This is a cattle trade fair held near Sunder-nagar in March every year.

10. *Phul Yatra Fair*—This fair is held in October every year at Kilar in the Pangi valley.

UTTARAKHAND

Religion

Hinduism is the main religion professed by the people of Uttarakhand. Other religious faiths followed by the people of this region are Sikhism, Islam, and Jainism. The proportional break-up of the population of Garhwal and Kumaun on the basis of religion is given below.

Religion-wise Break-Up of the Population of Garhwal and Kumaun

Religion	*Percentage of Total Population*	
	Garhwal	*Kumaun*
Hinduism	92.0	91.5
Sikkism	2.0	4.0
Islam	2.5	2.5
Christianity	2.0	1.0
Others	1.5	1.0
Total	100.0	100.0

Festivals

Life in the interior hilly areas of Uttarakhand is very different. Because of hard-work people have to put in to ele out a bring festivals and fairs are a welcome break from the arduous routine. These are also a representation of the social instincts of the people which have passed on from generation to generation. There is a festival or fair to celebrate each season. Important agricultural operations like ploughing, sowing and harvesting are also connected with festivals and fairs.

The main festivals celebrated by the people of Uttarakhand are:

Dussehra—This festival is widely celebrated in almost all parts of Uttarakhand. The epic *Ramayana* is enacted on the stage in villages, towns and cities. On Dussehra day, effigies of Ravana are burnt.

The Goddess Durga is widely worshipped on nine days preceding Dussehra. The people keep fast on this day. There are nightlong prayers at temples of the Goddess.

Diwali—Diwali or the festival of lights is celebrated all over this hilly region. It also marks the beginning of the Hindu new year. The festivities begin a few days before the Diwali day. Houses are cleaned and white-washed. At night, all buildings are illuminated with lamps and candles. Fireworks are lit on Diwali night and a day before Diwali. The people visit each other. Young people collect wood in the village courtyard and light a bonfire.

Magh—Magh is celebrated in late winter about four to six weeks after sowing of the winter crops. It aids in breaking the monotony of the long and drab winter season of the upper hills. People collect and sing in the village courtyard. They also dance and dine together. During the day, they visit each other. This festival is widely celebrated in the valley of the Yamuna river. In Punjab Himachal and Jammu it is celebrated as Lohri.

Basant Panchami—This festival is celebrated to mark the close of the winter season and arrival of spring or warmer season. As the days become longer, the people rejoice and this marks a general revival of life after the long and severe winter months. The wheat crop also begins to ripen and the people make themselves ready for the harvest.

This festival is usually celebrated in the middle of February. The goddess of learning (Saraswati) and springs are worshipped with traditional reverence on this day. In general, the people wear yellow clothes or at least one yellow apparel. Yellow scarves may be put on by women and children while menfolk don yellow caps or turbans. There is dancing and singing and local temples are worshipped on this day.

In many parts of the interior hills, two types of worship are performed on this occasion. Both the mother earth and crops or agriculture are worshipped. People place cowdung heaps in the fields on which ears of barley and wheat are kept. Earthen lamps and incense are lit on this heap to signify worship of the mother earth and crops or agriculture. They also tie ears of corn and barley to the doors and windows of buildings on this day. Sweet rice is eaten on Basant Panchami.

Bissu—This festival is celebrated in late spring, in parts of the Yamuna valley of western Garhwal. The people get ready for the harvest. They rejoice on seeing the crops ripen. Five-day celebrations are held on the occasion of Bissu. The people dance and sing in the village courtyard. This goes on till the early hours of the morning.

Holi—As in the rest of India, this festival of colours is widely celebrated in almost all parts of Uttarakhand, both in the urban and rural areas. Holi is celebrated to mark the end of winter. The people throw colours on each other on the occasion of Holi. They move in small groups and greet each other.

Hariyala or Hariyal—This festival is celebrated in some parts of Uttarakhand at the beginning of the rainy or monsoon season. Mostly it falls in the month of July. The people get ready for sowing paddy or maize. Grains are sown in pots by the head of the family amidst the chanting and singing of hymns about 10 days before Hariyala day. The grains sprout and the seedlings are put on the headgear on Hariyala day. The people greet each other on the occasion of this festival.

Fairs

Fairs are held in many parts of this hilly region from time to time. These fairs may be of the following types.

(i) religious fairs that are generally connected with places of worship;

(ii) fairs connected with festivals;

(iii) trade fairs and cattle fairs; and

(iv) general fairs.

Important fairs of Uttarakhand are given in the following table.

Important Fairs of Uttarakhand

Fair	*Area(s) in which held*
Vishu	Tons and Yamuna valleys at Dini Jad, Thana Danda, Lakanpal and Nagthat.
Mon	Yamuna valley at Purola, Jalori, Saundari, Bankholi, Meenar and Duniyara.
Jagra or Jatr	Arakot, Naitwar, Devru, Dandya Tangara, Lakhwar and Thana Danda.
Thaul	Upper tons valley, mainly at the hamlet of Osla.
Maker Sankranti	Bhagirathi fair, mainly at Uttarkashi where deities of the surrounding region are brought.
Mangshira Amavasya	Jalkur valley at Sem Mukheim.
Margshira	In the Mandakini valley at Vurha Kedar (Thati Kathur).
Surkhanda	At the temple of Surkhanda devi near Mussoorie.
Chandarbani	Near Pratapnagar in the Bhagirathi valley.
Kunjapuri	In the Bhagirathi valley at Kunjapuri.
Gauchar	Gauchar in the Alaknanda valley (largest fair of Uttarakhand).
Jhanda	Important Sikh fair at Dehradun.
Bampa	At Niti in the Alaknanda valley.
Visuvat Matamurti	At Karanprayag in the Alaknanda valley near Badrinath.
Kainchi	At Kainchi near Bhowali.
Nanakmatta	Nanakmatha (important Sikh fair).
Kishan melas	At Joshimath, Gauchar, Garur, Lata, Rudrapur and Champawat.
Religious fairs	At Gopeshwar, Joshimath, Gairsain, Adi-badri, Rishikesh, Kedarnath, Ansuiyamata, Nandprayag, Dwarahat, Bageshwar, Kalika and Tawaghat.

Thus, fairs in Uttarakhand, as everywhere else, play an important part in the life of the people of Uttarakhand.

NEPAL

Religion

Nepal is the meeting ground of Hinduism and Buddhism. The majority of the population of Nepal is of Hindu faith and Hinduism is also the state religion of the country. There are many temples in which Hindus and Buddhists worship together while most temples are worshipped only by Hindus. The three main gods revered in Nepal are Brahma, Vishnu and Mahesh while other gods and goddesses are also worshipped.

Buddhists have their own way of life. They worship in monasteries which have been constructed in different parts of the country.

Customs and Manners

The customs and manners of the people of Nepal are simple and traditional.

1. *Birth*—The birth of a child is an occasion for joy. Male children are welcomed with festivities and amongst the affluent, the whole village may be fed. The rejoicing continues for several days.

2. *Mundan ceremony*—This ceremony involves shaving off the hair of a baby or young child. It is a religious ceremony performed before the child attains the age of 5 years in the first, third or fifth year.

3. *Marriage*—Amongst most communities of Nepal, marriages take place within their own caste or community. The groom comes in a procession with his relatives and friends to the house of the bride where the marriage takes place. The couple take vows around a sacred fire.

4. *Death*—The death of a person is mourned by the whole village or community. The sons of the deceased shave off their heads and undergo special rituals during the period of mourning which may last from 13 days to a month. The dead are burnt on a pyre of wood in Nepal.

Festivals and Fairs

Important festivals and fairs of Nepal have been discussed in the following text.

1. *Shivratri*—This festival is held in honour of Lord Shiva who is highly revered in various parts of Nepal. Shivratri is celebrated at all Shiva temples and is the most important festival of Nepal. Shivratri falls around mid-February. On this day, devotees visit the famous Pashupatinath temple and bathe in the sacred Bagmati river.

2. *Loser*—Loser or Luser is the Buddhist new year celebrated by people living in northern Nepal and also by Buddhists in other parts of

the country. On this occasion, prayers are held in the gompas and community feasts are held. Community dances are also held.

3. *Holi*—This is the Hindu festival of colours celebrated all over Nepal on the occasion of the victory of Lord Krishna over the she-demon Holika. Holi falls in the middle of March every year. Prayers and colourful functions are held in Krishna temples and people apply colours on each other.

4. *Ghora Yatra*—This festival falls on the first day of the Hindu month of Baisakh in honour of the victory of Devtas over the demon Tundi whose ghost is believed to haunt the parade ground in Kathmandu. The King of Nepal presides over this function. This concedes with Baisakhi in many parts of India.

5. *Nav Varsha*—The solar new year is celebrated with great pomp and show in Kathmandu valley and other parts of Nepal. This festival falls in the middle of April every year. Procession of the gods are taken out in the towns of Kathmandu valley, particularly in Bhaktapur.

6. *Budh Jayanti*—This festival falls on the anniversary of Lord Buddha on the twenty-sixth day of May every year. Buddhists celebrate Budh Jayanti all over Nepal by offering prayer in gompas and also in their homes.

7. *Sitinakha*—This festival falls in the middle of June every year and is held in honour of Kumar, the god of war, who is the son of Lord Shiva. Communal tribal dances take place and rice transplantation is undertaken after this festival.

8. *Nag Panchmi*—This is a festival of the Nagas who migrated to Nepal from northwest under pressure of the Aryans. They worshipped snakes and their rituals were adopted by the Hindus. The festival of Nag Panchmi is celebrated in the middle of August every year. The snakes god is worshipped and food is left out for snakes. Drawings of snakes are made on the entrance of doors.

9. *Janai Purnima/Raksha Bandhan*—These are popular Hindu festivals falling towards the end of August. Hindu change the sacred threads and sisters tie thread around the wrists of their brothers. A colourful ceremony is held at the Kumbheshwar temple in Pattan.

10. *Gai Yatra*—This is a colourful festival of the Newars, celebrated towards the end of August each year. Cows are paraded by the family in which a death has occurred during the last one year. Dance rituals and skits are held in the rural areas.

11. *Janamashtami*—This festival marks the birth anniversary of Lord Krishna falling in the last few days of August. Janamashtami is celebrated with great pomp and show all over Nepal. It is usual for the people to fast the whole day and eat a special meal after midnight. Temples are decorated and continuous prayers are offered to the gods.

12. *Teej*—Falling in the middle of September, this is a festival of the Hindu women who remember the severe penances performed by Parvati, the daughter of the Himalayas, to win the affection of Lord Shiva, her husband in her earlier life as Sati, the daughter of Daksha Prajapati.

Hindu women keep fast on this day and special prayers are offered at the Pashupatinath temple.

13. *Indra Yatra*—This festival is celebrated in the third week of September every year in honour of Lord Indra, the king of the gods.

14. *Durga Puja*—Durga puja is the most widely celebrated festival in Nepal held in honours of the triumph of Lord Rama over the demon king Ravana of Lanka and the victory of the goddess Durga Bhawani over the demon Mahishasur. The religious ceremonies go on for ten days.

15. *Diwali*—The festival of lights and Lakshmi puja is celebrated all over Nepal, twenty days after the Dusshera festival. People light lamps in their homes and worship the goddess of wealth.

EASTERN HIMALAYA

The people of diverse religious faiths, customs, festivals and fairs inhabit the eastern Himalayas. The religion and customs of Buddhists living in the Darjeeling hills, Sikkim, Bhutan and Arunachal Pradesh resembles that of the Buddhists of Ladakh, Spiti and Tibet.

There is a considerable population of Hindus in the eastern Himalaya whose religious activities, customs and festivals are akin to that of Hindus living elsewhere.

The tribal communities of Arunachal Pradesh follow their own religious beliefs, customs, festivals and fairs which have come down to through centuries of traditions.

References

Bose, S.C. (1972). Geography of the Himalayas, NBT, New Delhi.

Nakano, T. (1984). Trekking in Nepal, Allied Publishers, New Delhi.

Negi, S.S. (1994). Garhwal: The Land and People, Indus Publishing Company, New Delhi.

Negi, S.S. (1995). Cold Deserts of India, Indus Publishing Company, New Delhi.

2

Lamaism and the Monks: Institutions, Temples and Monuments

Buddhism was introduced in Tibet, after millenia of Paganism (Bon religion) in the seventh century AD by king Strong-Btsan Sgam-Po in the seventh century AD. He was also a pagan king before he embraced Buddhism. He had done it on the advice of his Chinese queen, whose was a Buddhist. Scholars believe that philosophically and religion wise Tibet is an "ancient island floating on new ideas that pervade the world. Lamaism is a widely accepted nomenclature applied to Tibetan Buddhism.

Modified Religion

This new religion was widely adopted by Tibetans only when it was modified to suit local mentality by the apostle Padma Sambhava (born of lotus). To the already existing precepts of Tibetan Tantrism of a magico-superstitious nature, he added the precepts of Buddhism. The word *Tantrism* is derived from *Tantra* (literally a book), which denotes holy books of the Hindus of the Shiva cult. It may be an oversimplification to define Tantrism as a belief in the occult forces of magic and superstition. But this perhaps is the most expressive definition. The Tantras contain the text of dialogues between Shiva and Durga as well as many ritual prescriptions to control and display the occult powers of magic. Lamaism not only speaks of the Divinity and its Pantheon at the head of which is a triad of gods but also accepts and believes in the existence of many other supernatural forces, which hold their sway over man and are controlled by him in fits and starts. The apostle Padma Sambhava translated Buddhist precepts and adapted them to the Tibetan's superstitious notions. Thus, he gave birth to two fundamental canons: the *Kangiur* comprising of 108 books and the *Tangiur* having 225 volumes. *Kangiur* signifies the translated word (of Buddha) and has its source in Sanskrit and Pali texts; *Tangiur* means the translated doctrine and is derived from original Indian and Chinese texts. Both of them were composed around 1300 A.D. *Laricenmo,* a "high theological treatise" written by Tsonkhapa, the great reformer belonging to the "yellow sect", is also very important for Lamaites.

The number of the images of Buddha in big temples is 108. So are the lamps, the prayer wheel's the books of *kangiur,* the taps of the fountain of *Mkutinath* and the prayer wheels of *Manang.* In Lamaism, 108 is a magical number. Lamaism is considered to be the third and the last stage of Buddhist Tantrism, which is allied to it, and is founded on a monistic philosophy (single reality based on a single principle in which it can be resolved) on pantheistic bases. The world is created and dominated by a secret, invisible, unitary force which manifests itself in everything. With the help of *yoga* and mystical exaltation man can subdue this force and dominate the vital energy of the universe. By gradual stages the ascetic ends up in completely identifying himself with the force involved by him.

Lamaism: A Monastic Religion

Lamaism is predominantly a monastic religion. About a quarter of the Tibetan population takes to monastic way of life, temporarily or permanently, by frequenting monasteries or shutting themselves up in them. The effect of such a way of life on the citizens has enormous social and domestic implications. After a period of ascendancy Lamaism declined, but rose again around 1000 A.D., and got divided in different sects after the advent of the illustrious Indian patriarch Atisha. Then followed the conversion of the Mongols to Lamaism.

A new period of decline came to an end in the year 1400 with reforms effected by Tsonkhapa which gave rise to the "sect of the yellow church" so called because of the colour of the clothes and head gear of monks as opposed to the ancient "red church" which was also so defined after the colour of the clothes worn by ancient Lamas. About 1400 onwards there have been two spiritual heads in the Lama hierarchy: The Dalai Lama ("the Master as powerful as the ocean of wisdom") who also wields political power over the people, and the Panchen Lama ("the Master who excels among those who know") who is invested with the power of priestly wisdom and dignity. According to some fine hierarchical distinction the Panchen Lama is slightly above the Dalai Lama. The former concerns himself primarily with spiritual matters and hence is nearer the Divine Power. The latter's concern is with government and hence is given to more mundane affairs. The permanent residence of the Dalai Lama is at Lhasa in the great palace known as *Potala.* Panchen Lama, instead, has set up his residence at monastery of *Tashilumpo* at Shigatse. The Potala (God's own land)—the big sacred palace at Lhasa—contains in its hundreds of halls and rooms, the mortal remains of 13 or more dead Dalai Lamas who lie buried there. As a matter of fact, the more devout among the Lamaists maintain the Dalai Lama never dies. He "simply shows how to die" only to have an eternal reincarnation in another child Dalai Lama.

In *Zuglacan* or the Cathedral of Lhasa there is the *Djobo (giobo)* or an image of Buddha donated by the first king of Tibet (Strong-Btsan-Sgam-Po) who was converted to Buddhism by a Chinese emperor to whose daughter he had been married.

The Rivals

The Dalai Lama and Panchen Lama have always had a natural and inevitable rivalry between them. In the past this antagonism gave rise to sensational developments on account of political conflict born of the Dalai Lama's pro-English bias and the Panchen Lama's Chinese leanings.

Those who are called upon to the great task of perpetuating the Lama church in accordance with the Divine will are incarnations of the dead Lamas. The succession to headship in the Lamaist hierarchy takes place in accordance with the *Ciubilgunic* principle based on the incarnation dogma. So the Lamas who have lived upto today are not 15 to 20; but successive incarnations of only one *Chenrezi* (compassion and benevolence personified). The human body is like a coat that one takes off, changes or puts on again. The learned ones affirm that this system of succession guarantees the advantages not only of a hereditary line of descent but also of an election which is free of caste or social distinctions. The "Precious One" can equally take birth in a noble family or in an unprivileged plebian family.

Selecting Dalai Lama

At the death of a Lama there begins a search for the natural successor from among the children who display certain special signs and have a certain measure of intelligence worthy of being the reincarnation of the Illustrious One. While a normal person is allowed a maximum of 40 days to get reincarnated, in the case of Dalai Lama one can wait even for two years in order to find the successor designate. Generally, the families in which Dalai Lama is born receive a perpetual donation of large property to enable them to live in a manner suitable for a Dalai Lama's parents. Such families are called *Yapshi.*

The child identified as the new Dalai Lama has to recognise certain objects belonging to the deceased by selecting them out of perfect imitations. Among the objects the child has to recognise are: the bell *(tril-bu),* the arrow *(dorje),* the double liturgical drum *(nga-chung)* and the rosary *(threng-wa).*

Journey of Buddhism

Buddhism originating from India travelled to China first, though the far East from there it came to Tibet. It gave to Tibet not only its fine religious edifices but also highly rich and complex forms of art and culture. The Sherpas, migrating to the southern Himalayas brought with them this religio-philosophical and cultural patrimony of the Tibetan Buddhism. In spite of the fact that Sherpas from the neighbouring Tibet had migrated to the Khumbu region as early as the thirteenth and fourteenth centuries, a clear evidence of Buddhism in that area is available only in the seventeenth or eighteenth century.

The Sherpas started thinking of problems of the soul only after their immediate problems of physical survival had been solved after a tumultuous period of early settlement in new territories. It was in 1860 that the first temple in the entire region came into existence at Pangpoche; it was followed a few years later by the temple of Thami. The three most important temples of Khumbu region happen to be those of Pangpoche, Thami and Kerok; it is at these centres that the Buddhist faith was kept alive from generation to generation. The temple of Khumjung was constructed around the year 1900. This was succeeded, in more recent times, by the two temples of Nauche.

Constructing of Monastries

The construction of the Lama monastery at Tengpoche took place in 1921-22. The monastery was built at the bidding of Gulu Lama; in 1933 when the walls suddenly crumbled due to an earthquake, the 85-year-old saint died of grief. His body was cremated amidst the foundations of the ruined monastery so as to provide incentive for its immediate reconstruction. The credit of constructing the Pangpoche *Gompa* also goes to Lama Sanga Dorje, the sixth reincarnation of Lama Changma Dorje who assumed the duty of the abbot or prior of the monastery of Tengpoche in 1964-65. Sanga Dorje is nowadays considered the patron saint of the entire Khumbu region because to him have been attributed many miracles after his death and even during his early life. After his cremation his eyes, tongue and heart remained intact. They were enclosed in a silver case and today these relics constitute the greatest patrimony of the monastery of Tengpoche.

Architecture of a Gompa

The main square-shaped room of the *Gompa* is the *duang*. It has four columns and each side is about 12 metres in length. In the centre of this room is enthroned the figure of Buddha *Padma Sambhava* (born from the lotus) whom the Sherpas call *Guru Rimpoche* (the Precious Master). The small living *Bodhisattya* of the monastery also bears the same title. Inside the *duang* burn some lamps. The pilgrims offer small coins for the butter to be used to keep these lamps burning. Cones of coloured butter *(torma)* are always present on the lateral alter. Butter is the principal ingredient in various ceremonies performed by the Lama. In the form of a cone or pyramid *torma* symbolises the Buddha. In the same room *(duang)* are kept: the silver drums (*gyaling*); the secret drum made from the thigh-bone of a young virgin *(kangling),* the double drum *(nga-chung),* the silver bell *(trilbu);* and the two-sided magical drum *(damru).* The house for sexton *(konier)* is on the right side of the big open courtyard with *tarchen* in the centre.

First Gompa

The Lama religion in Khumbu (this first temple was followed by many others which were also under the charge of a *Chorumba)* bloomed in the last century. That is when the construction of first gompa took place. The foundation of the monastery of Tengpoche was also followed by other convents in the Khumbu region. The names of more recent monasteries are Chiwang, Thami, Tolaka, Gole, Thodung and Trakshindu. Some of these are so recent that the shine of paint is still fresh on them. The beautiful traditional murals depicting allegorical figures seem to have been given finishing touches "right now" by the artist. In the temples there are many figures in bas-relief. They flank the frescoes and paintings, painted with great skill according to immutable iconographic laws. It is noteworthy that for these paintings the monks have often had to take their cue either from Tibetan artists or Newaris—their compatriots.

Monasteries for Chomos

Side by side with the monasteries for the male monks has been noted the growth of similar institutions for the Buddhist nuns whose lives are dedicated to prayer, work and meditation. The most important, and perhaps the only one of its kind today, is the nunnery of Deboche *(Dewoche-Devuche)* which stands on a hill in Tengpoche at a distance of not more than half-an-hour's walk from it. The nuns who are called *chomo* live in their own houses around the monastery alternating work with periods of meditation. The monastery of Deboche contains some of the most beautiful religious paintings in the entire zone. According to belief, only about 15 nuns have broken their vow of chastity since the founding of the monastery. Ten of them got married to monks of the nearby Tengpoche monastery. Perhaps the temptation of leading a calm family life has been stronger than any vow.

Monks and nuns in their respective monasteries have their hands full. The engage themselves in learning and understanding rituals of the Lama faith, in reading holy books written in Tibetan language and in helping the novices in the formation of their religious character. The monks (or Lamas as they are usually called as an extended application of the name which is otherwise reserved only for the "master") come from well-off families. In fact their property, both movable and immovable is generally attached permanently to the monastery to assure them economic independence and also to provide some income to meet the needs of their daily collective life.

Duties of Lamas

Monks never sit idle. They are fully occupied from dawn to dusk; raising yak herds, collecting firewood, drawing water, cleaning, making repairs where necessary harvesting crops, winnowing cereals, cultivating fields and preparing butter and cheese. The monastery funds, augmented by the devotees' offerings, are meant to meet expenses only for ceremonies, tea and butter, as well as for the annual festival of mystic dances.

The happy annual get-together of *Mani Rimdu* takes place in the first half of December which forms part of the religious functions in which the Tengpoche dancers from many villages participate. After every catastrophe these very villagers restore and rebuild the monastery with their own hands and gather every year for spiritual dedication. Mystic dances are accompanied by the classic band of the Lama monks comprising of horns and drums.

There are not many monks in monasteries. They are mostly elderly and respectable. They guide novices who came to the monasteries for learning, but only temperary. The group of monks is the novices visit monasteries only temporarily to gain some ideas which may be useful after they return to their villages; because on re-entering family life they would be required to discharge some ordinary religious ceremonies at the request of co-villagers. Besides they may also be called upon to assist high functionaries during their pastoral visits to the villages.

Donations for Constructions

Every monastery is surrounded by a limited number of houses where novice monks have their temporary abode. These novices are called *trapa* to distinguish them from the Lama or the "master" who happens to be consecrated and under permanent vows. Funds for the construction of the monasteries, temples, walls *(mani), chorten* and stupas scattered all along the caravan routes are collected or provided by a Lama in addition to the offerings made by big landlords of neighbouring villages. The money spent on holy works entitles the donor to a number of indulgences for the benefit of his soul. The credit goes to the donor and not to the person who collects the donation. Many Lamas whom we came across had, at one time or other, been monks for some time. Later they had returned to family life. They are married people with children but for the rest of their lives they continue to feel the healthy influence of their "internal guide" to which they were exposed during their stay in the monastery.

Printing of Secred Books

Working in temples, monks patiently repair sacred furnishings, restore paintings on the walls, paste together pieces of painting fallen from the ceiling. In their friends' houses they take up the restoration of the *tankha* or *tangka* which are kept in the private chapel *(tha khang*—house of God). Every important monastery has its own "printing house" with wooden matrices (engraved with the writing in relief) which correspond to pages of the text. The sacred writings are reprinted in multiple copies with a process which can be called xilographic. An inked roller is passed over the matrix which then is ready to receive a piece of paper pushed there with uniform manual pressure.

Provided a Lama is not in a hurry, he can make a copy of any book desired to be kept in some monastery with these wooden matrices if they have not been lost. For obtaining a series of books kept in various monasteries one would need to visit all the monasteries to select the required books and to get them reprinted in xilography. The printing machines are not very refined but they certainly show ingenuity. The type of mark left by vegetable inks on a kind of paper not to be found in other places makes them pass as genuinely mystic works with visitors and devotees. Processing the tablets in the same way the monks make copies of other books also for the *tapas.* These copies, after being lent to the monastery for a short time, are recirculated in villages.

Gompa's Duties

When any villager need religious celebrations done the Lama of the village performs these duties, for which the villager pays him some money. In some villages a temporary Lama may be engaged even for twentyfive days in a month for religious services. Which means that he is unable to attend to any other work at home, in fields or pastures. Therefore the little money that is given to him as compensation is fully justified.

Because of the Chinese occupation of Tibet numerous Lamas of every hierarchical rank have shifted to Nepal. There is certainly a surplus of them in monasteries, *gompas* and in villages where they teach everybody to learn pure Tibetan script. The Sherpas, on the other hand, write in Nepalese script or in Devanagari in which Gurkhali, the national language, is written; this again is derived from Sanskrit with many Tibeto-Birman words. In the Khumjung village some Lamas can be seen interpreting their orders from sacred scriptures which had been brought from the Rongphu monastery. In the history of Lama religion Khumjung is known for having provided many reincarnations of dead Lamas from among its children. It is not generally known that reincarnation can sometimes be threefold. In other words, the body, the voice and the heart of a dead Lama can take rebirth separately in three different persons. One such case was detected in 1941.

Glorifying Buddha

At the entrance of a village where there is Buddhist population, or beside a riverbed or at a crossing, one often comes across a rock or block of big stones on which the invocation *Om Mani Padme Hum* is repeatedly inscribed. Such inscriptions are usually found on walls called *mani* walls or *mendong* along paths connecting one village with another. Sometimes at a village entrance or near a monastery the road passes across a small, square, two-door construction which opens on many colourful paintings glorifying Buddha and depicting scenes from his earthly and divine life.

The Sherpas love to fill their surroundings with sacred signs of Buddhism. The big cylinders or miniature prayer wheels of the *gompas* are worked by the water of streams or moved by winds on the heights. They believe that thousands of *mantras* (brief prayers) written inside or depicted outside are being constantly "read" by the elements of the cosmos. Numerous rows of cylinders placed along monastery walls are pushed into motion by the pilgrims. There are thousands of pocket-size prayer wheels; they hold inside them the traditional strip of paper on which the *mantras* are pyrographed. The big flags called *tarchens* flutter in the sky; a high pole fixed to the ground together with a vertically draped long cloth makes the wind "read" the prayers. During festivals small flags called *lung-to* are displayed in hundreds on doors and windows of houses. Big and small, humble and splendid *chortens* rise along the entire Himalayan facade to serve as a constant reminder of the people's great faith.

Love for the Neighbour

The *chautaras* constructed all along the roads display love for the neighbour. The *chautaras* are small walls with double steps meant to provide rest to the porters. They can keep their load on the higher step without having to take it off while they themselves can sit on the lower step. Generally the *chautaras* are erected at the top of a steep climb, or at a place commanding scenic view or near a small rivulet or fountain. The *kharkas* are shelter-huts built at a great altitude near mountain pastures or along big caravan routes to offer the travellers a momentary asylum. By building the *chautaras* and *kharkas* one is supposed to add to one's sum of indulgences.

What is a Chorten

What exactly is meant by a *chorten?* The broad answer without going into details is that it is derived from the Indian stupa; both represent cosmic symbols—in other words, an architecture of the universe in miniature. Just as the *mandala* is a microcosm or design of the universe with its essential elements represented in only two dimensions (*mandala* from Sanskrit meaning circle). Similarly the *stupa* and the *chorten* both assimilated from Buddhism, show the structure of the cosmos in three dimensions. The square basement represents the earth (geocentric is in fact a conception of the Buddhist religion with the revolving sun). The tapering or top hat-shaped cylinder stands for water. And numerous discs on a pivot perhaps indicate the six heavenly spheres which precede *devachen* or the Buddhist paradise. The reclining half moon indicates the atmosphere in the form of an inverted dome. The disc stands for the sun and the other—the infinite space. *Chorten* in Tibetan signifies "the guardian of the offerings." In a majority of cases, inside the *chorten* there is some relic, or on one side enclosed in a tabernacle is a votice image. The most famous *chorten* erected in the massive form of the Indian *stupa* lies in Gyangste (Tibet) and is called Kumbum; its name signifies "the nundred thousand images." Dozens of chapels and niches enclose 108 images of Buddha; frescoes and prayer wheels, *thankas* and votive lamps are placed in hundreds of perimeteral walls. The *Kumbum* is also called *tondol* because it is enough to have a sight of it to qualify for plenary indulgence of all one's sins.

In the Sherpa territory at every step one meets heaps of stones or pebble deposited by passerby. These are *lha-tho* (the house of God) which keep increasing in size and height. Upon some minor peaks are found other heaps of stones called *lha-bze* which serve as charms. These heaps are placed by devotees, stone upon stone, to appease *shidag,* the god of the peak who, if not piacated, could push the rocks and stones down on the travellers. So, in very remote times the Sherpas and Tibetans had already invented a form of mountaineering out of religious motives. The signs appear in the entire length and breadth of the Himalayas.

Spiritual Life and the Occult Forces

Before embarking on an important journey, the Sherpas sometimes make it a point to perform some atavistic ceremonies which Tibetans call "the elimination of obstacles" *(barche selva).* These functions carried out by special priests are accompanied by offerings of *torma* to the Divinity. Another divination *ta* or *pra* ceremony is sometimes combined with the one mentioned above. The aim of this ceremony is to know in advance what is going to happen during a journey and in the future life and undertakings of the person concerned. It is performed and concluded by a person who is prone to fits and trances in which he narrates his "visions" of things to come. The indispensable instruments for this ceremony are *dorje* (thunderbolt) and *dadar* (arrow with a number of coloured strings). So, a devotee of the Lama faith keeps himself constantly in touch with divine powers and with all the occult forces associated with them by a complicated system of interrelationships. The ceremony of "the removal of obstacles" is also performed when the Sherpa undertakes a *neko* (pilgrimage) for self-purification.

As already mentioned, the life of a Sherpa revolves round his religion which implies reincarnation of the souls of the dead into new bodies for other joys and sufferings. Every Sherpa has his store of indulgences, which may increase or decrease according to the performance of good or bad deeds. These indulgences can be accumulated to the extent of exonerating a person from rebirth. Such a person would enjoy a divine life without having to suffer earthly woes. So, the greatest wish of a Sherpa is to free himself from rebirth and enjoy eternal bliss in his heavenly abode. It is therefore not difficult to imagine what a great fund of good deeds (helping the poor, forgiving neighbours and so on) has to be collected by a Sherpa in the course of his earthly life. Thus, if a Sherpa commits some irregularity or indulges in adultery with girls dedicated to monastic life, his brethren do not reproach him. He simply loses his reserve of indulgences to face the inevitable consequences in his next birth.

Religious Practices

The Lamas and *trapas* perform their daily duties without so much as committing the smallest evil act. At every step they repeat prayers of love for the neighbour. Religious practices instinctively form part of the Sherpas' behaviour during their work-a-day life. They keep on performing them even during mountaineering expeditions in the non-too-easy company of Europeans. If everybody has a word of praise for the great hardships the Sherpa readily endures during expeditions, the main credit must go to their faith in Buddhism. When one talks of good and evil action with them one inevitably ends up with *pei*—which means the balance of good deeds after deducting evil actions from them. In conversation with some Sherpas who are in the know of holy secrets one often hears the word *sonam* which is a scholarly synonym of *pei.*

Thus, the divine hand goes on recording on everybody's personal scroll the bad deeds performed under the influence of evil spirits. Good actions are indicated on the same scroll by white strokes; those with only white strokes against their name and a big store of accumulated *sonam* can be certain of having access to the *devachen* (paradise above the six celestial spheres). They also have a chance to return to earth as a Lama reincarnate. The measure of saintliness and wisdom of such a Lama will be proportionate to the saintliness and wisdom achieved and displayed by him in previous life.

Among Sherpas sin is not associated with lack of respect for the Divine Being or disobedience to him as is generally the case with monotheistic religions. Rather it involves a failure to act according to social morality independent of any religious faith. So, the obligation not to commit sin is derived only from a profound sense of social propriety.

Positive Deeds

Observance of religious precepts and ritual; good deeds towards men; and kindness to animals, these are the categories in which the positive deeds of the sherpas are divided. Under the first category come the offerings of food and money for ceremonies, public and private reading of sacred texts, saying of prayers with wheels tied to walls or with individual prayer wheels, the gift of butter for the lamps in temples and of *torma* for rituals, use of musical instruments during ceremonies, the circumambulation of *chorten, stupa* and *mani* walls, offering of *chang* to perform the "*serchem*" (propitiatory ceremony of the dreadful gods). It has already been made clear that the construction of holy works (like *mani* walls, *chortens, gompas, stupas)* produces *sonam* only for the donor and not for the workers doing the actual work. Such a *sonam* can also be acquired by getting bridges made, wherever necessary, or by having shelters constructed for travellers along the caravan routes. The monks get *sonam* for their continuous renunciation of family life and other pleasures of life.

Sins

Theft, dishonesty in business, litigation, killing any living creature (including flies), sexual relations with nuns or persons married with others, threats, marriage against the bride's will, ill-treatment of animals, plucking flowers, setting a forest on fire, useless felling of trees and excessive use of alcoholic drinks, all these are considered serious sins committed by sherpas. The Sherpas do not believe in making the animals suffer unnecessarily even during certain necessary operations like castration. The slaying of cattle for food is done by butchers who do not belong to the Sherpa clan but are specially called in sometime from distant villages.

Hindus too have an almost similar concept. It is from there that it seems to have passed on to Buddhism. It is the concept of *karma,* which implies the theory of cause and effect on the level of human actions. Man is conditioned by what he does; his action is "the bosom which brings forth" his reincarnation. The initial concept of *karma* under the impact of Buddhist philosophical innovations undergoes a change. *Karm,* therefore, comes to imply the sum total of actions performed by man in earlier life. But according to the Sherpas, it goes beyond the "individual" and assumes a "collective" and transferable aspect. For instance, the merits of the *Bodhisatva* can wash off the demerits of sinners because they are accredited to collective *karma. Karma* is like a big lake of merits to which everyone adds a bucket of good actions, or from which everyone draws a bucket of sins. While *sonam* reminds us of the Egyptian concept of the judgment of souls after death (not dissimilar to the Christian belief of admittance into the three regions beyond death) *karma* relates to human life. It is wider in its range and is more liable to push men to do only good deeds. In every man there is an instinctive force to prevent and curb the sins of others. By employing this force it is possible, for everybody's benefit, to avoid the collective impoverishment of accumulated virtues through *karma.*

They considered disease and every misfortune the deed of evil spirits. This practice of propitiating and satisfying the invisible being is practiced even today. Sherpas in the past used to offer food to invisible beings to dissuade them from causing accidents or diseases.

Exorcisms

To gain control over the occult forces is a constant preoccupation of the Sherpas. Exorcisms are practised by the Lamas to liberate people from evil spirits called *shrindi* or *norpa.* Such exorcisms, are publicly performed in villages during the rite of *tsirim* in April and October. Among the Lamas there are some who have special aptitude for acting as prophets and predictors; others easily go in a trance and can thus see the spirit invoked. Some have the ability to read and interpret divine oracles; others still, with their ventriloquous skill, are able to make the invoked spirits who temporarily come to possess them, talk. The Tibetan and Sherpa literatures cite many cases (historically known and confirmed by circumstantial evidence) dealing with mediums, and record dates and names of the devotees and the Lamas who had entered in direct contact with supernatural forces.

The ability to predict future is a normal routine with some Lamas; it comes naturally without even the necessity of learning the mechanism. Naturally, many devotees make use of such Lamas on small payments. The local papers also report exceptional cases of women who become witches or *pem* insofar as evil spirits come to possess their bodies almost permanently. Unconsciously these women are led to inflict injury on people; for example, they can administer poison to guests. Needless to say they are shunned by everybody. It is also a general belief that touching the body of a witch, dead or alive, could bring bad luck for the whole life.

Propitiating the Klus

The Sherpas are also devotees of the so-called *klu* (the spirits of water) who in symbolic iconography are always represented as serpents. They are always well disposed towards men. However, they can be dangerous if they are neglected; for example, if one forgets to give them small offerings every day. The Sherpas, on noting that during summer Nauche's natural springs register a considerable fall in their water level, rush to the conclusion that in that particular season a fixed number of *klu* migrate to Tibet to return to Nepal during the rainy season and winter. Before being known as spirits of water, the *klus* were considered "goblins of habitations" and they were given a small daily offering at the household altar. The *klu* always shows a liking and attachment for the women of the house; when one of these gets married it is traditional to cover a small domestic sacrarium with heavy drapery so that the *klu* may not get wind of what is happening and so may not get displeased. Besides, the boys and girls keep dancing in front of the domestic altar for distracting *klu's* attention from the marriage festivities.

The Sherpas' daily life is so much enveloped in spiritualism that there is always some episode or incident, which deserves closer scrutiny. For us the mountain is a deserted and inanimate place. But for the Sherpas it is an abode of spirit and goblins who, since times immemorial, love to play tricks with those who venture in its confines. For example, when we attribute to sunrays or snow and ice the peeling of skin-patches from cheeks or the scorching of the faces of those who roam in high mountains, the Sherpas consider this as rather a naive explanation.

On their part, they are certain that these are the tricks played by some devils living in snow who waylay people and scratch their faces and tear down their skin, layer by layer. Visitors and travellers are not used to that sort of exposure to the sun. The sherpas are very sure that the ointment or a pomade which is applied to face to stave off peeling of the skin, is based on some ancient formula.

This claim has a point. The efficiency of the herbs available in the Himalayas is now dawning on the Europeans who use to scoff at the traditional system of skin-care.

The Yeti

Among the most mysterious entities, despite the numerous footprints found on snow in the Khumbu region, is the *yeti*, "the most venerable" snowman about whose existence nothing definite has so far been demonstrated, nor perhaps will it ever be done. A reader who would like to enter into a conversation with the natives on this subject, for scientific ends, would do well to acquaint himself with the various names with which the legendary creature is known (such as a wicked ogre, a good white witch and so on). It is also called *metch kangmi* (the stinking snowman) in Tibetan and Sherpa language; *metch* means stinking and dirty, *kang* means snow, *mi* stands for human or man. And then, *midre gangmi* is a hybrid compound of words used by the Tibetans; *midre* stands for bear-man, and gang or *kang-mi* stands for snowman.

It is worth noting that the natives imagine three different sizes of the snowman: average, big and small: *mi-teh* stands for medium height and *den-teh* for large; in Langtrang the expression *chumi* is used for the snowman as big as a child and *yilmu* for a bigger one. The English simply call it snowman. *Mahlangur Himal*—the great monkey of the mountains—is the name given by natives in the entire Everest chain.

Gemaka, on the other hand, stands for a masked character who dons a yeti scalp as headgear; this character appears sometimes in certain less common ceremonies.

Festivals and Ceremonies

Four images of divinity corresponding to the four seasons of the years have a special importance in the life of a Sherpa. *Ygri-gyemo* is the summer queen of azure colour; *gungi-gyemo* is the yellow winter queen, *tongy-gyemo* is the green coloured queen of autumn; and *chigi-*

gyeme the red queen of spring. These images are generally found in every gompa.

During the four seasons, certain ceremonies are performed at fixed times. The Sherpa community is called upon to attend and participate in these ceremonies. The village or the temple is the place where such festivals and ceremonies take place. They take on special importance when the Lama clergy alongwith a number of representatives participate. They are of great value even from a choreographic point of view. Some festivals last only for a day, others six days. On such occasions the work in the villages comes to a halt and everybody goes to the festival. A responsible person of the village called *Lawa* is entrusted with the charge of organising such festivals. He collects funds, fixes duties and turns for assistants, regulates various phases of the festival and arranges for the distribution of food among spectators.

A thing which one never misses in these ceremonies is *torma* which is given the shape of Divinity and then offered at the altars in great number. In April and October or beginning and end of farming operations, the rite called *tsirem* is performed in order to drive away evil spirits. This is celebrated in the village *gompas.*

Rate of Esho

At the end of April and beginning of May, every small village with a temple of its own celebrates the rite of *esho* for the protection of village fields. This ceremony coincides with the beginning of agricultural operations or with their earlier phases. It consists of the temporary removal of cattle from the village and creation of a magic wall around houses by means of exorcism to prevent evil forces from trespassing in cultivated fields.

At the end of May or beginning of June every village performs the *niungne* for obtaining forgiveness for sins. The ceremony lasts three days and, among other things, includes circumambulation of the *chorten* and *maṇi* walls by men and women who are provided with special food prepared by priests with donations from the community.

Dumja

In the second half of July, every village possessing a temple holds a two-day ceremony called *dumje* or the "festival of the village temple." Some men and boys stay back in the high altitude huts to take care of the cattle to enable the rest of the Sherpa population to participate in this ceremony. Although there is no specific on-the-spot declaration, this festival is traditionally held to celebrate the death anniversary of Lama Sanga Dorje—the patron saint of the entire Khumbu region and founder of the temple of Pangpoche. A similar rite dedicated to the founder is celebrated in February in Tengphoche monastery.

Yerchang (summer beer) or the summer festival is celebrating on the first of August in every village. It is reserved for people who, having no cattle to send to the pastures, are constrained to stay back in the village—a consolation drink for those who cannot be at the *yersa* (summer houses).

These ceremonies, too, are under the charge of a master of ceremonies (*lawa*). It is his duty to arrange funds, procure *chang* and *torma* for the votive offerings, and to compensate the lama for his liturgical services. *Phema* (butter and *tsampa* mixed in equal proportion) is also employed for votive offerings.

The greatest festival of the year is undoubtedly the *mani rimdu* or the festival of ritual dances at the monastery. This is celebrated alternatively at the monastery of Thami in May and at Tengpoche in November or beginning of December. This festival, which generally lasts for three days, is similar to *dumje;* the only difference being that at the *mani rimdu* there is a larger participation by the clergy, which makes it much more important. This festival came to be celebrated in the Khumbu region only from the mid-twentieth century. In 1940 it was celebrated at Thami for the first time. This ceremony, with its symbolic masked dances, is celebrated with as much pomp and show as at the Rongphu monastery.

3

Monastic Institutions and Priesthood

The monastery and its monks are forces of vital importance for Sherpa society and Sherpa culture. The village, with its inhabitants engrossed in the pursuit of husbandry and trade, represents only one side of Sherpa life. The other side is represented by monasteries and nunneries, by the lonely cave-dwellings of hermits and the small settlements of lamas within easy reach of the habitations of lay village-folk. Sherpa society embraces the laity as well as the many men and women who choose the religious life, and the one part is incomplete and incomprehensible without the other. Unlike the Brahman priest of Hindu society, whose place is invariably inside secular society, the Buddhist lama has the choice of either living in the midst of the laity, a villager among villagers, or of abandoning all secular ambitions and associations and devoting himself exclusively to spiritual pursuits. While personally withdrawing from lay society, he does not withdraw his services.

The worship of local deities, foremost in the religious thought of the untutored layman, is not excluded from the ritual performances of the monasteries. There is no cleavage between the Buddhist doctrine practised in the monasteries and the religion of the ordinary villager. Both have their roots in Tibetan religious traditions. The intellectual levels of the religious practices of monks and laymen are undoubtedly very different, but unlike in Tamang[1] society there is no trace of any conflict between village religion and the more sophisticated beliefs of learned lamas.

The Sherpa Civilisation

Strange as it may seem, none of the monastic institutions in Khumbu and Solu are older than a hundred years, and the two most prominent monasteries, Tengboche and Chiwong, were founded less than fifty years ago. That the last three generations have seen a most vigorous expansion of religious institutions cannot be doubted, and in Chapter I (pp. 10, 11) I have suggested that the great upsurge in religious activities had been made possible by favourable developments in the social and economic fields. The historical development of Buddhism in Khumbu and Solu is a problem intimately linked with that of the age of Sherpa civilization in its present form.

Lama Sanga Dorje

The Sherpas associate the oldest centres of Buddhist worship in Khumbu with the legendary figure of Lama Sanga Dorje, the sixth reincarnation of Changna Dorje (Vajra Pani), whose twelfth reincarnation is the present abbot of the Tibetan monastery of Rongphu. While all other reincarnations of Dorje Chang occurred in Tibet, local tradition has it that Lama Sanga Dorje was born in Mohang, a place on the path between Khumjung and Phortse, as the son of the great lama Bundachendzen. This lama, who is reputed to have been a Sherpa of Salaka clan, is himself the central figure of various legends. Thus, it is said that the great country god Khumbu-yulha regularly visited Lama Bundachendzen in his *gomba* in Mohang, but that the latter's wife, made suspicious by her husband's long conversations with a mysterious visitor, once surprised the god, who departed in a flash of light and never again appeared at Mohang. There is also a story of a contest of magic between Lama Bundachendzen and another lama resident near Khumjung, and all these traditions point to the fact that Lama Sanga Dorje, although thought responsible for the foundation of the first village temple in Khumbu, is not considered the first great lama who lived in this region. While his father, Bundachendzen, was able to converse in person with the great country god Khumbu-yulha, Lama Sanga Dorje had the power to fly through the air and perform other magical feats.

The Legend

Lama Sanga Dorje and his two brothers were debating as to which of them was the more powerful lama. Lama Sanga Dorje won the resulting competition in magical feats by using a ray of sunlight entering a room through a crack in the wall as a line to hang up his cloak. His fame greatly exceeds that of his two brothers, though the latter are also believed responsible for the foundation of *gomba,* namely those of

Kerok and Gomila. This story can be heard from sherpas in many places.

Lama Sanga Dorje is reputed to have stayed for some time at the present site of Tengboche, where he built a small *gomba.* But once he slipped on a rock, which still bears the marks of his feet, and taking this as an inauspicious sign, he left Tengboche and moved to nearby Pangboche, in the valley of the Imja Khola. There he built a *gomba,* the first great temple in the whole of Khumbu. Soon he collected monks around him, and his teaching is believed to have laid the foundation for much of the Buddhist learning in Khumbu.

The people of Pangboche point to many landmarks as the products of Lama Sanga Dorje's miraculous feats. Thus, they believe that the groves of old juniper trees to both sides of the *gomba* sprang from the hairs the saint cut from his head and scattered to the left and right of the site chosen for the temple. There is also a roof-like projection of rock, which he is believed to have pulled out of the mountainside to obtain shelter when he first arrived at Pangboche.

According to local tradition Lama Sanga Dorje's activities did not remain unopposed, and there is a story that a man of Jong-domba clan, alternatively believed to have been a *pembu* of Thami-chok or a resident of Khumjung, sent out two men to murder the saint. But Lama Sanga Dorje, who at that time lived in a hermitage at Nagarjung above Dingboche, saw the two men approach transformed his two dogs into a tiger and a leopard and thus killed the assassins.

Dorje's Death

Miracles have always been assigned to Lama Sanga Dorje. This happened in his life. This happened in his death, too. He died not in Pangboche but at Tshou, a place close to Rongphu. His body was not cremated; it evaporated in the form of a rainbow, and only his eyes, tongue and heart remained. These were enshrined in a silver casket by the local Tibetans, but on hearing of the death of their saint, the Pangboche people devised a trick to acquire the precious relics *(kudung)* for their own *gomba.* Sixteen men went to the shrine where they were kept, and while eight of them made its guardians drunk with beer and liquor, eight others seized the casket with the relics and carried it across the Nangpa La. The Tibetans, when recovered from their intoxication, pursued the Sherpas, but were beaten back by a hail of stones from the latters' slings. The relics were installed in the Pangboche *gomba,* and a second attempt by Tibetans, aimed at recovering the saints remains, was averted by negotiation. Ever since the silver casket with the relics has occupied the central place in the first-floor hall *(ser-song lha-khang)* of the Pangboche *gomba,* flanked by two caskets containing similar relics of two reincarnated Pangboche lamas, one of them the grandfather of Lama Ngawang Chotr, a man now in his early forties.

Lama Sanga Dorje had gathered a group of monks, who were celibate like himself but, when after his death he was not reincarnated for three years, another lama, named Rigsing Totuk Wongbu, established himself at Pangboche. He was married and the monks, following his example, also took wives, so that since that time Pangboche is a *gomba* of married lamas.

Reincarnation of Lama Sanga Dorje

Lama Sanga Dorje was reincarnated in Tibet, and the abbots of Rongphu monastery are considered the reincarnations of this saint, who—it must be remembered—was himself the sixth reincarnation of Dorje Chang. The present abbot of Rongphu is the twelfth-rein-carnation of Dorje Chang (and the sixth of Lama Sanga Dorje), and it is believed that there will be only two more reincarnations after which Lama Sanga Dorje will enter Devachen, i.e., the Western Paradise of Opame (Sanskrit: Amithaba), the Buddha of Boundless Light.

The Sherpa inhabitants of Pangboche lang claim to Lama Sanga Dorje as founder and patron of their religious institutions. But they are not the only ones. The people of Thami, too, point to this great saint as the founder of their *gomba* and preceptor of the lama who became the ancestor of a long line of married head-lamas. The story goes that at the time when Lama Sanga Dorje was contemplating the foundations of Thami *gomba,* which originally stood on the site now occupied by the head lama's house, he saw one morning a rainbow leading from the summit of Khumbu-yulha to this place above Thami, and took it as an indication of where the *gamba* should be built. He then installed one of his disciples as the lama to be in charge of the new *gomba,* and the latter's descendants, who were not celibate monks but married lamas have held this office ever since. The head lama whom I met in 1957 had a record of fourteen generations of lamas of his own family, and he believed that the foundation of the *gomba* occurred some four hundred years ago. This estimate tallies roughly with the idea that since then Lama Sanga Dorje has been reincarnated six times.

Proliferation of Monastic Institutions

Dr. David Snellgrove has suggested that Buddhism was introduced into Khumbu towards the end of the seventeenth century[2] and, if this proves correct, local ideas of the antiquity of the oldest *gomba* overestimate the time elapsed since its foundation by over one fourth, an error which may easily develop in a society with little sense of historic precision. In the context of our study the exact age of such *gomba* as those of Pangboche and Thami is of little relevance, but a phenomenon calling for an explanation is the proliferation of monastic institutions and the rapid increase in the numbers of celibate monks and nuns in the course of the past two or three generations.

Fifty years ago there existed in Khumbu no institution which might have been called a monastery or nunnery. There were the three ancient *gomba* of Pangboche, Thami and Kerok, and the more recently-founded *gomba* of Khumjung and Namche. Attached to each of these *gomba* were several lamas, and in the case of the Thami and Kerok *gomba,* one particular family of lamas had been in charge of the *gomba* for several generations. All the lamas were married men, and there were, as it seems, no monks *(thawa)* who had taken vows of permanent celibacy. Besides these married lamas there were hermits, who for a number of years occupied a cave-dwelling or solitary hut high above the inhabited valleys, but none of them seem to have attempted to turn their personal retreat into a settlement where others might join them in their life of meditation.

Lama Gulu

It was only in 1923 that Lama Gulu, the member of a prominent family of Khumjung and, as it seems a powerful personality, inspired the people of Khumjung to support him in the foundation of a *gomba* on the model of Tibetan monasteries. He did not embrace a religious career early in life. He married and had six children, five of whom died in childhood. It was only when he also lost his wife that he devoted himself more and more to the active practice of religion. He went to study in Tibet, and subsequently retired to Chamgaon, a small settlement on the slopes of Khumbu-yulha, some 800 feet above Khumjung, where convenient rock shelters easily convertible into cave-dwellings had sometimes served hermits and religious-minded women as a temporary retreat from village life. He inspired people of Khumjung to support him in the foundation of a gomba on the model of a Tibetan monastry. That was on 1023. It was there that he secluded himself for the traditional period of three years, three months and three days, and his example gradually led other men and women, to seek peace and spiritual advancement in the vicinity of so inspired a teacher. More and more people settled at Chamgaon, until it became a regular settlement of twelve to thirteen houses where people of Khumjung devoted themselves to religious practices.

Yet, these men and women who lived there without formal organization and discipline, did not form a regular monastic community. Only in his old age did Lama Gulu begin to contemplate the foundation of a proper monastery with an organized and disciplined religious life.

Founding of Tengboche

It was in connection with the founding of Tengboche that the abbot of Rongphu recognized Lama Gulu as a reincarnation of Lama Bundachendzen. The fact that his nature as a reincarnate lama was not discovered in childhood was explained by reference to an accident he had suffered in infancy. Old people remembered that as a small child Lama Gulu had fallen into a latrine, and this unfortunate defilement by human excrement was believed to have veiled his character as Lama Bundachendzen's reincarnation. When the two men met the abbot of Rongphu is said to have asked Lama Gulu not to salute him with the usual obeisance due to a reincarnate lama, for as Lama Gulu was a reincarnation of Lama Bundachendzen (the father of Lama Sanga Dorje), he stood to the abbot of Rongphu, the reincarnation of Lama Sanga Dorje, in the relationship of father. As Lama Bundachendzen is far less famous than Lama Sanga Dorje and Lama Gulu's nature as his first reincarnation for several hundred years is not widely known, the reincarnate abbot of Rongphu is nevertheless regarded with greater reverence than Lama Gulu's reincarnation, the present abbot of Tengboche. For Rongphu is the mother-institution, to which the young monks of Tengboche used to go for study and inspiration, and the charter of Tengboche, containing an account of the foundation and an enumeration of the rules governing its monastic life, bears the seal of the abbot of Rongphu.

Four men: Kushang (Thaktu) of Khumjung, Lama Karmamundu (Lama) of Junbesi, Chepal (Gole), the *gembu* of Khumbu, who lived in Namche, and a kinsman of his, Sun Chopal of Gole bore the cost of constructing the nearly founded gomba of Tengboche. To pay for the wall-paintings and other items of interior decoration as well as for the images Lama Gulu collected subscriptions in all the villages of Khumbu. So great is the Sherpas' generosity for religious purposes that an impressive three-storeyed building with a large paved courtyard surrounded by galleries arose within two months on a site several hours' walk from any permanent village. All the villagers of Khumjung, Kunde, Phortse, Pangboche and Namche came to help with the work, giving their labour free of charge.

Transfer of Property

As soon as the *gomba* was completed, Lama Gulu built a house for himself and other men, attracted by the prospects of an organized religious life, built small houses around the main temple. These houses were and still are individually owned, and may be sold by one monk to another. It is only in the event of a monk breaking his vows of celibacy and leaving the monastery that his immovable property within the *gomba* precincts falls to the monastery, from which it may be purchased by other monks.

Lama Gulu's brother's son and three other men of Khumjung, one man of Kunde, one man of Pangboche, one man of Namche, and one lama of Junbesi were the first members of the new monastic community of Tengboche. Several of these men had taken monastic vows in Rongphu monastery, and were living in Dzamda, a small settlement situated on a high and lonely site north of Thami, of a character similar to that of Chamgaon. While in Dzamda there was no *gomba,* Tengboche offered the chance of leading a full monastic life under the guidance of a lama renowned for his learning and saintliness throughout Khumbu.

The Earthquake

Within the first decade the number of monks in Tengboche had increased to twenty-five, and the monastery rapidly became the focal point of religious activities within a wide area. But ten years after its foundation a catastrophe occurred which might well have daunted the spirits of a people less resilient and devout than the Sherpas of Khumbu. In the great earthquake of 1933 the main temple collapsed and Lama

Gulu, then eighty-five years old, died shortly afterwards of shock. He was cremated in the ruins of the monastery, on the very site where the great hall *(duang)* of the *gomba* had stood.

The villagers of Khumbu again came to the help of the young monastery and, gave money and free labour. The gomba was to be rebuilt making it even bigger than it had been before the earthquake. And only three years passed before it was found that Lama Gulu was reincarnated in the son of a Khamba couple of Namche. The child's utterances about his former home in Tengboche had aroused first the parents' and then other people's attention, and when the monks of Tengboche placed some of Lama Gulu's clothes and other personal possessions, mixed up with similar articles of different origin before the child suspected to be a reincarnation of their late abbot, the little boy, then four years old, picked out all the genuine articles saying that they belonged to him. Satisfied with this proof the monks brought the child to Tengboche, and one of the higher monastery officials, the *umse* Gyaljen, who was Lama Gulu's brother's son, took the boy into his own house and devoted himself to his education. As the first reincarnate *(tulku)* lama of Tengboche, the Khamba boy was regarded with veneration from the very beginning. At the age of sixteen he was taken to Rongphu for further studies and when in 1956 he returned to Tengboche he was ready to assume—or in the Sherpas' view to reassume—his place as the head of the monastery.

The average age of the monks in 1957 was not more than thirty and it had a young lama as its head. Since its foundation thirty-four years previously many boys and young men of the villages of Khumbu, and particularly of Khumjung, Kunde and Namche, had come to the monastery to learn and to become initiated into a religious life. Not all were temperamentally suited to the contemplative existence of a monk. Some left the monastery to return to secular occupations, some married and settled down as village lamas, but others remained true to their monastic vows, content to make Tengboche their permanent home.

Monks who have no intention of returning to a secular life do not permanently live in seclusion. There are many occasions when they are called to the one or the other village, to recite from sacred scriptures for the benefit of a sick person, to participate in funeral ceremonies and memorial services, to conduct a rite in a village temple, and to help with the annual reading of the Kangyur. On all these occasions they are in close contact with the lay villagers, and they freely visit their families and kinsmen, staying for some days in their houses and advising them on practical as well as religious problems. Similarly lay folk from all villages of Khumbu as well as many parts of Pharak and Solu occasionally visit the *gomba,* anxious to obtain the reincarnate lama's blessing or intent on commissioning the performance of a sacred rite, be it to gain merit *(sonam)* or to honour the memory of a deceased kinsman, and smooth his path in the world beyond.

The Two Way Exposure

This inter-connection of the monastery and the lay world is a source of inspiration to the village lamas as well as to the more educated among the laymen. The great monastery festival, known as Mani-rimdu, places even before the most simple of villagers some basic notions of Buddhist doctrine in the form of dramatic and most impressive representations.

The monk community of Tengboche might have grown to even greater size had it not been for the presence of a settlement of nuns, known as Devuche, less than half an hour's walk north-east of the monastery. Four years before his death Lama Gulu agreed to the foundation of a nunnery in a pleasant valley a few hundred feet the ridge of Tengboche, and there some of the wealthy families of Khumjung, Kunde and Namche built small house, for daughters or sisters attracted by the prospect of a religious life close to the revered abbot of Tengboche. But the proximity of young monks and young nuns had consequences perhaps not foreseen by Lama Gulu, and the high rate of marriages between Tengboche monks and Devuche nuns formed a serious brake to the growth of the new community of monks.

Before we deal in detail with the social composition of these two religious settlements, we must briefly consider contemporary developments in the western part of Khumbu. At Thami, the largest village in the valley of the Bhote Kosi, a family of married or *gyupi* lamas had for many generations—fourteen generations according to their own estimate—been in charge of a *gomba* tracing its origin to Lama Sanga Dorje. This *gomba* was a small building, and the only lamas living in the neighbouring houses were members of the present head lama's lineage. Even when Lama Tundu, the latter's father succeeded to the position of abbot there were no celibate monks at Thami, and several lay families dwelt in the settlement clustering round the small *gomba.* But in the year 1920

Lama Tundu decided to shift the *gomba* to a place where a bigger structure could be erected and the reincarnate abbot of Rongphu, the same man who had chosen the site for Tengboche, encouraged him in this undertaking. Thami *gomba* developed into a monastic a monastic establishment catering for a wider circle of students and lamas. It ceased to be a family institution.

To became a Monk

Young men desirous of becoming monks soon collected. Most of them came from the villages of Thamichok, and small houses, built into the rocks of the steep mountain slope, began to spring up round the new *gomba.* Among the first novices were several sisters' sons of Lama Tundu, but others had no ties of kinship to the lama's family, but gathered there on account of Lama Tundu's reputation and the facilities for a communal religious life provided in the newly built *gomba.* By 1957 Thami *gomba,* the official name of which is Gon-de Dziri-chu-ko, had grown into a monastery comprising married lamas as well as celibate monks, or *thawa,* with a full complement of monastery officials, and the facilities for staging performances of the great Mani-rimdu dance festival.

Emergency of Monastic Institutions

The inspiration for this development—like the inspiration for the foundation of Tengboche—clearly came from Rongphu, the famous monastery of the Nyingmapa sect on the Tibetan side of the Mount Everest group, and no year passed without some of the Thami monks going for several weeks, or even months, to Rongphu for study and religious practices. It was in Rongphu that these *thawa* first took their vows and later received instruction in the ritual dances of the Mani-rimdu.

The first performance of this festival at Thami monastery took place in 1942, but for several years it was confined to the *gomba* services and the blessing of the crowd by the abbot. Only from 1950 onwards were the monks able to stage also the elaborate dramatic dances, which give the Mani-rimdu the character of a colourful folk festival. The first half of the twentieth century saw the emergence of monastic institutions not only in Khumbu, but also in various parts of Solu. Monasteries and nunneries have sprung up at Chiwang, Trakshindo, Tolaka, Gole and most recently Todhung. Their foundation within the past fifty years lends to show that the establishment of monasteries at Tengboche and Thami at about the same time cannot be due to purely local cause.

Formation of Monastic Communities

Before we enter upon a discussion of the organization of a monastery such as Tengboche, it is appropriate to analyse the composition of such a small and closely-knit community of men and boys, who have renounced secular life in familiar surroundings in order to devote themselves to the practice of religion. Does such a community constitute a random aggregation of individuals united solely by the common desire for spiritual advancement, or are some of the *thawa* linked by ties of kinship, and do family connections play a part in setting young boys on the path to a monastic career?

An analysis of the community of *thawa* in Tengboche provides the answer to some of these questions. In 1957 there were, apart from the reincarnate abbot, thirty-two monks in Tengboche. Eight of these came from Namche, two of them being step-brothers while one was the father's brother's grandson of Kushang (Thaktu), who had provided part of the funds for the construction of the monastery. Only three of the monks resident in 1957 came from Khumjung, but judging from the large number of *ex-thawa* born in Khumjung and living in various villages, Khumjung provided in earlier years a much larger percentage of the Tengboche monks. Kunde was the home village of seven thawa, two of these stood in the relation of uncle and brother's son, two were brothers, and with one of these monks lived his widowed father, a lama who in his youth had also been a monk in Tengboche. Pangboche, a village with a high percentage of lamas, was represented only by three monks, and Phortse, though at no great distance from Tengboche, surprisingly only by one *thawa*.

It is understandable, on the other hand, that only one of the monks came from Thami, a village with its own flourishing *gomba.* Finally there were two young step-brothers of the reincarnate abbot among the student monks. They were the sons of his father and a Tibetan mother, and had grown up in Tibet, where their father had settled after separating from the *tulku* lama's mother. The latter lived with her son in Tengboche, an exception from the ban on women being made in the case of a reincarnate lama's mother, and with her was her twelve-year-old son from a second husband. This step-brother of the abbot also received training in Tengboche and in August 1957 he went to Rongphu to take monastic vows. A reincarnate lama inspires the members of his family to the monastic in which resides and prompts them to take vows.

Close Links

This analysis of the community of Tengboche monks in 1957 shows the close link between a monastery and the villages in the vicinity. With the exception of the abbot's Tibetan step-brothers not one of the monks hailed from any village outside Khumbu, and the vast majority came from the three villages of Namche, Khumjung and Kunde. It shows moreover that many monks have kinship ties to at least one other member of the community, and this tendency becomes even clearer when we include in our consideration those monks who either died or left the monastery. For we then see that among those *thawa* who in 1957 had no-close kinsmen in the monastery, some came to Tenghoche at a time when they could share the house of a close relative.

If we extend our analysis over the thirty-three years between the foundation of the monastery and 1957 we will find that the composition of monk community gains great depth. In that period 91 *thawa* were admitted to the *gomba;* 8 died there, one founded a monastery of his own at Trakshindo, and 44 *thawa* either voluntarily left Tengboche to return to secular life and marry, or were compelled to leave on account of clandestine associations with women brought to the *gomba* officials' notice. The large number of *thawa,* who left the monastery for the one or other reason leads us to the conclusion that the state of monk is not considered as a man's final choice, but that in many cases it is but a phase in a career, comparable almost to some years spent in an institution of higher education.

If we add all the figures of *thawa* who had passed through Tengboche to those resident in 1957, we find that altogether 17 came from Namche, 18 from Khumjung, 13 from Kunde, 9 from Pangboche, 2 copy of the bill voter card photo from Phortse, one from Thami, 4 from Solu and Pharak, and 2 from Tibet.

The Extended Family

Many families of Namche, Khumjung and Kunde furnished more than one *thawa.* We find among the past and present *thawa* three brothers of Chusherwa clan of Kunde, four members of one Thaklu family of Khumjung, a man of another Thaktu lineage of Khumjung, as well as four cases of father and son. Kinship connections with one of the senior *thawa* greatly facilitates a boy's entrance into the monastery and reduces the financial burden to his parents. For in such a case a boy will usually stay with his relative for several years and may ultimately even inherit his house. Considering that the majority of the *thawa* of Tengboche come from the wealthier and more prominent families of the three villages Namche, Khumjung and Kunde, it is obvious that the web of consanguineous and affinal kinship ties connecting most of these families extends also to the monk community of Tengboche.

The reincarnation of Tengboche's founder Lama Gulu, who had belonged to one of the leading Khumjung families, occurred not within the same circle, but in a family of Khambas recently immigrated from Tibet. The same social stratum from which most of the monks in Tengboche were recruited, also provided the majority of the nuns *(ani)* of Devuche. In 1957 there were twenty nuns resident, but only nine of these had the qualifications to take an active part in the services in their *gomba.* The others were either devout women without sufficient learning, who had not taken any vows, or nuns disqualified by a breach of their vow of celibacy. Fourteen of the nuns had never been married—though two of these had *themba* children—and six had been married but came to Devuche after their husband's death or the break-up of their marriage. Nine of the nuns came from Khumjung, seven from Namche, three from Kunde and one from Phortse. Neither Pangboche nor the Thamichok area was represented in the small community. Among the twenty nuns there were four pairs of sisters, and one mother and her daughter. The percentage of nuns who had remained for the whole of their lives in Devuche was no greater than that of monks who had resisted the temptations of a secular life. Since the foundation of Devuche in 1930 fourteen nuns had left the nunnery and got married, and in ten of these cases they had married ex-*thawa* of Tengboche. But the number of nuns in Devuche remained fairly stable, for there was a hard core of those unlikely to find husbands even if they were thus inclined, and newamers took the place and acquired the houses of those who left the nunnery.

Composition of the Community

If one studies religious societies one would found that food is provided at their places above by that society. In sharpa monastries, it is not so. One of the principal factors determining the composition of a community of monks as well as that of a nunnery, is the general rule that monks and nuns must provide for their own maintenance and their own lodgings. The monks in a Sherpa monastery, though provided with tea during the daily services, have each their own household maintained by two or three *thawa* living in one house. The parents of a novice either buy or build him a house, or arrange for him to live with an older kinsman or friend. They provide the young *thawa* with food and other necessities, and when it seems probable that he will persist in a monastic career they give him a share in their property similar to that given to an elder son at the time of his marriage and separation from the parental household. Whatever immovable property a monk receives as his share he usually sells, investing the money in such a way as to give him a steady income of agricultural produce. The high rates of interest paid by Sherpas—25 per cent being the usual rate—enable a single man to live on the income from even a modest capital and, as there is always a demand for cash loans, no monk or nun has difficulty in finding borrowers who will promise annual deliveries of provisions as a form of interest payment.

Affluent Thawas

Since a thawa has to make his own arrangement, this system allows only the sons of fairly wealthy people to enter a monastery as a *thawa,* and the same applies to the nuns wishing to settle at Devuche. A poor man can maintain himself in a monastery only if he finds work as the servant of a more affluent *thawa,* but such opportunities are limited. Few monks are rich enough to maintain such a servant: there are usually younger kinsmen only too willing to serve a father's or mother's brother in return for instruction and their keep. Among the monks resident in 1957 there was none who had to maintain himself by serving the other monks, but a Tibetan *thawa* without any income of his own, had lived in Tengboche for many years supporting himself by carrying water and doing other menial jobs for his fellow monks. He had nevertheless the same status as other monks and remained in Tengboche until his death.

Motive behind becoming a Monk

Boys of perhaps not more than twelve or thirteen are sent to a monastery by their parents and usually left in charge of an older kinsman, and young men who become *thawa* on their own initiative. In the former case parents of some means may wish their sons to receive a sound education, leaving them the option of staying in the monastery and in due course taking religious vows, or of returning to their home and employing their learning perhaps in a career of village lama. The presence among the monks of a senior kinsman facilitates a boy's maintenance at a monastery, and such family connections obviously play a role in deciding parents to detail one son to a career of religious studies. The prestige value of learning and religious knowledge is certainly not without influence in such a decision, but an equally strong motive is the genuine conviction that a life spent in the service of religion and devoted to the accumulation of merit predestines a person for a desirable fate in future lives.

A rich man with much property to pass on to his children is not likely to encourage an only son to become a *thawa,* but if there are several sons the departure of one leaves no gap and may even ease arrangements for the management of the paternal property. If we consider the boys and young men of Khumjung and Kunde who, in 1957, had either already become *thawa* or intended to take up a monastic career in Tengboche, we find that out of twelve only one was the sole son of his parents. But in this case there was the strong motivation that the boy's father's brother had acted, during the reincarnate lama's minority, as head of the monastery and wanted his nephew to live with him. Two of the prospective *thawa* were second sons out of three sons; one the third son among seven; three the second sons out of two and one the fourth and last son. In one case both the eldest and the second sons of a rich man had become *thawa*, but there were three younger brothers to remain with the parents. Family circumstances are, therefore, also taken into consideration.

The Case in Point

The way in which an elder kinsman can attract a boy to a monastic life is exemplified by the case of the eldest son of Phur Temba (Paldorje), a moderately prosperous man of Khumjung. This boy was being taught how to read and write by his maternal uncle Jangbu, who was a monk in Tengboche. It was understood that if the boy proved intelligent and Jangbu liked him he would leave him all his property, which included a house in Tengboche and sufficient investments to support him. Any of close blood relations, if willing to take monastic vows, would thus have a home and adequate means to lend a life free of worldly cares.

Where the decision to enter a monastery is taken by a young man himself, a predilection for intellectual pursuits is probably one of the most frequent motives. A young Sherpa of more than average intelligence, whose interests lie in the literary sphere rather than in trade, finds in a monastery more scope for his special talent than in any other environment. Whether he has a bent for a contemplative life, enjoys the study of scriptures, proves skilful in the organization of ritual performances or has a talent for the running of monastery affairs, as a *thawa* he can follow his interests and finds ample opportunity for the development of his intellectual gifts. The attraction of a materially rather comfortable life is not likely to rank high among the incentives, for young men wealthy enough to be able to maintain themselves at a monastery, would not suffer any hardships even if they remained in their parental houses. Far more important is, no doubt, the prospect of attaining to positions of dignity and influence, for the social status of a lama reputed for his learning is high. Sherpas will vie with each other in inviting such a person for the performance of rites and will consider it an honour to offer him hospitality and generous gifts.

Why become a Monk?

Yet we would misinterpret Sherpa mentality, if we assumed that expectations of worldly success and recognition were the main motives that led young men to choose a career as monks and lamas. There is no doubt a deeply religious strain in Sherpa society, and the conviction that the acquisition of merit assures future bliss no less than present peace of mind and joyousness, is not confined to a few hermits and reincarnate lamas. One has only to stand a few days in a Sherpa monastery to realize that the expedition of a happy and contented life is no illusion. The monks one meets there, old as well as young, seem so cheerful and full of zest that one can hardly doubt their satisfaction with the mode of life they have chosen. Though the direction of their endeavours may be 'other-worldly' they enjoy to the full the permitted pleasures their monastic life has to offer, and the artistic merits of their immediate environment are proof of a highly developed and basically life-affirming sense of aesthetic appreciation.

There is, moreover, the important fact that the youthful enthusiasm of those attracted by a life of study and religious practices has not to contend with the scepticism of a more worldly minded majority, for although only a few Sherpas are prepared to follow Buddhist doctrine in all its implications, no one doubts the validity and the superiority of a life of renunciation and 'other-worldliness's to the secular life of the ordinary villager.

Atternatives

The two types of life mutually exclusive and choices once made can be turned. The example of the founder of Tengboche shows that even those who for many years were householders and family men, can embrace a religions life and attain to much high spiritual perfection that they take re-birth as reincarnate lamas. Conversely, there are many monks who after some years in a monastery return to secular life, but continue to study and practise their knowledge of ritual performances, They make fresh effort to gain new merits by periods of fasting and long isolation.

As some members quit the monastery to seek satisfaction of natural desires permissible only in the outside world, without however abandoning faith in religious practices, others join the monastery either in early youth or in middle age after having lived some secular life and finding it wanting in emotional or intellectual satisfaction. The composition of a monastic community is therefore never static. There is even provision for those too old to join the monastery as *thawa* and take the regular vows. Mature men can join the monk community as *korba* or lay members, and in this capacity they can lead a life of study and religious practices without sharing in all the privileges and responsibilities of regular monks. It is not unusual for widowed village-lamas to enter a monastery in this capacity. Even lamas, who in their youth had been *thawa,* but left the monastery in order to marry, may be allowed to rejoin the monks' community in the capacity of *Korba.* In order to do that they must either be widowed or must have formally separated from their wives. As *korba* they may not participate in *gomba* services and consequently receive none of the tea and food served to the *thawa* at the expense of the monastery. They are free, to act as lamas and participate in rites and ceremonies performed outside the monastery. They do not they receive any share of the donations given to the monks.

In 1957, there were two *korba* in Tengboche, Ngawang Chundu and Ngawang Yonden. The former was one of the seven original *thawa,* who had to leave the monastery on account of an association with a woman of Pangboche. When she deserted him, he sought and obtained permission to live in Tengboche as *korba.* The other was Ngawang Yonden, who had also been a *thawa.* After leaving the monastery and marrying twice, he returned to Tengboche and shared the house of his son, who was a regular monk. When reentering a monastery as *korba* such a lama must once more take a vow, but whereas a middle-aged man who had never been a *thawa* can be accepted as a proper monk, no one who has once broken his vow of celibacy can be accepted in any other capacity than as *korba*. In distinction to the *korba*, the fully privileged monks are described as *tshowa*, which means literally 'those who partake of *tsho* (offerings)'

Monastic Vows and Monastery Organization

While young boys may be sent to a monastery for the purpose of study without committing them to a clerical career, no one can be a full member of a monastic community without having taken vows of celibacy and abstention from certain worldly occupations. The superior vows can be administered only by reincarnate abbots or other lamas of high spiritual achievements, but a preliminary vow, which a prospective monk has to take when entering a monastery, can be given into the hands of any senior lama. Few formalities are connected with its administration. No questions are put to the candidate, and his future preceptor simply says: 'From now on you will have a new name and be called so-and-so; you must now promise not to engage in tilling the soil and not to marry." The candidate promises to observe these rules, and is henceforth known as *gyengi* ('living upon virtue') and is entitled to participate in *gomba* services.

While living in their parental homes until the age of eighteen or twenty, some young men have studied privately. They may omit taking the vow of *gyengi*, and begin their monastic career by at once taking the next higher vow, known as *rabdzung*. It is therefore not necessary for all monks to pass through *gyengi*. The only qualification for admittance to this vow is the ability to read Tibetan, and once a young man has taken this vow he is considered a *thawa* or monk, even if his learning is still very rudimentary.

The Ceremoney

A lama become 'great' when he crosses the age of thirty years. He must have taken the next higher vow which is *gelung*. He can with the help of four lamas who have also taken the vow *gelung* can administer the vow of *rabdzung*. As in 1957 the reincarnate abbot of Tenghoche was in his early twenties, and there was no other lama of adequate status and age in Khumbu, candidates for the administration of the vow of *rabdzung* had to go to Rongphu or await the visit of a Tibetan lama of high status. Such a visit occurred some years ago, when the abbot of a Sakyapa monastery visited Tengboche, and conducted the initiation of several *thawa*. It was more usual, however, for candidates to make the journey to Rongphu. In August 1957 twelve young boys and one girl from Khumbu went to Rongphu and there took the vow of *rabdzung*, which the reincarnate abbot of that monastery administered during the same ceremony to about sixty prospective monks and nuns. It is obvious that during a mass initiation of this kind, the questions put to the candidates are asked for the sake of formality rather than to elicit information about the young men's and women's qualifications for a religious life.

The Interogation

The traditional procedure is observed and the abbot's first assistant begins the male candidate's interrogation with the following questions:

'Have you ever committed any crime? Have you killed one of your parents or a lama?' Such a murder is an absolute bar to the administration of the *rabdzung* vow, while other types of murder and manslaughter can be expiated.

If the answer is satisfactory, the second monk asks:

> 'Have you any grey hair on your head?' (A candidate with grey hair cannot be admitted to this vow, as men and women past middle age are not to be ordained. It must be remembered, how-ever, that most Sherpas retain black hair until well over the age of fifty.)

The third monk then asks:

> 'Are you free of any marital tie? Have your parents permitted you to become monk?'

If the candidates can give positive answers to both these questions, they are asked by the fourth monk:

'Are you free of debts? Are you under no obligation towards any government authority? Has no court of law pronounced any order against you?'

When these questions have also been satisfactorily answered the senior lama conducting the ceremony asks.

'Are you prepared to shave your head and to have a new name?'

All this is a formalty. The candidates affirm their willingness. The lama then confers upon each his *thawa* name, and invests him with a monk's habit, which the candidate or his parents have handed to the lama before the beginning of the ceremony. The lama also burns a piece of paper, on which is written the candidate's previous name. If the candidate had previously been made a *gyengi,* he may be given the same or a new name. The lama finally advises the candidates to remain celibate, to abstain from trading and cultivate the land and not to commit any sins. Each candidate solemnly promises to observe all these rules, and by taking the *rabdzung* vow he becomes a proper *thawa.* There is no definite age a candidate must have reached before taking this vow, but before he can proceed to the next vow, known as *gelung,* he must at least be twenty years old. In practice, however, most *thawa* are of mature age before taking this vow. It is only a confirmation of the previous vow, and the questions asked by the 'great' lama and his four assistants are virtually the same. But those who have taken the *gelung* vow, and are therefore sometimes referred to as *gelling.* can themselves act as a 'great' lama's assistant in administering the vow provided they are not less than thirty years old.

In September 1957 there were in Tengboche monastery five monks who had taken the *gelung* vow, and nineteen who had taken the vow of *rabdzung.* At that time there were no boys, who had taken the initial vow of *gyengi* only, for even *thawa* of fourteen and fifteen years of age had already had the opportunity of going to Rongphu and taking the *rabdzung* vow. In the small monastery of Trakshindo, founded in 1946 by a monk of Tengboche, there were in 1957 thirteen *thawa* who had taken the *rabdzung* vow and two—exclusive of the founder, Lama Chuldim—who had taken the vow of *gelung.* These two, as well as six of the former, had made the journey to the Tibetan monastery of Rongphu for the purpose of taking their vows, whereas seven had their *rabdzung* vows administered by the abbot of a Sakyapa monastery on the occasion of his visit to Tengboche.

The Model

Just as the ritual performances in the monasteries of Tengboche and Thami are replicas of the corresponding performances in Tibetan monasteries of the Nyingmapa sect, and the monks study and recite from books identical to those used in such places as Rongphu, so the organisation of these institutions has been modelled according to the Tibetan monastic pattern. But whereas in the large monasteries in Tibet there were hundreds and even thousands of monks and students, the numbers of *thawa* in Sherpa monasteries are small, with the result that in order to fill all or most of the traditional offices as many as 25 or 30 percent of the monks must serve as monastery officials. The abbot of a monastery is either a reincarnate lama, known as *tulku* lama and never referred to by his name, or a head lama *(lama chc)* such as the hereditary lama of the Thami *gomba.* An spends his time in studying religious scriptures, teaching some of the monks, receiving pilgrims and visitors and presiding at major rites and festivals. He does not concern himself with the day-to-day affairs of the monastery. An abbot impresses his personality on the monks under his authority and the fortunes of a monastery depend to no small degree on the leadership of its abbot. It is obvious, therefore, that the founder of a monastery, such as Lama Gulu, must take a more active part in shaping the new community of monks than an abbot who succeeds to the headship of an established monastery.

Next in rank to the abbot is an official known as *loben.* He has no definite function, but advises other monks in matters of ritual, and sits at ceremonies above the other *thawa,* without being directly in charge of the proceedings. Whenever the abbot is absent and during the years of a reincarnate lama's minority, the *loben* officiates as the head of the monastery.

The official immediately below the *loben* is the *umse,* who conducts all the services in the *gomba,* leads the recitation and is generally in charge of the ritual. While the *loben* is usually one of the most senior monks, and may hold the office for many years, the *umse* can be a comparatively young man knowledgeable in scriptures and historical matters, and his appointment is usually for three years.

The Gerku

The monastery official next in rank to the *umse* is known *gerku.* He is responsible for the maintenance of discipline, has the right to punish offenders against monastery rules, settles disputes arising between *thawa,* and keeps the accounts of monastery funds. He is usually elected for one year only, but may be re-elected if the abbot and the other monks are satisfied with his conduct of affairs. Responsible to the *gerku* are one or more officials known as *nierwa.* They are in charge of the trading and other economic affairs of the monastery, and may be described as managers or stewards. The *nierwa* hold the cash, but have to show accounts to the *gerku.* They are elected for one year, and can normally not be re-elected. If there is a profit from the trading deals they have conducted it goes to the monastery, but if they have incurred a loss through their own fault they may be asked to make it up out of their personal property. In small monasteries there may be only one *nierwa,* but in monasteries which have landed property and cattle and engage in trade, the number of monks dealing with business matters must be at least two, one in charge of the internal management, and one free to go on trading journeys. Once out on these journies, a monk may take several weeks to come back.

In Tengboche, which compared with Tibetan monasteries is by no means big, there were in 1957 no less than seven monks with the title of *nierwa.* One was in charge of the kitchen and the regular *gomba* services; one was specifically responsible for the making of the tea, which plays so great *a* role in sustaining the *thawa* during the long ritual performances; one was in charge of the money offered by benefactors for *mang-se,* i.e., the supply of tea to the monks, and having invested such contributions had to collect the interest; two *nierwa* were responsible for the maintenance and repair of the buildings and one of them collected for this purpose contributions within Khumbu and Solu, whereas the other travelled to Tibet and Kalimpong to raise funds for the monastery. Finally there were two *nierwa* in charge of the cattle and the land, owned by Tengboche.

Managing the Donalions

The need for men specifically responsible for the management of a monastery's economic assets becomes obvious if we consider that some gifts of wealthy men are neither in cash nor in goods suitable for direct consumption. Some twenty years ago, for instance, a rich trader of Namche donated to Tengboche a herd of one hundred yak, and to care for such a herd requires considerable organization. A monk may gradually pass through all the ranks of monastery officials, and finally be senior even to the *loben* without holding any specific office. Thus, in 1957 the second son of the abbot of Thami *gomba* ranked above all the *thawa* and was the chosen successor of his father, while his youngest brother held the post of *loben* and his eldest brother's son acted as *gerku.*

In Tengboche where, unlike in Thami, there are no married lamas and the succession is by reincarnation instead of by lineal succession, elderly monks who have passed through all the higher posts, but made room for younger men, have no clearly defined status, and are usually referred to by the title of the last senior post they held. Apart from the higher ranks connected with administrative responsibilities there are ranks of lower order, through which the younger *thawa* have to pass before they become eligible for one of the responsible posts. These ranks are named after the part played by the various *thawa* at *gomba* services.

For the first three years after his admission a boy works as *cha-de* or server of tea, and it is usually only after one or two years that he advances to *majen* or cook. When he has done his apprenticeship in these menial capacities, he is promoted to *nga-wa* or drummer, and from now on he sits in the *gomba* in the line of monks reciting and playing instruments. He remains *nga-wa* for one or two years, and then rises to the rank and function of *sang-dung-ba* or blower of long, telescopic horns. This rank he will normally hold for two or three years, until he gains promotion to *geling-ba* or flageolet player, a rank he may hold for about three years. The lower ranks are attained in accordance with the knowledge of books a monk has mastered and with the acquisition of such skills as the making of ritual requisites.

Any monk who has reached a certain stage in his studies may present himself before the abbot, *loben* and *umse* and give proof that he has attained proficiency in his subjects. If he passes this test, he becomes eligible for promotion. There are no public examinations, as those held in the great Tibetan monasteries, and in a small community like that of Tengboche the senior officials are undoubtedly well aware of the progress and qualifications of the individual junior monks, and it seems that at times they even dispense with the formal test to be held before the abbot. By the time a monk has attained the rank of flageolet player *(geling-ba)* he is eligible for election as *nierwa* or even *gerku*. The age at which a monk may attain one of the higher posts depends on the size and composition of the individual monastic community. In the recently founded monastery of Trakshindo, for instance, there were in 1957 not sufficient even middle-aged monks to fill the majority of senior posts. It was a community of young men; the *loben* was forty-two years old, the *umse* thirty-one, the *gerku* twenty-eight, and the only *nierwa* twenty-three.

In small monasteries where officials and junior *thawa* are daily in close contact, and many of the inmates, recruited from a few nearby villages, are linked by ties of kinship or traditional friendship, there is not the same need for the enforcement of strict and impersonal discipline as in the giant monasteries of Tibet.

There exists nevertheless provision for the punishment of those who offend against the monastery discipline or disregard the orders of the officials. In the case of an offence having been committed, the *gerku,* who is responsible for discipline, investigates the case, and then consults with the *umse* regarding an appropriate punishment. To expiate a minor fault the offender is usually ordered to provide tea for all the monks, and this punishment is known as *mang-se.* Money fines are imposed for major offences, and if someone is very obstinate and does not submit to their punishment, the *gerku* may even order him to be flogged. This, however, is a most exceptional occurrence, and I have not heard of any concrete case where corporal punishment was inflicted.

Monks are not supposed to smoke at all, and they may not drink liquor or beer within the monastery precincts. Breaches of these rules are subject to fines, but if it becomes known that a monk has relations with a woman he is expelled from the monastery. Anyone who has proof of such a violation of a monk's vow of chastity may remove from the *gomba* the offender's personal cushion on which he used to sit during services and which is symbolic of a man's status of *thawa.* The case is then reported to the *gerku,* who will compel the offender to confess his sin to the abbot, and ask for his discharge from the monastery. For in such cases there is no alternative to expulsion.

In the event of a *gerku* being found guilty of a breach of monastery rules, all the *thawa* must sit in judgement on him, and the punishment to which he is liable is twice that to which an ordinary *thawa* would be subjected had he committed the same offence. Expulsion of a *thawa* on account of relations with women involves confiscation of any immovable property the offender may possess within the monastery precincts. If he owned a house, this falls to the monastery and the expelled owner has no right to sell it. If, on the other hand, a monk wants to leave his monastery in order to join another institution, he may get leave to do so and sell his house provided he pays a fee of Rs. 40.

To the monastery which he wants to enter, he has to pay a fee of at least Rs. 40. He must, moreover, offer scarves to the *loben, umse* and *gerku.* A change-over from one monastery to the other is not a frequent practice, but it occurs occasionally when a monk has quarrelled with his abbot or when he is attracted by a new foundation close to his home village. Thus, the present *loben* of Trakshindo monastery was for ten years a monk in Rongphu, but as a native of Ringmo, a village close to Trakshindo, he returned to Solu to participate in the development of a new monastery in his home district.

Visits to other monasteries, on the other hand, are a regular feature in the lives of many monks. Until the time when the Chinese communists destroyed monastic life in Tibet, it was usual for the *thawa* of Thami to go to Rongphu for further study, and during their stay there they had to hire a house and provided their own food. But they could take part in the services, and Tibetan lamas coming to Thami were granted the same privilege. Periods of foreign travel and study were sometimes very prolonged.

Of the eighteen *thawa* of Trakshindo, two spent six years in monasteries of the Tibetan province of Kham, and seven received some training in Tengboche. Many of the Sherpa lamas are widely travelled, and the universality of Tibetan Buddhism enables them to feel at home wherever its doctrine is practised and the same scriptures form the basis of monastery ritual. The organization of nunneries is modelled on that of monasteries, but communal activities and services are fewer, and the discipline is, on the whole, less strict. There is no figure corresponding to a reincarnate lama or permanent abbot, but the head nun, known as *loben,* is elected from time to time. There are also nuns holding the posts of *umse* and *gerku,* but—at least in the small nunneries of Khumbu—none in the lower ranks corresponding to *cha-de* or *nga-wa.* Before a girl can be admitted to a nunnery as a proper nun *(ani),* she must take the same *rabdzung* vow as that taken by monks. In August 1957, for instance, when twelve young men went to Rongphu to take this vow, one girl of Kunde, sister of a rich man, attended the same initiation ceremony, and look the *rabdzung* vow which enabled her to enter the nunnery of Devuche.

Those Nuns who have in some manner found guilty of a breach of their vow of chastity are excluded from the *gomba* services, but they sometimes stay on in their houses, and—when they leave the nunnery—have the right to sell these to other nuns. Although occasionally a 'great' lama may perform *a* rite of 'Life-Consecration' *(Tshe-wong)* in the *gomba* of a nunnery, the nuns are capable of conducting all the normal services including such rites as the Niungne, and on these occasions they play the same instruments as those used by lamas. Like monks, the nuns of Devuche are sometimes invited to perform a mourning or memorial rite in one of the villages of Khumbu. In such a case they proceed in a body to the house, where their services are required, and perform the ritual in much the same way as lamas.

Monastic Routine in Tengboche

The charter of the Tengboche monastery, a document bearing the seal of Lama Tenzing Nurbu of Rongphu, the fifth reincarnation of Lama Sa..ga Dorje, lays down the rules according to which the life of the community should be organized. The formulation and arrangement of these rules appear somewhat haphazard. It is obvious that they do not by any means represent a complete code of behaviour to be observed by the monks. But as a reflection of what the reincarnate lama of Rongphu and the founder of the monastery must have considered important points, they are worth quoting. In the original document the rules are not numbered. In summarizing the points it will be convenient to arrange them under the following numbers:

1. The *thawa* must be punctual in attending the *gomba* services, and assemble as soon as the gong is sounded. Any *thawa* who is late must prostrate himself 100 times.
2. No woman may live within the precincts of the *gomba,* and no *thawa* may anywhere share a house with a nun.
3. When a thawa is alone he should meditate on his own chosen divinity.
4. Every *thawa* should observe a fast on the fifteenth and thirtieth day of each month.
5. Every *thawa* must learn by heart the three books Deshags-Kundu[3], Ngundru-ral-tso and Cho-tse.
6. Every *thawa* should study the books Konchok-chundi,[4] Rena, Thukdub, Drowa-Kundrol,[5] Rigsin, Zangthal, Gyaldzen-lak-len, a book of instructions and Gurutangmar, a book of texts for ceremonies.
7. Every *thawa* must learn to make *torma,* play cymbals, drums, trumpets and flageolets.

8. Every *thawa,* after learning all these skills must show before the abbot, *loben* and *umse,* that he has mastered them, and if he passes the test he shall be promoted.
9. Every *thawa* must learn to recite the book Dombsun-scta. (*domba*—vow, instruction for monks).
10. During *gomba* services the *thawa* must wear sleeveless gowns. It is desirable that *thawa* should wear sleeveless gowns even outside the monastery.
11. At the first blowing of the conch shell all *thawa* must file into the *gomba* hall, and start reciting without talking to each other.

Attendance of the *Gomba* Services

From these rules it appears that on any ordinary day the only compulsory corporate activity of the members of a monastery is attendance of the *gomba* service which is held in the morning. For the rest of the day the monks go about their individual business, reading books, studying with their preceptor or teaching pupils, meditating, engaging in one of the religious crafts, such as painting, or dealing with more practical tasks of monastery management, catering, accounts or trade. As each monk has his own household, there is, except at the *gomba* services, no occasion for common meals, and gatherings of monks for purposes other than formal worship are confined to casual visits of individual monks to each other's houses.

At the time of planting or harvest the younger monks work in groups on the monastery's fields, and at that time they mess together in the houses belonging to the *gomba* in such places as Dingboche. The duration of such activities is however, short, and during other times of the year co-operation in practical matters is limited to such incidental tasks as the building of a bridge across the Dudh Kosi or the repair of the monastery buildings. Regular co-operation of all the monks is compulsory, however, in the various rites and ceremonies traditionally held at fixed times of the year. An abstract of the calendar of rites and festivals will give an idea of the manner and frequency of such co-operation:

Dawa Tangbu (corresponding approximately to March)

(a) *Losar* celebrations are held on the 1st to 3rd day of the month.

1st day: a service is held, *torma* are made, and the abbot entertains all the monks to a meal.

2nd day: the monks are entertained from *gomba* funds.

3rd day: the monks hold a common meal to which all have subscribed.

(b) *Tsedub duwa,* a prayer service is performed for the benefit of the country, the king and all the people, lasting for ten days.

(c) *Tsho,* a memorial rite is performed for the late abbot of Rongphu, lasting from the 17th to the 19th day.

Dawa Niwa (April)

No special rites.

Dawa Sumba (May)

No special rites.

Dawa Shiwa (June)

No special rites.

Dawa Ngawa (July)

The abbot and many monks go to Namche Bazar. They celebrate the Dumje festival for five days.

Dawa Tukpa (August)

Niungne rite lasting for three days.

Dawa Dumba (September)

Dorsung-duwa, a *tsedub* rite lasting for ten days.

From the 15th *Dawa Ngawa* to the 15th *Dawa Diimba* the monks observe *yerne dembu* (summer retreat).

Dawa Gyepa (October)

No special rites.

Dawa Guwa (November)

The last day of this month is the first day of the Mani-rimdu festival.

Dawa Chuwa (December)

(a) *Mani-rimdu* rites and dance festival take place from the Ist—15th day:

Ist—5th day: *torma* making and recitations
6th—11th day: recitations
12th—13th day: dancing
14th day: *Tinsak* (fire-sacrifice)
15th day: *Tshe-wong* (rite of 'Life-Consecration')

(b) 29th day: Recitation of *Kangso* throughout the night; this is a rite of propitiation of local gods.

Dawa Chuchikpa (January)

(a) 29th day: *Sherab ninpo,* a *kurim* rite.

(b) Last day of the month: first day of the *Tsho,* memorial rite is performed for the late abbot, Lama Gulu.

Dawa Chuniwa (February)

(a) 1st—3rd day: *Tsho (=gong-dzok,* memory of death)

(b) 25th—29th day: *Lokpar,* a rite identical with the Dumje, festival performed in village temples in Dawa Ngawa.

(c) 30th day: *Delakunjung lhapsang,* a *kurim* rite.

Ceremonies and Festivals

There are some seasonal festivals and rates also. Ceremonies are held throughout the year on specific days of the month . Thus, on the eighth day of every month a *lhapsang* known as *Gye-nga-lhapsang* is performed, and on the twenty-fifth day, a *tsho* rite held. In the days of the late Lama Gulu there was also a *tsho* rite on the tenth day of every month, but this practice was abandoned as a measure of economy. The presisting abbot was anxious to resume the celebration of this monthly rite. It is quite possible that the practice has been revived.

The Summer Retreat

The summer retreat *(yerne dembu),* which lasts from the 15th of Dawa Ngawa to the 15th of Dawa Dumba; it is a period of intensified religious concentration. During these two months no woman may enter the monastery precincts except with special permission of the abbot, and the monks may not leave Tengboche unless there is an emergency. But even in this case, they should be back before nightfall. The prohibition of killing any living being extends during this time even to plants. The monks may not remove weeds from their gardens and should not even pass urine on the grass lest they harm it. There are two daily services in the *gomba* during this time, and the monks are served at monastery expense twice a day with tea and once with gruel *(koli).* At the end of this period, i.e., on the 15th of Dawa Dumba, there is general feasting, playing and dancing, and this day of rejoicing when everyone may do what he likes is called *gyakye tongup.*

Maintenance

Members of a monastic community have to provide for their own maintenance. Therefore they have to allowed a great deal of liberty in the way they spend their time outside the regular *gomba* services. Though this system of individual independence has its positive features, it undoubtedly militates against the planning of scholarly and religious activities under a central authority. The young reincarnate abbot of Tengboche realized this weakness of the accepted system, and has reviewed this practice an innovation designed to give him more direct control over a nucleus of monks selected for their intellectual abilities.

His aim was to provide from a special fund for the maintenance of a small elite group, throughout the year, and to exercise over their studies and other activities of this group a much closer control than over those of other monks. Such monks, entirely maintained from monastery funds, known as *seta to-up* were a feature of many Tibetan monasteries, and add, as it seems, greatly to the prestige of an institution. In 1957, the *seta to-up* group consisted of nine young monks and had been in existence for only two months. The fund to maintain them, which was separate from the general monastery funds, was not yet large enough to provide these monks with their entire board. The reincarnate abbot was hopeful of collecting sufficient contributions ultimately to maintain fifteen *thawa* in this way.

The members of the *seta to-up* group were to be given leave only twice a year, during the months of Dawa Shiwa (June) and Dawa Gyepa (October). The members spend most of their time in studies of religious scriptures. At these times of the year they were to be allowed fifteen days' leave, to collect money and provisions, either from their parents' house, or by going round the villages and collecting the interest of their investments or even charitable contributions. Though fed by the monastery, even such *seta to-up* have to provide their own clothes, and to buy or build their own houses. They must therefore have some private means, and the system of *seta to-up* is certainly not designed to open the monastery to the sons of very poor families, but to give the abbot a more direct control over a group of monks freed from the petty cares of their supplies of food.

Laymen and Reincarnate Lamas

In Tibet, the principle of reincarnation determines. For at least five centuries the succession to high ecclesiastic office. The earliest authentically documented case is that of the first Grand Lama of the Gelugpa Church, Geden-dub, who died in A.D. 1475. According to contemporary belief, he was reborn in a child identified by oracular signs, and this boy was duly installed as the second Grand Lama. The heads of the Gelugpa Church, who since 1640 were also the temporal rulers of Tibet, have ever since been chosen on the basis of the belief that the deceased priest-king is reborn in an infant recognizable by his ability to identify objects associated with his previous life. This manner of establishing an uncontested succession to major ecclesiastical posts soon spread throughout Tibet, and countless reincarnate lamas functioned as the heads of monastic institutions. They were known as *tulku.*

The Practice Spreads

The Sherpas have also taken up this principal of reincarnation. They have long been used to revere the abbot of Rongphu monastery as the reincarnation of their patron saint Lama Sanga Dorje, but it would seem that the appearance of reincarnate lamas in Khumbu and Solu is a comparatively recent phenomenon. Until the foundation of monastic institutions during the first half of the twentieth century, there were indeed no ecclesiastic personalities of sufficient eminence to make their rebirth in a child a matter of public concern, nor would a reincarnate lama have found the proper setting for his activities.

However, with the foundation of monastic institutions in Khumbu all this changed. Not only in Khumbu, which is only a few days' walk from Rongphu, the seat of a famous succession of reincarnate lamas, but even in Solu, the southernmost projection of the Buddhist sphere the same thing happened. In 1957 there were within these regions four publicly recognized reincarnate lamas, and the monastery of Chiwong had only recently lost its reincarnate lama to the larger and more important Tibetan monastery of Tathyo.

Succession by Incarnation

According to the ideas current among Buddhists of the Nyingmapa sect, a man's personality (*sem*)[6] after death takes one of six paths leading to the six spheres of the world beyond. On the fork of three paths Urken Rimpoche awaits the departed and sends everyone according to his merit along one of the seven paths. But when a great lama, whose merit would entitle him to go to Devachen the 'Abode of Gods', arrives at the fork, Urken Rimpoche leads him only a short way along the white path to heaven. He then arrests his progress and tells him: 'Your time to go to Devachen has not yet come. You must take rebirth again and return to your task on earth. In future times you may go to Devachen. The eschatological concepts is followed for succession to the office by reincarnation (cf. p. 246). Such a lama, though fully entitled to heavenly rewards for past merit, is then reincarnated for the benefit of humanity, but unlike other beings in a new birth, he retains his knowledge of past experiences. His wisdom is hence superior to that of any lama relying on the learning of a single life.

The Example

Is an example of the competition between monasteries for the presence of a reincarnate lama *(tulku).*

Karma Ongel (Salaka), a young Sherpa held to be a reincarnation of Lama Tensing Nurbu, an abbot of Rongphu, who was himself a reincarnation of Lama Sanga Dorje or—as some believe—even of the famous translator Vairocana. He was born in 1938 in Changmitang near Tengboche as the *themba* son of an ex-nun of Devuche. His mother Ani Lhamai was of Lama clan and came from the Solu village of Thalsa. Her paternal father was Phinzo Lama, who—as we shall see presently—was also reincarnated. Lama Tensing Nurbu, though abbot of a Tibetan monastery, was himself from Solu, and stood to Ani Lhamai in the classifactory relationship of father's brother. Karma Ongel's father was a Salaka man from Solu, who at first paid little attention to his *themba* son, and did nothing to support the mother. After she had to leave Devuche, she lived in a minute house in Changmitang, and added to her small income by working for other people.

The boy, when only three years old, started began to say that Changmitang was not his home, that he was a Rongphu lama, and wanted to go to Rongphu. Often he cried, because his mother would not take him to Rongphu, and at first she used to scold and even beat him, when he pestered her in this way. But ultimately she told other people about the boy's odd behaviour and they advised her to take the child to

Rongphu. When they arrived in Rongphu, the child said at once: 'This is my *gomba,* these are my books', and seemed to recognize many things in the monastery. The monks in Rongphu, who no doubt were looking out for a reincarnation of their late abbot, listened sympathetically to the mother's account, and agreed to go with her and the child to Khumbu, and to arrange there for the usual test. Taking the beads and some of their late abbot's other belongings with them they went to Khumbu, and there confronted the child with a collection of articles containing among many of similar type also those of the Rongphu lama. The child chose without hesitation the genuine articles, and thus proved himself as a reincarnation of the late abbot.

However, the boy and his mother could not be invited to take residence in Rongphu, because in this case the matter was complicated by another claimant, born in Tibet, who at about the same time had successfully passed a similar test. Double, and even triple reincarnations are by themselves not unknown for every personality is made up of *ku* (body), *sung* (voice) and *liti* (heart). The theory is that these components can be reincarnated separately. Many of the Rongphu monks favoured the Khumbu-born *tulku,* but the problem had to be referred to Lhasa, and it is said that the father of the other claimant was a man of some influence, and hence brought about a decision in favour of his son, who was duly installed as abbot designate of Rongphu.

Ani Lhamai was not unhappy with what happened. She knew a trick had been played by those influential people. She took her son to Solu and lived with relatives near the monastery of Chiwong. There is a story, according to which the boy, who continued to demand to be taken to Rongphu, once, when about ten years old, accompanied some Sherpa monks to Tibet, and at a place called Singi-tak near Shigatse met some of the nuns of Rongphu. Seeing him, the nuns began to cry, protesting that they knew him to be the true incarnation of the heart *(lu)* of Lama Tensing Nurbu, but that now an inferior reincarnation had taken his place in Rongphu. The young lama said: 'Do not cry; I will still remain with you, and I shall build a *gomba* in this very place.' At this, all those present marvelled, for at Singi-tak there was neither water nor suitable building material. But the boy thrust his stick into the ground and said: 'Dig here and you will find stones for building a *gomba.*' And when the people dug, they found stones excellent for house building. But they pointed out that there was no water, and again the reincarnate lama pointed to a place on the ground and, when the people removed a little soil, they found an ample current of water.

A small *gomba* was built there, and the young *tulku* lama stayed there for some time, attended by the nuns and supplied by the local population. Finally the monks of Chiwong offered him the abbotship of their monastery. It was there that he received his formal education. He was a cheerful, though slightly self-conscious boy, not very different from other student monks of his age. But two years later he went for further studies to Tibet, and the abbot of the monastery of Thatyo, a monastery one day's journey from Rongphu, was so impressed by his personality that he offered him the succession to the abbotship of Tathyo. Being over eighty years old, the abbot soon withdrew from active affairs, and in 1957 the young reincarnate lama was de facto abbot of Thatyo. As Thatyo was a monastery with over eighty monks, while in 1957 there were only fifteen resident monks in Chiwong, this position was of far greater importance than the one which the reincarnate lama had held in Solu. It is said, moreover, that he was also offered the position of abbot of the Naphta monastery in Tibet. Regrettably he succumbed to an illness and died young, but on his death-bed he foretold an early reincarnation.

Reincarnations can run in family. Phinzo Lama, the grandfather of Ani Lhamai, the young *tulku* lama's mother, was himself reincarnated in Ngawang Yonde Nurbu, the younger brother of Lama Tundu, the late abbot of Thami *gomba*. Ngawang Yonde Nurbu went to live in Chiwong, but when he began an association with a nun related to the family of Sange Lama of Phaphlu, the patron of Chiwong, he came into conflict with this powerful personality, and left Chiwong for the newly-founded monastery of Toloka. He married the nun, whose name was Giami, and lived in Toloka until his death. Giami then married Randul Lama (Gole), a disciple of her late husband, and a son she bore to him was found to be a reincarnation of Ngawang Yonde Nurbu. The boy, who was generally recognized as a *tulku* lama and after studying for three years in Tibet, he lived at Toloka in the monastery known as Tar-ling. This monastery seems to be modelled on the pattern of Thami *gomba* rather than on that of Chiwong or Tengboche. Among the inmates there are married lamas as well as *thawa,* and even the reincarnate lama could marry, but that if he did so he could not ordain *thawa* such as the reincarnate abbot of Tengboche would soon be able to do.

The monks' community of Thodung *gomba,* built by Lama Dawa

Kipa of Lama clan in 1948 was more recently founded. It prides itself also on having a reincarnate lama, a small Sherpa boy born to the west of Solu. He recognized as the reincarnation of a Drugpa lama.

Even lamas and nuns of less exalted status may be reborn in children, who recall some experiences of their past life. Reincarnations, therefore are not confined to the abbots of monasteries. Thus, Lama Kiri (Sherwa) of Khumjung, a lama of learning and repute, but without monastic affiliations, was reborn in the son of Lama Lhakpa of the Kerok *gomba.* The child's mother was from Khumjung, and distantly related by marriage to Lama Kiri. When she brought her son to Khumjung, he pointed out the house in which Lama Kiri had lived, and insisted that it had belonged to him. He remembered also certain incidents of Lama Kiri's life, but as no question of succession is involved in such cases, there are no tests like those required to establish the claim of a reincarnate abbot.

In the last generation, there was a case of reincarnation in Rongphu, which supports the Sherpa idea that a monk's marriage and return to secular life, does not necessarily involve a very serious loss of merit if he is permitted his preceptor to do so. The *loben* of Rongphu, who was obviously one of the most senior and highly respected monks, asked permission to marry a nun with whom he had fallen in love. Leave was granted and the couple got married. Both died after a few years of married life, and both were reincarnated at about the same time. Their reincarnations are now again a monk and a nun, and it would be of interest to know whether any bond of sympathy reflects their love in a previous existence.

Children conscious of their previous life have shown that even laymen who never claimed any sanctity are sometime reincarnated. Such reincarnations, however, are of little practical importance. While a reincarnate abbot takes over the personal property as well as the official position of his predecessor, the reincarnation of a layman has no claim to the property owned in his previous life. Yet, there is some indication that such a claim would not be considered entirely fantastic. In many cases the heirs, who inherited the property, usually give to the new incarnation of their late father or kinsman a set of new clothes. This is in reincarnation's recognition of his right to a share in the property, which he might have owned in his previous birth.

There were in 1957 two generally known reincarnations of this type, as well as two children considered as reincarnations only by a small circle of relatives in the village of Khumjung. The best known case was that of Lama Karma (Thaktu), a young man about thirty years old. The story goes that a nun in Devuche, who had a *themba* son who died before she entered the nunnery once asked the abbot of Rongphu in what shape her child might have been reincarnated. The reply was that in one of the highest houses of Khumjung there lived a lama, and that in his son—the present Lama Karma—her child was reincarnated. This indication was corroborated by the small boy himself, who several times spoke of his mother who was a nun and lived in Devuche. The nun was delighted to know of her child's rebirth and presented the boy with clothes and other gifts. But with this ended the acknowledgement of their connection in the child's previous life, and there are no signs of any lasting relationship of intimacy and mutual affection between the nun and Lama Karma.

The other lay-reincarnation in Khumjung, is Phu Dorje, the son of a Khamba couple of rather humble status. When the boy was four years old he said that he had been the father of the then very important and influential *pembu* Yulha Tarkia (Thaktu). When he saw the *pembu* riding past his parents' house, he shouted from the window: 'This is my son, and this is the horse I used to ride'. The parents, fearing the *pembu's* anger, tried to prevent the child from making such remarks. But the boy was not to be restrained, and went on to describe the property and the house he had owned in his previous life. The child's strange remarks came to the *pembu's* ears, and he fetched the boy to his house and gave him a present of clothes. The *pembu's* son, who told me the story, said that the boy claimed to be a reincarnation of his grandfather, expressed no wish to remain in the house he had owned in his previous life, but that in Tibet such a reincarnation of a layman may be accepted as a member of the reincarnated person's family and brought up in his former home.

Less well known than these two cases is the alleged reincarnation of a lama and a nun of Phortse in the two small daughters of Nga-wang Tundu (Mende) an ex-monk of Tengboche, married to an ex-nun of Devuche. The fact that a man should be reincarnated in a girl-child is not considered an entirely improbable event, for reincarnations are known to have occurred in children of the opposite sex. I do not know, however, what would happen if the abbot of a monastery was found to be reincarnated in a girl-child.

Reincarnation of Laymen

The kinsmen of a lama of learning reputation for holiness sometimes expect him to be reborn and wait for the appropriate signs. Thus, it was told of Lama Ngawang Chotr of Pangboche that he expected his father, who had died two years previously, to be reincarnated before long. His father was a highly respected lama, and the son of a reincarnated lama, whose heart, eyes and tongue were enshrined in a silver casket in the Pangboche *gomba* by the side of the similar relics of Lama Sanga Dorje. Ngawang Chotr had kept the heart of his father, no doubt with a view to placing it in the *gomba* as soon as there were sure signs of his reincarnation.

The Village Clergy

While the monasteries are today the main focal points of Sherpa religious life, the performance of seasonal and domestic ritual is mainly the responsibility of the lamas resident in the villages. The position of such a village lama must not be confused with that of a priest who is the hereditary or appointed representative of the community in the religious sphere. There is in a Sherpa village no position comparable either to that of a parson or priest appointed by a superior religious authority, or to that of a priest with hereditary ties to locality gods such as found in many Indian tribal societies. A village lama is simply a person who has received religious instruction enabling him to perform certain rites and is resident in the village as a householder. He may have been taught by another village lama or he may have spent some years as a novice or a *thawa* in a monastery before returning to secular life.

A village lama need not have taken any vows nor does he require to be elected or appointed like one of the secular village dignitaries. The fact that he is available in the village and capable of ministering at such seasonal rites as Osho, Dumje or Yer-chang, as well as at the usual domestic rites assures him employment whenever there is need for the services of lamas. At the beginning of his career a village lama will act as assistant at rites conducted by a senior and more experienced lama. But as his knowledge and his skill in the reciting of liturgical books increases, he will gradually assume roles of greater responsibility, and may even be asked to perform minor rites independently. If there are several experienced lamas in a village, such a chance may not come early, but where there is a shortage of lamas, even a young and not very learned lama may have to minister on many occasions.

Marital Status of Village Lamas

In most cases village lamas are married and it is the desire to legalize an irregular union which induces a monk to give up his monastic career and settle down as a married householder. Some such ex-monks are today highly respected village lamas, whose services are much in demand even outside their own village community. But marriage and his position as householder and owner of land and cattle do not prevent a village lama from striving after further spiritual perfection, and the honour and prestige which goes along with virtue and wisdom. The recognized manner of acquiring further knowledge and spiritual power is the practice of *tsam,* which involves isolation in a hermitage or, more rarely, seclusion in one's own house.

Losum, Dasum Sheaksum

The duration of a *tsam* may be of any length, but the most effective is an isolation for three years, three months and three days, referred to as *losum, dasum, sheaksum.* During such a period of isolation a lama may be visited only by a disciple, servant or kinsman, who brings him supplies of food and ritual accessories, and by superior monks or lamas, who can guide him in his spiritual exercises. Part of the practice of *tsam* are times of fasting when the hermit takes no other nourishment than three times a day a small quantity of milk mixed with water and certain herbs. While in isolation a lama spends his days in the study and recitation of sacred scriptures, and in meditation.

In 1957 there was no lama in Khumbu engaged in a long period of *tsam.* In a cave above the village of Jorsale (Sherpa: Thumbu), a few hours walk south of Namche Bazar, there was the hermitage of Lama Nurbu of Salaka clan, who was engaged in a *tsam* of three years, three months and three days. But there was no lama in Khumba engaged in long period of *tsam.* He had built himself a fairly substantial hermitage, which stood in the mouth of a large cave, and in his house ten minutes' walk below lived his wife and children. His youngest son, a boy of eighteen looked after the lama's bodily needs, brought him food cooked in his house or cooked for him in the hermitage. This period of *tsam* was intended as a temporary exercise and the lama's wife told me that after its completion her husband would rejoin his family and the company of people.

TYPES OF TSAMS

A different type of *tsam* was being practised by an ex-monk of Tengboche, who lived as her seventh husband with Ngawang Samden, in a small, but comfortable house above Pangboche. For one whole year he did not leave this house and its small garden, but he had the company of his wife and received visitors. Ngawang Samden told me that at the end of her husband's *tsam,* she would observe the same voluntary seclusion and her husband would maintain the connection with the outside world and bring up supplies.

Spiritual and Social Incentives

There are many married lamas who have never undergone the rigorous discipline of a prolonged *tsam,* but such lamas are considered incapable of conducting independently rites for which great spiritual powers are required, such as the rite of 'Life-Consecration' known as *Tshe-wong*. Hence, there is not only a spiritual but also a social incentive to embark on the arduous enterprise of nearly total isolation from the world of laymen. The lama who has successfully completed his seclusion of three years, three months and three days, can be sure of the increased respect of his co-villagers and his fame is likely to spread throughout Khumbu and Pharak. His services will be more in demand and more generously rewarded than those of village lamas of lesser reputation, and material rewards will thus follow upon the spiritual progress resulting from the practice of *tsam.*

It is not necessary nor desirable that village lama should be adopt at learning and meditation. They have often a very full programme of ritual duties. The extent and nature of such duties as well as their material rewards can best be demonstrated by a specific example. Moderately learned lama of Khamba origin had from the end of April until early October the following engagements. It is table which is followed everywhere, according to the local situations.

28 April	Co-operation in the performance of the *tsirim* rite, aimed at the expulsion of evil spirits, in the *gomba* of Khumjung.
1-2 May	Co-operation in the recitation of *Totup* on the occasion of the death of Ang Tenzing.

3 May	As above and co-operation in the funeral of Ang Tenzing.
4-7 May	Co-operation in the performance of *napur* for Ang Tenzing.
10 May	Co-operation in a rite connected with the death of Ang Teshi (Thaktu) in Kunde village.
11-13 May	Co-operation in the performance of *shetu* rite for Pasang Putr in Namche Bazar.
14-19 May	Co-operation in the *napur* rite for Ang Teshi (Thaktu) in Kunde.
23 May	Co-operation in a *tsho* rite commissioned by the widow of a Khumjung man for her late husband's benefit, and performed in the Khumjung *gomba.*
25 May	Co-operation in a similar *tsho* rite performed in a private house of Khumjung.
26-27 May	Co-operation in recitation of *do-dzunga* in the house of the late Ang Tenzing's son.
28 May-1 June	Co-operation in *napur* rite for Mingma (Pal-dorje), who had died on an expedition.
2-5 June	Co-operation in *shetu* rite for Ang Teshi (Thaktu) in Kunde.
6 June	Completion of *shetu* and *gyewa* for Ang Teshi in Kunde.
7 June (morning)	Recitation of *kurim* in the house of Lama Kiu who was seriously ill.
7-9 June	Co-operation in *shetu* rite for Ang Tenzing.
10 June	Completion of *shetu* and *gyewa* for Ang Tenzing.
11-15 June	Co-operation in a *shetu* rite commissioned by a man of Namche Bazar in the name of his wife and father.
15 June	Completion of *shetu* rite in Namche Bazar and *gyewa.*
16-17 June	Co-operation in recitation of *Dordzi chopa* for Chortin, recently drowned.
20 June	Co-operation in funeral rites of Lama Kiu.
21-23 June	Recitation of *niti* in his own house on the occasion of his eldest daughter's 25th birthday.

27 June-1 July	Co-operation in *shetu* rite for Chortin.
4-10 July	Co-operation in the rites and ceremonies of the Dumje village festival.
12 July	Co-operation in *lhapsang* rite performed by the abbot of Tengboche in order to purify the house of Dawa Tenzing, whose son Mingma and wife Chortin had died in accidents.
14 July	Co-operation in *Tshe-Wong* rite performed in the Khumjung *gomba* by the abbot of Tengboche.
16-19 July	Co-operation in *shetu rite* for Lama Kiu.
20 July	Completion of *shetu* and *gyewa* for Lama Kiu.
21 July	Recitation of a *kurim* in the house of Urken (Khamba) for the welfare of his household.
24 July	Recitation of a *kurim* in the house of a sick man.
25 July	Recitation of a *kurim* for the benefit of a woman entering her 49th year.
31 July	Journey to Machherma.
1-6 August	Performance of *Yer-chang* rite at Machherma.
7 August	Journey from Machherma to Khumjung.
10-11 August	Recitation of *doma* in his own house for the benefit of a sick man.
15-19 August	Some hours of each day are spent in the recitation of *doma* for the general welfare of his own family. (This was done because there was no other work).
22-24 September	Recited with seven other lamas the 16 volumes of *Bum* in a private house of Namche Bazar. This is done as *kurim* rite for the benefit of the son of the house, who was ill.
1-3 October	Recited with eight other lamas the 16 volumes of *Bum* in a house of Namche Bazar, whose owner commissions every year such a recitation for the general welfare of his family.
4-6 October	As above in the house of another man of Namche Bazar.

Ritual Tasks

From the above list it appears that Sharap Lama was engaged in ritual tasks on 26 days in May, 25 days in June, and 18 days in July. During these months there occurred the deaths of several well-to-do persons, and the subsequent funerary rites account for the greater part of Sharap Lama's and other lamas' activities. These months can therefore hardly be taken as normal, but neither do the three days spent in September in reciting sacred scriptures in the house of a wealthy merchant of Namche Bazar represent the normal ritual activities of a lama during a full month. The average lies in between these extremes, and we can assume that most village lamas will spend between one-half and one-third of their time on purely ritual tasks, whereas for the rest of the time they are free to devote themselves to agriculture or trade.

A Lama does not get a big amount when he performs certain rites. He gets a modest amount. When reciting *shetu* in the house of a rich man, Sharap Lama received about Rs. 1½ in cash per day, which is only 50 per cent more than the wage of a farm labourer, but part of the reward consists in the lavish food and drink with which the lamas are entertained throughout a performance. Yet, on the whole it appears that village lamas no less than monks are modest in their demands on the laity, and that they will readily participate in the performance of rites in private houses whenever called upon, and accept whatever fee the host or organizer of the rite is prepared to pay them. They do not, moreover, expect cash payments when performing any of the village rites, but usually receive a share of the grain or other food offered at the time.

Often an individual will give a lama a quantity of beer with the request to recite a *kurim* in furtherance of any specific prospect. Thus, an oldish rich man of Khumjung who set out on a journey across the Nangpa La at the time of the monsoon presented Lama Lakba of Kerok *gomba* with beer made with about 10 lb. of maize and asked him to recite the book of Dorje *kotop ngabum* to obtain good weather for the two days of the journey across the pass. The lama accepted the commission and the weather duly improved. Similar requests to village lamas are by no means infrequent, for in Sherpa belief there are few activities which cannot benefit from the recitation of the one or other *kurim*, and it is in illness, misfortune and many a risky activity that a Sherpa turns to lamas for help. In the choice of those whom he invites to his house or commissions to recite a specific text in their own home, he is not bound by any hereditary ties or village custom. He can turn to one of the lamas of his own village, or approach a lama of a neighbouring village or the abbot of a monastery. There is no institution comparable with the tie between a Hindu and his family priest *(purohit)* nor does residence in a village give a lama any specific right to employment by the people of the locality.

The *gomba* dignitaries, such as *umse, chorumba* and *chorpen* may be laymen. A lama does not by virtue of his religious knowledge and skill hold any position of authority in the village in which he resides. Thus, in Khumjung all three of these offices were filled by laymen, and the village lamas, though called upon to act at ceremonies and rites held in the *gomba,* had no status in its administration. In his capacity as a householder any village lama may, however, be elected to one of the village offices, and lamas may thus function as *Osho naua, shingo naua* or *pembu.* But their function in such a position is quite separate from their priestly tasks. They in other words, are not village dignitaries, but act as private practitioners providing their priestly services wherever they are required.

Village Lama

Not hold any recognized or traditionally defined position within the village community, and owe any influence they may possess solely to their personality or reputation of knowledge and saintliness. Though a village without some resident lamas must inevitably experience many difficulties, there is no organized effort on the part of the village community as a whole to attract lamas or get some of its own members instructed in Buddhist scriptures and ritual. This is left to the initiative of individuals and hence more or less to chance. There may be times when a village community comprises several eminent lamas, and others when that same village depends for all more important rites on the ministration of lamas from neighbouring villages. The position in Khumjung has recently undergone such a change.

Kusho Kapkye, a Khamba, who immigrated from Tibet some thirty years previously, and had the reputation of considerable learning, Lama Kiu of Gardze clan, then eighty years old, Sharap Lama, a Khamba, who had immigrated from Tibet some twenty-five years previously, Lama Karma of Thaktu clan, who was the son of a lama of Kunde, and Ongchu Lama, a man of Solu, and son-in-law of Sange Lama, who was one of the Khumjung *pembu* but had retired to Tengboche. These were the lamas in Khumjung in 1953. Kusho Kapkye ranked as the senior lama, and presided at major rites. When he died in 1955, this role fell to Lama Kiu, who despite his great age and frailty presided at *gomba* rite and funeral services as late as May 1957. When he died in June of that year, there was no lama of sufficient status to conduct the service at his funeral, and an old lama from Phortse had to be called. In November 1957 Sharap Lama died suddenly, thus leaving the village with only Lama Karma and *Ongomba* Lama, both of whom were rather worldly personalities and lacking the spiritual status which qualify a lama for the independent performance of major rites.

In the neighbouring village of Kunde, which shares with Khumjung one *gomba* and co-operates in the performance of all village rites, there was only one lama, Lama Jangbu, a widower with grown-up children, whose reputation for learning was also not very high. Yet, he was senior to the two lamas of Khumjung, and in the absence of lamas of higher status it fell to him to preside at ceremonies in the *gomba.* Yet, even at the celebration of the Dumje festival, which occurred shortly after the death of Lama Kiu, and at a time when Sharap Lama was alive and in excellent health, the organizers of the festival felt that the help of a more experienced lama was required, and they prevailed upon Gelung Ngawang, a former *loben* and acting head lama of Tengboche, who then lived in a hermitage above Dingboche, to undertake the journey to Khumjung and preside at the Dumje rites. Similar arrangements will presumably have to be made until Khumjung has once more a resident lama of learning and high spiritual status.

In Khumjung, there was Ngawang Tundu, who for many years had been a monk at Tengboche but who returned to secular life on account of his marriage to an ex-nun of Devuche. Though he had the full religious training of a monk and like many other ex-monks of Tengboche, could have set up as a respected village lama, he devoted himself entirely to the care of his large herd of yak and the cultivation of his land, and never even joined the lamas of the village in their recitations at village rites. Therefore, there map have been qualified, experienced or educated lamas who had stopped practising.

Unlike the clergy of an organized church or the monks of a Buddhist monastery, the village lamas are not subject to any ecclesiastic authority. Yet, co-operation at all ritual occasions appears to function smoothly, and there seem to be no quarrels over the question of precedence. Greater knowledge of texts and ritual practices is readily recognized and this, together with the recitation and spiritual status gained by the practice of *tsam,* determines a lama's place among other village lamas co-operating in the same ritual. The most senior lama, who formally conducts the rite, always sits nearest to the altar, and the others take their places in order of seniority. The use of the title Lama for the ordinary village priest is somewhat inconsistent with the monastic practice of reserving this title, which corresponds to the Sansksrit *guru* or master, to the abbot of a monastery, who is usually referred to as *lamache* or 'great lama'.[7]

Ordinary Monks and Lamas

Ordinary monks are not described as lamas, and if someone speaks, for instance, of the 'Tengboche lama' he means inevitably the abbot. All those clerics resident in villages who engage regularly in the performance of religious rites, on the other hand, are freely accorded the title lama, even though some of them may be much less learned than the average monk. The qualifications which entitle a religious practitioner to the courtesy title of Lama are not clearly defined, and at the early stages of a village lama's career there will be some villagers who refer to him already by this title while others continue to call him by his ordinary name. But as he establishes himself as an experienced performer of rites and ceremonies, he will gradually become known as Lama 'so-and-so', or the title Lama will be affixed to his name.

Emergency Lamas

In Khumjung, there were in 1957 several men with some knowledge of sacred books and ritual practices who were never referred to as lamas, though on the occasion of funerals or certain other services they might sit in a line with the lamas and join in the recitation of liturgical texts. Most prominent among them was the painter Kapa Kalden, who though a man of learning no less than of artistic gifts, never aspired to the title of lama, and never undertook independently any ritual task. Some of the others, however, occasionally accepted the commission of reciting a text for a private purpose, and they were also employed at the annual public recitation of the Kangyur at village expense. It is not unlikely that the one or other of these young men will continue his studies and ultimately qualify for the tasks of a regular village lama. Most likely some time later by completing their studies and meditation, they would have taken up the duties of a regular village lamas.

Women Village Lamas

There are no female counterparts to the village lamas. The nuns of such nunneries as Devuche correspond to the monks of the monasteries. Among the inhabitants of most villages there are no doubt one or two religiously-minded women described as nuns *(ani),* who shave their hair and dress like the nuns of a nunnery, but they do not play any active role in ritual performances and are often virtually illiterate. Unable to join a nunnery on account of poverty, or unacceptable to a nunnery because of their lack of learning, they lead within the village a devout and celibate life, and usually help in the houses and in the fields of kinsmen who provide for their bodily needs. Even if learned in the sacred scriptures such an *ani* resident in a village can never attain to a position comparable to that of a village lama, and the only commission she might occasionally be entrusted with is the recitation of a *kurim* for the purpose of warding off illness or any specific danger. Sherpa religion provides no scope for ministrations of individual women following a religious calling, though nuns of an established nunnery are occasionally invited to perform mortuary rites.

Village Temples

In every main village there is either a temple *(gomba)* or at least a building which contains a giant, brightly painted prayer-wheel. Such religious buildings are invariably painted a dull pink, and their roof is surmounted by a gilded spire. While the structures housing prayer-wheels only serve the private devotions of those squatting before the wheel and turning it to the accompaniment of their prayers, the village temple is the centre of many celebrations which have their secular as well as religious aspects. Most temples consist of a courtyard surrounded by galleries the main hall containing the altar and library of sacred books, and one or two minor buildings in which the kitchen and storerooms are accommodated. The position of these main features depends on the character of the site.

Description of the temple in Khumjung will give a general idea of a Sherpa *gomba.* This temple stands in a small grove of juniper trees at the foot of the hill slopes rising on the northern side of the village. Five stone steps lead to a double-leaved wooden door set into the stone wall of the courtyard, and through this door one enters the covered gallery surrounding an open courtyard 35 feet square. The gallery covered by an inward sloping roof of wooden planks is about 5 feet wide and raised 2 feet above the level of the courtyard. In its centre stands a flagpole. On the right side of the courtyard, and accessible only through it, stands a double-storeyed house for the sacristan *(konier)*. Whenever rites performed in the temple necessitate the preparation of food, its two ground-floor rooms are used as kitchen and store. Three steps lead from the courtyard to the single entrance door of the main hall *(duang)* of the temple, which is approximately 40 feet square. Passing through this door one faces the main altar. At a right angle to this stand two long benches, on which at rituals lamas and prominent villagers sit facing each other. The roof of the *duang* rests on four stout wooden pillars, on each of which hangs a painted banner *(thanka)*, the gift of a villager long dead.

Buddha Padmasambhava

'Lotus-Born' Buddha Padmasambhava, a historical figure connected with the establishment of Buddhism in Tibet, who is known to the Sherpas as Guru Rimpoche ('Precious Master') and regarded as a manifestation of Pawa Cheresi in the central figure on the altar. Other statues of divinities arranged on an altar-table running along the entire back wall of the main hall are those of the Great Saviour Pawa Cheresi (Sanskrit: Avalokitesvara), of the Saviouress Drolma (Sanskrit: Tara); of Mandarava and the 'Goddess Ocean of Wisdom' Kando-ye-shes-chogyel, the two wives of Guru Rimpoche, and of an unnamed reincarnate nun. On a separate altar in the right hand corner stands a large statue of Jambhala (Nor-lha) the god of wealth. These statues, which are made of plaster and painted in gold and various colours, are not of high artistic merit, and compare unfavourably with the many exquisite frescoes in Tibetan style, painted by Sherpa painters. Temples and private chapels of Khumbu have these in plenty.

The Library

Wooden shelves line the entire side wall to the left of the entrance. This is in the shape of pigeon holes. East of the holes contains a volume of the temple library. The latter consists of Tibetan block prints of the 108 volumes of the Kangyur, the Buddhist canon, of part of the Tengyur, the commentaries, and several other sacred works. Most of the books, as well as several of the statues, are gifts of individual villagers. To donate ritual objects or works of religious art to a temple is a usual way of acquiring merit, and even the restoration of temples or individual statues is often paid for by pious persons anxious to add to their store of merit or to express their gratitude for rescue from danger. Thus, in 1957 a young Sherpa who had survived a serious illness contracted on a mountaineering expedition, paid for the regilding of the faces of some of the statues in the *gomba.*

PRAYER WHEEL HOUSE

Carved wooden masks worn by dancers representing divinities and demons at the time of the Dumje festival are deposited in the Temple. Some of these are hung up on pillars while others lie on a special shelf.

Built on to the main hall of the *gomba,* but not accessible either from this hall or even the temple courtyard, is a structure 27 feet long and 12 feet wide, which houses a prayer-wheel 8 feet high and 6 feet in diameter. While the frescoes in the hall of the *gomba* are not remarkable, and indeed of much poorer quality than many frescoes in private chapels, the walls of the interior of the prayer-wheel house bear frescoes of much better style. Among these are panels featuring the Great Saviour 'Glancing Eye' Pawa Cheresi (Avalokitesvara), the 'Precious Master" Guru Rimpoche (Padmasambhava), the 'Lord of Death' Shinje-chogyal (Yamaraj); Tungsha Tonba, the five celestial Buddhas; Guru Trakpo, the fierce aspect of Guru Rimpoche, and the Supreme Buddha 'All Good' Kuntubzang-po (Samanthabhadra). Village Kunde, has a prayer-wheel house of its own, which stands in a central place and is the only purely religious building of that village. The gomba is shared by the people of the two villages of Khumjung and Kunde.

Dumje Festival

A century ago there were in Khumbu only two temples, namely the one at Pangboche, believed to have been founded by Lama Sanga Dorje, and a small temple at Thami. Only in those two villages was the Dumje festival celebrated, and the people of Khumjung, for instance, went for the celebration of the Dumje to Thami. Not until the end of the nineteenth century—no exact dates are available—was a village temple built in Khumjung, and the one in Namche Bazar is of an even more recent date. Khumbu was then without any monastic establishment, and it was only in the first half of the twentieth century, that the great and elaborately decorated *gomba* of Thami and Tengboche were built.

Taking a one form the construction of these new temples, many wealthy men of Khumbu built houses with elaborately furnished and painted private chapels, and all along the paths sprung up religious structures, such as *chorten*, *mani*-walls, rock engravings, and houses containing water-driven prayer-wheels. *Chorten* are stupa like monuments consisting usually of a square base built of stone, a semi-spherical stone structure enclosing printed scriptures and sometimes some relics of a great lama, and rising above this a short spire, sometimes carrying a crescent moon. In most main villages there are one or two such *chorten*, usually standing close to a principal path leading into the village, but *chorten* are also found near subsidiary settlements and even on paths far from human habitation.

This is not a stand alone case. This applies to the *mani*-walls so characteristic of all the Buddhist regions of Nepal. They consist of an understructure of rough stone supporting innumerable upright stone slabs. The inscriptions on these slabs, carved in relief, include the sacred formula *om mani padme hum* and other prayers, and their erection provides merit for the person who bears the cost of the construction and of the work of carving the tablets. The economic effort required for the construction of all these religious buildings and structures within a comparatively short span, must be rated all the higher as the population of Khumbu, numbering 2,205 in 1957, was even one generation ago undoubtedly still considerably smaller. Quite apart from any natural growth owing to the immigration of numerous Khamba families which settled in Khumbu only within the last thirty or forty years, the population increased rapidly.

Sustaining Monks and Nuns

Out of the surplus of income over domestic expenditure the farmers and traders of Khumbu not only paid for the construction of temples, monasteries and religious monuments, but they also maintained a growing number of monks and nuns, who did not directly contribute to production. In 1957 the number of monks and lamas in Tengboche and Thami *gomba* was sixty, and that of nuns in Devuche and Thami *gomba* twenty-five. Apart from these there were in all the villages of Khumbu lamas who, though householders and landowners, devoted only part of their time to the farming of their land, and spent days and often weeks in ritual activities, for which they received payment by the laymen of the community.

Thus, the economic efforts of some 500 lay-households provide sufficient food and other necessities to support entirely some eighty-five monks and nuns, and contribute to the maintenance of several village lamas, much of whose income is derived from the fees paid by other householders for ritual services.

NEW DEVELOPMENT

Although Buddhism has been well established in Khumbu for at least 300 years, the foundation of monasteries and nunneries as well as the construction of new village temples and many religious monuments have taken place within the last fifty to eighty years. This points to economic events which favoured a sudden spurt of non-productive activities, and in my opinion there can be little doubt that these events were brought about by the introduction of the potato and the resulting increase in agricultural production. Obviously the sudden development of a surplus in food supplies must be regarded as permissive and not as causative of the flowering of the religious life. It would seem that among the Sherpas, as among Tibetan Buddhists, the religious impulse is so strong that any margin of resources left after essential needs have been met is largely devoted to religious purposes. This seems to have happened not only in Khumbu, but also in Solu where no less than five monastic establishments—Chiwong, Trakshindo, Gole, Tolaka and Thodung—have sprung up during the past forty years when the development of potato cultivation did not only improve the local food supplies but provided a commodity for a profitable export trade to India.

NOTES

1. Cf. C. von Furer-Haimendorf, 'Ethnographic Notes on the Tamangs of Nepal' *Eastern Anthropologist*, Vol. 9, 1955/56, pp. 166-77.
2. *Buddhist Himalaya*, Oxford, 1957, p. 213.
3. 'Unity of All the Blessed,' (Tib. *bDe-gshegs kun-' dus*).
4. 'Union of the Precious Ones,' (Tib. *dKon-mchog-spyi-' dus*).
5. 'Universal Saviour,' (Tib.' *Gro-ba-Kun-sgrol*).
6. *Sem*, written in Tibetan *sems*, is the equivalent of the Sanskrit *chit*, and means literally 'mind.'
7. Cf. also L.A. Waddell, *The Buddhism of Tibet*, p. 173, London, 1895.

4

Lamaism in Sikkim

I. HISTORIC SKETCH OF THE LAMAIC CHURCH IN SIKKIM

Lamaism The State Religion of Sikkim

Lamaism or Tibetan Buddhism is the State religion of Sikkim, and professed by the majority of the people.[1] Indeed, the lamas since entering the country about two and half centuries ago have retained the temporal power more or less directly in their hands; and the first of the present series of rulers was nominated by the pioneer lamas.

No Detailed Account Previously Published

No detailed account of Sikkim Lamaism has hitherto been published.[2] In regard to the ritual also and general history of Lamaism, I have often differed from such authorities as Koppen[3] and Schlagintweit, as I have enjoyed superior opportunities for studying the subject at first hand, with living lamas.

Priestcraft

As Lamaism is essentially a priestcraft, it has been dealt with it mainly in its sacerdotal aspects, and touch little upon its higher ethics and metaphysics of which most of the lamas are wholly ignorant. And throughout this paper the term "lama" has been used in its popular sense, as a general term for all the clergy of the Tibetan Buddhist Church, and not in its special sense of the superior monk of a monastery or sect.

Sources of Information

Sources of information have been taken note of by the author notes taken during several visits to Sikkim and a prolonged residence at Darjeeling in the society of lamas. For many of the local details he feels especially indebted to the learned Sikkim Lama and the Tibetan Lamas, with whom he had consulted most of the indigenous and Tibetan books which contain references to the early history of Sikkim and Tibet. These vernacular books contain no very systematic account either of the introduction of Lamaism into Sikkim or of its origin in Tibet. Their contents are largely mixed with myth and legend. However by careful sifting and comparative treatment it is possible to get a residue which may be treated as fairly historical, seeing that the periods dealt with are so relatively recent.

Buddhism

Buddhism arose in India and flourished there for about fifteen centuries, until it was forcibly suppressed by the Muhammadan invaders in the latter end of the 12th century A.D. According to the best authorities, Buddhism was founded at Benares about the 5th century B.C., when the newly-fledged Buddha preached his first sermon and made his first converts on the site now marked by Sarnath stupa.

Spread of Buddhism

The new religion soon spread over the North-Western Provinces and Oudh and extended down the Gangetic valley to Bihar. Its wide dissemination dates from the epoch of the Great Indian Emperor Asoka, in the 3rd century B.C., who had his capital at the city of Patna in Bihar. Asoka made Buddhism the State religion. Besides diligently promoting it in his own territories, he sent thousands of missionaries into neighbouring countries to preach the faith. From Asoka's son, Mahendra, Ceylon claims to have obtained its Buddhism and the Pali alphabet; while the Asoka missionaries Uttara and Sauna are similarly claimed by Burma. Not only the neighbouring countries.

Cashmere, Afghanistan, Mongolia, China and Japan

Buddhism spread through Afghanistan, Cashmere, and its adjoining principalities, into Mongolia and China, and through China to Japan, from Afghanistan monks went upto Greek and Egypt exercising on all the wilder tribes a marked civilizing influence. It was established in China about 61 A.D.

Its Extension to Tibet

Up to the 7th century A.D. the people of Tibet were without a written language and were pure savages. Early in the 7th Century A.D. was born Srong-tsan-gampo, whose ancestors since two or three generations had established their authority over Central Tibet, and had latterly harassed the western boundaries of China; so that the Chinese Emperor was glad to make peace with the young prince and gave him a princess of the Imperial house in marriage. Srong-tsan-gampo had two years previously married the daughter of the King of Nepal; and both these wives being staunch Buddhists, they speedily converted Srong-tsan-gampo, who under their advice sent messages to India. Thus Seventh Century is considered to period when Buddhism started take roots in Tibet.

The Great Councils

Four great councils are reported to have been held for the suppression of heresy:

(1) The Council held at Rajagriha under the presidency of Maha Kasyapa immediately after Buddha's death.

(2) The Council of Vaisali held about 350 B.C. under Yashada.

(3) The Council of Pataliputra (Patna) held about 250 B.C. under Asoka's orders, with Mogaliputra as president,

(4) The Council of Jalandhara held in the 1st century A.D. under the auspices of King Kanishka of Kashmir and the Panjab.

The Great Schisms

The second Council dealt only with discipline. The third Council defined the Buddhist canon as now current in Ceylon and Burma and Siam. The fourth developed exorcism, and from it arose the *Dharani* formulae for schism of the "Northern" and "Southern" schools.

The Southern School

The Southern school is the more primitive and of purer form; it includes the Burmese, Ceylonese, and Siamese forms of Buddhism. Its sacred language is Pali.

The Northern School

The Northern school comprises the forms of Buddhism current in Kashmir, Mongolia, China, Manchuria, Japan, Nepal, Tibet, Bhutan, and Sikkim. Its sacred language is Sanskrit.

Its Nature

The schism was brought about by the *Mahayana* doctrine, a theistic and metaphysical form of Buddhism introduced by a monk named Asvagosha and specially advocated by *Nagarjuna*, whose name is most intimately identified with it. Its chief work is the *Prajna paramita* (Tib. *Sher-chin),* which recognises several grades of theoretical Buddhas and of numerous divine Bodhisatwas, or beings who have arrived at perfect wisdom *(Bodhi)*, yet consent to remain a creature *(satwa)* for the good of men, and who must therefore be worshipped, and to whom prayers must be addressed.

Mythology and Mysticism

The Mahayana school gave both to mythology and mysticism, and its extension amongst races of devil worshippers. Like Hinduism, it admitted within its pale the gods and demons of the new nations it sought to convert. *Mysticism* reached its fullest expression in the *Tantrik* doctrines (a mixture of Siva-worship and magic) which spread throughout India about the 6th and 7th century of our era, affecting alike Buddhism and Hinduism. Arya Asanga, a Buddhist monk of Peshawar, who lived about 300 A.D., is supposed to have introduced Tantricism into Buddhism.

Tantricism

The Tantriks teach yogism and incantations addressed mostly to female energies, by which men may gain miraculous powers, which may be used for purely selfish and secular objects. Just as they assigned female "energies"—the Hindu *Saktis* or divine mothers—as companions to most of the gods and some alone, wives were allotted to the several Buddhas and Bodhisatwas.

Image-Worship

At an early date, Buddhists worshipped the tree under which the Buddhahood was attained, and the monument which contained Buddha's relics. These images of the two objects together with the wheel are symbolic of Buddha teaching.

Introduction to Tibet

Northern Buddhism had almost reached this impure stage when it was introduced into Tibet about the middle of the 7th century A.D. Hiuen Tsiang states that the Mahayana school then predominated in India and tantrik and mystic doctrines had mushroomed. Lamaism dates from over a century later than the first entry of Buddhism into Tibet, and in the meantime tantricism had greatly increased. About the same time the doctrine of the Kalachakra or supreme Deity, without beginning or end, the source of all things, [*Adi Buddha Samantabhadra* (Tib. *Kun-tu-zang-po*)] was accepted by the Lamas.

The Founder of Lamaism

Lamaism was founded by the wizard-priest *Padma Sambhava* (Tib. *Pedma Jungne), i.e.,* "The lotus born;" usually called by the Tibetans *Guru Rimbochhe* or "The Precious Guru;" or simply "*Guru*" the Sanskrit for "teacher."

Visit to Tibet of the Founder, Guru Rimpochhe

It was in connection with the building of this monastery that Padma Sambhava first came to Tibet. King Thi-Srong De-tsan's endeavours to build the monastry were all frustrated by earthquakes which were attributed to demons. On the advice of the Indian Buddhist monk Shantarakshita, the king requested wizard-priest Padma Sambhava of the Yogacharya School to come to Tibet. Priest Padma Sambhava was considered to be a famous sorcerer.

Padma Sambhava, who was a native of Udyana, or Ghazni, a region famed for sorcery, promptly responded to the Tibetan king's request and arrived at Samye. With the *dorje* (Sansk. *Vajra)* or thunderbolt, and spells from the Mahayana he, vanquished and converted the devils, built the monastery in 749 A.D., and established the first community of lamas.

What is Lamaism

Lamaism may be defined as a mixture of Buddhism with a preponderating amount of mythology, mysticism, and magic: the doctrine of incarnate lamas and the worship of canonized saints, now such prominent features of Lamaism, are of recent origin. It was readily accepted as it protected the people from devils.

Lamaic Sects

Atisha, the Great Refomer of Lamaism

The Lamaic sects date from the visit to Tibet of the Indian Buddhist monk Atisha (1038-1052 A.D.), who preached celibacy and moral abstinence, and deprecated the practice of the magic arts. Some reformed, some did not and went on loving their own way.

The reformed sect was called the *Kah-dam-pa?*[4] or "those bound by the orders," and three and-a-half centuries later, in Tsongkhapa's hands, it became less ascetic and more ritualistic under the title of *Ge-luk-pa,* now the dominant sect in Tibet.

The unreformed residue were called the *Nying-ma-pa* or "the old sect."

Ge-Luk-Pa Sect: Its Peculiarities, Tsongkhapa

Tsongkhapa[5] gathered together the scattered members of the Kadampa and housed them in monasteries, under rigorous discipline. He made them carry a begging-bowl and wear a garment of a yellow colour after the fashion of Indian Buddhists. He instituted a ritualistic service, in part, apparently, perhaps borrowed from the Nestorian Christian missionaries, who were settled at that time in Western China. The tutelary deities are Dorje-hjig-*b*yed, *b*De-mchhog and *g*Sang-wa-*h*duspa; the guardian demons are "*m*Gronpo phyag-truk," or the six-armed protector, and Tam-chhen Chhos-gyal.

Kargyupa Sect

Lama Marpa, had visited India in eleventh century AD and had obtained special instruction from the Indian pandit Atisha and Atisha's teacher Naropa. After returning home, he founded Kargyupa sect.

Its Peculiarities

The distinctive features of the Kargyupa sect are that they inhabit caves and profess meditation and the following doctrines:

(a) Their guardian deity is "The Lord of the Black Cloak."[6]

(b) Their tutelary deity is Demchhok[7] (Skt. *Sambhara), or* "Chief of Happiness."

(c) Their mode of meditation or system of mystical insight is *Chhag-chhen,*[8] or in Sanskrit *Mahamudra;* and their highest teacher is the mythical Dorje-Chhang[9] (Skt. *Bajra-dhara*), or "the holder of the Dorje."

(d) Their hat is called *gom-zha pu khyu,* or "the meditation hat with the crossed knees."

The Kar-ma-pa

The diagram of Kar-gyupa sects relation of the sub-sects to the parent sect. The *Kar-ma-pa* adopted the Nyingmapa *ter-ma* or Las-*h*prod-ling-pa.

The Di-Kung-pa

The *Di-kung-pa* take their title from the Dikung Monastery founded by Rinchhen-phun-tshog about the middle of the 12th century. Their Nyingmapa *ter-ma* is Padma ling-pa.

The Ta-lung-pa

The *Ta-lung-pa* branched out from the Dikungpa and take their title from the Talung Monastery founded by *Ngagadbang-chhos-gyalpo* in 1179. They differ from their parent Di-kung-pa in admitting also the *ter-ma* work adopted by the Kar-ma-pa.

The-Duk-pa

The *Duk-pa* are of three forms. The oldest is the *Upper Duk-pa* which originated by *h*Gro-*m*gon-*r*tsang-pa-*r*gyal-ras (The patron of Animals, The Victory-clad Tsang-po) or *s*Prul *s*ku-*d*bung-*b*sam-wang-po of the Ralung Monastery in Gnam province of Tibet about the middle of the 12th century. To emphasize the change, the monastery was called *Duk*-Ralung, and a legend of the thunder-dragon *Duk* is related in connection therewith. It adopted the same *ter-ma* as the Dikungpa, but there seems some other distinctive tenet which have not yet been elicited. The *Middle Duk-pa* and the *Lower Duk-pa* arose very soon after.

The *Middle Duk-pa* took the *terma* book of Sangyas-ling-pa. This is the form of Kar-gyu-pa, which now prevails in Bhutan under the name of *Duk-pa* or *Southern Duk-pa.* Its chief lama is Zhab-drung Ngag-*d*bang-nam-gyal, a pupil of "Kun-*m*khyen padma *d*kar-po" or "The Omniscient White Lotus," who, in the 17th century A.D., settled at "*l*chags rit *r*ta *m*go" in Bhutan. He soon displaced the Karthok-pa and other forms of Nyingmapa Lamaism then existing in that country. These are reputed to have been founded there directly by Lo-pon himself, who entered Bhutan *via g*Zhas-ma gang and left it by *m*Dung-tsang, and at *d*gon-tshal phu*k* are still shown his footprints on a rock.

The Sakya-pa Sect

The Sakya-pa Sect, Its Title, Specialities and Sub-Sects

The *Sakya-pa* takes its name from the Sakya Monastery in Western Tibet, founded by *h*Khon-*d*kon-*m*chhog-*r*gyalpo. The name Sakya[10] refers to the light yellow colour of the scanty soil in that locality, which is rocky and almost bare of vegetation. The founder mixed together the "old" and "new" dispensations in regard to the *tantras,* calling his tantrik system gsang-*s*ngags-*g*sar-nying, or "the new-old occult mystery." The Nyingmapa books adopted by the Sakya-pa are called *Dorje phurpai chhoga;* and from the newer school were taken Dem-chhok, Dorje-kando, Den-zhi, Maha-maha-ma-yab, Sangye thopa, and Dorje-dutsi. Its special meditative system is "*Lam-h*bras." Its guardian demons are *m*gon-po-gur or "The Guardian of the Tent" and *m*gon-po-zhal. Its hat is called Sa-zhu. Now, however, the Sakya sect and the Nyingmapa are scarcely distinguishable from each other. Its sub-sects are as follows:

Ngor-pa

The *Ngor-pa,* founded by Gun-gah Zang-po, issued from the Sakya-pa at the time of Tsongkhapa. It has many monasteries in Kham. Its founder discarded the Nynimapa element in its tantrik system, retaining only the "new."

Jonang-po, Taranath

The *Jonang-po,* issued from the Sakya-pa, in the person of Je-kun-gah-tol chhok, who was re-incarnated some centuries later as the great historian lama Taranath, now the highest incarnate lama of the Mongols and Chinese. This latter lama built the monastery of Phuntsholing about a mile to the north of Jonang in Upper Tsang, which was one of the many seized by the great Dalai Lama Lo-zang gyatsho and forcibly converted into a Gelukpa institution. This sect does not practically differ from the Ngor-pa. The distinction is only one of founders.

Nyingmapa's Entry into Sikkim

The *Nyingmapa* peculiarities have already been indicated in a general way. Further details will be found under the head of Sikkim Lamaism. It was the Nyingma form of Lamaism which first found its way into Sikkim about 250 years ago.

Lamaism in Sikkim

Legendary Account of the Guru's Visit to Sikkim

It is believed in Sikkim that Guru Rimbochhe visited Sikkim during his travels in Tibet and its western border lands. The introduction of Lamaism into Sikkim dates from the time of *Lhatsun Chhembo's* arrival there about the middle of the 17th century A.D. By this time

Lamaism had become a most powerful hierarchy in Tibet, and was extending its creed among the Himalayan and Central Asian tribes.

Lhatsun Chhembo

Lhatsun Chhembo was a native of Kongbu in the lower valley of the Tsangpo, which has a climate and physical appearance very similar to Sikkim. His name means "The great reverend God." His religious name is *Kun-zang nam-gye* or "The entirely victorious Essence of Goodness." He is also known by the title of *Lhatsun nam-kha Jig-med,* or "The Reverend God who fears not the sky," with reference to his alleged power of flying. He is also sometimes called *Kusho Dsog-chhen Chhembo,* or "The great Honourable Dsog-chhen"—*Dsog-chhen,* literally "The Great End," being the technical name for the system of mystical insight of the Nyingmapa, and *Kusho* means "the honourable."

His Early History

He was born in the fire-bird year of the tenth of the sixty-year cycles, corresponding to 1595 A.D., in the district of Kongbu in South-Eastern Tibet. Having spent many years in various monasteries and in travelling throughout Tibet and Sikkim, he ultimately in the year 1648 arrived in Lhassa and obtained such great repute by his learning as to attract the favourable notice of Gyalwa Ngak-Wang, the greatest of the Grand Lamas, who shortly afterwards became the first Dalai Lama.

At this time another lama of the *Kartok-pa* sub-sect came by Kangla nangma searching for a path into Sikkim, and also tried without success the *sPreu-gyab-tak* (i.e., "Monkey-back rock," with reference to its semblance to a monkey sitting with hands behind its back) and Dsong-ri, and the western shoulder of *sKam-pa Khab-rag*—a ridge of "*Kabru*", which runs down to the Rathong river. He then arrived at the cave of "the very pleasant grove," and met the saint, who told him that as he was not destined to open the northern gate, he should go round and try the western.

Miraculous Reconnaissance and Entry

Then Lhatsun Chhembo, traversing the Kangla nangma and finding no road beyond the cave of *Skam-pa Khabruk,* flew miraculously to the upper part of "Kabru" (24,000 feet), and there blew his kangling, and after an absence of two weeks flew down to where his servants were collected and guided them by a road *via* Dsongri to Norbugang in Sikkim.

Meeting Two Other Lamas

He arrived in Sikkim with two other Nyingmapa lamas. By "the western gate" of *Singlela* came a Kartok-pa lama named Sempah Chhembo,[11] and a lama of the Ngadakpa sub-sect, named Rigdsin Chhembo,[12] who had opened "the southern gate" by way of Darjeeling and Namchi respectively. The place where these three lamas met was called by the Lepchas *Yok-sam,* which means "the three superior ones or noblemen" a literal translation of "the three lamas".

Their Appointment and Coronation of a King of Sikkim

The three lamas held here a council at which Hlatsun Chhembo said, "Here are we three lamas in a new and irreligious country. We must have a 'dispenser of gifts'[13] (i.e., a king) to rule the country on our behalf." Then the *Nga-dak-pa* lama said, "I am descended from the celebrated Terton Nga-dak Nyang-rel, who was latterly a governor; I should therefore be the king." While the Kartok-pa lama declared, "As I am of royal lineage I have the right to rule." Then *Hlatsun Chhembo* said, "In the prophesy of Guru Rimbochhe it is written that four noble brothers shall meet in Sikkim and arrange for its government. We are three of these come from the north, west, and south."

Towards the east, it is written, there is at this epoch, a man named *Phuntshog,*[14] a descendant of brave ancestors of *Kham* in Eastern Tibet. According, to the prophesy of the Guru we should invite him." Two messengers were then despatched to search for this Phuntshog. Going towards the extreme east near Gangtok they met a man churning milk and asked him his name. He without replying invited them to sit down and gave them milk to drink. After they were refreshed, he said his name was Phuntshog. He was then conducted to the lamas, who crowned him by placing the holy water vase on his head and anointed him with the water; and exhorting him to rule the country religiously, gave him Hlatsun's own surname of Namgye and the title of *Chho-gyal* (Skt. *Dharma-raja)* or "religious king." Phuntshog Namgye" was at this time aged 38 years. He became a lama in the same year, which is said to have been 1641 A.D.

His Appearance (Plate III), His Incarnation

In appearance Lhatsun is usually represented as seated on a leopard skin mat, with the right leg hanging down and his body almost naked one of his title is *He-ru-ka-pa,* which means "unclad." His complexion is dark blue. A chaplet of skulls encircles his brow. In his left hand is a skull cup filled with blood, and a trident topped with human heads rests in front of the left shoulder. The right hand is in a teaching attitude. He is believed to be the incarnation of the great Indian teacher Bhima Mitra.

Development of Lamaism in Sikkim, Subsequent to the Epoch of Lhatsun Chhembo

Its Peculiarities

The religions ousted by Lamaism were the Pon (Bon), usually identified with Taouism, and the earlier demon and fairly worship of the Lepchas, which can scarcely be called a religion. Numerous traces of both of these primitive faiths are to be found embodied in Sikkim Lamaism, which owes any special features it possesses to the preponderance of these two elements. Only two sects of lamas exist in Sikkim, viz., the Nyingmapa and the Kargyupa as represented by the Karmapa. There are no Duk-pa monasteries in Sikkim, nor does there seem ever to have been any.

The Nyingma-pa

The Nyingma-pa or "the old school" represents the primitive and unreformed style of Lamaism. It is more largely tinged with the indigenous pre-Buddhist religious practices; and celibacy and abstinence are rarely practised.

Its Sub-sects in Sikkim

In Sikkim there are three sub-sects of Nyingma-pa, viz.—(1) the *Lhatsun-pa,* to which belong most of the monasteries with Pemiongchi at the head; (2) the *Kartok-pa* with the monasteries of Kartok and Doling; and (3) the *Nga dak-pa* with the monasteries of Namchi, Tashiding, Sinon, and Thang-mochhe.

Lhatsun-pa

The Ter-ma of the *Lhatsun-pa* is the same as was adopted by the Karmapa, viz., the work *Le-tho Ling-pa* discovered *(i.e.,* composed) by *Ja-tshon-pa* in Kongbu. But the Pemiongchi lamas also follow the *Mindolling* monastery in giving pre-eminence to the *ter-ma* work of Dag-ling-pa as a form of ritual.

Kartok-pa

The *Kartok-pa* taking their name from the title of their founder lama *Kah-tok, i.e.,* "The Understander of the Precepts," give pre-eminence to the *terton* work *Long-chhen rab chung*. It has been suggested that Darjeeling, properly Dorjeling, may owe its name to the terton Dorje-lingpa, who visited the Kartok-pa Do-ling (properly Dorjeling) monastery in Sikkim, of which the old Darjeeling monastery was a branch.

Nga-dak-pa

The *Nga-dak-pa,* also taking their name from their founder "The owner of Sway or Dominion," who was of royal lineage, give pre-eminence to the *terton* work of *Rig-dsin go dem*[15] as a code of ritual.

Specialities of Nyingma-pa

All sections of the Nyingma-pa agree in professing the creed called Dsog-chhen-bo, or "The Great End; it is probable, however, that the Sanskrit *Maha-joga* is intended. This Dsog-chhen-bo doctrine is a purely theoretical distinction, in great part relating merely to the posture of the hands in meditation and little understood by the great majority of the members. The obvious and practical Nyingma-pa characteristics are (a) their special worship of Guru Rimbochhe; (b) their highest god is *Kuntu zang po* (Skt. *Samantabhadra),* "the Highest Goodness;" (c) their special tutelary deity is *Dub-pa kah gye;*[16] (d) their special guardian deity *Pal-gon de-nga*; (e) and their peculiar red hat is named *Ugyen penzhu,* and (f) with these characteristics they exhibit, as a class, a greater laxity in living than any other sect of lamas.

The Guru's Eight Forms

In spite of his uncelibate life, his semi-demoniac temper, and his being altogether void of any of the admirable traits of Buddha. By the Nyingma-pa, the great wizard Guru Pema is worshipped as "a second Buddha." It is just possible, however, that he is painted blacker than he really was, for most of the practices and rites which are credited to him were really the composition of the *tertons* or "revealers of hidden scriptures" many centuries after his time. He is worshipped under eight forms, called *Guru Tsen-gye,* or "the eight worshipful names of the Teacher." These, together with their usual paraphrase, are here given:

I. *Guru Padma Jungne,*[17] "Born of a lotus" for the happiness of the three worlds.

II. *Guru Padma, Sambhava,*"Saviour by the Religious

Doctrine." (N.B.—This title is the pure Sanskrit equivalent of No. I).

III. *Guru Padma Gyelpo,* "The King of the Three Collections of Scriptures" *(Skt.* "Tripitaka").

IV. *Guru Dorje Do-lo,*[18] "The *Dorje* or Diamond Comforter of all."

V. *Guru Nyima Od-zer?*[19] "The Enlightening Sun of Darkness."

VI. *Guru Shakya Seng-ge,* "The Second Sakya—the Lion," who does the work of eight sages.

VII. *Guru Seng-ge-da dok,*[20] "The propagator of religion in the six worlds—with "the roaring lion's voice."

VIII. *Guru Lo-ten Chhog-Se,*[21] "The Conveyer of knowledge to all worlds."

Head Monasteries of the Nyingma-pa Sect

The chief monastery of the Pemiongchi sect, and its associated lamas, is at Mindolling in Central Tibet. The chief monastery of the Kartok-pa is at Der-ge in Kham (Eastern Tibet), excellent prints; celebrated for its and that of the Nga dak-pa at Dorje-tak, the greatest of the Nyingma-pa headquarters about two days' journey south-east of Lhassa. Until recently, Pemiongchi was in the habit of sending batches of its young lamas to Mindolling for instruction in strict discipline and rites; for some years now this practice has been allowed to lapse.

The Karmapa Sub-Sect

Karmapa in Sikkim, Tenets

The Karmapa, was one of the earliest sub-sects of the Kargyupa. It differs from its parent, Kargyupa, in the adoption of the Nyingma "hidden revelation" found in Kongbo, and entitled Le-to Ling-pa or "the locally-revealed merit." And from the Duk-pa, another sub-sect of the Kargyupa, it differs in not having adopted the Nyingma terton works Padma ling-pa and Sangye ling-pa. The Karmapa sect was founded by Milaraspa's pupil Rangchug dorje. Their chief monastery is at To-lung tshur phu, founded in 1158 A.D. and about one day's journey to the north-west of Lhasa. They are Kargyupas, who have retrograded towards the Nyingma-pa practices. Marpa, the nominal founder of the Kargyupa sect, was married. A few of the Karma-pa lamas are celibate.

When Established in Sikkim

The first Karmapa monastery in Sikkim was built at Ralang about 1730 A.D. by the Sikkim ruler Gyur-med Namgyal at the special request of the Ninth Karmapa Grand Lama—*d*Bang-chug-*r*dorje—in Tibet during a pilgrimage of the king in Tibet. Their other monasteries are at Ramtek and Phodang, and the "Phodang" monastery in the Bhotiya *basti* of Darjeeling which is a chapel of ease to Phodang.

Their Temples

The central image in a Karmapa temple is usually that of the founder of the sub-sect, viz. Karma " Bakshi," otherwise their temples do not differ from those of the Nyingma-pa sect.

II. GENERAL DESCRIPTION OF SIKKIM MONASTERIES

Monasteries of Three Kinds

Monasteries in Sikkim are of three kinds, viz.—(a) *Tak-phu,*[22] literally a "rock-cave" or cave-hermitage; (b) *Gompa,*[23] literally "a solitary place" or monastery proper; and (c) the so called "*gompas*" founded in or near villages. These latter are, as a rule, merely temples *(hla-khang)* with one or more priests engaged in ministering to the religious wants of the villagers.

The Four Great Caves of Sikkim

The four great caves of Sikkim hallowed as the traditional abodes of Guru Rimbochhe and Lhatsun Chhembo, and now the objects of pilgrimage even to lamas from Tibet, are distinguished according to the four cardinal points, viz.

The north *Lha-ri nying phu,* or "the old cave of God's hill." It is situated about three days' journey to the north of Tashiding, along a most difficult path. This is the most holy of the series.

The south *Kah-do Sang phu,*[24] or "cave of the occult fairies". Here, it is said is a hot spring, and on the rock are many footprints ascribed to the fairies.

The east *Pe phu,*[25] or "secret cave." It lies between the Mainom and Tendong mountains, about five miles from Yangang. It is a vast cavern, reputed to extend by a bifurcation to both Tendong and Mainom. People go in with torches about a quarter of a mile. Its height varies from five feet to one hundred or two hundred feet.

The west *De-chhen phu*[26] or "cave of Great Happiness." It is in the snow near Jongri, and only reachable in the autumn.

The Gompa, or Monastery Proper

"Gompa," as has been noted, means "a solitary place" and most of the "Gompa," still found in solitary places. Isolation from the world has always been a desideratum of Buddhist monks; not as an act of self-punishment, but merely to escape mundane temptations.

Its Isolation

The extreme isolation of some of the gompas has its counterpart. These are the Alpine monasteries in Europe in the Alpine monasteries amid the ever-lasting snows. One of these gompa is To-lung which for the greater part of the year is quite cut off from the outer world and at favourable times is only reachable from the south by a path of flimsy rope and bamboo ladders leading across the face of precipices. Thus, its solitude is seldom broken by visitors. The remote and almost inaccessible position of many of the Sikkim gompas renders mendicancy impossible; but begging-with-bowl seems never to have been a feature of Lamaism, even when the monastery adjoins a town or village.

Conditions Necessary for its Site

The site occupied by the monastery is usually commanding and frequently picturesque. It should have a free outlook to the east to catch the first rays of the rising sun. The monastery building should be built in the long axis of the hill, and it is desirable to have a lake in front even though it be several miles distant. These two conditions are expressed in the couplet:

> "Back to the hill-rock,
> And front to the tarn."[27]

The door of the assembly room and temple is *coeteris paribus* built to face eastwards. The next best direction is south-east, and then south. If a stream directly drains the site or is visible a short way below, then the site is considered bad, as the virtue of the place escapes by the stream. In such a case the chief entrance is made in another direction. A waterfall, however, is of very good omen, and if one is visible in the neighbourhood, the entrance is made in that direction, should it not be too far removed from the east.

General Plan of the Buildings

The monastic buildings cluster round the temple, which is also used as the Assembly Hall or *du-khang,* and corresponds to the *vihara* of the earlier Buddhists. The temple building and its contents form the subject of the next chapter. Most of the outer detached buildings are dormitories for the monks, and have nothing to distinguish them from the ordinary houses of Sikkim, except, perhaps, that their surroundings are sometimes a trifle cleaner and more comfortable looking, and occasionally a few flowers are to be seen. One elderly monk and two or three novices usually occupy one house, and each house cooks its own meals independently. There is no common refectory in the small monastic establishments of Sikkim. The menial lay servants are usually housed some distance among from the main establishment.

Its Surroundings

Lining the approaches to the monastery are rows of tall "prayer" flags, and several large lichen-clad chhortens and long mendong monuments.

Chhortens

The *chhortens*[28] literally, "receptacle for offerings" (Skt. *Da-garbha, Chaitya* or stupa[29]), are solid conical structure originally intended as relic-holders, but now are mostly erected as cenotaphs in memory of Buddha or canonized saints, and they have a suggestively mournful appearance. The original form of the stupa was a simple hemisphere with its convexity upwards and crowned by one or more umbrellas. Latterly they became more complex and elongated, especially in regard to their capitals. The details of many of the Lamaic Chaityas are capable of an elemental interpretation, symbolic of the five elements into which a body is resolved on death.

Thus, *vide* figure in margin modified from Remusat, the lowest section, a solid rectangular block, typifies the solidity of the *earth,* above it *water* is represented by a *globo fire* by a triangular tongue, *air* by a crescent—the inverted vault of the sky, and *ether* by an acuminated circle. The Chaityas of Sikkim are mainly of two forms. Each *chhorten* consists of a solid hemisphere—the true relic-holder—which stands on a plinth of several steps. The hemisphere is surmounted by a narrow neck bearing in a lotus-leaved basin a graded cone usually of 13 tiers, which are considered to represent umbrellas—the symbol of royalty;

they are by others said to represent the 13 Bodhisatwa heavens of Nepalese Buddhist cosmography. And the whole is topped by a horizontal disc bearing a smaller vertical disc set within a crescent, which popularly are said to typify the sun and moon, but which may have the elemental character already noted.

In the most common form, the hemisphere has its curved surface directed downwards. The second form especially common in Nepal, bears a closer resemblance to the older form of stupa, but its capital is more elongated, and it and the cone or pyramid is separated from the hemisphere by a square neck which bears on each face a pair of eyes which typify omniscience. In most of monasteries found in Sikkim, the chorten wears a doleful look, but wealthier monasteries, the chhortens are occasionally whitewashed.

The Great Tashiding Chhorten

The most holy chhorten in Sikkim is at Tashiding, It is the largest of the group figured by Hooker.[30] So sacred is it that the mere act of beholding it is supposed to cleanse one from all sin, according to its name. Its full title is *Thong-wa rang to,*[31] or "Saviour by more sight." It owes its special sanctity to its reputedly containing some of the funereal granules[32] of the mythical Buddha antecedent to Shakyamuni, viz.—*O-sung,*[33] the relics having been deposited there by Jik-mi Pawo, the incarnation and successor of Lhatsun Chhembo. As a result of this repute, it is a favourite object of pilgrimage.

Mendongs

The *mendongs* are faced with blocks bearing in rudely cut characters the six-syllabled mystic sentence "*Om mani padme hung*"—the same which is revolved in the "prayer-wheels." Occasionally it also bears coarsely outlined figures of the three favourite protecting divinities of Lamaism, the *Ri-sum Gonpo,* or "the Three-*Defensores Fidei,*" viz.—the four-handed *Cheresi* (Skt. *Avalokita), Jai-yang* (Skt. *Manjugosha),* and *Chakna Dorje* (Skt. *Bajrapani).* As it is a pious act to add to these "*mani*" slabs, a mason is kept at the larger temples and places of special pilgrimage. His job is to carves the necessary number of stones according to the order and at the expense of the donating pilgrim.

Pradakshina Mode of Passing Religious Buildings

The above monuments must always be passed on the right hand, according to the ancient Hindu ceremonial of *pradakshina,* as a tribute of respect. Thus, it is that the prayer cylinders must always be turned in a similar direction.

Lama's Throne

In addition to the foregoing objects there is frequently found in the vicinity of the monastery a stone seat called a "throne" for the head lama while giving *al-fresco* instruction to his pupils. One of the reputed thrones of Lhatsun Chhembo exists at the Pemiongchi chhorten. Here the camp of visitors is usually pitched.

Ransomed Animals

There is no regular asylum for animals rescued from the butcher to save these from imminent death. Occasionally such ransomed cattle are to be found in the neighbourhood of monasteries where their pension-expenses have been covered by a donation from the party cured. The animals have their ears bored for a tuft of coloured rags as a distinctive mark.

Murwa Fields

Not far from most monasteries are fertile fields of *murwa (Eleusine corocana).* From this made the country beer, a beverage which the Sikkim monks do not deny themselves.

List of Sikkim Monasteries

In the following table is given, what is described as, a complete list of monasteries in native Sikkim with the number of the monks in each, from official information supplied by Lama Ugyen Gyatsho:—

List of Monasteries in Sikkim

	Map name	*Vernacular name*	*Meaning of the name*	*Date of building*	*Number of monks*
1.	Sanga Chelling	gsang sngags chhos gling	The place of secret spells	1697	25
2.	Dubdi	sgrub-sde	The Hermit's cell	1701	30
3.	Pemiongchi	pad-ma yang tse	The sublime perfect lotus	1705	108
4.	Gantok	btsan-mkhar	The Tsen's house	1716	3
5.	Tashiding	bkra-shis-lding	*(The large Tashiding temple* is the temple of the religious king or "*Dharma raja*")	1716	20
6.	Senan	gzil-gnon	The suppressor of intense fear	1716	8

7.	Rinchinpong	rin-chhen *s*pungs	The precious knoll	1730	8
8.	Ralong	ra-*b*lang	—	1730	80
9.	Mali	mad-lis	—	1740	15
10.	Ram the.	Ram-tek	A Lepcha village name	1740	80
11.	Fadung	pho-brang	The chapel royal	1740	100
12.	Cheung tong	*b*tsun-thang	The Meadow of Marriage (of the two rivers), or of Dorje Phagmo.	1788	8
13.	Ketsu perri	*m*khah *s*pyod *a*pal ri	The noble heaven-reaching mountain.	—	11
14.	Lachung	thang mo-chhen	The large plain	1788	5
15.	Talung	*r*do lung	The stony valley	1789	90
16.	Entchi	rab-*b*rten *g*ling	The high strong place	1840	15
17.	Phensung	phan-*b*zang	The excellent banner or good bliss.	1840	100
18.	Kartok	*b*kah-*r*tog	The Kartok (founder of a schism).	1840	20
19.	Dalling	*r*do-*g*ling	"The stony site" or the place of the "Dorjeling" terton.	1840	8
20.	Yangong	*g*yang *s*gang	"The cliffy ridge" or "the lucky ridge."	1841	10
21.	Labrong	*b*la-brang	The lama's dwelling	1844	30
22.	Lachung	pon-po *s*gang	The Bon's ridge	1850	8
23.	Lintse	lhun-*r*tse	The lofty summit	1850	15
24.	Sinik	zi-mig	—	1850	30
25.	Ringim	ri-*d*gon	Hermitage hill	1852	30
26.	Lingthem	ling-tham	A Lepcha village name	1855	20
27.	Changhe	*r*tsag-nges	—	—	—
28.	Lachen	La-chhen	The big pass	1858	8
29.	Giatong	zi-hdur	—	1860	8
30.	Lingqui	ling-*b*kod	The uplifted limb	1860	20
31.	Fadie	*h*phago *r*gyal	The sublime victor	1862	8
32.	Nobling	nub-gling	The western place	1875	5
33.	Namchi	*r*nam-*r*tse	The sky-top	1836	6
34.	Pabia	*s*pa-*h*bi-*h*og	—	1875	20
35.	Singtam	sing-ltam	A Lepcha village name	1884	6

The Older Monasteries, Pemiongchi and its ta Sang

The oldest monastery in Sikkim is Dub-de. It was founded by the pioneer lama Lhatsun Chhembo. Soon afterwards shrines seem to have been erected at Tashiding, Pemiongchi and Sang-nga-chho-ling over spots consecrated to Guru Rimbochhe, and these ultimately became the nuclei of monasteries; Sangngachholing and Pemiongchi being first built. As Sangngachholing is open to members of all classes of Sikkim-Bhotiyas, Lepchas, Limbus, and also females and even deformed persons, it is said that Pemiongchi was designed, if not actually built, by Hlatsun Chhembo as a high-class monastery for *ta-sang* or "pure-monks" of pure Tibetan race, celibate and undeformed. Pemiongchi still retains this reputation for the professedly celibate character and good family of its monks. Its monks alone in Sikkim enjoy the title of *ta-sang,* and to its lama is reserved the honour of anointing with holy-water the reigning sovereign.

Monasteries According to Seet, Lepcha Monasteries, Nuns

The great majority of the monasteries belong to the Nyingmapa sub-sect of Lhatsun-pa, only Namchi, Tashiding, Sinon, and Thangmochhe belonging to the Ngadakpa sub-sect, and Kartok and Do-ling to the Kartokpa sub-sect of Nyingmapa. All of these are practically subordinate to Pemiongchi, although Namchi and Kartok gompas are nominally the heads of the Ngadakpa and Kartokpa respectively. Pemiongchi also exercises supervision over the Lepcha gompas of Ling-them, Zimik, and Phaggye. Lepchas are admissible also to Ragin as well as Sangngaphholing Nuns are admitted to a few monasteries. Most of the time, their number is extremely small, and individually they are illiterate, old, and decrepit.

Only three monasteries belong to the Karmapa, viz., Ramtek, and Phodang, and Ralang, of these Phodang is now in reality the chief, although Ralang is the parent monastery.

At present the most flourishing monasteries in Sikkim are the Nyingmapa, Pemiongchi, and the Karmapa Phodang.

The Names of the Monasteries

The names of the monasteries, as will be seen from the translations given in the second column, of the table, are mostly Tibetan and of an ideal or mystic nature. Some, however, are physically descriptive of the site and a few are Lepcha place-names also of a descriptive character.

Proportion of Lamas to the Buddhist Population

The lamas number nearly one thousand, and are very numerous in proportion to the Buddhist population of the country. In 1840, Dr.

Campbell estimated[34] the Lepchas and Bhotiyas of Sikkim at 3,000 and 2,000 respectively; but Mr. White in his census of Sikkim in March 1891 gives the population roughly as—

Lepchas	5,800
Bhotiyas	4,700
Nepalese, and others	19,500
	30,000

As the Nepalese are all professing Hindus, the lamas are now dependent on the Bhotiyas and Lepchas for support, and one gets a proportion of one lamaic priest to every 10 or 11 of the indigenous population. But this does not represent the full priest-force of those two races. It takes no count of the numerous devil-dancers and Lepcha priests patronized by both Bhotiyas and Lepchas.

III. THE TEMPLE AND ITS CONTENTS

The Temple

The temple had no place in primitive Buddhism. It is the out-come of the worship of relics and images, and dates from the later and impurer stage of Buddhism.

Its Names

Its proper name is *Lha-khang* or "God's house;" but as it serves the purpose of an assembly room and school, it is also called respectively *Du-khang*[35] (a meeting-room) and *Tsug-lak-khang*[36] (an academy), although the former name is strictly applicable only to the hall in the lower flat in which the monks assemble for worship.

Exterior

It is the chief and most conspicuous building in the monastery. But it is isolated from the other buildings. It is usually surrounded by a paved path to allow of pious circumambulation, and it is sometimes shaded by a cypress tree. Built in the Sikkim style of architecture, it is a heavy ungainly building with squarish base, tapering whitewashed stone walls, and a huge projecting flattish roof of thatched bamboo. In the wealthier monasteries the thatch has lately been replaced by corrugated iron, which does not improve the appearance of the building. As the wide projecting caves render the roof liable to be blown off, the latter is tied down to the ground at the four corners by long pendant ropes. The roof is surmounted by one or a pair of small bell-shaped domes of gilt copper: if a pair, they are placed one on either end of the ridge, and called *jira;*[37] if a solitary one in the middle of the ridge, it is called *gyal-tshen.*[38]

They are emblematic of the umbrella-banner of victory and good fortune. The building is usually two stories in height with an outside stair on one flank, generally the right, leading to the upper flat. In front is an upper wooden balcony, the beams of which are rudely carved and its doors variously ornamented.[39] The necessary orientation of the building has already been noted. In approaching the temple door, the visitor must proceed with his right hand to the wall, in conformity with the Hindu ceremonial custom of *pradakshina*. In niches along the base of the building, about three feet above the level of the path, are sometimes inserted rows of prayer-barrels, which are turned by the visitor sweeping his hand over them as he proceeds.

Entrance

One enters the main door by a short flight of steps. On ascending the steps, the entrance is at times screened by a large curtain of yak-hair hung from the upper balcony, which serves to keep out rain and snow from the frescoes in the vestibule.

Vestibule Figures

Entering the vestibule, we find its gateway guarded by several fiendish figures. These are—

I. The Demon of the Locality, usually a *Tsen* or male demon of a red colour, but differing in name according to the locality.

II. Especially vicious demons of a more or less local character. Thus, at Pemiongchi is the *Gyalpo Shuk-den* with a brown face and seated on a white elephant. He was formerly the learned lama Panchhen Sod-nam*s* grak*s*-pa, who being falsely charged with licentious living and deposed, his spirit on his death took this actively malignant form and wreaks his wrath on all who do not worship him—inflicting disease and accident.

III. A pair of hideous imps, one on either side, of a red and bluish-black colour, respectively, named *Ki-kang* or *Shemba Mar-nak,*[40] who butcher their victims.

IV. Here, also are sometimes portrayed the twelve *Tan-ma,*-aerial nymphs peculiar to Tibet, who sow disease and who were among the chief fiends subjugated by "The Guru."

The Guardian Kings of the Quarters

Confronting the visitor in the vestibule are the four colossal images (frescoes) of the Kings of the Quarters, who guard the Universe and heavens against the outer demons. They are clad in full armour and of defiant mien. Two are placed on each side of the doorway. Their names are

1. Yul-khor srung[41] (Skt. *Dhrita-rashtra),* the white guardian of the east and King of the Gandharvas (Dri-za).
2. Phag-kye-po[42] (Skt. *Virudhaka*), the yellow guardian of the south and King of the Kumbhandas (Grul-bun).
3. Je-mi-zang (Skt. *Virupaksha*), the red guardian of the west and King of the Nagas (*k*Lu).
4. Nam-tho-sre (Skt. *Vaisravana),* the green guardian of the north and King of the Yakshas (*g*Nod-*s*byin).

According to the later fashion of the gelukpa sometimes the guardian of the north is given a yellow complexion, and the guardian of the south a green complexion, thus making the complexion of the guardians to coincide with the mythic colours of the quarters.

Prayer-Barrels

In the smaller temples, which possess no detached *Mani lhakhang,* one or more huge *mani* prayer-barrels are set at either end of the vestibule, and mechanically revolved by lay-devotees, each revolution being announced by an affixed lever striking a bell. As the bells are of different tones and are struck alternately, they form at times a not unpleasant chime.

Door

The door is of massive proportions, sometimes rudely carved and ornamented with brazen bosses. It opens in halves, giving entry directly to the temple.

Interior

The temple is a large hall, with a double row of pillars separating it into a nave and two aisles. The nave is terminated by the altar. The whole of the interior, in whichever direction the eye turns, is a mass of rich colour, the walls to right and left being covered with frescoes of deities, saints, and demons, mostly of life-size, but in no regular order; the beams are mostly painted red, picked out with lotus rosettes and other emblems. The brightest of colours are used, but the general effect is softened in the deep gloom of the temple, which is dimly lit only by the entrance door.

Central Triad of Images, Shakya, Guru Rimbochhe, His Two Wives, Che-resi

Three colossal gilt images in a sitting attitude, are placed above the altar. "The Three Rarest Ones"[43] or trinity of the of Lamas. These three images should be *Shakyamuni* in the centre, with *Guru Rimbochhe* to the left (of the spectator) and *Che—resi* to the right. Shakya Muni is of a yellow colour with blue curly hair, and is occasionally attended to by standing figures of his two chief disciples, Maugdalputra on his left and Shariputra on his right, each with an alarm-staff[44] and begging-bowl (Tib.. *Hlun-sed,* Skt. *Patra)* in hand. *Guru Rimbochhe* or *Padma Jungne* (the Lotus-born) usually sits in front of a screen of lotuses and wears his typical mitre-like hat shaped in the fashion of a lotus flower. He holds a *dorje* (the thunderbolt of Indra, the Hindu Jove) in his right hand and a human skull-cup of blood in his left, and resting on his left shoulder is a trident decorated with human heads. He is almost always attended by his two ministering wives, viz. the Tibetan fairy *Khando Ye-she Tsho-gyal,* holding a skull-cup of blood on his left, and the Indian *Lha-cham Mandarawa,* holding a jar of wine for the Guru's use on his right. *Che-resi,*[45] the patron god of Lamaism and of Tibet, and incarnate in the Dalai Lama, is represented white in colour, with four hands, the front pair of which are joined in devotion, the upper right hand holds a crystal rosary, and the upper left a lotus flower.

It towers high above every other object in the country. It is also the first to receive the rays of the rising sun and the last to part with the setting sun. *Kangchhendsonga* literally means "the five repositories or ledges of the great snows," and is physically descriptive of its, five peaks—the name having been given by the adjoining Tsangpa Tibetans, who also worshipped the mountain. But Lhatsun Chhembo gave the name a mythological meaning, and the mountain was made to become merely the habitation of the god of that name, and the five "repositories" were real store-house of the god's treasure. The peak which is most conspicuously gilded by the rising sun, is the treasury of gold, the peak which remains in cold grey shade is the silver treasury, and the other peaks are the stores of gems and grain of sorts and holy books. This idea of treasure naturally led to the god being physically represented somewhat after the style of 'the god of *wealth.*' He is on the whole a good-natured god, but rather impassive, and is therefore less worshipped than the more actively malignant deities.

Lha-tsun Chhembo the pioneer lama of Sikkim; or other lama-saint of Sikkim, or of the special sect to which the temple belongs.

Sir Monier Williams[46] have mentioned existence and others[47] of the images of Gorakhnath in Tashiding, Tumlong, and other Sikkim temples is quite a mistake. No such image is known. The name evidently intended was Guru Rimbochhe.

Material or Images

The large images are generally of gilded clay, and the most artistic of these come from Pa-to or "Paro" in Bhutan. A few are of gilded copper and mostly made by Newaris in Nepal. All are consecrated by the introduction of pellets of paper inscribed with sacred texts.

Frescoes

Amongst the frescoes on the walls are displayed the *Neden chu-tuk,* or the sixteen disciples of Buddha: and also numerous lama-saints of Tibet.

Framed Paintings

There are also a few oil-paintings of divinities framed in silk of grotesque dragon pattern with a border, from within outwards, of "the primary" colours in their prismatic order of red, yellow, and blue. These pictures have mostly been brought from Tibet and Bhutan. They are creditable specimens of art.

Plan of Interior, Seats of Officers

The general plan of a temple interior is shown in the foregoing diagram. Along each side of the nave is a long low cushion about three inches high, the seat for the monks and novices. At the further end of the right-hand cushion on a throne about 2½ feet high sits the *Dorje Lo-pon,*[48] the spiritual head of the monastery. Immediately below him, on a cushion about one foot high, is his assistant who plays the si-nyen cymbals. Facing the Dorje Lo-pon, and seated on a similar throne at the further end of the left-hand cushion, is the *Um-dse*[49] or chief chorister and celebrant and the temporal head of the monastery; and below him, on a cushion about one foot high, is the *Uchhung-pa* or Deputy Um-dse, who plays the large *tsho-rol* or assembly cymbals at the command of the *Um-dse,* and officiates in the absence of the latter.

At the door-end of the cushion on the right-hand side is a seat about one foot high for the *Chho tim pa,*[50] a sort of provost-marshal who enforces discipline, and on the pillar behind his seat hangs his bamboo rod for corporal chastisement. During the entry and exit of the congregation he stands by the right side of the door. Facing him at the end of the left-hand cushion, but merely seated on a mat, is the *Chhab-dupa* or water-giver, who offers water to the monks and novices, for washing their hands and lips after each round of soup. To the left of the door is a table on which is set the tea and soup served out by the unpassed boy-probationers during the intervals of worship.

At the spot marked "13" on plan is placed the lay figure of the corpse whose spirit is to be withdrawn by the Dorje Lo-pon. At the point marked "12" is set the throne of the king or of the Labrang incarnate lama—the *Kyab-gon* or protector of religion—when either of them chances to visit the temple.

Decorations

On each pillar is hung a small silk banner with five flaps, usually in vertical series of threes called *phen,*[51] and on each side of the altar is a large one of circular form called *chephur.*

Side-Chapels

In some of the larger temples are side-chapels for the special shrine of Dorje-phagmo or other favourite divinity. The shrines of the deities and demons to whom flesh is offered are usually located in a detached building.

Upper Flat

Upstairs are the images of secondary importance, and here among the frescoes covering the walls are usually found the *Gon-pos,* or demoniacal protectors of Lamaism. These latter are of ferocious aspect, enveloped in flames and wielding various weapons. They are clothed in human and tiger skins, and adorned with snakes and human skulls and bones. Chief among these are (1) the blue-faced *Lhamo,* the Kali form of the Hindu Devi; (2) her consort *Mahakala,* a destructive form of Shiva; (3) the horse-headed *Tamdin,* the Hayagriva of the Hindus and spouse of Dorje-phagmo.

"The Cycle of Existence"

Prominent among the frescoes is the *Si-pa-i Khor-lo*[52] or "Cycle of existence," showing the regions of re-birth and the tortures of the damned. This picture is so very interesting and important that it demands more than passing notice.

The Pictorial Wheel of Life

The *Si-pa-i-khor-lo* or "Cycle of Existence"—for a copy of the Tashiding temple-picture[53]—is a graphic exposition of metempsychosis, one of the most fundamental laws of Buddhism—the secret of Buddha having consisted in the means he devised for escaping from this ceaseless round of re-births with its attendant sufferings. This picture is one of the purest Buddhist emblems that the lamas have preserved to us. And by its means I have been able to restore the fragment of a cycle in the verandah of Ajanta Cave No. XVII hitherto uninterpreted, and merely known as "the Zodiac." This picture portrays in symbolic and concrete form the three original sins and the recognized causes of re-birth *(Nidanas),* so as to ensure their being vividly perceived and avoided; while the evils of existence in its various forms and the tortures of the damned are intended to intimidate evil-doers.

As the Sikkim copies of the picture misplace the order of the Nidanas, and are deficient in many details. The circular form of the large disc symbolizes the ceaseless round of wordly existence. It is held in the clutches of a monster, whose head is seen overtopping the whole. This angry demon, who grips the disc with his claws and teeth, typifies the passionate clinging of the people to existence. In the centre of the disc are symbolized the three original sins, and around the margin the twelve linked chain of causes of re-birth; while the remainder of the disc is divided by radii into six compartments, which represent the six regions of re-birth.

These pictorial symbols of the abstract conceptions of the early

Buddhists are extremely valuable in showing what is the traditional interpretation of the ambiguous Sanskrit and Pali metaphysical terms for the *Nidana* found in the Indian Buddhist books. Its real interpretation has formed a subject of much controversy amongst Western scholars.

The three original sins are depicted as (a) a *pig*, which has hold of the tail of (b) a *cock*, which has seized the tail of *(c)* a *snake*, which in its turn has hold of the pig's tail, thus forming a circle which revolves continuously around the world. The *pig* symbolizes the ignorance or stupidity; the cock, animal desire or lust; and the snake, anger.[54] If these sins are avoided. Virtue results and merit is accumulated.

The causes of re-birth—the Nidanas—are categorically given as twelve in the form of a linked chain, the result of the first cause being the cause of the second, and so on; the ultimate result being suffering.[55] The illustrations with their lamaic paraphrases are:

I. A blind old woman groping her way[56] = *marig-pa* (Skt. *Avidya)* or- "want of knowledge," which is the cardinal cause of existence leading people to mistake for happiness the miseries of existence.

II. A potter with his wheel making pots = *du-che* (Skt. *Sanskara)* or *impressing*—literally "preparation or fashioning + action," showing the fruits of worldly labour are perishable objects—action being misdirected as a result of ignorance.

III. A monkey eating fruit = *nam-she* (Skt. *Vijnana)* or "entire knowledge" of good and evil fruits—tasting every fruit in the sense of a roving libertine without system: thus engendering *consciousness.*

IV. A dying man with a physician feeling pulse[57] = *ming-zug* (Skt. *Nama-rupa)* or "name and body," *i.e.*, individual being. Its fleeting character is shown by the man being about to lose his individuality and name in death.

V. An empty house = *kye-chhe* (Skt. *Shadayatana)* or "the five mortal sense organs and mind," illustrates the organs and the will which are the result of individual being—the hollowness of these is typified. The Ajanta painting depicts this by a mask, which is a much more appropriate symbol.

VI. A pair of lovers kissing = *reg-pa* (Skt. *Sparsha*) or contact which results from the exercise of the sense organs and will.

VII. An arrow entering a man's eye = *tshor-wa* (Skt. *Vedana)* or "perception," the result of a contact. It includes joy and sorrow as well as pain.

VIII. A man drinking wine = *sre-pa* (Skt. *Trishna)* or "desire for more," including thirst and affection, which results from the exercise of the perceptive faculty.

IX. A man gathering a large basketful of flowers = *len-pa* (Skt. *Upadana)* "taking": grasping indulgence in worldly matters—the result of desire.

X. A pregnant woman = *srid-pa* (Skt. *Bhava)* or "continuity of existence," a desire for inheritance—the result of the clinging to worldly life and wealth.

XI. A mother in childbirth = *kye-wa* (Skt. *Jati)* or birth as a result of No. X.

XII. A human corpse being carried off = *ga-she* (Skt. *Jaramarana)* or "decay and death" with all their sufferings, which are the result of birth.

The six forms of re-birth—gro-bai *rigs* (Skt. *Gati)*—are shown in the inner circle. In the order of their superiority they are:

1. The gods or *lha* (=Skt. *Sura* or *Deva*)—the highest form of existence.
2. The Titans, literally "ungodly spirits" or *lha-ma-yin* (= Skt. *Asura)*.
3. Mankind or *mi* (Skt. *Nara)*.
4. The Beasts or *du-do* (Skt. *Tirjyak)*.
5. The Tantalized ghosts—*yi-dag* (Skt. *Preta)*.
6. The inhabitants of hell, *nyal-wa* (Skt. *Naraka)*, the lowest of all.

Classification of Good and Bad

The first three forms of existence are classed as good and the last three are bad; all are under the immediate care of a Buddha, who stands in the centre of each compartment, and is a form of the Bodhisatwa

Che'-re'-si *(Avalokita),* who is incarnate in the Dalai Grand Lama at Lhasa.

The place of one's re-birth is determined solely by one's own deeds—although the lamas now make faith and charms and ritual take the place of the good works of the earlier Buddhists. If the virtues are in excess of the sins, then the soul is re-born in one or other of the first three forms: as a god if the virtue be of the first degree, as an ungodly spirit if the virtue be of the second degree, and as a human being if the virtue is of the lowest order. Those whose sins preponderate are re-born in one or other of the last three forms, the most wicked going to hell, and the least wicked to the beasts.

The judgment is in every case meted out by the impartial "*Shinje chho gyal*" or "Religious King of the Dead," a form of *Yama,* the Hindu god of the dead, who holds a mirror in which the naked soul is reflected, while his servant *Shinje* weigh out in scales the good as opposed to the bad deeds; the former being represented by white pebbles, and the latter by black.—This incident usually occupies the upper portion of the hell-compartment of the *Si-pa-i khor-lo* picture.

The Regions

The details of these several regions are briefly as follow:

I. *The Gods.* These are the gods of Indra's heaven of Hindu mythology rendered finite. Their life is the longest of all beings; but they, too, are within the operation of the law of continuous metamorphosis, and may be re-born in hell or in any other of the six regions. Their abode is the Mt. Meru (Tib. *Ri-rab)* of the Hindus, a mythical and invisible mountain-heaven[58] in the centre of the universe according to Hindu cosmogony. The picture of the region of the gods shows a three-storied palace in the heavens of Indra, Desire occupying the lower, Brahma the middle, and the indigenous *Da-lha,* the Tibetan war god, the upper compartment. This curious perversion of the usual order of the heavens is notable, as the Lamas have placed the embodiment of passion—their war-god—above Brahma.

Attributes of the God and Godesses

These gods are surrounded by other gods, all with shining bodies and the special attributes of a god of this heaven, namely, (1) goddess-companions; (2) a lake of perfumed nectar *(amrita),* which is their *elixir vitae* and source of their bodily lustre; (3) the *pag sam shing* or wish-granting tree, which bestows at once any fruit or food wished for; (4) the wish-granting cow, which yields instantly any, drink wished for; (5) the horse of knowledge, which *Pegasus*-like carries his rider to the worlds of the present, past, and future; (6) his splendid dress and ornaments; (7) a fine palace; (8) a charming garden with flowers, which form his wreath, and pretty animals and singing birds. Along the border, separating this world from that of the *lhamayin* (Asuras) are some of the gods armed with spears and other weapons under the direction of the war-god *Da-lha* resisting the encroachments of the *lhamayin* of the lower world.

A charitable human being, who has been virtuous and pious during his earthly life may be re-born as a god and enjoy bliss for an almost incalculable time—one god's day being one hundred human years. And he is born into heaven in a full-grown state. But when his merit is exhausted, then his lake of nectar dries up his wish-granting tree and cow and horse die, his splendid dress and ornaments disappear, his garden and flowers wither, his body, no longer bathed by nectar, loses its lustre, and his person becomes loath some to his goddess companions and the other gods, who shun him and he dies miserably. If he has led a virtuous life during his existence as a god, then he may be re-born in heaven, otherwise he goes to a lower region and may be even sent to hell.

II. *The Titans* (Lhamayin) *or ungodly spirits* These are the Titans or *Asuras* of Hindu mythology, and occupy the base of Mt. Meru, and are therefore intermediate between heaven and the earth. They have numerous joys and comforts; but are discontented, and envy the greater bliss of the gods, with whom they are continually fighting for some of the fruits of the heavenly wish-granting tree, which has its roots and trunk within their region.

This region contains a fortified house, with a lake and flowers and numerous animals. This is represented with a light fellow atmosphere. The people are all clad in full armour, and are engaged mostly in fighting with the gods across their frontier. Many of them are dead, or dying, or horribly mangled by the weapons of the gods, the most deadly of which is a wheel with teeth like a circular saw; which is thrown like the Sikh quoit. As existence here is rather miserable, although it is above mankind, only the proud and envious are re-born here. Rebirth, however, from this region mostly occurs in hell owing to the wicked life led during existence here.

III. *Mankind.* The atmosphere of this region is blue or colourless. It shows the miseries of human existence, which have to be endured by all alike, from prince to pauper: family troubles, striving after wealth, position, or necessities of life.

The following phases of life are depicted amongst others:

1. *Birth.*
2. *Old age.* Decrepit old man and woman hobbling along.
3. *Disease.* Sick man, with doctor feeling his pulse, or sick attempting to drink.
4. *Death.* A dying man surrounded by weeping relatives, with a lama doing worship near his head, and another monk ascertaining whether the breathing has ceased. Another scene depicts the dead body being carried off, preceded by a lama, who carries the end of a scarf affixed to the corpse, and in the lama's hand are a *damaru* (hand-drum) and a thigh-bone trumpet, while in the distance is the funeral pyre to cremate the body.

Other scenes illustrate worldly pleasure and business. A criminal being punished for crimes. A man sitting under a tree in front of his house, drinking tea or wine, and children at play, and hills in the distance. Traders bargaining, also a drunken man, a borrower

IV. *The Beasts.* The atmosphere of this region is darker, but it has hills and trees and also some men, as it is merely a different aspect of the human world. As Ruskin Bond Ruskin says "the fish is freer than the man;" but the lamas think otherwise. They class all aquatic animals as " the Bonded Animals," and only terrestrial and flying animals are "The free." Hence, the animal region is divided into an aquatic and a land-section, each peopled by characteristic animals. This is a state of greater misery than the human, as the animals prey on one another, and man also kills many of the animals and uses others as beasts of burden or for other utilitarian purposes.

The picture shows land animals of various kinds, some devouring others, and some human hunters killing game animals. In the water are fish and a variety of animals, also preying on one another.

V. *The Yidags or Tantalised Ghosts.* The atmosphere of this region is very dark and doomy. This is the special place of those who on earth were miserly, envious, and uncharitable. They have jewels and food and drink in plenty, but cannot enjoy them, and are always gnawed by hunger and thirst as they are given bodies with microseonical mouths and gullets. And when any food is taken it is transformed to sharp knives and saws, which lacerate the bowels and come out externally, making large painful wounds. Others have fires constantly burning in their mouths.

VI. *The Hells.* The atmosphere of the hell is black. Only eight hells are mentioned in the older Buddhist works, but the lamas describe and figure eight cold and eight hot hells, and give two extra hells named *nyi-tshewa,* which includes the state of being flies and insects in the human world and *nye-khorwa*, a milder hell filled with fiery ashes and rubbish and bodies in which those escaping from hell must dwell for a further period. In the upper portion of this region is figured the King and Judge of the dead in the act of trying the spirits of the dead, with the good recording angel on his right hand, counting out the good deeds by white pebbles from his purse, and the incarnation of evil on his left hand displaying before the Judge the bad deeds as a pile of black pebbles. In front is the scaleholder, who weighs the good as against the bad deeds. Those who have sinned in anger are sent to the hot hell, while those who have sinned through stupidity go to the cold hell, and each receives some appropriate punishment for misdeeds during life.

The hot hells are to the left (of spectator) and the cold to the right.

I. The Hot Hells:

1. *Yang-So* (Skt. *Samjiva)*= "again revived." Here, the bodies are torn to pieces and then revived only to have the process repeated *ad libitum.*
2. *Thi-nag* (Skt. *Kalasutra)* = "black lines." Here, the bodies are nailed down and 8 or 16 black lines marked along body, which is then sawn in sections along these lines by a burning hot saw. Another punishment here is the especial one of the slanderer or gossiper, who has his or her tongue enlarged and pegged out and constantly harrowed by spikes ploughing through it.
3. *Du-jom* (Skt. *Samghata)* = "concentrated oppression." Here,

bodies are squeezed between animal-headed mountains or monster iron books (this is an especial punishment for monks, laymen, and infidels who have disregarded or profaned the scriptures). Others here are pounded in iron mortars.

4. *Ngu-bod Chhenpo* (Skt. *Maharaurava)* = "greater weeping and screaming." Here, they are cooked in pots containing molten iron.
5. *Tshewa* (Skt. *Tapana)* = "heat." The body is cast upon and transfixed by red-hot iron spikes.
6. *Rabtu-tshawa* (Skt. *Pratapana)* "highest heat." A three-spiked burning spear is thrust into body, and later rolled up within red-hot iron plates.
7. *Nar-med* (Skt. *Avichi)*= "endless torture." This is the most severe and longest punishment. The body is perpetually kept in flames, though never consumed.

II. The Cold Hells which have no place in the mythology of the Indian and Southern Buddhists are:

1. *Chhu-bur chen* = "blistered and wrinkled." The torture here is constant immersion of the naked body in icy cold water. The body becomes covered with chilblains.
2. *Chhu-bur dolwa* = The chilblains are forcibly cut and torn open, producing raw sores and deep chaps.
3. *A-cchu* = "achu!" an exclamation of anguish. It vents itself in this expression and which resounds throughout this hell.
4. *Kyi-hud* = A worse degree of cold. In this the tongue is paralysed and the exclamation "*kyi-hu!*" alone possible.
5. *So-tham-pa.* = The teeth and jaws are rigidly clenched through cold.
6. *Ut-pal tar-ge-pa.* = Livid sores which become everted like blue utpal flowers.
7. *Pe-ma tar ge-pa.* = The raw sores become red like lotus *(padma)* flowers.
8. *Pe-ma chhen-po tar-ge-pa.* = The flesh falls away from the bones like the petals of the great red lotus *(padma),*

> leaving raw sores which are continually gnawed and pecked by birds with iron beaks.

The stay in hell is necessary for those who have sinnel. Sins committed during the previous existence have to be expiated only then one comes out of it. From hell the usual course is back to earth, by the merit of good works done in a former existence. The lamas explain this by saying that it is like the discharge of a criminal who has expiated his offence in jail: on release he gets back his clothes and any other personal properties he can justly lay claim to, and the benefit of any virtuous deeds he had formerly done.

History of the Si-pa-i khor-lo

The history of the *Si-pa-i khor-lo* as given by the lamas is that Buddha on one occasion plucked a stalk of rice, and with its grains illustrated to his disciples his arguments on the 12 causes of existence and the continuous metamorphoses of animated beings in the six regions; and that later he personally directed the preparation of the picture in what is now known as the 'new' style which was specially intended for the conversion of the king of U-tra-ya-na (? Udhayana) and latterly introduced into Tibet in the 11th century A.D. by the Indian monk Atisha, who had received it from the followers of Phagpa Thog*s*-med or Arya Asadga.

The "older" style, that is, as regards Tibet, is reported to have been the copy sanctioned by Lopon Lu-tub or Guru Nagarjuna, the founder of the Mahayana system, and a copy of it was brought to Tibet by Bande Ye-shi in the 8th century A.D. in the reign of the Thi-srong-de-tsan, and reproduced in the monastery of Samye. The present picture in the Samye monastery is said to measure about 15 to 20 feet in diameter, and differs from the "newer" style chiefly in the absence of a figure of Buddha in the upper right-and corner and of the Munis in each of the six regions.

The Altar and Its Objects

The Altar

The altar or *chho-sham*[59] occupies the remote end of the nave of the temple. Above its middle is placed the chief image. A canopy, called *nam-yul* or "sky-country," on which are depicted the dragons of the sky, is stretched above the altar, and a large silken parasol, called *duk* or umbrella—the oriental symbol of royalty—is suspended over the head of the central image. This umbrella slightly revolves in one or other direction by the ascending currents of warm air from the lamps.

Its Tiers

The altar should have at least two tiers. On the lower and narrow outer ledge are placed the offerings of water, rice, cake, flowers, and lamps. The musical instruments and certain other utensils for worship, are placed on the higher platforms. This platform extends upto the images.

Its Accessories

There is spouted water-jug *chhab-pum* which stands in front of the altar.[60] This is used for filling the smaller water vessels, a dish to hold grain for offerings *ne-ze,*[61] an incense-holder *po-dsin,*[62] and a pair of flower vases. And on the right (of the spectator) on a small stool or table is the rice *mandala* cone, with its three tiers, daily made up by the temple attendant, and symbolic of an offering of all the continents and associated islands of the world according to Hindu and Buddhist cosmography, with Mount Meru (Tibetan *Ri-rab),* the abode of the gods, as the culminating point.

The Offerings

The ordinary water and rice offerings are set in shallow brazen bowls, called *chho-ting,*[63] composed of a brittle alloy or brass, silver, gold, and pounded precious stones. Their number is five or seven, usually the former. Two out of the five bowls should be filled with rice heaped up into a small cone; but this must be daily renewed by fresh rice. In its place fresh water is usually employed instead, as rice in Sikkim is very expensive.

Food Offering

Another food-offering is a high, conical cake of dough, butter, and sugar, variously coloured, named *torma* or *zhal-ze,* that is, "holy food." It is placed on a metal tray supported by a tripod. To save expense a painted dummy cake is usually employed.

Candles

The temple-lamp or *chho-kong*[64] is a short pedestalled bowl, into a socket in the centre of which is thrust a cotton wick, and it is fed by melted butter. As the great mass of butter solidifies and remains mostly in this state, the lamp is practically a candle. The size varies according to the means and the number of the temple votaries, as it is an act of piety to add butter to the lamp. One is necessary, but two or more are desirable, and on special occasions 108 or 1,000 small lamps are offered. The "essential offerings," or *Nyer-cho chho-pa,*[65] which are needed in every form of worship are seven in number, and must be placed in line and in a definite order.

Order of Offerings

The cymbals are placed on the inner platform. On the top of the rice heaps of Nos. 3 and 4 should be placed respectively a flower, preferably the large-winged seed of the legume of the so-called *pag-sam* shing or "wish-granting tree," and a stick of incense. And in the bowl marked "No. 6" should be placed perfumed water: but these details are only observed on special occasions. Ordinarily the bowls are filled with plain water.

These offerings have each received a special Sanskritic name descriptive of their nature, viz.

1. *Ar-gham* (or Ar-ganga), in Tibetan *chho-yon,*[66] or excellent drinking river water.
2. *Pa dyam,* in Tibetan *zhab-sel,*[67] or the cool water for washing feet.
3. *Pukh-pe* (or Pushpe), in Tibetan *me-tok,*[68] flower.
4. *Dhu-pe,* in Tibetan *du-po,*[69] incense fumes.
5. *A-loke,* in Tibetan *mar-me,*[70] lamp or light.
6. *Gan-dhe,* in Tibetan *ti-chhab,*[71] perfumed water for anointing body.
7. *Nai-wi-dya,* in Tibetan *zhal-ze,*[72] sacred food.
8. *Shabta,* in Tibetan *rol-mo,*[73] cymbals.

This order is reversed in *Kargyupa* and *Gelukpa* temples when doing a certain kind of *yidam* or tutelary deity's worship. These eight offerings appear to be symbolic of the eight *Matris* or Divine mothers. And with them may also be compared the 16 stages of the Hindu worship of a deity which I append in a foot-note[74] for reference.

Accompanying Worship

On placing the above offerings in position in the order noted, the benefit of a full service of worship is obtained by merely chanting the following hymn:

"*A-wa-ta-ya, A-wa-ta-ya. Om bajra! Argham, Pa-dyam, Pukh-pe*", "*Dhu-pe, A-loke, Gan-dhe, Nai-wi-dya, Shab-ta, Prati-dsa-yi Swaha!*" Which being interpreted is:—"Come! Come! *Om! Bajra* (the thunderbolt)! Partake of these offerings! excellent drinking river water, cool water for washing your feet, flowers for decking your; hair, pleasing incense fumes, lamp for lightening the darkness, perfumed water for anointing your body, sacred food, the music of cymbals! (here the cymbals are sounded.) Eat fully! *Swaha!*"

Special Banquet to the Host of Gods and Demons

The Banquet entitled Kon-chhok cli du,[74a] or "sacrifice to the whole assembly of the Rare Ones," is a more elaborate arrangement of food offerings to the whole assembly of the gods and the demons, which is frequently held in the temples. This feast is observed by all sects of lamas, Nyingmapa, Gelukpa, &c., and is an interesting sample of devil-worship. The Nyingmapa fashion is here detailed, but it differs from the Gelukpa only in providing for a slightly larger party of demoniacal guests, the Gelukpa inviting only the following, viz., their chief Lama, *i.e.*, Tsongkhapa, their tutelary deity Dorje-jik-che, Buddha, Chang-sem, the deified heroes, the fairies, the guardian demons' of the Gelukpa creed, the god of wealth, the guardian demons of the caves where the *terma* (hidden revelations) are deposited, the twelve To'-ma or aerial nymphs who sow disease, and the special "country" and "locality" gods and the five sister demons of Mount Everest.

When Given

This sacrifice should be done in the temples for the benefit of the lamas on the 10th and 15th of every month. On behalf of laymen it must be done *once* annually at the expense of every individual layman who can afford it; and on extra occasions, as a thanksgiving for a successful undertaking, and as a propitiation in sickness, death, and disaster.

Its Arrangement

Large coloured and ornamented Baling cakes for (1) the chief Lama-Saint *Guru Rimbochhe,* (2) the tutelary deity, in this case *Guru tak-po,* a fierce demoniacal form of the Guru, and (3) the fairy with the lion face are in the inmost row. For the Guru there is also placed on either side of his cake a skull-cup, the one to his right containing country wine, here called *Amrita* or "nectar" (in Tibetan—literally "devils' juice"), and the contents of the other are called *Rakta* or blood—infused tea is usually offered instead of blood. In the second row are the cakes for the guardians and protector of Lamaism, usually with Buddha's cake (No. 4) in centre.

No. 5. The Lion-faced demoness.
" 6. The four-armed "Lord," a form of Mahakala.
" 7. The god of wealth.
" 8. The "Ruler" of Tibet's guardian (and in Sikkim the special guardian of the *Nga-dakpa* monasteries).
" 9. The demon Blacksmith (red and black colour, rides a goat and carries an an land a bellows, was made a protector of lamaism by Lo-pon).
" 10. The Lord of the Rakshas.
" 11. The Locality protector.
" 12. The *Naga* demi-gods, white and black.
" 13. The female fiend-nun of Di-kung monastery.
No. 14. The five everlasting Sisters of Mount Everest.
" 15. The spirits of the Tank-drowned ones.
" 16. The homestead demon-owner.
" 17. The country god Kangchkend-songa (mountain).
" 18. The black devil, red devil and *Naga* of Darjeeling or special locality of temple.
" 19. The demons who cause disease.
" 20. The twelve aerial nymphs who cause disease.
" 21. The demon owners of the "Ter" caves where the hidden revelations are deposited.
" 22. The black and red devils and *Naga* of parent monastery of the priests of this temple.

An indefinite number of *tshok* cakes are placed in the fourth and outermost row which are especial dainties as an extra course for all. These cakes contain ordinary *torma* cake of cooked rice or barley, with the addition of some wine, and a mixture of cooked flesh and all sorts of eatables available.

The stages of the worship in this feast are as follows:

1st. Invitation to the deities and demons to come to the feast (Skt. *avahan).* This is accompanied by great clamour of drums, cymbals, horns and fifes, so as to attract the attention of the gods and demons.

2nd. Requesting the guests to be seated (Skt. *asan).*

3rd. Begging them to partake of the food offered.

4th Praises the goodness and admirable qualities of the guests. This is done while the guests are partaking of the essence of the food.

This delicacy *tshog* is then offered to all, on four plates, a plate for each row of guests,

6th One plateful of a special delicacy is reserved for the Lamas. This delicacy *tshog* is then offered to all, on four plates, a plate for each row of guests, being reserved for the lamas.

Then is done the ceremony of *Kang-so,*[75] or "expiation for religious duties left undone," which wipes off all arrears of religious duty. Here, the *ku-nyer* or novice appointed for the occasion throws skywards, amid great noise of instruments, several of the *tshok* cakes to all the demi-gods and demons not specially included in the feast. One *tshok* cake is then given to each iama in order of rank, from the highest to the lowest, as the food has been consecrated by the gods having eaten of it. They must, however, leave a portion, which is collected carefully, in a plate, in order, from the lowest to the head lama. A whole *torma* cake, is placed on these collected fragments and a worship entitled *Hlak-dor* is done, when the whole of these crumbs—the leavings of the lamas—are contemptuously thrown down to the earth outside the temple door to those evil-spirits who have not yet been subjected by Lo-pon or subsequent lamas.

Other Articles on Altar

On the top of the altar are placed the following articles:

(i) A miniature *chhorten* (=chaitya).[76]

(ii) One or more sacred books on each side of altar.

(iii) A *dor-je,* the lamaic sceptre and type of the thunderbolt of Indra (Jupiter), and a bell *tilbu*[77]. The *dorje* is the counterpart of the bell, and when applied to the shoulder of the latter should be of exactly the same length as the bell-handle.

(iv) The holy-water vase—*thu-pum*[78]—and a metal mirror—*me-long*—hanging from its spout. The holy-water of the vase is tinged with saffron, and is sprinkled by means of a long stopper-rod, which is surmounted by a fan of peacock's feathers and the holy *kusa* grass.

(v) The divining arrow, bound with five coloured silks, called *da-dar.*[79]

(vi) A large metal mirror—*me-long*—to reflect the image of the spirits.

(vii) Two pairs of cymbals. The pair used in the worship of Buddha and the higher divinities are called *si-nyen,*[80] and are of about 12 inches or more in diameter, with very small centre bosses. They are held vertically when in use, one above the other, and are manipulated gently. The pair of cymbals used in the worship of the inferior deities and demons are called *rol-mo,* and are of short diameter with very much broader bosses. They are held horizontally in the hands and are clanged with full strength of the arms and shoulders.

(viii) Conch-shell trumpet—*tung*[81]—used with the si-nyen cymbals.

(ix) Pair of copper hautboy-fifes—*gye-ling.*[82]

(x) Pair of long telescopic copper horns—*ra-dung.*[83]

(xi) Pair of human thigh-bone trumpets—*khang-ling.*[84] These are sometimes encased in brass, with a wide copper flanged extremity on which are figured the three eyes and nose of the ogre-demon, the oval open extremity being the demon's mouth. In the preparation of these thigh-bone trumpets the bones of criminals or those who have died by violence are preferred, and an elaborate incantation is done, part of which consists in the lama eating a portion of the skin of the bone. That way the blast becomes powerful.

(xii) Pair of tiger thigh-bone trumpets—*ta-dung.*[85] These are not always present, and the last three instruments are only for the worship of the inferior gods and demons.

(xiii) Drums—

(a) A small hand-drum or *nga-chhung*[86] or *damaru,* like a large double egg-cup. Between its two faces are attached a pair of pendant leather knobs and a long-beaded flap for handle. When the drum is held by the upper part of the cloth handle and jerked alternately to right and left, the knobs strike the faces of the drum. When a pause has to be industed between prayers, the drum is used. It is used daily.

(b) The big drum is called *chho-nga,*[87] or religious drum. These are of two kinds, one of which is suspended in a frame and beaten only occasionally and in Buddha's worship. The other is carried in the hand by means of a stem, thrust through its curved border. These are beaten by drumsticks with straight or curved handles.

(c) The human-skull-drum is made of *skull-caps* and isof same style as the smaller drum (a) above described.

The Lama's Table

Lama's Table

To the right front of the altar stands the lama's table called *dun-chog,*[88] about 2½ feet in length and one foot in height. A cushion is placed behind it, and on this is spread a tiger or leopard-skin rug as seat.

Dorje Lo-pon's Table

The extensive arrangement here figured is properly that of the Dorje Lo-pon's table. Only three monks are allowed tables in the temple, viz.

The Dorje *Lo-pon,* or abbot.

The *Um-dse,* or chief celebrant.

The *Chho-timba*, or provost-marshal.

Um-dse's

The Um-dse's table faces that of the Dorje Lo-pon, and contains only a *tu-bum* or holy-water vase, bell, dorje and the large *tsho-rol* cymbals.

Chho-timba's

The table of the Chho-timba stands in front of the latter's seat, near the door, and contains an incense goblet or *sang-bur,* bell and *dorje*.

Lamaic Rosaries

Its Origin

The rosary is an essential part of a lama's dress. As a Buddhist article, the rosary is especially peculiar to the Northern school of Buddhists and the outcome of the esoteric teachings of the Mahayana school, instilling belief in the potency of muttering mystic spells and other strange formulas. In the very complicated rosaries of Japan[89] it has attained its highest development. It is not enumerated in the Southern Scriptures among the articles necessary for a monk. But incidental mention is made by Shway Yoe[90] of a rosary with 108 beads; and several of the Burmese monks I have met possessed a rosary called "Bodhi," consisting of 72 black sub-cylindrical beads, which I understood were composed of slips of leaf inscribed with charmed words and rolled into pellets with the aid of lacquer or varnish.

The rosary is not conspicuous amongst Southern Buddhists but among Tibetans it is everywhere visible.

Its Uses

It is also held in the hand of the image of the patron god of Tibet—Che-re-si (Skt. *Avalokita),* and its use is not confined to the lamas. Nearly every layman and woman is possessed of a rosary on which at every opportunity they zealously store up merit; and they also use it for secular purposes, like the sliding balls of the Chinese, to assist in ordinary calculations: the beads to the right of the centre bead being called *ta-thang* and registering units, while those to the left are called *chu-do* and record tens, which numbers suffice for their ordinary wants.

Description of the Rosary and its Appendages

Vernacular Name

The vernacular name for the rosary is "*phreng-ba,*" pronounced *theng-wa* or vulgarly *theng-nga,* and literally means "a string of beads."

The Number 108

The rosary contains 108 beads of uniform size. The reason for this special number is explained to be merely a provision to ensure the repetition of the sacred spell a full hundred times, and the extra beads are added to make up for any omission of beads through absent-mindedness during the telling process or for actual loss of beads by breakage; but the number is of mystic significance. Che'-re'-si and Dol-ma have each 108 names; although it is not usual to tell these on the rosary.

One hundred and eight is the usual number of lamps and cakes offered at great shrines; and in the later Kham editions of the lamaic scriptures—the "*kah-gyur*"—the volumes have been extended from 100 to 108. The Southern scriptures state that 108 Brahmans were called by Gotama's father at the birth-feast to cast the embryo Buddha's horoscope, and the Burmese footprints of Buddha sometimes contain 108 subdivisions.[91] The Vaishnavs amongst Hindu have rosaries containing 108 beeds. It seems this mystic number was borrowed, like so many lamaic practices from the Hindu rituals.

The Head Beads

The two ends of the string of beads before being knotted are passed through three extra beads the centre one of which is the largest. These are collectively called dok-dsin[92] or "retaining or seizing bead"—*vide* "a" in figures. The word is sometimes spelt *m*do-hdsin, and pronounced *do-dsin,* which means "the union-holder." In either case the meaning is much the same. These beads keep the proper rosary beads in position, and indicate to the teller the completion of a cycle of beads.

This triad of beads symbolizes "the Three Holy Ones" of the Buddhist Trinity, viz., Buddha, Dharma (the Word), and Sangha (the Church, excluding the laity). The large central bead represents Buddha, while the smaller one intervening between it and the rosary beads represents the Church and is called "Our special Lama-monitor,"[93] the personal Lama-guide and confessor of the Tibetan Buddhist; and his symbolic presence on the rosary immediately at the end of the bead-cycle is to ensure becoming gravity and care in the act of telling the beads, as if he were actually present. The ge-luk-pa or "reformed" sect of lamas usually have only two beads as dok-dsin, in which case the terminal one is of much smaller size, and the pair are considered emblematic of a vase from which the beads spring.

The Counters

A pair of strings of ten small pendant metallic rings as counters—*vide* "b" in the figures is attached is the rosary. One of these, strings is terminated by a miniature *dorje* (the thunderbolt of Indra) and the other by a small bell—in tantric Buddhist figures the dorje is usually associated with a bell. The counters on the dorje-string register units of bead-cycles, while those on the bell-string mark tens of cycles. The counters and the ornaments of the strings are usually of silver, and inlaid with turquoise.

These two strings of counters are called dang-dsin[94] or "count-keepers," but vulgarly they are known as chub-she[95] or "the ten markers." They may be attached at any part of the rosary string but are usually affixed at the 8th and 21st bead on either side of the central bead.

Use of Counters

When about to tell the beads, the counters on each string are slid up the string. On completing a cycle of the beads the lowest counter on the dorje-string is slid down into contact with the dorje. And on each further cycle of beads being told a further counter is slipped down. When the ten have been exhausted, they are then slid up again and one counter is slipped down. The counters thus serve to register the utterance of 108 X 10 X 10 = 10,800 prayers or mystic formulas. The number of formulas daily repeated in this way is enormous. The average daily number of repetitions may in the earlier stages of a lama's career amount to 5,000 daily, but it depends somewhat on the zeal and leisure of the individual.

A layman may repeat daily about five to twenty bead cycles, but usually less. Old women are especially pious in this way, many telling over twenty bead-cycles daily. A middle-aged lama friend of mine has repeated the spell of his tutelary deity alone over 2,000,000 times. It is not uncommon to find rosaries so worn away by the friction of so much handling that originally globular beads have become cylindrical. Affixed to the rosary are small odds and ends, such as a metal tooth-pick, tweezer, small keys, &c.

Material of Beads

The materials of which the lamaic rosaries are composed may to a certain extent vary in costliness according to the wealth of the wearer. The Khen-pos or abbots of large and wealthy monasteries have rosaries of pearl and other precious stones, and even of gold. Turner relates that the Grand Tashi Lama possessed rosaries of pearls, emeralds, rubies, sapphires, coral, amber, crystal, and lapislazuli. The material of the rosary can only vary within rather narrow limits, its nature being determined by the particular sect to which the lama belongs and the particular deity to whom worship is to be paid.

Yellow Rosary

The special rosary of the ge-luk-pa or "reformed school," also called "the yellow-hat sect" (sha-ser). The beads are formed from the ochrey-yellow wood of the *chang-chhub,* literally "the Bodhi tree" or tree of supreme wisdom, which is said to grow in Central China. The wood is so deeply yellow that it is doubtful whether it be really that of the *pipal (Ficus religiosa)* which was the Bodhi tree under which Gautama attained his Buddhahood. These beads are manufactured wholesale by machinery at the temple called by Tibetans Ri-wo-tse-nga and by the Chinese *U-tha-Shan* or "The Five Peaks," about 200 miles south-west of Pekin. Hue gives a sketch[96] of this romantic place, but makes no mention of its rosaries. This rosary is of two kinds, viz. the usual form of spherical beads about the size of a pea, and a less common form of lozenge-shaped perforated discs about the size of a sixpence. This rosary is usable for all kinds of worship, including that of the furies.

The *Bo-dhi-tse*[97] rosary is the one chiefly in use among the nying-mapa, or "old (i.e., unreformed) school" of lamas. It is remarkable that its name also seeks to associate it with the Bodhi tree, but its beads are certainly not derived from the *Ficus* family. Its beads are the rough brown seeds of a tree which grows in the outer Himalayas. This rosary may also be used by the ge-luk-pa in the worship of the fiercer deities. It can also be used for all kinds of worship.

White Rosary

The white rosary *tung-theng,*[98] consists of cylindrical perforated discs of the conch shell (Tib. *tung),* and is specially used in the worship of Che-re-si—the usual form of whose image holds a white rosary in the upper right hand. This is the special rosary of nuns.

Crystal

The rosary of plain crystal or uncoloured glass beads is also peculiar to Che-re-si.

Sandal

The red sandal-wood rosary—*Tsen-den mar theng,*[99] consists of perforated discs of red sandal-wood *(Adenanthera pavonina)* or other wood of a similar appearance. It is used only in the worship of the fierce deity Tam-din (Skt. *Hayagriva),* a special protector of Lamaism.

Coral

The coral rosary *Chi-ru-theng*[100] is also used for Tam-din and by the nyingmapa sects for their wizard-saint Padma Sambhava's worship. Coral being so expensive, red beads of glass or composition are in general use instead. With this rosary, it is usual to have the counters of turquoise or blue beads.

Human Skull

The rosary formed of discs of the human skull—the *tho-theng,*[101] is especially used for the worship of Dorje Jik-che (Skt. *Yama),* one of the forms of the King of the Dead. It frequently has its discs symmetrically divided by *raksha* beads into four series. There is no rosary formed of finger bones as has been sometimes stated.

Elephant-stone

A porous bony-like concretion which is sometimes found in the stomach of the elephant. The "elephant-stone" rosary—lang-chhen do-pa—is preferal from that concretion. It also being suggestive of bone, is used in worship of Yama. The real material, however, being extremely scarce and expensive, a substitute is usually had in beads made from the fibrous root of the bow-bambu (Zhu-shing) which has on section a structure very like the stomach-stone, and its name also means "stomach or digestion" as well as "bow."

"Rak-sha"

The *rak-sha* rosary,[103] formed of the large brown warty seeds of the *Elceocarpus Janitrus,* is specially used by the nyingmapa lamas in the worship of the fierce deities and demons. The seeds of this tree are normally five-lobed and it is interesting, from a botanical point of view, to find how relatively frequent is the occurrence of six lobes. Such abnormal seeds are highly prized by the Tibetans as being the offspring of the miraculous seeds of Padma Sambhava's rosary—the legend stating that the saint's rosary string broke while at his Halashi hermitage near the Kusi river in Nepal, and several of the detached beads remained unpicked up; and from these have resulted the six-lobed seeds. The demand for such uncommon seeds being great, it is astonishing how many of them are forthcoming to diligent search. This rosary is also commonly used by the indigenous Bon-po priests. The Tibetan name of *rak-sha* is derived from the Shivaic Hindu's *rudraksh.*

Nan-ga Pani

The *nang-ga pa-ni* rosary is only used by the ngak-pa or wizards in their mystical incantations for the worship of Nam-se, the God of Wealth (Skt. *Kuvera).* It consists of glossy jet-black nuts about the size of a hazel, but of the shape of small horse-chestnuts. These are the seeds of the *lung- thang* tree, which grows in the sub-tropical forests of the south-eastern Himalayas. They are emblematic of the eyes of the Garuda bird, the chief assistant of Vajra-pani (Jupiter) and the great enemy of snakes—hence is supposed to be derived the Sanskritic name of the beads, from *naga,* a serpent. Its use in the worship of the God of Wealth is noteworthy in the association of snakes. He is mythological guardians of treasure—with the idea of wealth. The rosary of *snake-spines* (vertebrae), is only used by the (ngak-pa) sorcerers for purposes of sorcery and divination. The string contains about fifty vertebrae.

Rosaries and Complexion

The complexion of the god or goddess to be worshipped also determines sometimes the colour of the rosary-beads. Thus, a turquoise rosary is occasionally used in the worship of the popular goddess Dol-ma, who is of a bluish-green complexion. A red rosary with red Tarn-din, a yellow with yellow Jam-yang; and Nam-se, who is of a golden yellow colour, is worshipped with an amber rosary.

Lay Rosaries

According to the taste and wealth of the owner the rosaries can be composed of any sort of bead. They are mostly of glass beads of various colours, and the same rosary contains beads of a variety of sizes and colours interspersed with coral, amber, turquoise. The number of beads is the same as with the lamas, but each of the counter strings are usually terminated by a dorje both strings record only units of cycles, which suffice for the smaller amount of bead-telling done by the laity.

Mode of Telling the Beads

Telling the Beads

When not in use the rosary is wound round the right wrist like a bracelet, or worn around the neck with the knotted end uppermost.

How Called

The act of telling the beads is called *tang-che,* which literally means "to purr" like a cat, and the muttering of the prayers is rather suggestive of this sound. In telling the beads the right hand is passed through the rosary, which is allowed to hang freely down with the knotted end upwards. The hand with the thumb upwards is then usually carried to the breast and held there stationary during the recital. On pronouncing the initial word "Om," the first bead resting on the knuckle is grasped by raising the thumb and quickly depressing its tip to seize the bead against the outer part of the second joint of the index finger. During the rest of the sentence the bead, still grasped between the thumb and index finger, is gently revolved to the right, and on conclusion of the sentence is dropped down the palm-side of the string. Then with another "Om" the next bead is seized and treated in like manner this way the whole cycle is completed.

On concluding each cycle of the beads, it is usual to finger each of the three "keeper-beads," saying respectively "Om! Ah! Hung!" the mystic symbols of the lamaic trinity.

The Mystic Formulas for the Beads

The Mystic Formulas

The mystic formulas for the beads follow the prayer properly so called, and are believed to contain the essence of the formal prayer, and to act as powerful spells. These prayers are more or less wholly unintelligible to the worshipper. They usually containing the name of the deity addressed.

The formula used at any particular time varies according to the particular deity being worshipped. But the one most frequently used by the individual lama is that of his own *yi-dam* or tutelary deity, which varies according to the sect to which the lama belongs.

The formulas most frequently used are shown in the following table:

	Name of deity	*The Spell*	*Special kind of rosary used*
1.	Dor-je jik-che.[104] Skt. *Yama (antaka).*	Om! Ya-man-ta-taka hung phat!	Human skull or "stomach stone."
		Om! Bajrapani hung phat!	Raksha.

2.	Cha-na dorje.[105] Skt. *Vajrapani.*	Om! Bajra dsan-da maha ro-khana hung!	Do.
3.	Tam-din.[106] Skt. *Hayagriva*	Om pad-ma ta krid hung phat!	Red sandal or coral.
4.	Che'-re-si or Thuk-je-chhenbo.[107] Skt. *Avalokita.*	Om! mani pad-me hung!	Conch shell or crystal.
5.	Dol-ma jang-khu.[108] Skt. *Tara;*	Om! Ta-re tut-ta-re ture swa-ha!	Bodhitse or turquoise.
6.	Dol-kar.[109] Skt. *Sitatara.*	Om! Ta-re tut-ta-re mama a-yur punye-dsanyana pusphpita ku-ru swa-ha!	Bodhist.
7.	Dor-je phak-mo.[110] Skt. *Vajra varahi.*	Om! sar-ba Bud-ha dakkin-ni hung phat!	Ditto.
8.	Ozer-chen-ma.[111] Skt. *Marici.*	Om! Ma-ri-tsye mam swa-ha!	Ditto.
9.	Gon-po nag-po.[112] Skt. *Kalanatha.*	Om! Sri Ma ha-ka-la hung phat swa-ha!	Raksha.
10.	Nam-se.[113] Skt. *Kuvera.*	Om! Bai-sra-ma-na ye swa-ha!	Nangapani.
11.	Dsam bha-la.[114] Skt. *Jambhala.*	Om! Dsam-bha-la dsalen-dra ye swa-ba!	Ditto.
12.	Seng-ge-da.[115] Skt. *Singhanada.*	Om! a-hrih Sing-ha-nada hung phat!	Conch shell or crystal.
13.	Jam-yang.[116] Skt. *Manjughosa.*	Om! a-ra-pa-tsa-na-dhi!	Yellow rosary.
14.	Dem-chhok.[117] Skt. *Samvara.*	Om! hrih ha-ha hung hung phat	Bodhitse.
15.	Pad-ma jung-ne.[118] Skt. *Padma sambhava.*	Om! bajra gu-ru padma sid-dhi hung!	Coral or bodbitse.

The concluding word *phat,* which follows the mystic hung in many of these spells, is cognate with the current Hindustani word *phat,* and means "may the enemy be *destroyed utterly.*"

Origin of the Formula "Om Mani"

The laity seldom use with their rosaries other than the well-known lamaic formula "*Om! ma-ni-pad-me Hung*" *i.e.*, "Hail! to the Jewel in the lotus! *Hung*" This may be due to want of knowledge or lack of proper studies and meditation. This refers to the Bodhisatwa Cheresi (Skt. *Padmapani),* the patron-god of Tibet, who, like Buddha, is usually represented as seated or standing within a lotus flower and who is believed to have been born from such a flower. It has, however, many mystic meanings. And no wonder this formula is so popular and constantly being repeated by both laity and lamas, for its mere enunciation is credited with stopping the cycle of re-birth, and reaching directly to Nirvana. Thus, it is stated in the Mani-kah-bum with extravagant rhapsody that this formula "is the essence of all happiness, prosperity, and knowledge, and the great means of deliverance," and that the *om* closes re-birth amongst the gods, *ma* among the Titans, *ni* as a man, *pad* as a beast, *me* as a "yidag," and *hung* as an inhabitant of hell. And in keeping with this view each of these six syllables is given the distinctive colour of these six states of re-birth, viz. *om,* the godly *white; ma,* the titanic *blue; ni,* the human *yellow; pad,* the animal *green; me,* the "yidag" *red; hung,* the hellish *black.*

This formula is of comparatively modern origin; its first appearance seems to be in the legendary history (*b*kah bum) of King Srong-tsan-gam-bo, which was one of the so-called "hidden" treatises, and probably written about the 14th or 16th century A.D.[119] With this formula, which is peculiar to Tibet, may be compared the Chinese and Japanese spells "*Namo Butsu*" (=Skt. *Namo Buddhaya, i.e.,* salutation to Buddha!) and *Namo O-mi-to-Fu,* (=Skt. *Namo Amitabha, i.e.,* salutation to the Boundless Light!—a fanciful form of Buddha). The Burmese, so far as I have seen, seem to use their rosary merely for repeating the names of the Buddhist Trinity, viz., 'Phra" or Buddha, "Tara" or Dharma, and Sangha. And the number of beads in their rosary is a multiple of 3 X 3 as with the lamas. On completing the cycle, the central bead is fingered with the pessimistic formula "*Anitsa, Dukha, Anatha.*" This means every object of desire is transitory, painful, and unreal.

List of the Masks

The Masks

In the Sikkimese vernacular a mask is called *bak.*[120] The masks for the religious dances in Sikkim are carved out of the tough light wood of the giant climber called *zar;* while in Tibet, where wood is scarce, they are composed of mashed paper and cloth. In all cases they are fantastically painted and varnished, and usually provided with a yak-tail wig.

The masks found in Sikkim temples are the following:

I. King of the Ogre deities *Ku*[121]	1.	*Yeshe gons-po*[122] or Mahakala.	Colour red.
	2.	*Guru dak-mar,* a fierce form of Guru Rim bochhe.	Colour red.
	3.	*Lhamo Mak-zor ma,* or Maharani, the *Kali* form of Devi.	Colour blue.
	4.	*Lang,*[124] the Bull.	Colour black.
II. The angry Ogre deities *To-wo.*[123]	5.	*Tag,*[125] the Tiger.	Colour brown.
	6.	Sengge, the Lion.	Colour white.
	7.	*Khyung,* the Garuda-bird.	Colour green.
	8.	*Teu,* the Monkey.	Colour ruddy brown.
	9.	*Sha-wa,* the Stag.	Colour fawn.
	10.	*Yak,* the Yak.	Colour black.

The above are all of hideous appearance and huge size having a vertical diameter of at least twice the length of an ordinary human face, and a breadth in proportion. Each has projecting tusks and three eyes, the central eye being the eye of fore-knowledge. Those of an anthropoid form have a chaplet of five skulls, with pendant bead ornaments of human bones.

III. The Ghouls	11.	*Tur* or Grave-yard ghosts. A monster human skull of yellowish colour. A pair of these are needed.
IV. The Earth demons—servants of above.	12.	*Sa-chak pa.* Large hideous masks with only two eyes.
V. The Indian Teacher—buffoons.	13.	*A-tsa-ra* (Skt. *acharya*= teacher). These are of ordinary human size, white in colour, with moustaches and hair done up into a coil. Their wives are red or yellow complexioned.

Dress of Masquers

The dresses which are worn with the first two classes of masks are ample robes of rich brocade and satin, with gilt embroidery. The dress of the skeletons is tight fitting white calico with red bands to imitate the ribs and limb bones. The weapons carried by the maskers are made of wood carved with dorje patterns. The staves of the skeletons are topped by a death's-head.

The object and meaning of the masked play are described under the heading of Lamaic Festivals.

The Lamaic Library

Lamaic Encyclopaedias-Kan-gyur

The larger monasteries in Sikkim all try to possess a copy of the two great lamaic encyclopaedias, *(a)* the *Kah-gyur* or vulgarly *Kan-gyur,*[126] *i.e.,* "The translated Commandments," and *(b)* the *Tengyur*[127] or "Translated doctrinal Commentaries" by reputed saints. All of the treatises contained in the Kah-gyur and most of those in the Tengyur were translated from the Sanskrit of the later Buddhist Church in India and Kashmir, and a few from the Chinese Buddhist, mostly in the 9th and 12th centuries; but the Tengyur contains also much later works. The translations were done by the Indian Pandits and Tibetan translators *(lotsavas)* and Chinese priests. For six hundred years they were lying scattered either in monasteries or gompas where work was done or with the families the scholars who had done the translators. They were collected in their present form only about the beginning-of the last (18th) century of our era.

Tengyur

The common edition of the Kah-gyur is printed from wooden blocks at Narthang, about six miles from Tashelhunpo, and fills 100 bulky volumes of about 1,000 pages each. A later edition, printed at Der-ge in Eastern Tibet (Kham), contains the same matter distributed in volumes so as to reach the mystic number of 108. The Tengyur contains 225 or more volumes, and has treatises on the Indian philosophic schools, grammar, logic, astrology, medicine, & c. The cost at the printing establishment is about ten rupees *per* volume.

The expense of such a library being so great, Pemiongchi and Labrang are the only monasteries in Sikkim which possess a complete set of both encyclopaedias. But several monasteries possess a full set of the Kah-gyur scriptures.

Divisions of Kah-gyur

The *Kah-gyur* as regards its contents is divided into three great sections, viz.

I. The *Dulva* (Skt. *Vinaya)* or Discipline, in 13 volumes.

II. The *Do* (Skt. *Sutra)* or Sermons of the Buddhas, in 66 volumes.

III. The *Sher-chin* with its divisions (Skt. *Abi-dharmma)* or Transcendental Wisdom, in 21 volumes.

These divisions broadly correspond to the classification of the Southern Buddhist Canon into the Tripitaka or 'three baskets or collections;' but the lamaic versions are all of a highly inflated and tantrik type, and the *Gyut* or tantrik charms and incantations to the number of 22 volumes, which has no counterpart in the Southern scriptures, has been introduced into the *Do* class of the Kah-gyur.

As might be supposed from the leading part which mysticism plays in the lamaic creed, the sections of the Kah-gyur which are most highly prized are the *Do* and the *Sher-chin* or Transcendental Wisdom of the tantrik kind.

"Bum," "Nyi-thi", "Gye-tong-ba", Dorje-chopa"

Not every monastery in Sikkim has sufficient to buy the full Kah-gyur—and these in Sikkim form the majority—possess the following parts of the Sher-chin, viz., the 12 volumes called *Bum,* literally "100,000" precepts of Transcendental Wisdom, forming the main body of the Sher-chin. Also the abridged edition of the same in three volumes called *Nyi-thi,* literally "the 20,000" precepts, adapted for those individuals who are unable to peruse the full text. And for the common use of the junior clergy a still smaller abstract in one volume exists under the name of *Gye-tong-ba*—literally, "the 8,000" precepts of Transcendental Wisdom. This is the volume which is carried on the lotus of Jam-pal, the God of Wisdom. The *Dorje-chopa* or the "Diamond cutter" is a sloka which is commonly printed in separate form. A tract of about six leaves containing the most popular portions of the Sherchin is prepared for the youngest boy-novices.

Do-mang

Mystic formulas are called out from Do Division of the Kah-gyur. The are mostly in Sanskrit which perhaps Sanskrit scholar of to-day cannot understand. These are deemed most potent as charms, and these form the volume named *m*Do-mang *gzung bsdus* or curtly *Do-many* or "assorted aphorisms"—literally "many *sutras.*" These formulas are not used in the worship of the Buddhas and superior gods, but only as priestly incantations in the treatment of disease and ill-fortune. Being thus the forms of worship of which the laity have most experience, small pocket editions of one or other *Sutra* are to be found in the possession of all literate laymen, as the mere act of reading these charms suffices to ward off the demon-bred disease and misfortune.

The books of ordinary worship and ritual, and the school-text books for the boy-probationers and novices, are also an essential part of the monastic library. They must be daily repeated till their contents are fully learned by heart.

Pedma Kah-thang, and c., "Namthars"

Each monastery also possesses one or more of the legendary accounts of the great wizard-saint of the Nyingmapa lamas, viz., Lo-pon Rimbochhe, or Pedmajungne', who is believed to have visited Sikkim. These are entitled *Pedma kah-thang* (The displayed orders of the Lotus-born One) or *Tang-yik Sertheng* (The golden Rosary of plain Epistles); also more or less fragmentary bits of the works of the pioneer lama of Sikkim—Lha-tsun Chhembo, especially his *Ne-yik* or "Story of the Sacred Sites of Sikkim," and his manual of worship of the great mountain god Kangchhendsonga (Ang. *Kanchinjingna).* Monasteries of the Karmapa and Dukpa sects contain the "Kargyupa Golden Rosary" and the *namthars* or biographies of the special lama-saints of the Karmapa or of the Bhutan lama-saints. Each monastery possesses a manuscript account of its own history *(deb-ther).* This history however is kept safe and hidden and is not shown to visitors.

Lepcha Scriptures

A few Lepcha sacred books are to be found in the Lepcha monasteries. A few Lepcha laymen have also got them. They are mostly translations from the Tibetan. The titles of the chief ones are (1) *Tashi Sung,* a fabulous history of Guru Rimbochhe; (2) *Guru Chho Wang,* a terton work of Tibet; (3) *Sakun de-lok,* the narrative of a visit to Hades by a resuscitated man named Sakun; (4) *Ek-doshi manlom*—forms of worship.

Miscellaneous Books

Individual lamas possess some special books these they have acquired over time according to their private means and inclinations, such as the *Manikahbum,* a legendary history of Che-re-si, the patron god of Tibet, and of the origin of the mystic sentence "Om Mani," c.;

the songs of the great mendicant sage *Milarepa,* books on the worship of Dolma and other favourite and tutelary deities. The specialist in medicine has one or more fantastic medical works, and the *Tsi-pa*[128] or astrologer has the *Baidyur karpo* and other books on astrological calculations.

The books are deposited in an open pigeon-holed rack-work. Each book consists of several hundred leaves, and each leaf is of tough unglazed country paper, about two feet long by half a foot broad. The leaves forming the volume are wrapped in a napkin; and the package then placed between two heavy wooden blocks, as covers, which bear on their front border the name of the book in letters graved in relief and gilt. The whole parcel is firmly bound by a broad tape and buckle tied across its middle. These ponderous tomes are very unwieldy and not easy of reference. When being read the book is held across the knees, and the upper board and the leaves as read are lifted towards the reader and repiled in order in his lap. Before opening its fastenings, and also on retying the parcel, the monk places the book reverently on his head, saying, "may I obtain the blessing of Thy Holy Word."

IV. THE MONKHOOD

Under this heading are detailed the Curriculum for the Monkhood, the Lamaic Grades and Discipline, and the Daily Routine of a lama's life in Sikkim.

I. THE CURRICULUM

Popularity of the Church

In nearly every Bhotiya[129] family in Sikkim, one son is devoted to the Church. This practice is fostered by the deep religious habit of the people and the attractions offered by the high social position and privileges enjoyed by the lamas. It makes them superior to the highest lay official and free from ordinary tribunals. A certain amount of reflected honour also attaches to the family which has afforded the lama.

In the Family

The rule is for the second son to become a lama, while the eldest son marries in order to continue the family name and property, and be the bread-winner.

Course of Training

The course of training now detailed obtains at Pemiongchi as that monastery is regarded as a standard one, which the other monasteries try to live up to.

Age

Preliminary Examination—Physical.—The boy-candidate for admission is usually brought to the monastery between the age of eight and ten years, and very seldom over twelve years.

Parentage, Physical Examination, Tutor

There are very elaborate procedures for admission to this order. The parentage of the boy is enquired into At Pemiongchi only those candidates who are of relatively pure Tibetan descent are ordinarily admitted to that monastery. The boy is then physically examined to ascertain that he is free from deformity or defect in his limbs and faculties. If he stammers or is a cripple in any way or bent in body, he is rejected. When he has passed this physical examination he is made over by his father or guardian to any senior relative he may have amongst the monks. Should he have no relative in the monastery, then by consulting his horoscope one of the monks is fixed upon as being his most suitable tutor; and this tutor receives from the boy's father a present of tea, eatables, and beer. The tutor then takes the boy inside the great hall where the monks are assembled, and publicly stating the parentage of the boy and the other details, and offering presents of beer, he asks the permission of the *db*U-chhos, or elder monks, to take the boy as a pupil. When approved, the boy becomes a probationer. There is normally no difficulty in this approval.

His Position, Tuition and List of Text-Books

Probation. As a probationer the boy is little more than a private school-boy under the care of his tutor. His hair is cropped without any ceremony, and he wears his ordinary lay dress. He is taught by his tutor the alphabet (the "Ka, Kha, Ga," as it is called), and afterwards to read and recite by heart the following small booklets of about six or seven leaves each[130]:

Leu *b*dun ma or "The Seven Chapters"—A prayer-book of Guru Rimpochhe. Bar-ohha*d* lam *g*sel or "Charms to clear the way from Danger and Injury"—a prayer to "The Guru" in twelve stanzas.

Sher-phyin—An Abstract of Transcendental Wisdom in six leaves.

*s*Ku-rim—a sacrificial service for averting a calamity.

Mon-lam—Prayers for general welfare.

*s*Dig shag or "The Confession of Sins." The mere act of reading this holy booklet even as a school exercise cleanses from sin. Most of the monasteries possess their own blocks for printing this pamphlet. Both the text and its translation have been given by Schlagintweit.

*r*Dor goho*d*,—a *Sutra* from the Book of Transcendental Wisdom.

Phyogs-*b*ohui-phyogs-dra*l* or "Description of the Ten Directions"	6	pages.
Namo Guru—"Salutation to The Guru"	5	"
*m*Ohhod-*h*bul—To give offerings	6	"
*g*Torma—Sacred cake	8	"
*b*Sangs *b*sur—Incense and butter-incense	5	"
*l*To-mohho*d* —Rice offering	4	"
Rig-*h*dsin *s*ngon-*h*gro—The First essay of the Sage	4	"
*d*rag-*d*mar *s*ngon-*h*gro—The Primer of the Red Fierce Deity	4	"
*b*Kah *brgyed*—"The Eight Commands" or precepts	4	"
*b*De *g*ahegs kun *h*dus—The Collection of the Tathagathas	4	"
Yeshes *s*ku *m*ohho*g*—The best Fore-knowledge	5	"
*r*Tsa-gdung *b*shag-*g*sal—The root-pillar of Clear Confession	4	"

There are maxims which are very essential to be learnt. The probationer is instructed in these maxims which are of a moral kind.

Some Precious Maxims

The four Precipices in Speech. If speech be too long, it is tedious; if too short, its meaning is not appreciated; if rough, it ruffles the temper of the hearers; if soft, it is unsatisfying.

On Speech

The Requirements of Speech. Speech must possess vigour or it will not interest; it must be bright or it will not enlighten; it must be suitably ended, otherwise its effect will be lost.

The Qualities of Speech. Speech must be bold as a lion, gentle and soft as a hare, impressive as a serpent, pointed as an arrow, and evenly balanced as a *dorje* held by its middle (literally '*waist*').

The four Relations of Speech. The necessary question should first be stated. The later arguments should be connected with the former.

Essentials should be repeated. The meanings should be illustrated by examples.

The great religious king Srong-*b*tsan-*s*gam-po has said, "speech should float forth freely like a bird into the sky, and be clothed in charming dress like a goddess. At the outset the object of the speech should be made clear like an unclouded sky. The speech should proceed like the excavation of treasure. The arguments should be agile like a deer chased by fresh hounds, without hesitation or pause."

Human Gatherings

Collections of human beings occur for three purposes, namely, (I) happiness, (II) sorrow, and (III) worldly gossip. The gatherings for happiness are three, namely, (1) for doing virtuous acts, (2) for worship in the temples, and (3) for erecting houses and for feasts. The gatherings for virtuous acts are four, viz., the gathering of the monks, the gathering of the laity for worship, writing and copying holy books, and giving away wealth in charity. There are six kinds of gatherings for worship, namely, the gathering of the rich, the gathering in a separate place of the common men, the gathering for thanksgiving of those who have escaped from their enemy's grasp, traders who have escaped returned safely and successfully, sick men from the devouring jaws of death, and youths on gaining a victory.

Low Conduct

The eight acts of Low-born persons. Using coarse language, impoliteness, talking with pride, want of foresight, harsh manners, staring, immoral conduct, and "stealing.

The Ten Faults

The ten Faults. Unbelief in books, disrespect of teachers, making one's self unpleasant, covetousness, speaking too much, ridiculing another's misfortune, using abusive language, being angry with old men or with women, borrowing what cannot be repaid, and stealing.

The Three Improper Acts

"*The three Improper Acts.*—To speak of a subject of which one is ignorant, to take an oath, to give poison to any one."

Test of Results

After two or three years spent in this training, during which corporal chastisement is emparted regularly, if the boy is then found to be hopelessly stupid, he is dismissed; while should he prove to be fairly intelligent, he is admitted to the regular noviciate. The object of this probationary stage is to weed out unpromising individuals.

The Noviciate

Its General Character

The novice or " Gra-pa," pronounced "Ta-pa," [literally "student" or "learner," and seldom called *d*gen-yen or *d*ge- thsul *(Skt.* Sramana)] is, now for the first time brought under monastic rules. Certainly ceremonies are performed after which he is ceremoniously shaved, takes the vows, assumes the dress of a monk, and receives a religious name.

Appraising of Descent

The candidate for the noviciate is searchingly interrogated by the *db*U-chhos (or elder lamas) regarding his descent, his entrance donation and presents being proportionate to the impurity of his descent. If he has a good strain of Tibetan blood, he is let off cheaply and *vice versa;* but it is the paternal descent which is most regarded: mixed blood on the mother's side being tolerated to a considerable extent.[131]

Preliminary Presents, &c.

When the boy's descent is satisfactorily appraised, the *db*U-chhos of the Great Assembly Hall are requested to place the boy under the "sgris" or General Rules. On permission being accorded, the parent or guardian of the boy prepares a feast of food and beer for the monks. After a few months another present of food and beer, accompanied by a flesh gift of a pig or bullock, must be made, with the request for a *g*tor-*b*zings in the temple. A suitable date for this is fixed by the help of astrology.

Formal Acceptance of Candidate

After that a magic circle or *mandal*[132] is prepared. On the following morning all the monks (dge-dun) before early mass drink tea at the expense of the candidate. After early mass, when all the monks have departed except the elders (*db*U-chhos), the parent or guardian of the boy with his relatives, who has been waiting outside, now requests an interview with the elders (*db*U-chhos), and accompanies his request with a present of a slaughtered pig and a load of beer, a load of parched gram (zib-*h*bras), and about half a maund of rice. On these being accepted; the boy is brought in and is made to recite some of the books he has learned, especially "the Eight Precepts," "the Refuge formula," "the performance of religious kindness," and the celebration ritual of "sKu-rim" and "Mon-lam." Then is done the ceremony of *b*Ges-*s*prad and the proclamation *b*Kab-*bs*go.

Tonsuring, Baptism, &c.

The boy is then tonsured (in Pemiongchi this is done with the identical razor used by the pioneer lama Lhatsun Chhembo). He then is given a religious name, and takes the usual vows of poverty, celibacy, followed by the declaration that "From to-day I have entered on a religious life." The ceremony concludes with a present to the "*g*nas zhag," of two bricks of Chinese tea. If somehow the tea is not available then some money paid.

Introduction to Assembly as a Bride

For the midday mass, the boy dresses. He is then brought to the Great Assembly Hall, in the three pieces of monkish vestment (chho*s*-go*s*) and carrying a bundle of incense sticks. He is chaperoned by a monk (gonpa) named the "bride-companion" (ba-grag*s*), as this ceremony is regarded as a marriage with the Church. He sits down on an appointed seat by the side of the bride-companion, who instructs him in the rules and etiquette (*s*gri*s*) of the monkish manner of sitting, walking, &c and other behavioural requirements.

Confirmation of Noviciate

The man begins, and on its conclusion beer is brought inside in a skull-cup, and distributed to the assembled monks under the name of *gzo*-chhang. (It is considered improper to bring the ordinary bamboo jugs of beer into the Assembly Hall.) Then a pig and a bullock are given by the boy's people, as well as a money present. If the boy's relatives are wealthy, this sum should amount to two rupees for each of the two *db*U-chhos and one rupee to each of the 108 monks. But if the boy's relatives are poor, the total amount may be limited to sixty rupees. Should, however, this money and "flesh" presents not be forthcoming, the boy's admission cannot be confirmed.

On the third day, that particular one of the boy's relatives who is the "dispenser of gifts" (*s*byin *b*dag*s*) must visit each of the two *db*U-chho*s* at their respective chambers, taking an offering of rice, beer, and flour. Each *db*U-chho*s* gives about ten rupees as a return present for the articles received. Then the boy's relatives return to their homes.

His Life as a Novice

The boy is now subject to the monastery rules and discipline; he must practise and learn by heart the books of the magic circles (dKyil *h*kor). He shares in most of the privileges of the other monks, getting his share of meat and lay offerings of money and gifts of alms—these latter two are, however, appropriated by his lama-tutor. He resides in the monastery, getting occasionally leave of absence for a month or so to visit his home. He must implicitly obey his tutor, and the relatives of the boy must come frequently to pay their respects to the tutor, bringing presents of cooked food, and other eatable items.

First Professional Examination

Examinations. Within a year of his admission to the order he should attempt to pass the first professional examination, and in the following year or two the second examination for promotion. Until he passes these examinations he must perform the menial office of serving out tea and beer to the elder monks in the Great Assembly Hall.

How Conducted

When the examinations are conducted, all the monks in the monastery are present during the examination, they observe complete silence. The test is for the candidate to stand up in the assembly and recite by heart all the prescribed books. The ordeal is a very trying one, so that the candidate is given a companion to prompt and encourage him. The first examination lasts for three days; 'and nine intervals are allowed daily during the examination, and these intervals are utilized by the candidates in revising the next exercise, in company with their teacher.

The Text-Books for First Examination

The books for the First Examination comprise the worship necessary for three "magic circles," viz.—The *first* is the magic circle of *d*Kon-*m*chhog *s*pyi *h*dus Rig-*h*dsin *h*dsah *m*tshan *s*nying-poi chhos *h*khor.[133] This book contains about sixty pages, and its recitation takes nearly one whole day. It comprises the chapters:

(1) Tshe-*s*grub or The obtaining of long life.

(2) Zhi-khro—The mild and angry deities.

(3) Guru-drag—The fierce form of Padma Sambhava.

(4) Seng-*g*dongma—The lion-faced demoness.

(5) Chho*s* *s*kyong Mahakala Yeshe*s* *m*gonpo.

(6) Thang-lha,[134] *m*Dso*d*-*l*nga, Lha-chhen and *s*Man *b*stun—Local and mountain deities.

(7) *bs*Kang *bs*hag*s*, tshogs and Tashi *s*mon-lam.

His Further Academic Instruction

The new mont now is instructed in the preparation and adornment of *torma,* or sacred food for the gods and demons; and in the blowing of the copper trumpets, in the manipulation of the cymbals, and in dancing and rhetoric, and in any science which he fancies. He is at liberty to choose for himself a teacher. The "sciences" usually taken up are astrology, medicine, and painting, but the majority of the newly-fledged monks are content with the position of an ordinary monk.

His Sacerdotal Functions

Until, however, he commits to memory the following books, he will never become a successful chaplain or family priest (*m*chhod-*g*nas), which is a paying business and the goal of most of the monks. For those lamas who can recite by heart all the Litanies and other sacerdotal ritual, without consulting their books, are much more popular and sought after than those who read their ritual service. He therefore tries to learn by heart— "The real story of animal beings by Sagon, who had returned from the dead" (Sagon *h*gro *d*ngos zhi), and the Litany of Avalokita— The Powerful Great Pitier (gar-*db*ang Thug-*r*je chhenpo), and " The exhorting Mani," which are used on the occasion of a death. Also "The ripe (magic) circle which draws to the best and most pleasing dwelling" (*s*min-byed-*db*yang gi-*d*kyil-*h*kor *db*ang *m*chhog-*g*nas *h*dren).

The majority of the lamas exercise sacerdotal functions, and are priests rather than monks. Many of the lamas are permitted to reside in their villages for the greater part of the year, ostensibly as village-priests for the convenience of the people. They must, however, return at definite intervals to their parent-monastery, which keeps a roll of all its members. Those individuals who absent themselves for unduly long periods, get a punishment for stay by away for long without permission.

Penalty for Violation of Celibacy

The regulation enroling celibacy is the one which is often violated. But in most of the institutions other than Pemiongchi celibacy is not observed. Should it be proved that a Pemiongchi monk consorts with women, he will be expelled by a chapter, unless it be his first offence and he prays publicly for forgiveness, and then is awarded some penance and pays a fine of 180 rupees according to the rules of the *l*Chags-yig. He must also pay over again the entrance fees and presents as before.

II. LAMAIC GRADES AND DISCIPLINE

Lower Offices

The consecutive offices through which the young lama must pass to reach the highest grades are the following:

I. *Conch-shell Blower*—for about one year. These go in pairs.

II. *Pourer of holy water,* or Chhab-hdren—for one year.

III. *Image care-taker* or *s*Ku-gnyer—for three years.

The *Ku-nyer* is also charged with the duty of dusting and arranging the objects on the altar and making the offerings of water, lamps, sacred food, &c., and the removal of the same.

Higher Offices, U-chho or Ya-pa

On completing his service in this last office, he passes out of the stage of gra-pa (pronounced *ta-pa)* or learner, and becomes an *db*U-chho*s* (pronounced "u-chho") or "Head of Religion." And by the laity he now is called *Ya-pa* or "Reverend Father." From this class of *db*U-chho*s* are selected the officials to fill the special offices of IV and V, and one from the Pemiongchi monastery acts for a term of a few years as family priest to the Sikhim Raja, doing especially the *s*Kang-*g*so worship.

The Commissariat Officer—Chi-nyer

IV. The Commissariat Manager or *s*pyi-gnyer (pronounced *Chi-nyer)* are tenable for three years. There are two of these, and they are in charge of the lay menials of the monastery. When the menials have any complaint, it must be made through the Commissariat Manager, who privately informs one of the *db*U-chho*s* of the details, and afterwards it is laid before the assembly of *db*U-chho*s* under the presidency of the U-mdse and Dorje *s*Lob-*d*pon. The orders, which are then passed, are communicated by the two Commissariat Managers to the menials concerned.

The Provost Marshal—Chho-tim-ba

V. Provost Marshal or Chhos khrims-pa (pronounced *Chho-rtim-ba),* an appointment tenable for one year. This office requires qualities of pre-eminent learning, popularity, tact, and the ability to enforce discipline and respect. The Provost Marshal is appointed by the vote of the monks *(tapa).* These select one of the yapas or superior monks, and recommend him to the Sikkim Raja in a memorial, which they all sign. The Raja's minister then informs the nominee that he has been appointed Provost Marshal for the current year, and that into his charge have been placed all the books of the Library, including the *l*Chag*s*-yig Rules, and certain advice is given him, accompanied by the presentation of an exceptionally long and honourable scarf; a refreshment of tea and beer is given. He is given refreshment of tea and bear. After that he is ceremonially long and honourable scarf.

One of his duties is to read the *l*Chag*s*-yig Rules to the assembled monks, and also lecture to them occasionally on religious and civil history and discipline.

He is the recognised head of the monks and their spokesman. When any person requests that the "Banquet to the whole assembly of the Gods and Demons" (Tshogs-*h*khor)—be performed, all the monks assemble and do the necessary worship and make the magic circles. It is the *Chho-tim-ba* who declares the object of the sacrifice, viz., for one or other of the four conditions—birth, old age, sickness or death.

The *second* comprises the magic circle of the collection of the Tathagathas and "the powerful great pitiful one" (Avalokita)—*b*De-*g*shegs-kun *h*dus-gar-*db*ang, Thug*s*-rje chhen-po, of about 40 pages.

Then follow the magic circles of the fierce and demoniacal deities Guru-drag-*d*mar, Khrowo-rol wai *g*tor-zlog and Drag-poi-las Gurui-*g*sol-*h*debs len-*b*dunma, Kha *h*don chhos *s*pyo*d*.

Penalties of Failure to Pass

Those who fail to pass this examination are taken outside are disgraced and beaten by the Chhos-khrim*s*-pa. Repeated failure up to a limit of three years necessitates the rejection of members from the order. Should, however, the boy be rich and wish re-entry, he may be readmitted on paying presents and money on a higher scale than formerly, without which no re-admission is possible. If the rejected candidate be poor and he wishes to continue a religious life, he can only do so as a lay-devotee doing drudgery about the monastery buildings. Or he may set up in some village as an unorthodox lama-priest.

The majority fail to pass at the first attempt. Failure on the part of the candidate attaches a stigma to his teacher, while in the event of the boy chanting the exercises correctly and with pleasing voice in the orthodox oratorical manner, his teacher is highly complimented.

The Second Examination is conducted like the first one. It lasts for two days this examination "the iron letter" *(i.e.*, inflexible rule) *l*chag-yig is solemnly read out before the examination.

The Text-Books for Second Examination

The books to be recited by heart at the Second Examination are the following:

(1) The worship of "The Lake-born *Vajra*" (*m*Tsho-*s*kyes-*r*dorje), *i.e.*, Padma Sambhava and the *Guru*-Sage who has obtained understanding (Rig-*h*dsin *r*tog *s*grub-guru).

(2) The three roots of sagedom (Rig hdsin *r*tsa-*g*sum)—

(a) Rig *h*dsin lhamai-las.

(b) Tshe-*s*grub khog *db*ugs.

(c) *g*Sang *s*grub dongyi *s*nying-po.

(3) The deeds of Dorje Phagmo (*r*Dorje phagmoi-las), the great happiness of zag-med (zag-med bde-chhen), and the four classes of the Fierce Guardians—chhos srung drag-po *s*de *b*zhi. The names of these demons are—on the east, *k*Lu-*b*dud Munpa nagpo; on the south, Srinpo Lanka-*m*grim-*b*chu; on the west, Mamo Sha-za phra-gral nag-po; on the north, *g*Shenpa *s*Pu-gri-*d*marpo.

(4) The subjugation of the host of demons—The offering to the Dhyani Budhas *b*dud *d*pung zil non, Kun-*b*zang, *m*chhod-*s*prin.

(5) The sacrificial ceremony *bs*kang *bs*hags, viz., Rig-dsin *bs*kang-*bs*hags, Phagmai *bs*kang *bs*hags.

(6) The prayer of the glorious "Tashi"—the Lepcha name for Padma Sambhava—Tashi-*s*mon-lam.

The above books reach to about fifty-five pages.

(7) The circle of the eight Commanders of the collected Buddhas. bKah *b*gya*d b*de *g*shegs *h*duspai *d*kyil-*h*khor kyi las and Khrowo-rol wai *g*tor-zlog gyi *s*kori *b*kah *b*rgyad. This has about 40 pages. [The names of the eight Commanders, *b*Kah-*b*gyads, are—(1) Chhe-*m*chhog, (2) Yang-dag, (3) gShin *r*je, (4) *r*Ta-mgrin, (5) Phurpa, (6) Mamo, (7) *h*Gad stong, (8) Rig-*h*dsin).]

When the young monk recites by heart all these books satisfactorily, and so passes this examination his training period is over. He is not subject to any further ordeal of examination.

Ordinary Practice

It should be noted, however, that outside Pemiongchi practically no examination obtains. All that is done is merely to insist on the young monks endeavouring to commit to memory as many of these books as possible.

His Position and Privileges

The Monkhood.—On passing these two examinations, the successful candidate becomes a junior monk, and is supposed to keep "The Ten Precepts"[135] but he is still called a gra-pa or "learner." [The term *d*ge-*s*long or "the virtuous beggar," which may be considered as representing the *Bhikhu* of Indian Buddhism, is not in use in Sikkim; and in Tibet it is restricted to those lamas who profess the strict observation of the 253 obligations]. He is presented with a scarf of honour by the monks, and is considered a member of the Order—even although he be under 20 years of age. From that date, he is relieved of the menial office of serving out tea and beer, and he takes a higher seat in the Assembly Hall., He now directly receives his share of the money and other lay gifts which had hitherto been the perquisite of his tutor. He has the privilege of drinking beer which he should not previously have tasted—although abstinence from intoxicating drinks is one of "the eight precepts." He may even drink the beer off the same table as his teacher. He learns to pay complete attention to what his teacher says, place implicit reliance on his sayings, and give him the deepest respect.

He is usually re-appointed for one or more terms, as there is difficulty in finding suitable men for this appointment.

After filling the above office he is eligible for the two highest appointments in the monastery, viz.

VI.—Principal and *Chief Celebrant* or *db*U-*m*dsad (pronounced *Um-dse);* and

VII.—Patriarch or *r*Do-rje *s*Lob-*d*pon (pronounced Dorje Lo-pon).

The Um-dse

These two offices are held for life. The holders enjoy equal rank and receive the same stipend and perquisites, They sit opposite each other in the assembly room. However, the Um-dse is always the more learned of the two, and is necessarily something of a man of the world. He supervises the whole establishment and controls the discussions, and it is to him that the peasantry resort for advice and settlement of their disputes.

The Dorje Lo-pon

The Dorje Lo-pon does not take part in secular matter. He has to uphold the dignity of the religion. He does the mechanical work of meditation and some of the higher ritual, one of his chief duties being to abstract the soul of the dead and despatch it on the right path to heaven or for a new rebirth.

Bishop

The Incarnate Lama of *bLa*-brang monastery is supposed to exercise the functions of a Bishop of Sikkim; but he has only the title of Protector of Religion—the titles of *Do-dam-pa* or "bishop," *Khenpo* (mkhan-po) or "abbot" are not used in Sikkim.

III. MONASTIC ROUTINE

The daily routine of the Sikkim monk differs somewhat, according to whether (a) he be living apart from his monastery, say, as a village priest, or (b) as a resident in a monastery, or (c) as a solitary hermit. I will describe the practices in this order.

As a Village Priest

Night Devotion

On waking monk immediately must arise from his couch even though it be midnight, and commence to chant the mi-*r*tak-*r*gyu*d*-*bs*kul, taking care to pronounce all the words fully and distinctly. This contains the instructions of his special Lama-preceptor (*r*tsa-wa-*b*lama), and in the recital the monk must call vividly to mind his spiritual guide. Then he says a prayers in which he makes a number of requests for himself

"Meditative" Postures

After that he assumes the meditative posture of "the seven attitudes," in order to subjugate the five senses. These attitudes are: (1) sitting with legs flexed in the well-known attitude of Buddha; (2) the hands resting one above the other in the lap; (3) head slightly bent forwards; (4) eyes fixed on the tip of the nose; (5) shoulders "floating like the wings of a vulture;" (6) spine erect and " straight like an arrow;" (7) tongue arched upwards to palate like the carving petals of the eight-leaved lotus. While in this posture he must think that he is alone in a wilderness. This is a tapasya which perfects after very hard meditation.

Expulsion of the Three Original Sins

The three original sins of the body are then got rid of according to the humoural physiology of the ancients in the three series of *db*uma, roma, and *r*kyang-ma. After taking a deep inspiration, the air of the *roma* veins is expelled three times, and thus "the white wind" is let out from the right nostril three times in short and forcible expiratory gusts. This expels all Anger. Then from the left nostril is thrice expelled in a similar way "the red air," which rids from Lust. The colourless central air is thrice expelled, which frees from Ignorance. On concluding these processes, the monk must mentally realize that all ignorance, lust, and anger—the three Original Sins—have disappeared like frost before a scorching sun.

Mummery

He then says the "a-lia-ki," keeping his tongue curved like a lotus petal. This is followed by his chanting the *b*lami *r*nal-*h*byor or the Yoga of the Lama," during which he must mentally conceive his Lama-guide as sitting overhead upon a lotus flower.

Ritual

Then, assuming the spiritual guise of his *Yidam* or tutelary deity, he chants the Four Preliminary Services—the *s*ngon-gro *b*zi-*h*byor. These are the Refuge formula or *s*kyab*s* = *h*gro—which cleanses the darkness of the Body, the Hundred Letters or Yige-*br*gyapa, which cleanses all obscurity in Speech; and the magic circle of rice—the *Mandala,*—which cleanses the Mind; and the prayer *g*sol-*h*debs, classifying the lamas up to the most perfect one, confers Perfection on the monk himself.

This is followed by the chanting of bla-grub, " the obtaining of the Lama," and " the obtaining of the ornaments *s*nyen-grub."

Repetition of Mantras

The mild deity in this worship is called "The Agreeable One" (*m*thun) and the demon (drag-po) is called "The Repulsive" (*b*zle-pa). The demoniacal form must be recited that full number of times which the lama bound himself to do by vow before his spiritual tutor, viz., 100, 1,000, or 10,000 times daily. Those not bound in this way by vows repeat the charm as many times as they conveniently can.

Further Devotion

Having done this, he may retire again to sleep

He cannot ensure that these are the early hours of night and that the night is not far advanced. But if the dawn is near, he must not go to sleep, but should employ the interval in several sorts of prayer (*s*mon-lam).

At Dawn

As soon as day dawns, he must wash his face and rinse his mouth and do the worship above noted, should he not have already done so; also the following rites:

Offerings

1st. —Prepare sacred food for the six sorts of beings (Rigs. strug-gi-*g*torma) and send it to Ngo-wo-yidag—The Tantalized Ghosts.

2nd. —Offer incense, butter-incense, and wine-oblation (*g*ser-skyem). The incense is offered to the good spirits—firstly, to the chief god and the lama; secondly, to the class of "king" gods; and thirdly, to the mountain god Kang-chhen dsonga (*Ang.* Kanchinjingna). Then offerings are made to the spirits of caves (who guarded and still guard the hidden revelations therein deposited), the *d*gra-lha or "gods of Battle," the Yul-lha or country gods, the *gzi-b*dag or local gods, and the *sde-brgyad,* "the eight classes of deities." The butter-incense is only given to the most malignant class of the demons and evil spirits.

Morning's Occupation

Some breakfast is now taken, consisting of *thugpa* or weak soup, followed by tea with parched grain. Any especial work which has to be done will now be attended to, failing which some *d*ge-*s*byor or other service will be chanted. And if any temple or chaitya (chhorten) he at hand, these will be circumambulated with "prayer-wheel" revolving in hand and chanting *mantras.* After that if any villager requires priestly services these are performed.

Evening Service

In the afternoon around 2 p.m. a meal of rice is taken, followed by beer by those who take it, or by tea for non-beer drinkers. About six o'clock P.M. is done the *g*tor-*bs*ngo*s* service, in which, after assuming his tutelary deity, he chants the *s*ngon-gro and the *s*kyab-gro. Then is done a chhoga (a form of celebration-worship) with bell and small drum in hands, followed by an invocation to all the host of Lamas, yidams and Chhos-*s*kyong *(Defensores Fidei),* on the assembly of all of whom there is done the worship of the magic-circle of a tutelary deity *(Yidam).*

At 9 or 10 P.M. he retires to sleep.

In Monastic Residence

Morning Muster for Mass

In the morning, after offering the sacred food, incense, and butter-incense, a conch-shell is blown. On hearing this all the monks must come out of their chambers (gra-shag). On the second blast all collect in the Great Assembly Hall, and during this entry into the hall the Provost Marshal (chhos-*k*hrimba) stands beside the door with his rod in hand. All the monks seat themselves in Buddha fashion, each on his own mat. The monk's feet must not project and his clothes must not hang down or rest upon the mat. Each must face straight his front with eyes fixed on the tip of his nose. And the most solemn silence must be observed. The slightest breach of these rules is promptly punished by the rod of the Provost Marshal or, in the case of the younger novices, by the *s*Ku-*g*nyer.

Service of Tea, Grace before Drinking

When all have been properly seated, then two or three of the most inferior novices who have not passed their examination and who occupy back seats, rise up and serve out tea to the assembly,[136] each monk producing from his breast pocket his own cup and having it filled up by these novices. Before drinking it all must wait for the Um-dse to say the Grace. All the assembly joins in this offering.

A usual grace is—

"We humbly beseech Thee! that we and our relatives throughout all of our life-cycles may never be separated from the Three Holy Ones! May the blessing of The Trinity enter into this drink!"

Then sprinkling a few drops on the ground with the tips of the fore and middle fingers:

"To all the dread locality demons of this country, we offer this good Chinese tea! And May the doctrines of Buddha be extended!" Let us obtain our wishes."

Service of Soup

The tea is then drunk and the cup is refilled two or three times. The service of tea is succeeded by soup named "*g*sol-jam thugpa," and served by a new set of the novice underlings. When the cups are filled the Um-dse, joined by all the monks, chants the "thug-pai *m*chhod-pa," or "the Sacrificial Offering of the Soup." Three or four cups of soup are supplied to each monk. The hall is then swept clean by junior monks.

Celebration of Mass

The Um-dse then inspects the magic circle (*d*Kyil-*h*khor) to see that it is correct, and this ascertained he commences the celebration. He always heads the service, the rest of the congregation repeating it word by word closely after him and. using a *Psalter.* This service consists of the *s*ngon-*h*gro, *s*kyabs-*h*gro and las-*s*byang, on the conclusion of which the assembly disperses. As a sample of this part of the worship, I here translate a short version of the *s*Kyab*s*-*h*gro (roughly *"KYAM-DO").*

THE REFUGE FORMULA

The Refuge Formula

With the passing of time, Buddhism took a depraved form. It

included study and steadily a host of defied saints, deities and demons of Tibet and also introduced many of India Yogacharya and Mahayana saints.

We—all beings—through the intercession of the Lama, go for refuge to Buddha!

We go for refuge to Buddha's Books (Dharma)!

We go for refuge to The Assembly of the Lamas (Sanghha)!

We go for refuge to the host of the Gods and their retinue of the Yidam (tantalized ghosts), *m*Khah-*h*gros (fairies), and the Defenders of THE Religion who people the sky!

We go for refuge to the victorious Lamas who have descended from the Sky *(i.e.,* all inspired Lamas)!

We go for refuge to The Lama who is the holder of Wisdom and the Tantra! *(i.e.,* The holder of *Padma Jungre* as personified by Wisdom and Tantra.)

We go for refuge to the All-Good Father-Mother, *Samanta-bhadra*—Yab-yum Kun tu-*b*zang-po! (The primordial Buddha-God.)

We go for refuge to the divinely adorned Mild and Angry Loving Ones—Long*s*-*s*ku-zhi-khro-rab-*h*byam!

We go for refuge to the *Maha Vajradhara* Incarnation (of Shakya-muni)—*s*prul-*s*ku-Dorje-*h*chhang-chhen!

We go for refuge to The Diamond Sworded Guide '*Vajrasatwa*'—*s*Ton-pa-Dorje-Sems-pa!

We go for refuge to the victorious *Sakyamuni*—*r*Gyal-wa Sakya-Thub-pa!

We go for refuge to the Fierce *Vajrapani*—Phyag-na-Dorje-gtum-po!

We go for refuge to the Converted Mother *Devi Marici*—Yum-*h*gyur-lha-mo od-zer-chan ma!

We go for refuge to the Learned *Acharji Manjusri*—*s*Lob-*d*pon *h*Jam *d*pal *b*shes-*b*snyen!

We go for refuge to the *Pandita Sri Singha*—Pan-chhen-Shri-Singha!

We go for refuge to the *Pandita Bimala Mitra*—Panchhen Bhi-ma-la-ri-tma!

We go for refuge to the Incarnate Lotus-born *Padma Sambhava*—*s*prul-*s*ku-Pad-ma-*h*byung-*g*na*s*!

We go for refuge to (his wife) the *Dakini* of the Ocean of Fore-knowledge—*m*Khah-*h*gro-ye-*s*hes-*m*tsho-*r*gyal!

We go for refuge to the Religious King *Dharma raja* Thi-srong-de-tsen—Chhos-*r*gyal-Khri stong-*l*de*u*-*b*tsan!

We go for refuge to The Apocalyse Finder—Terton Myang-ban-ting-*h*dsin-*b*zang-po!

We go for refuge to The Guru's disciple, the Victor *Sthavira* Dang-ma—*g*nas-*b*rtan-*l*dang-ma-hlun-*r*gyal!

We go for refuge to the Reverend Sister, the powerful Lioness Lady *Singeshwara*—*l*che-*b*tsun Seng-ge-*d*bang-phyug!

We go for refuge to the Incarnate *Jina* Zhang—ton *s*prul-sku-*r*gyal-wa-zhang-*r*ton!

We go for refuge to The Gu-ru, clever above thousands— *m*Khas-pa-nyid-*h*bum!

We go for refuge to *Dharma Gurunath Ber.*nag—Chhos-*b*dag-gu-ru-jo-*h*ber-nak *m*gon-po!

We go for refuge to The Illusive Lion *Gyaba*—Khrul-zhig-seng-ge-*r*gyab-ba!

We go for refuge to the Great Devotee 'The Clearer of the misty moon'—Grub-chhen-zla-wa mun sel!

We go for refuge to the Indian Sage *Kumaraja*—Rig-*h*dsin-ku-ma-ra-dsa!

We go for refuge to the *Jina* Prince of the Scentless Rays—*r*Gyal-*s*res-Dri-*med*-*hod*-zer!

We go for refuge to the Incarnate 'Noble Banner of Victory'—*s*prul-*s*ku-*d*Pal-*h*byor-*r*gyal-*m*tshan!

We go for refuge to the Omniscient renowned *Chandrakirti*—Kun-*m*khyen-Zla-wa-grag*s*-pa!

We go for refuge to The Three Incarnate Kind brothers—Drin-chhen-*s*prul-*s*ku-*m*chhed-*g*sum!

We go for refuge to the Bodhisatwa, The Noble Ocean—Byang-sem*s*-*d*Pal-*h*byor-*r*gya *m*tsho!

We go for refuge to the Incarnate Sage, the religious Vajra—*s*prul-*s*ku-Rig-*h*dsin-chhos-*r*dor!

We go for refuge to The Entirely accomplished and renowned Speaker—Yong*s*-*h*dsin-ngag-*d*bang-grags-pa!

We go for refuge to *Mahaguru Dharmaraja*—*b*La-chhen-Chhos kyi-*r*gyal-po!

We go for refuge to the Religious king of accomplished knowledge[137]—Chhos-*r*gyal-yon-ten-Phuntshog*s*!

We go for refuge to The Banner of obtained Wisdom—*m*Khas-grub-*b*Lo-gro*s*-*r*gyal-*m*tshan!

We go for refuge tò The Unequalled useful Vajra—Tshung med-*g*zhan-phan-Dorje!

We go for refuge to the Radical *(Mula)* Lama Asoka—Mya-ngan-med-*r*Tsa-wai-*b*La-ma![138]

We go for refuge to the Lama of the Three collections of the Mula Tantra—*r*Tsa *r*Gyud-dus-*g*sum-*b*La-ma!

We go for refuge to the accomplished Sage *Satwa* Phuntshogs—Sems-*d*pah Phun-tshogs-rig-*h*dsin!

We go for refuge to The Beloved Religious King *hsTan-hds*in, the holder of the doctrines—Chho*s*-*r*gyal-Byams-pa-*bs Tan*-*h*dsin!

We go for refuge to the Reverend Sky *Vajra*—*m*Khas-*b*tsun-Nam-*m*khah-Dorje!

We go for refuge to the *Shri-Ratna-Bhadra-Satwa*—Sems-*d*pah-Rin-chhen-*d*Pal-*b*zang!

We go for refuge to the collection of mild and angry Yidams (Tutelary gods)!

We go for refuge to the holy doctrine of *Maha Anta* or the Great End—*r*Dsog*s*pa-chhen-po!

We go for refuge to The male and female Saints of the Country!

We go for refuge to The Fairies (*m*Khah hgro), Defenders of Religion (Chhos-*s*kyongs), and Guardians (*b*Srung*s* ma)!

Oh! Lama! Bless us as you have been blessed; Bless us with the blessing of the Tantras!

We beg you to bless us with *OM*, which is the body. We beg you to purify our sins and pollutions of the body. We beg you to increase happiness without any sickness. We beg you to give us the real undying gift of life!

We beg you to bless us with *AH,* which is the command. We beg you to purify the sins and pollution of speech. We beg you to give us the power of speech. We beg you to confer on us the gift of perfect speech!

We beg you to bless us with the *HUM* (pr. *Hung),* which is the MInd! We beg you to purify the pollution and sins of the mind! We beg you to give us the real gift of pure heart. We beg you to empower us with the four powers!

We pray you to give us the gifts of the True Body, Command and Mind!

"—OM—AH—HUNG!—

Give us such blessing as will clear away the sins and pollution of bad deeds!

We beg you to soften the evils of bad causes!

We beg you to bless us with the prosperity of our body, *i.e.,* health.

Bless us with mental guidance.

Bless us with Buddhahood soon.

Bless us by cutting us off from (worldly) illusions.

Bless us by putting us into The Right Path.

Bless us by making us understand all religious things.

Bless us to be useful to each other with kindliness.

Bless us with the ability of doing good and delivering the animal beings from misery.

Bless us to know ourselves thoroughly.

Bless us to be mild from the depths of our heart.

Bless us to be brave as Yourself.

Bless us with the Tantras as Yourself!

Now, we, the innumerable animal beings, conceive that we have become pure in thought like Buddha; we think that we are working for the welfare of the other animal beings. We, now having obtained the qualities of the collection of the gods and the roots of the Tantras, and the zhi-wa, *r*gya*s*-pa, *d*bang and Phrin-las, pray that all the animal beings be possessed of happiness and be freed from misery. Let us all animals (human beings) be freed from lust, anger, and attachment to worldly affairs, and let us perfectly understand the true nature of religion!

Now, O! Father-Mother! The unadorned Dharma Kaya *Sumanta bhadra*-Yab-yum Chhos-*s*ku-Kun-*b*zang! The richly adorned Mild and Angry Loving Ones—Long*s*-*s*ku-zhi-khro-rab-*h*byam*s*! The incarnate sages of the Skull Rosary—*s*prul-*s*ku-rigs-*h*dsin-thod-*h*phreng-*bs*tsal! and the Mula Tantra Lama—Tsa-*r*gyu*d*-*b*la-ma! I now beg You to depart!

O! Ghosts of heroes, *d*Pa-o! Female fiends, Dakkini Demoniacal Defenders of the faith, Chho*s*-*s*kyong*s*! The Holy Guardians of the Commandments—Dam-chan-*b*kah-i-*b*srung-ma! And all those that we invited to this place! I beg You All now to depart!

O! The powerful King of the Angry Deities, Khro-wo-i-*r*gyal-po-*s*tob-po-chhe! The powerful Ishwara and the host of the Country Guardian Gods—*m*thu-*s*tob*s*-*d*bang—phyug-yul-*h*khor-srung! And all those others that were invited to this place with all their retinue! I beg you All now to depart!

"May glory come Tashi-shok!

"Let Virtue Come! d Ge-o!"

Other Services

About 8 A.M. the conch-shell blast again summons the monks to the Assembly Hall, where, after partaking of refreshments of tea and parched grain in the manner already described, a full celebration (chhoga) is done. And on its conclusion the monks disperse.

About 10 A.M. a Chinese drum is beaten to muster the monks in the Assembly Hall. At this meeting rice and meat and vegetables: are served out as before, and with this is also served beer called *g*sos-*r*gyab, the *l*to-*m*chhod being-done as formerly A full celebration is then performed and the meeting dissolves.

In the afternoon a conch shell is blown for tea and a Chinese drum beaten for beer, the monks assembling as before and doing a full celebration of the worship of Mahakala Natha (*m*gonpo) and the Guardians of Religion respectively. When sacerdotal celebrations on behalf of lay individuals have to be done, they are introduced within the latter celebration, which is interrupted for this purpose. After each of these extra celebrations the monks remain outside the Assembly Hall for a very short time and then re-assemble. On finishing the extra chhogas, the chhoga of the Religious Guardians is then resumed and concluded.

In the evening another assembly, preceded by tea as refreshment, conducts the celebration of *s*kang-shags with 108 lamps. Another and final assembly for the day is made by beat of drum, and rice and flesh-meat is served out. The refreshments and meals usually number nine daily.

In Hermitage

Hermits

In the case of the hermit-lama (or *m*tshams*s*-pa), of which there are very few in Sikkim, he is engaged all day long in mortifying his passions and worldly desires, repeating mantras and practising those postures and magic rites which, according to the Tantrik school, give miraculous powers These retes are also considered a short cut to Nirvana.

Their Meditation

According to the book entitled, *The complete Esoteric Tantra* the reputed work of Padma Sambhava, the order of these exercises, is as follows:

1st.— The mode of placing the three mystic words (i.e., ku, *sung*, and *tuk).*

2nd.— The Nectar-replying rosary.

3rd.— The jewelled rosary-guide for Ascending.

4th.— Secret counsels of the four Yogas.

5th.— The great Root of the Heart.

6th.— The Lamp of The Three Dwellings.

7th.— The bright Loosener of the Illusion.

8th.— The water-drawing "dorje."

9th.— The secret guide to the fierce Dakini.

10th.— *The* drawing of the Essence of the stony nectar.

11th.— Counsel on the Dakinis' habits.

12th.— Fathoming the mystery of the Dakinis.

13th.— Counsel for the Khandoma Fairies heart root.

14th.— The Four Words for the path of Pardo.[139]

15th.— The Pardo of the angry demons.

16th.— To recognise the Gyalwa Rig-na or The Five Former Buddhas. Then Nirvana is reached.

The hermit-lamas of Sikkim usually leave their hermitage for some months annually to visit villages and places of pilgrimage. A true hermit who has cut off all connection with the world is called *s*gom-chhen or "great devotee."

Temporary Hermitage and its Exercises

Initially, it was essential that every young lama spond three years, three months and three days in the hermitage. This was the period of his training to accustom himself to ascetic rites. But slowly and slowly this practice has been dispensed with. If at all it is done, a period of three months and three days is considered sufficient. During this seclusion he repeats the mantra of his tutelary deity an incredible number of times. *s*Ngon-gro-*b*zi-*hb*yor, complete in all its four sections, must be repeated 100,000 times. In the "Kyab-do" portion he must prostrate himself to the ground 100,000 times. The repetition of the Yige-*br*gya-pa itself takes about two months; and in addition must be chanted the following voluminous services:

Phyi-*h*grub, nang-*h*grub, *g*sang-*h*grub, *b*la-*h*grub, *s*nyen-grub, *h*phrin-las, and *b*zi-*h*grub.

As a sample of the form of lamaic ritual employed in the worship of a special divinity, I give here a translation of the manual entitled—

The Worship of Dolma, the Deliveress

Her Popularity

Dolma is one of the most popular of the deities, and a large proportion of the laity can repeat her services by heart. She is known to Northern Buddhism by the Sanskrit name of Tara of which Dolma is a literal Tibetan translation, meaning "The Unloosener (of difficulties)" or "The Saviouress." And it is to this attribute of being ever ready to help and easily approachable that she owes her popularity. Most of the other deities cannot be approached without the mediation of a lama; poor common man or woman had another way. They could directly appeal to Dolma for help.

Semblance to the Virgin Mary

The striking similarity between Dolma and "The Virgin Mary of Roman Catholicism has excited comment. Dolma like The Virgin Mary, occupies a maternal relation to the Buddhas, and is an intercessor, a ready bearer of prayers easily approachable and able and willing to relieve or soothe petty troubles. The name Dolma is a favourite personal name for Buddhist women.

Origin of Her Worship

Worship of Dolma seems to started about the 7th century A.D., when Tantric ideas began to tinge Indian Buddhism. It seems that the name was evidently suggested by the Hindu myth of *Budha,* or the planet Mercury, whose mother was Tara; and either by wilful or accidental confusion the idea got transferred to *Buddha.* Buddha had, about this time, also received a place in the Hindu Pantheon.

Her Forms

There are now two recognized classes of the goddess Dolma, viz.

(a) The *Green* Dolma—"*The* Dolma" of the Tibetans, of which King Srongtsan-gampo's *Nepalese* wife was an incarnation, and

(b) The *White* Dolma—who is especially worshipped in China and Mongolia and very seldom in Tibet. King Srongtsan-gampo's *Chinese* wife is believed to be an incarnation of this form.

The White Form

The white form is seated like a Buddha, and has seven eyes, one being in the forehead in addition to the ordinary facial pair, and one in and in the sole each foot.

The Green Form

"*The* Dolma" of the Tibetans in the gereen form—is usually represented in the form of a bejewelled young Indian woman of a green complexion seated on a lotus, with her left leg hanging down and holding a long-stemmed lotus flower. She is, however, given a variety of other forms, mild and demoniacal, to the number of twenty-one or more. The demoniacal forms are very similar to those of the Hindu Durga. These several forms are evidently the objective representations in concrete fashion of the numerous titles of the goddess:—thus Locana, Mamaki, Vajradhatviswari, Pandara, Ugratara, Ratnatara, Bhrikutitara, Visvatara, &c. Latterly her names have been extended to reach the mystic number of 108.

Her Manual of Worship

Her Manual of Worship, it is believed in the inner circle of Buddhism has been composed by the first of the seven mythical Dhyani Buddhas, viz., Vipashyi. The appendix, however, is signed by Gedun Dub, the Grand Lama, who built Tashi-lhunpo monastery *circa* 1445 A.D., so that it is possible he composed this version.

The Manual is here translated:

"Exhortation to Dolma's Worship

If we worship this high and pure-souled goddess when we retire in the dusk and get up in the morning, then all our fears and worldly anxieties will 'give way,' and our sins be forgiven. SHE— The conqueror of myriad hosts, will strengthen us. She will do more than this! She will reach us directly to the end of our transmigration to Buddha and Nirvana!

She will expel the direst poisons and relieve us from all anxieties as to food and drink, and all our wants will be satisfied; and all devils and plagues and poisons will be annihilated utterly; and the burdens of all animals will be lightened! If you chant her hymn two or three or six or seven times, your desire for a son will be realized! Or, should you wish wealth, you will obtain it, and all other wishes will be gratified and every sort of demon will be wholly overcome!"

Her Worship

Her worship is divided into seven stages, viz.

(1) Invocation—Calling her to come.

(2) Presentation of offerings of sacred food, water, flowers and rice, and occasionally a *mandala* or magic circle offering.

(3) Hymn in her praise.

(4) Repetition of her spell or *mantra.*

(5)&(6) Prayers for benefits present and to come.

(7) Benediction.

I

Invocation

"Hail! O! emeraldine Dolma!
Who art the Saviour of all beings!
I pray Thee descend from Thy heavenly mansion, at Potala,
Together with all Thy retinue of gods, titans, and deliverers!
I humbly prostrate myself at Thy lotus feet!
Hail to Thee, Our Holy Mother!"
Deliver us from all distress!

II

Presentation of Offerings (Sacrificial)

"We hail Thee! O Rever'd and Sublime Dolma!
Who art adored by all the kings and princes
Of the ten directions and of the present, past and future
We pray Thee to accept these offerings
Of flowers, incense, perfumed lamps,
Precious food, the music of cymbals,
And the other offerings!
We sincerely beg Thee in all of Thy divine Forms
To partake of the food now offered!
On confessing to Thee penitently their sins
The most sinful hearts, yea! even the committers of the
Ten vices and the five boundless sins,
Will obtain forgiveness and reach
Perfection of soul—through Thee!
If we (human beings) have amassed any merit
In the three periods, the present, past and future,
We rejoice in this good fortune, when we consider
The unfortunate lot of the poor (lower) animals
Piteously engulphed in the ocean of misery.
On their behalf, we now beg to turn the wheel of religion:
We beseech Thee by whatever merit we've accumulated
To kindly regard all the animals.
And for ourselves!
When our merit has reached perfection
Let us not, we pray Thee
Linger longer in this world!"

III

Hymns in Praise of Dolma

(In her Twenty-one Forms)[140]

"Adoration to Arya Tara!
And Avalokita (her spiritual father),
Rich in power and the store-house of pity!
Hail! rever'd and sublime Dolma!
We adore Thee!
"Hail! Dolma! Thou ever ready heroine!
Born, like a lightning-flash, from the pitying tear[141]
Shed for humanity by The Lord of the three worlds
The Lotus-born!
Hail! to Thee whose face is shining
As a hundred harvest moons
Lit by the splendid light of
A full thousand fulgent stars!
Hail! O! Thou whose hand is decked with
The Blue and Golden, water-lotus!
Thou beneficent and zealous Soother of difficulties,
Thou monopoliseth the realms of woe, as well as action.
Hail! O! Thou with head adorned by Tathagatha[142]
Conqueror of the Universe!
Thou hast overcome Thine enemies without exception
And shown Thyself a saintly Victor.
Hail! By Thy mystic *Tut-ta-ra-hung.*[143]
Thou possesseth the realms of earth and sky.
Thou treadest under foot the seven worlds
And makest one and all to bend!
Hail! The mighty gods adore Thee—
Indra, Agni, Brahma and the Lord of the Winds;
The risen ghosts and the dread ' Ti-za';
The horde of harmful spirits praise Thee!
Hail! By Thy mystic *'tre'* and *'Phat'*
Thou destroyest the cunning schemes of Thy opponents.

With Thy right leg flexed and the left extended,
Thou consumest Thine enemies with devouring fire!
Hail! With Thy awful word '*tu-re*'[144]
Thou banishest the bravest of devils!
Thou completely routeth enemies!
With the mere frown of Thy tear-born face

V. SOME MAGIC RITES AND CHARMS

Tibetan Superstitions

Magic and Mystic Rites Here Described

Magic and mysticism enter largely into lamaic ritual and especially into the priestly ministrations for the laity. Under this head a few of the more prominent magic rites, are viz. the "*Mandala*" offering in effigy of the Universe, which forms part of the daily worship of every lama; the casting of lots for soothsaying purposes, charms against sickness and accidents of sorts, ill-luck, and the printed charms for luck, which form the "prayer-flags" and tufts of rags affixed to trees, bridges, and other places.

The "Mandala" or Magic Circle-Offering of the Universe

The Daily Offering of the Universe

It is a matter of history how Asoka, the greatest of Indian Emperors, thrice offered India to the Buddhist church and thrice redeemed it with his treasure and jewels. The lamas, however, are much more magnificently generous than Asoka, for every day each lama offers to the Buddhas and other saints and demons not only the whole of India, but the entire universe, including the heavens and their inhabitants. This is done in effigy, but the offering is considered to be nonetheless effective than if were it actually made in reality. To render this ceremony intelligible, we must refer to the lamaic ideas on the cosmogony of the universe and othr places.

The Universe According to the Lamas

The Universe of the Lamas

The universe according to the lamas—and they closely follow Hindu notions on the subject—is graphically depicted in the chart facing.

General Description

The system of worlds forming one universe *(sakwal)*, of which there are many consists of a series of fabulous continents circularly disposed around the great central mass is girdled externally by an iron wall, 312½ miles[145] high and 3,602,625 miles in circumference, which shuts in the light of the sun, moon, and stars; outside this wall is perpetual darkness until another universe is reached. The primary support of each universe is a "warp and woof" of blue air like crossed *dorjes*, upon which rests "the body of the waters "and in this latter ocean are set the "continents" with bases of "solid gold," and underneath the central Mount Meru are the Hells.

Dimensions

The dimensions are as follow: Mount Meru towers 80,000 miles above the ocean, and it extends for the same distance below the waters. Enveloping it is an "enchanted ocean" (rolwai *m*tshò) 80,000 miles in width and the same in depth. To this succeeds a wall of golden mountains named the "Track of the Neck-Yoke," 40,000 miles high and the same in width, and beyond this is an enchanted ocean of the same dimensions. Externally to these are consecutive circles of alternating pairs of golden mountains and enchanted oceans of gradually diminishing dimensions as to width, depth, and height, viz. of 20,000, 10,001, 5,000, 2,500, 1,250, and 625 respectively. These are the "continents" in the outer occeans which have mentioned in Buddhist scriptures.

The Continents

These "continents" are really worlds, for under the heading of *Jambuling* (Skt. *Jambudwip)* is included the whole known world both oriental and occidental. All the other "continents" specified by the lamas are therefore purely fabulous, as in Hindu mythology. The chief continents are four in number, one being situated exactly in each of the four directions, and each continent has a smaller satellite on either side, thus bringing the total up to twelve.

The description of these continents briefly is:

> On the *East* is "Lus-*h*pags" (Skt. *Videha)*, or "vast body." This is shaped like the crescent moon, and is white in colour. It is 9,000 miles in diameter, and the inhabitants are described as tranquil and mild, and of excellent conduct, and with faces of same shape as this continent, *i.e.*, crescentic like the moon.

On the *South is* "Jambuling" (Skt. *Jambudwip),* or our own world. It is shaped like the shoulder-blade of a sheep, and is blue in colour. It is the smallest of all, being only 7,000 miles in diameter. Here are found riches and plenty, but also acts of sin as well as virtue. The inhabitants have faces of the same shape as the continent, *i.e.,* sub-triangular.

On the *West* is "ba-*g*lang *s*pyod" (Skt. *Godhanya* or "Wealth of Oxen"), which in shape is like the sun and red in colour. It is 8,000 miles in diameter. Its inhabitants are extremely powerful, and (as the name literally means, *cow + ox + action)* they are believed to be specially addicted to eating cattle, and their faces are round like the sun.

On the *North* is "*s*gra-mi-*s*nyan" (Skt. *Uttara Kuru* or "Elevated *Kuru*"-tribe) of square shape and green in colour, and the largest of all the continents, being 10,000 miles in diameter. Its inhabitants are extremely firece and noisy. They have square faces "like horses"; and live on trees, which supply all their wants. They become tree-spirits on their death; these trees afterwards emit "bad sounds" (this is evidently, like many of the other legends, due to a puerile and false interpretation of the etymology of the word).

The satellite continents resemble their parent one in shape and are half its size. The left satellite of Jambuling, viz. Ngayabling, is the fabulous country of the Rakshas, to which Padma Sambhava is believed to have gone and be still there reigning. And each of the latter presents towards Mount Meru one of the following objects respectively, viz., The Mountain of Jewels; The wish-granting tree (*d*pag-*b*sam kyi shing), The wish-granting cow ("*h*dod-*h*zo-i-ba"), and "The self-sprung crops" (ma-*s*mos-pi lo-thog) already referred to as divine objects in the description of "The Cycle of Existence."

Mount Ri-rab (Meru), Its Compartments, The Heavens

In the very centre of this system "The King of Mountains, Mount Ri-rab" (Meru), towers erect "like the handle of a hand millstone," and underneath it are the hells. It is composed of jewels: its eastern face is of silver, the south of jasper (Baidhuriya) stone, the west of ruby, and the north of gold. It has four lower compartments before the heavens are reached. The lowest of these compartments is inhabited by the "*g*nod *s*byin," usually interpreted as Yaksha, but really "givers of injury," and therefore bad genii—and these hold wooden plates. Above this is "the bead or wreath-holder's" region [phreng thog (Skt. *Sragdhara),* which seems to be a title of the Garudas]. Above this is the region of the Nagas, above whom are "the eternally fuddled ones" (*r*tak myos).

Above whom are the four Great Guardian Kings of the Quarters.[146] Above Mount Meru, at an elevation of 160,000 miles from the base, are the heavens of the gods, amongst the lower of which are the 33 sensuous heavens of Indra. Above Indira's and Mara's heavens of desire are the less sensuous heavens of Brahma's *d*gah-*l*dan "Paradise," *h*phru-*d*gah, and *g*zhan *h*phrul *d*wang byed, and above all these is The God of Gods, The Primordial Buddha—*Kuntu-zang-po* (Skt. *Samanta-bhadra)* or "The Best of All" in the highest Brahmaloka called *h*g-min (Skt. *Akanista),* (pronounced "O-min") or "The Supreme".

The Eight "Matri" Goddesses

Inhabiting the air, on a level with Indra's heaven, is the circle of The Eight Goddesses—(or *Hlamo)* the *Matris* of the earlier Hindus. These goddesses are all of beautiful appearance, and are thus named and described:—

1. "*s*Geg-mo-ma" (Skt. *Lasya)* of white complexion, holding a mirror and in a coquettish *(sgeg-pa)* attitude.
2. "*h*Phreng-ba-ma" (Skt. *Mala)* of yellow colour, holding a rosary (*h*phreng-ba).
3. "*g*Lu-ma" (Skt. *Gita)* of red colour, holding a lyre symbolizing music (*g*lu).
4. "Gar-ma" of green colour in a dancing attitude.
5. "Me-tog-ma" (Skt. *Pushpa)* of white colour, holding a flower (me-tog).
6. "*b*Dug-*s*pos ma" (Skt. *Dhupa)* of yellow colour, holding an incense (*b*Dug-*s*pos) vase.
7. "*s*Nang-gsal-ma" (?.Skt. *Dipa)* of red colour, holding a lamp.
8. "Dri-chha-ma" (Skt. *Gandha)* of green colour, holding a shell-vase of perfume (dri).

"The Seven Precious Things" of an Emperor

Immediately outside these goddesses, and also suspended in the air in fixed positions, are *"The Seven Precious Things"*[147] of a Chakravartin-raja, or universal monarch, viz.

(1) h*Khorlo rin-po-chhe* (Skt. *Chakra ratna),* or the victorious *Wheel* of a thousand spokes.

(2) *Nor-bu rin-po-chhe* (Skt. *Mani ratna)* The mother of *Jewels.*

(3) *Tsun-mo rin-po-chhe* (Skt. *Stri ratna),* The jewel of a *Wife.*

(4) *bLon-po rin-po-chhe* (Skt. *Mahajan ratna),* The good *Minister.*

(5) g*Lang-po rin-po-chhe* (Skt. *Hasti ratna),* The jowel of a white *Elephant.*

(6) r*Ta-mchhog rin-po-chhe* (Skt. *Ashwa ratna),* The best *Horse* jewel.

(7) d*Mag-pon rin-po-chhe* (Skt. *Sena-pati ratna),* The jewel of a *General.*

To these have been added an eighth, viz.

(8) *Bum-pa-ter*—the *Vase* for storing all the riches of the three worlds.

In the inmost circle immediately around Ri-rab are:

Nyima or The Sun, consisting of "glazed fire," with its chariot drawn by ten horses.

Da-wa or the Moon, composed of "glazed water," with its chariot and seven horses.

Rin-po-chhe Duk or the Jewelled Umbrella of Sovereignty.

Gyal-tshen (Skt. *Dhwaja)* or Banner of Victory.

In the centre of all, in the heavens of Indra, is the store of the entire treasure of the gods.

THE MODE OF OFFERING THE MANDALA

The mode of offering the Universe in effigy is as follows:

The Ceremony of Making the Mandala

Having wiped the 'mandal' tray with the right arm or sleeve, take a fistful of rice in either hand, and sprinkle some on the tray to lay the Foundation of the Universe of mighty Gold. Then set down the large ring, which is the Iron Girdle of the Universe. Then in the middle set down a dole of rice as Ri-rab (Mount Meru). Then in the order given in the attached diagram are set down a few grains of rice representing the 38 component portions of the Universe, each of which is named at the time of depositing its representative rice. The ritual for all sects of lamas during this ceremony is practically the same. The text of rituals which is folllowed by the Kargyupa of the Bhotiya *Basti* Gompa at Darjeeling is noted here.

The Mental Part of the Process

During this ceremony it is specially insisted on that the performer must mentally conceive that he is actually bestowing all this wealth of continents, gods, etc., upon his lamaic deities, those deities, he must convince himself in his mind are quite outside the system of the Universe.

The Mandala Service

The words employed during the offering of the Mandala are the following.

"Om! Bajra bhrummi ah Hum!

"On the entirely clear foundation of solid gold is *Om! bajra—rekhe-ah Hum.*

"On the middle of the outer iron wall is *Hum* and Ri-rab (Meru), "the King of Mountains. (1)

"On the East is Lus-*h*phags-po, (2)

"On the South *h*Jam-bu-*g*ling, (3)

"On the West Ba-lang-*s*pyod, (4) and

"On the North *s*Gra-mi-*s*nyan. (5)

"On either side of the Eastern continent Lus-*h*phags are Lus (6) and Lus-*h*phags. (7)

"On either side of the Southern continent are *r*Nga-yab (8) and

*r*Nga-yab-*g*zhan. (9)

"On either side of the Western continent are Yonten (10) and Lam-*m*chhog-*h*gra. (11)

"And on either side of the Northern continent are *s*Gra-mi-*s*nyan (12) and *s*Gra-mi-*s*nyan-gyi-*m*dah. (13)

"There are mountains of jewels (14), wish-granting trees (15), wish-granting cows (16), unploughed crops (17), the precious Wheel (18), the precious *Norbu* jewel (19), the precious Queen (20), the precious Minister (21), the precious Elephant (22), the precious Horse (23), the precious Battle-chief (24), the Bumpa of the great treasure (25), the Goddesses *s*geg-pa-ma (26), *h*Phreng-wa-ma (27), *g*Lu-ma (28), Gar-ma (29), Me-tog-ma (30), *b*Dug-spos-ma (31), sNang-*g*sal-ma (32), Dri-chhal-ma (33), the sun (34), moon (35), jewelled umbrella (35), the ensign of victory (37), which is entirely victorious from all directions. In the middle are the gods (38), the most accomplished and wealthy of the beings!

I offer you all these constituent parts of the Universe all complete! O! noble, kind, and holy Lama! O! tutelary *Yidam* gods of the magic circle, and all the Collections of Buddhas and Bodhisatwas!

I beg you all to receive these offerings for the benefit of the Animal beings!

I offer you O! Buddhas! the four continents and Ri-rab (Meru) adorned with the sun and moon on a foundation of incense and flowers. Let all the Animal beings enjoy happiness!

I offer you O! You whole assembly of accomplished Supreme Beings of the outside, inside, and hidden regions, the entire wealth and body of all these mythical regions. I beg you all to give us the best of all real gifts, and also the real gift of *r*Dsogs-pa-chhen-po (the mystic insight sought by the Nyingmapa)!

I offer up this fresh magic circle, through the virtue of which let no injury beset the path of purity, but let us have the grace of

N.B.—The figures in brackets correspond to those in the diagram and indicate the several points in the magic circle where the Jinas of the three times, and let us, the innumerable Animal beings, be delivered from this illusive world!

I offer up salutations, offerings, confessions of sins, and repentance. What virtue has been accumulated by myself and others, let it go to the attainment of our great end. *Idam-ratna mandala kamniryah teyami!*

"I humbly prostrate myself three times to all who are worthy of worship, with my whole heart and body."

"Tashi Shok! Let Glory Come"

In order to complete the view of this Daily Service of Offerings called:

The Presentation of Offerings or *m*CHH*od h*Bul

The Daily Service of "Presentation of Offerings"

I here give that portion of the celebration which preceded the *Mandala,* as the *Mandala* is only its concluding portion:

OM! swabhawashudha sarba dharma swabhawashudha-hang! The dwelling-place of the sphere of the supreme ok-min-*s*tug-po-*b*kod is well furnished with good foundations and adorned on every side with lotuses and jewels.

"By enunciating the word Hung! there flow out these offerings, viz., excellent sacrifice (*m*chhod-yon), cool water (zhabs-*g*sil), flowers (me-tok), incense (*b*dug-spos), lamps (mar-me), perfumed water (dri-chhab), holy food (zhal-zas), music of cymbals (rol-mo), the five sensuous gifts (*h*dod-yon-Inga), the seven kinds of jewels (rin-po-chhe-*s*na-*b*dun), the eight glorious symbols, A-dah-na of Dorje-hla-mo-bchu-trug-mchhog, *r*du-*r*di-ra of various sorts, and many other offerings of endless variety, which are pleasing to the senses, sufficient to fill all the celestial regions." (Then here with melodious voice and hands in proper attitude make the offering up of)

I. THE EIGHT ESSENTIAL OFFERINGS

The "Essential" Offerings

Nyer-*m*chho*d*—and chant—"All" the excellent offerings of every variety that are available in the three empty regions and others, I arrange with great reverence, and offer up to all the Jinas (rGyal-was) with their princes. O! I beg you to take them for the benefit of the Animal beings. *Om! sarba Tathàgatha Arghang-pra-ti-tsa swa-hah!*

"All the cool Foot-bathing water (zhab*s*-gsel) of every variety that is available in the three worlds and others, I arrange with great reverence, and offer up to all the Jinas and their princes. O! I beg you to take them for the benefit of the Animal beings. *Om! sarba Tathagatha-Padyam-pratitsa swa-hah!*

All the Flowers (me-tog) of every variety that are available in the three empty (worlds) and others, I arrange with great reverence, and offer up to all the Jinas and their princes. O! I beg you to take them for the benefit of the Animal beings. *Om! sarba Tathagata-Puh-pe pratitsa swa-hah!*

"All the Incense (*b*dug-*s*pos) of every variety that are available in the three empty (worlds) and others, I arrange with great reverence, and offer up to all the Jinas and their princes. O! I beg you to take them for the benefit of the Animal beings. *Om! sarba Tathagata Dhuh-pe pratitsa swa-hah!*

All the Lamps (*s*nang-*s*sal) of every variety that are available in the three empty (worlds) and others, I arrange with great reverence, and offer up to the victors and the princes. O! I beg you to take them for the benefit of the Animal beings. *Om! sarba Tathagata A-lo-ke pratitsa swa-hah!*

All the Scented water (dri-[illegible]hab) of every variety that are available in the three empty (worlds) and others, I arrange with great reverence, and offer up to all the victors and the princes. O! I beg you to take them for the benefit of the Animal beings. *Om! sarba Tathagata Gandhe pratitsa swa-hah!*

All the holy Food (zhal-za*s*) of every variety that are available in the three empty (worlds), I arrange with great reverence, and offer up to all the victors and princes. O! I beg you to take them for the benefit of the Animal beings. *Om! sarba Tathagate Ne-waide Pratitsa swa-hah!*

All the Music (*s*sil-*s*nyen) of every variety that are available in the three empty (worlds) and others, I arrange with great reverence, and offer up to all the victors and the princes. O! I beg you to take them for the benefit of the Animal beings. *Om! sarba Tathagata shapta pratitsa swa-hah!*"

II. THE OFFERING OF THE FIVE SENSUOUS EXCELLENT THINGS

The Five Sensuous Excellent Things

(*Dod-yon*) I here offer the best things of every variety which are most pleasing to the senses in shape and colours, to the circle of the gods with all my heart and reverence. O! please receive them and (in return) I beg you to give me the best and the highest attainment *(i.e.,*

Nirvana). *Om! sarba Tathagata Rupa kama guna badsara-" pu-dsi-te-ah Hum!*

I offer the rarest things of all the directions with pleasing voice and chaste words to the circle of the gods with all heart and reverence. O! I beg you to receive them, and I pray you to confer on me the best and highest attainment. *Om! sarba Tathagata Shapta kama guna badsara-pu-dsi-te-ah Hum!*

I offer you the old grains of sandal wood, spice (*bd*kar), *&c.*, of the best scent of every variety to the circle of the gods with all heart and reverence. O! I beg you to receive it, and I pray you to confer on me the best and highest attainment. *Om! sarba Tathagata Gandhe kar-ma guna badsara-pu-dsi-te-ah-Hum!*

I offer all the things with moisture and taste, and all the best tastes suitable to the body and mind, to the circle of the gods with great respect and reverence. O! I beg you to receive it and I pray you to confer on me the best and highest attainment. *Om! sarba Tathagata Nai-we-te-dkar-ma guna badsara-pu-dsi-te-ah Hum!*

I offer all that is pleasing and soft to the touch, and which makes the body and the mind happy, with great respect and reverence. O! I beg you to receive them, and I pray you to confer on me the best and highest attainment. *Om! sarba Tathagata Parsha kama guna bad-sara-pu-dsi-te-ah Hum!*

III. THE OFFERING OF THE SEVEN PRECIOUS THINGS

[(Rinchhen *sna-b*dun) NOTE.—"These are to be distinguished from 'The Seven Banners' (Gyaltshen sna dun) which are detailed in foot-note.[148]]

The Seven Precious Things

I offer this precious Wheel to all those that have gone to happiness, *i.e.*, the Buddhas. Let us be stopped from further rebirths in this world; and let us be able to turn the wheel of religion. *Om! sarba Tathagata Chakra ratna pu-dsi-te-ah Hum!*

I offer this precious *Norbu* jewel to all the Buddhas. O! let us be separated from hunger and poverty, and let us be possessed of accomplished wealth. *Om! sarba Tathagata Mani ratna pu-dsi-te-ah Hum!*

I offer the prècious Queen-Wife to all the Buddhas. O! let us "understand the meaning of wisdom, and let us be connected with "means and wisdom. *Om! sarba Tathagata Stiratna pu-dsi-te-ah "Hum!*

I offer the precious Minister to all Buddhas. O! let our thoughts be firm and good, and let us be acquainted with all the branches of knowledge. *Om! sarba Tathagata 'Girti' ratna pu-dsi-te-ah Hum!*

I offer the precious *Elephant* to the Buddhas. O! let us have the highest and supreme *yana* as our vehicle, and let us become acquainted with the All-knowing one. *Om! sarba Tathagata Hasti ratna pu-dsi-te-ah Hum!*

I offer the precious '*best Horse*' to all the Buddhas. Oh! let us be delivered from the rebirths of this world, and let us be possessed of miracles, power, and Buddhahood. *Om! sarba Tathagata Ashwa ratna "pu-dsi-te-ah Hum!*

"I offer thė precious *General* to all the Buddhas. Oh! let us be separated from the noisy din, and let us attain the most pleasing of sounds. *Om! sarba Tathagata Khatri-ka ratna pu-dsi-te-ah Hum*!"

IV. THE OFFERING OF THE EIGHT GLORIOUS SYMBOLS

The Eight Glorious Symbols

(Tashi-ta gye).—Hum! I offer to The Three supreme Holy Ones the precious glory of the glorious *golden umbrella* which shines over the heads of the Buddhas according to their signs and accomplishments. Let the glorious umbrella come over the heads of all the Animal beings!

I offer to the Three supreme Holy Ones, the glorious *Banner of Victory* (rgyal-mtshan), which shines over the heads of the Buddhas. Let the Animal beings gain glorious victory over the devils!

I offer to the Three supreme Holy Ones, the glorious *Golden Fish,* which shines in the eyes of Buddhas. Let the glory of the Animal beings possessed of the five eyes come!

I offer to the Three supreme Holy Ones, the glorious *conch-shell* which shines over the commands of the Buddhas. Let Animal "beings be possessed of the melodious commands of the glorious" Religion!

I offer to the Three supreme Holy Ones, the glorious *vase* of "treasure, which shines over the neck of the Buddhas. Let the Animal" beings be possessed of the undying treasure of the glorious life to come!

I offer to the Three supreme Holy Ones, the precious *lotus,* which shines over the tongue of the Buddhas. Let the Animal beings be possessed of glorious knowledge!

I offer to the Three supreme Holy Ones, glorious symbol *Sri-'bi-u,'* which shines over the heart of the Buddhas. Let the Animal beings be possessed of unchangeable piety!

I offer to the Three supreme Holy Ones, the precious glory of the precious *wheel,* which shines over the feet of the Buddhas. Let the Animal beings obtain the true path to good conduct!

(Here follows the *Mandala* service already detailed above.)

Divination by Lots

Lucky and Unlucky Days and Times, Omens

The elements of luck and chance are allowed to influence nearly every action of both lamas and laity. Each hour and day of the week possesses a lucky or unlucky character, and the days of the month according to their order introduce another set of lucky and unlucky combinations. Omen are eagerly watched for and noted.

Divination

In addition to the consideration of the foregoing influences it is an almost universal practice to take a special Divination by lot for even ordinary and most trivial affairs. Divination is done by both lamas and laity. Most laymen as well as lamas possess small divining manuals called mo or "*mo*-pe," *i.e.,* short for "mo-pecha," or "The *mo* book." These books show the portent attached to the particular number which is elicited and also the initiatory spells. Divination is commonly made by lamaic cards, by the rosary, by seeds or pebble counters; less commonly by dice, and rarely by sheep's shoulder-blades.

By Cards

The cards used for divination purposes are small oblong strips of card-board, each representing several degrees of lucky and unlucky portents suitably inscribed and illustrated, and to each of these is attached a small thread. In consulting this oracle, an invocation to a favourite deity is made, frequently the goddess Dolma, and the packet is held by the left hand on a level with the face, when, with eyes closed, one of the threads is grasped, and its attached card is drawn out. In accordance with the practice, average of three draws is considered the luck of the proposed undertaking, or the ultimate result of the sickness or the other question of fortune sought for.

Divination by the Rosary, Preliminary Spell

Mostly illiterate people practise divination by the Rosary. Some time Bon priests also practise it. The preliminary spell is:—"*gsol! ye-dhar-ma! Om-sha-sha mu-ne-ye-swa-hah! Kra-mu-ne-ye swa-hah! madah-shu-mu-ne ye-swa-hah*!" After having repeated this, breathe upon the Rosary and say "*Namo-Guru!* I bow down before the kind, merciful, and noble Lama, the three Holy Ones, the *yidam* (tutelary deity), and before all the collections of Dakinis, Religion protectors and Guardians of the Magic Circle, and I beg that you will cause the truth to descend on this lot. I also beg you, O! Religious Protectors and Guardians, Brahma, Indra, the ten religious protectors, Nanda and Takshaka, the Naga Kings, including the eight great Nagas, the sun, the eight planets, the twenty-eight constellations of stars, the twelve great Chiefs of the Injurers, and the great owners of the localities, let the true light descend on my lot and let the truth and reality appear in it."

Manipulation of Rosary

After having repeated the above, the rosary is taken in the palm and well thubbed between the two revolving palms and the hands clapped thrice. Then, closing the eyes, a portion of the rosary is seized between the thumb and finger of each hand, and opening the eyes the intervening beads are counted from each end in threes. According to the remainder being 1, 2, or 3 in successive countings depends the result. Thus:

Results

(1) *If One as a remainder comes after One* as the previous remainder, everything is favourable in life, in friendship, in trade, &c.

(2) *If Two comes after Two* it is bad:—"The cloudless sky will be suddenly darkened. There will be loss of wealth. So Rim-*h*gro must be done repeatedly and the gods must be worshipped, which are the only preventions."

(3) *If Three comes after Three* it is very good:—"Prosperity is at hand in trade and everything."

(4) *If Three comes after One* it is good:—"Rice plants will grow on sandy hills, widows will obtain husbands, and poor men will obtain riches."

(5) *If One comes after Two* it is good:—"Every wish will be fulfilled and riches will be found. If one travels to a dangerous place one will escape every danger."

(6) *If One comes after Three* it is good:—"God's help will always be at hand, therefore worship the gods."

(7) *If Two comes after Three* it is not very good, it is middling:—"Legal proceedings will come."

(8) *If Three comes after Two* it is good:—"Turquoise fountains will spring out and fertilize the grounds. Unexpected food will be obtained. Escape is at hand from any danger."

(9) *If Two comes after One* it is bad:—"Contagious disease will come. But if the gods be worshipped and the devils be propitiated, then it will be prevented."

By Seeds or Pebbles

The most ordinary mode of divination is by counters of seeds or pebbles in sets of 15 or 21. These may be used with or without a dice-board. If a dice-board be used, it consists of small squares drawn on paper to the number of 15 or of 21, and each square has got a number within a circle corresponding to a number in the *mo-pe* or divination book. The counters are white and black pebbles or seeds, only one black one to each series. After the invocation to the special deity and shaking up and mixing all the seeds in the closed palm, they are then told out between the forefinger and thumb of the still closed palm on to the squares in the numerical order of the latter, and the number on which the black seed comes out determines, by means of the *mo-pe* book, the divination result of the particular fortune sought for.

15	14	13	12	11
6	7	8	9	10
5	4	3	2	1

In Fifteen: "Gya-nak-sman-chhu"

The set of fifteen squares is called "Gya-nak-*s*man-chhu," or "The Chinese medicinal water." It consists of a triples series of five squares, with the numbers arranged as in the above sketch. But properly, as its name implies, the seeds should be dropped into a vessel of water and no dice-board is thus needed. This divination is used especially in sickness, hence it is called "medicinal." But the manual most commonly consulted for the prognosis and treatment of sickness is the "Hlamo-*b*rgya*d*-*r*tsi*s*," or "The Account of the Eight Goddesses."

This book gives a fixed prognosis and prescription of remedial worship for each of the 30 days of the month in series of fours. Thus, for its reference only the day of the month is needed and no dice or seeds are necessary. Another manual named "du*s*-tshod-*r*tsis" gives similar information in regard to the particular time of the day of the occurrence in question. These two manuals are, however, considered only Astrological books and not "*mo*" or divination manuals.

In Twenty-One

The set of twenty-one squares is called "The Twenty-one Dolmas", after the twenty-one forms of that obliging goddess.

Image of Dolma

17	18	19	20	21
16	15	14	13	12
7	8	9	10	11
6	5	4	3	2 1

A figure of the goddess is given above the centre of the diagram, who is specially invoked in this divination. The numbers run as in the diagram here given. As a sample of the oracles are given here a few of the divination-results from Dolma's series. If the black seed falls on 1, 2, 8 or 9, the divination is as follows:

No. 1. *The Jewel.*If you do not go to sea then you will get the jewel. For merchants' and thieves' adventures it is good. For your own house and soil it is excellent. But, if you are sick, it is somewhat bad. For travelling you should first feed people and dogs. You will obtain a son and get temporal power. Your wishes will ultimately be obtained. You have as an enemy a thief.

No. 2. *The Turquoise Spring*. The dried valley will yield springs and plants will become verdant, and timely rain will fall. The absent will soon return. Do the *d*pang-*b*sto*d* worship of the Enemy God (sgra-lha) and the worship of your special god (*m*chhod lha). These worships are good for marriage.

No. 8. *The Conch Chaitya*. In the supreme *Ok-min* heavens it is good for the lower animals, in the three worlds of existence is long life and auspicious time. Your desires will be realized. Life is good. If you are ill, whitewash the Chaitya and worship in the Temple. The enemy is present in the vicinity. For merchants are treaters the time is rather late. If they are careful no serious loss will happen. It is very good for health.

No. 9. *The Invalid.*—If an actual invalid it is due to the demon of the grand-parents. Agriculture will be bad. Cattle will suffer. To prevent this, offer the "black" cake of the three heads (gtor nag mgo sum) and do Yang-kuk or "calling for Luck." For your wishes, business, and credit it is a bad outlook. For sickness do "Tse-dub" or "Obtaining Long Life." Mend the road and repaint the "*Mani*" stones. Household things and Life are bad. For these read the "do-mang" also Du-Kar and Dok. The ancestral devil is to be suppressed by Srī-*g*non. This is not the time to take on the enemy. Now conflicts must be avoided. Long journies must not be undertaken.

The titles of the other numbers somewhat indicate the nature of their contents, viz.

3. Golden *Dorje*.
4. Painted vase.
5. Turquoise parrot.
6. Verdant plants.
7. Lady carrying child.
10. White Lion.
11. Golden vase.
12. Turquoise Dragon.
13. Garuda.
14. Tigress.
15. Sun and Moon.
16. Enemy with bow and arrows.
17. Fiendess with red mouth.
18. *h*gong king-devil.
19. Peacocks
20. Glorious white couch.
21. The great king.

In Twenty-Eight

The above are the forms of dice-boards used by the laity and the lower clergy. The more respectable lamas use a circular disc with twenty-eight divisions in the form of three concentric lotus flowers, each of the petals of the two outer whorls bearing a number which corresponds to a number in the divining manual which is called "Las-*b*yed *m*thong-ba kun-*l*dan," or "The one who sees all actions." The margin of the disc is surrounded by flames. This more artistic arrangement. As a sample of this oracle are given here the detail of No. 1 and list of the presiding divinities of the other number.

No. 1, *Bhagawan* (a title of Buddha). "You are of the wise class, or if not, you will get a wise son. Your god needs to be worshipped fully, and what you desire will be realized, and you will obtain long life and freedom from sickness. And if you are a male this blessing will last for nine years. If you are a female then, nine monks must be engaged to read the nyithi, and four monks must do the *dok-pa,* clapping of hands to drive away the evil spirits; for in the south is a King Demon who is angry with you and your heart is disturbed and your temper bad. On this account do the worship of the King Demon and wear his charm. Your children will be affected by evil spirits but there is no chance of their death. You may lose your money or your ornaments. Your valuable goods are likely to go, therefore do the worship of *Nor-thub* or 'the obtaining of wealth.'

The names of the divinities of the other numbers, which give some indication of the nature of the divination, are:

2. Cheresi.
3. Ugyen Rimbochhe.
4. Dolma.
5. Chakna Dorje.
6. Yeshe Norbu.
7. Chandan.
8. Indra.
9. Manjusri.
10. Dorje leg-pa.
11. Sirge Shashi.
12. Dorje Gyatham.
13. Yuduk Ngonmo.
14. Tongngan Lhamo.
15. Tamchhen Naypo.
16. Lungpa Kyithik.
17. Durpag Nag.
18. Garwa Bishu.
19. Gyacha kua.
20. Nad-*b*dak Remati, God of sickness.
21. Tsunpa.
22. Chhui Lhamo.
23. Tuk-zig-pa.
24. Sipi Kukhor.
25. Damcha Dzema.
26. Dreo Dagyak.
27. Purnang Ukpu.
28. Ngag-nag.

By Dice

There two types of Dice used in divination and fortune-telling viz., (a) ordinary ivory or bone dice marked with black dots from 1 to 6 as in European dice, and (b) a solitary wooden cube, on each of the six sides of which is carved a letter corresponding to a similar letter in the manual.

Ordinary Ivory Dice

The ordinary ivory dice are used in a set of three with the *Hlamo. Mo* or "The Goddess Divination Manual," which provides for results from 3 to 18. These three dice are usually thrown on the book itself from the bare hand after having been shaken up in the closed palm.

Wooden Dice

For divination by the manual of Manjusri (Jam-*d*pal), The solitary wooden dice is used. It contains on its six sides the six letters, compound or otherwise, of Manjusri's spell, viz.

A	RA	PA	TSA	NA	DI

The wood of this dice should be made of either Manjusri's sacred "bla" tree, or *chandan,* or rose-wood, or if none of these woods are available, then the dice should be made of conch-shell or glass. In the manual key to this dice, the portent of each letter is divided into the following sections, viz. House, Favours, Life, Medical, Enemy, Visitors, Business, Travel, Lost Property, Wealth, Sickness, &c., which cover all the ordinary objects for which the oracle is consulted. As an example I here extract the portents of A:

'A' is the best of all for great lamas and for lay officers, and what you will perform will have a good result. For low people it means a little sadness therefore worship your favourite god.

House section. All your household will be happy and lucky, and for a time your house will be safe; but where the cattle dwell, there a thief and rogue will perhaps come. To avoid this repeat, or get repeated (by lamas), 10,000 times the spell (*g*zung) of Arya Marici Phagpa-hod-zer-chan-ma—

Favours section. You wish favours. You will not get them at once. You will get them gradually. To remove the difficulty in the way of getting these repeat, or get repeated, 100,000 times the gzung of gra-lnga, and also of Devi lo-gyon-ma this latter is *Om! pisha-tsi-par-na-sha-wa-ri sarba dso-la-ta-sha-ma-na-ye swa-ha!*, and do the *Dug-kar* with its contained *b*zlog *b*sgyur (clapping of hands) celebration.

Life (Srog). This is good. But the *g*don demon from the east and south came with a blue and black article you got. To clear away this cloud do, or get done, 100,000 grib-sel and do the Naga worship and read, or get read, 1,000 times Sherab-Nyingpo.

Medical. Taking the medicine prescribed for you for a long time secretly you will recover. Also burn a lamp nightly from sunset to sunrise as an offering to the gods.

Enemy. You will not suffer, as your god is strong and will protect you.

Visitors. probable. They are coming, or news of their visit will soon be received.

Business. If you quickly do business it will be profitable—delay will be unprofitable.

Travel. The actual leaving of your house will be difficult, but if you persevere you will travel safely.

Lost property. If you go to the north-west you will get the lost "property, or news of it.

The Gamble of Rebirth

For determining the successive regions and grades of one's future rebirths. Fifty-six or more squares of about 2 inches a side are painted side by side in contrasting colours on a large sheet of cloth, thus giving a chequered area like an ordinary draught or chess board This is a peculiar application of the dice. Each of these squares represents a certain phase of existence in one or other of the six regions of rebirth, and on it is graphically depicted a figure or scene expressive of the particular state of existence in the world of man, or beast, or god, or in hell, etc. Each square bears in its centre the name of its particular form of existence, and it also contains the names of six other possible states of rebirth from this particular existence, the names of each of these grades of rebirth being preceded by one or other of the following six letters: A, S, R, G, D, Y, which are also borne on the six faces of the wooden cube. This forms the solitary dice for this gamble.

The seeker is in human existence. For him the dice is thrown, and the letter which turns up determines the region of the next rebirth *(see* the list in next paragraph). Then proceeding from it the dice is again thrown. The turned-up letter indicates the next state of rebirth from this new existence, and so on from square to square *ad infinitum.*

For the lamaic layman there thus appear only six states of rebirth ordinarily possible, viz.

A. *s*ngags-lam *h*gro, *i.e.*, the path of the sorcerer.

S. Nyin tshog*s* lam.

R. dud *h*gro or the "bent goer's," *i.e.*, the beasts.

G. Bonpo lok chhos, *i.e.*, a follower of the Bon or pre-lamaic form of religion in Tibet. It is called Lok chhos or "the reverse religion," because much of their ritual is the reverse of the lamaic form; thus chaityas are circumambulated in the reverse direction, and prayer wheels are turned in the reverse way and the "*om mani*" is repeated backward, and the swastika has its ends turned in the reverse fashion.

D. Mutogpa, *i.e.*, as an Indian heretic.

Y. Sridpai-bar-do—a ghostly state.

The dice accompanying the copy of this board seems to have been loaded so as to show up the letter Y, which gives a ghostly existence, and thus necessitates the performance of many expensive rites to counteract so undesirable a fate.

The Grand Coup

Extra to the ordinary six states of possible rebirth are the extra-ordinary states of rebirth to be obtained by the grand *coup* of turning up the *A* five times in succession or the *S* 13 times in succession. The former event means direct rebirth in the paradise of Padma Sambhava and his mythical Buddha *Kuntu zangpo* (Skt. *Samanta bhadra),* while the latter event is rebirth immediately into the grander paradise of the coming Buddha *Champa* (Skt. *Maitreya).*

The Lamaic Zadkiel

There are four or five versions of forecasts for each year of the twelve-year cycle in addition to a separate set for each year of the sixty-year cycle Every year has its general character for good or evil foretold in the astrological books, but like most oracular utterances, these prophecies are couched in rather ambiguous terms. There is thus considerable latitude allowed for accounting for most phenomena. In 1890, during that great visitation of locusts which swarmed over India and into plague of locusts was down in the lamaic forecast for that year.

I examined the old printed books and found that in one of the more common versions of the twelve-year cycle a plague of *chhaga* was foretold for that year, and *chhaga* is a short form of the word for "locust." It seemed that it could not come out in the forecast more often than about once in six to twelve years.

Talismans and Amulet Charms

Talismans as Curative Medicine

Amulet-charms are talismans, are innumerable. There are special sorts for nearly every kind of disease, accident or misfortune, and the eating of the paper on which a charm has been written is an ordinary form of combatting disease. The letters used in such cases are called *za-zig* or "Eatable letters," and are magic sentences printed or written on paper in what is called the "Fairy" character—an old form of Devanagari. In other cases merely the washings of the reflection of the writing in a mirror constitutes the physic. Thus to cure the evil eye as shown, by symptoms of mind wandering and demented condition—called "byad-bgrol"—It is ordered as follows:—Write with Chinese ink on a piece of wood the particular letters, and smear the writing over with myrobalams and saffron as varnish, and ever 29 days reflect this inscribed wood in a mirror. During reflection wash the face of the mirror with beer and collect a cupful of such beer and drink it in nine sips. This ritual must be followed without break.

Amulets

Every individual has always one or more of these charms, usually folded up into little cloth-covered packets tied around with coloured threads in geometrical pattern and worn around the neck. Others are kept in small metallic cases called "ka-o." They are fastened to the girdle or sash, and others are affixed overhead in the house or tent to ward off lightning, hail, and other natural calamities and for cattle special charms are read and sometimes pasted on the walls of the stalls.

General Form of Charm

Most of these charms against accident, disease, and ill-fortune are in the form. They are is called the bLa-ma *d*gongs-*h*dus, or "the Assembly of the Hearts of the Lamas," as it is believed to contain the essence of the most powerful religious aphorisms. It consists of a series of concentric circles of spells surrounded by flames, amid which in the four corners are the symbols of (a) a *dorje* or thunderbolt's sceptre; (b) the precious trifid-jewel; (c) a lotus flower and (d) a flaming dagger with a *dorje* hilt. The translation of the inscribed aphorisms is here given.

In the Outmost Circle.—"Guard the Body, Mind and Speech of this charm-holder! *Rakhya, rakhya, kuruye swaha! Angtadyatha! Om muni muni mahamuniye swaha.*" (Here follows "The Buddhist Creed":—)

"OM! Ye dharma hetu parbhava
Hetum teshan Tathagato
Hyatha data teshan chayo nirodha
Evam vadi Maha Sramana."[149]

(Here follows the Dhyani Buddhas:—) *"Birotsana Om bajra Akshobha Hung, Ratna Smbhava Hri, Bargudhara Hri, Amoga Siddha Ah!"*

In Second Circle.—"Om! nama Samanta Buddhanam, Wama Samanta Dharmanam, nama Samanta Sangghanam. Om Sititabatrai. Om Bimala, Om Shadkara, Om Brahyarigar bajra ustsikhatsa krawarti Sarbayana manta mula barma hana dhanamha. Namkilaniba makriayena keni chatkramtamtata sarban ratsin ratsin dakhinda bhinda tsiri tsiri giri giri mada mada hung hung phat phat."

In Third Circle.—"Guard the Body, Mind and Speech of this charm-holder! *Mama* rakya rakhya kuruye swaha. (Here follow the letters of the alphabet:—) 'Ang, a, a, i, τ, u, u, ri, ri, li, li, e, ai, o, au, ang, a, ka, kh, g, gh, ng, ts, tsh, ds, dsa, nv, ta, th, d, da, na, t, th, d, dh, n, p, ph, b, bh, m, y, r, 1, w, sh, sh, s, h, khy!"

In Fourth Circle.—"Hung, Hung," &c.

In Fifth Circle.—"Hri, Hri," &c.

In Sixth Circle.—*"Om! A! Hung! Hri! Guru! Deva!' Dakkini! Sarbasiddhipala Hung! A!"*

As most of these specific charms are evidently derived from ancient Indian sources, these being of the nature of Sympathetic Magic, probably dating back to Vedic times, are given several examples:

Thus to make the

Charm protective against Bullets and Weapons,

The directions are as these:—With the blood of a wounded man draw the annexed monogram (DD) and insert in the vacant space in the centre of the aforesaid print of "The Assembly of the Hearts of the Lamas." The sheet should then be folded and wrapped in a piece of *red* silk, and, tied with a piece of string, be worn around the neck or an unexposed part of your breast immediately next the skin, and never removed.

Charm for Leprosy. On a piece of paper made from the bark of the poisonous laurel write with a mixture of the blood of the individual and the ulcerous discharge and urine of a leper the monogram (?CHCH) and insert into the centre of the print, and fold up and wear around neck.

Charm for Clawing Animals (i.e., Tiger, Cats, Bear). On a miniature knife write with a mixture of *myrobalams* and musk water the monogram (?Zah) and tie up in the print, &c. (Here the knife seems to represent the animal's claw).

For Dog-bite. With the blood of a leopard write the monogram Hri and insert into the print, and fold up and enclose within a piece of leopard skin and wear around neck. (The leopard preys on dogs).

For Cholera (or "vomiting, purging, and cramps"). With the dung of a black horse and black sulphur and musk water write the monogram (? za) and insert in the print and fold up in a piece of snake's skin and wear. (The dung may represent the purging, the black colour the deadly character, and the snake-skin the virulence of the disease).

For Small-pox. With the juice of the Som (?pine) tree write the monogram (?OM), and sprinkle over it some pulverised bone of a man who has died from small-pox, and insert, &c.

For Domestic Bickering. Write the monogram (?RE) and insert in the print and fold up and bind with a thread made of the mixed hairs of a dog, goat, and sheep, and enclose in a mouse's skin. (This seems to represent union of domestic elements).

For External Quarrels. With the blood of a bearded goat write the monogram (?TAMGI) and insert in print and wrap in a piece of a horse's skin and enclose in an otter's skin.

For Poison.—With blood of a peacock write the monogram (?GRA) with the moustache of a hare.

For Slander and Scandal. 'With earth taken from the travellers' *sarai* (halting place) fire, or if this is not procurable, with some of the menses of a courtesan, write the monogram (?ZOMA) and insert in print and fold up, (Travellers' *sarai* fires and courtesans are regarded as especial places of gossip and scandalmongers respectively).

To cleanse from Sin of Perjury. Write the monogram (?SA) and insert in print and fold up with the ear of a hare, the tongue of a hyaena, and the ear of a sow, and wrap in a piece of the robe of an unburied corpse, and wear it below the waist on in the shoe.

For Bad Dreams. With the tears or with the urine of a person possessed of second-sight write the monogram (ZI) and insert in print and bind up in piece of the wearer's own cloth with one of his own eyelashes, and pass the parcel through the hands of persons of nine different castes.

For Bad Omens. With blood of an owl write the monogram (?AMRA) and insert in print along with monkey's hair, and bind in a piece of fox's skin.

For Fever. With cold camphor and musk water write the monogram (?LO) and insert, &c.

For Cold. With the three hot spices (black pepper, long pepper, and ginger) and water write monogram and insert, &c.

For Lightning and Hail. Write the monogram (?GA or CHA) with female menstrual blood and insert in print and bind in a piece of the skirt of a widow.

For the Nagas. Write the monogram (s) on a piece of birch-bark,[150] with a paste of musk and sweet marsh flag and incense, and insert in print and bind in a frog's skin and wear. (Note here the use of a water-plant and frog's skin in relation to the deities, of water—the Nagas).

For the Yakshas. On a piece of red silk write the monogram (?TI) and insert in print and wrap up with filings of the fire precious things and a small dough image of your enemy, and wear (the Yakshas are associated with wealth and also guardianship).

For Seminal Emissions. With a ruby write the monogram and insert in print, and bind it with a blue and red thread spun by a virgin maid and wear round neck.

For Bad Planets. With the ashes of a cremated human body which had died on an unlucky day (e.g., died on a Sunday or a Saturday) made into paste with water, write the monogram place it on a small sheet of copper, which has been perforated in nine spots, and wrap up with a small wooden image of a penis and wear. (The nine perforations represent the nine planets of Hindu astronomy. The use of this charm is very common in the Tsang province of Tibet, where the wooden image is worn externally).

For Theft. With the blood of a thief or a black dog, write the monogram (?LI) and insert in print and wrap inside a mouse-skin and tie to a post in the house. (The mouse is a thief, and the charm seems to be on the principle of setting a thief to catch a thief.)

For Foul Smells. On white silk, with a paste of the six perfumes, write the monogram SAM and insert in print and fold up and bind on crown of head. Then the Jinas of the ten directions will assist and the bad smells will disappear and prove innocuous.

For Fire-side Cooking Smells offensive to House Gods. With the blood of a hybrid bull-calf write the monogram GAU and insert in the print and fold up in a piece of the skin of a hedge-hog.

GARUDA CHARM AGAINST PLAGUE AND OTHER DISEASES

Charm Against Plagues

This charm carries of a monster figure of the Garuda, The King of Birds, with a snake in its mouth, and each of its outstretched plumes bears a text. This charm also contains the "Buddhist Creed." The charm-inscription runs:

> "*Om! Bhrum satrirbad namkhamjamram,*
>
> *Om! bisakhrilimili hala, swaha!*
>
> *Om! bisakhrilimilihalaya skachig!*
>
> Guard the holder *(i.e.,* the wearer) of this from all the host of diseases, of evil spirits and injuries, including contagious diseases, sore-throat, cough, rheumatism, the black 'rgyughg-yel,' *h*brum-bu, and all kinds of plague of the body, speech, and mind!
>
> *Ye dharma hetu prabhava.*
>
> *Hetum teshan Tuthagato.*

Hyatha-data teshantsayo nirodha.

Evam radi Mala Sramana.

Habatse habatse hum sod.
Suru suru hum sod.
Sukarjuka hum sod.
Sati karur hum sod.
Kularakhyi hum sod.

Guard the holder.
Om! thamitharati sadunte dswaramghaye swaha!"

Here the fierce demon Tamdin, clad in human and animal skins, bears on his front a disc with concentric circles of spells.

SCORPION CHARM AGAINST INJURY BY DEMONS

Charm against Injury by Demons

This charm is in the form of a scorpion, whose mouth, tipped by flames, forms the apex of the picture. On its shoulder are seated the especial demons to be protected against—*vide* illustration in plate XVI, for details. The inscription runs:

"*Ayama durur tsa shana zhamaya.*
Hum! Om! A! Hung! Artsignirtsig!
Namo Bhagaiwati Hum! Hum! Phat!"

"A guard against all the injuries of '*r*gyalpo,' 'drimo' (a malignant demon specially injuring women), '*b*tsan' (or red demons), 'sa-dag' (or earth-demons), *k*lu (or *naga),* including '*g*nyan' (a plague-causing subordinate of the *naga).*

"Against injury by these preserve!"

The figures are hemmed in by the mystic syllables:—"*Jsa! Hung! Hung! Bam! Ilo!*"

CHARM AGAINST DOG-BITE

Charm against Dog-bite

The huge Tibetan mastiffs are let loose at night as watch-dogs, and roaming about in a ferocious state are a source of much alarm to travellers, who therefore carry the following charm against dog-bite. It consists of a picture of a dog fettered and muzzled by a chain, terminated by the mystic and all-powerful *dorje.* It contains the following inscribed Sanskrit *mantras* and statements:—"The mouth of the blue[151] dog is bound beforehand! *Om-riti sri-ti swahah! Om-riti sri-ti swahah!"* (this is again written twice along the body of the dog).

"*Om! badsara ghanana kara kukuratsa sal sal nan marya smugs smugs kukuratsa khaihamtsa le tsa le mun mun sar sar rgyug kha tha mu chhu chhing hehhang ma raya rakkhya rakkhya!* (It is) fixed! fixed!"

CHARM AGAINST EAGLES AND BIRDS OF PREY

Against Eagles

When eagles play havoc with the young herds of the pastoral Bhotiyas of the Sikkim uplands and Tibet. for this the people use the charm, They tie it up near their huts. The central figure is a manacled bird, representation of the eagle or other bird of prey; and around it is the following text:

"A guard against all injuries of the covetous, sky-soaring Monarch Bird. (It is) fixed! fixed! *Om smege smege bhumbhum ngu!"*

CHARM FOR KILLING ONE'S ENEMY

The full details are here translated:

Charms for Killing One's Enemy

"*Om!* Salutation to the revered Manjusri!" The necessary materials for the killing of one's enemy are the following:

1. An axe with three heads, the right of which is bull-headed, the left snake-headed, and the middle one pig-headed.

2. On the middle head a lamp is to be kept.

3. In the pig's mouth an image of a human being made of wheaten flour (a *linga).* The upper part of the body is black and the lower part red. On the side of the upper part of the body draw the figure of the eight great planets, and on the lower part of the body the twenty-eight constellations of stars. Write also the eight parkha, the nine mewa, the claws of the Garuda in the hands, the wing of the eagles and the snake tail.

4. Hang a bow and an arrow on the left and load him with provisions on the back. Hang an owl's feather on right and a rook's feather on left; stick a piece of the poison tree on the upper part of the body, and surround him with red swords on all sides. Then place a red Rgyangbu wood on the right, a yellow one on the left, a black one in the middle, and many blue ones on several places.

5. Then sitting in quiet meditation recite the following:

Hung! This axe with a bull's head on the right will repel all the injuries of the *s*ngagpas and Bonpos—sorcerers; the snake on the left will repel all the classes of plagues; the pig head in the middle will repel the *sa-dag* and other earth-demons; the *linga* image in the mouth will repel all the evil spirits without remainder and the lamp on the head will repel the evil spirits of the upper regions. O! the axe will pierce the heart of the angry enemy and also of the hosts of evil spirits!!!

Hung! The upper body of the axe is black. It will repel the hosts of *b*dud demons; the 'lower part of the body which is red will repel the mamos, she-fiends, and diseases; the eagle-winged part of the body will repel the eight classes of demons; the snake-tailed body will repel the sa-dag, naga and the gnyan demons; the Guruda-clawed hands will repel the hosts of she-demons; the arrow on the right will repel all the inauspicious cases, and the bow in the left will repel all the hosts of the The-u-brang demon. O! the axe will tear of apart the angry enemy and all the hosts of the injuring demons!!!

Hung! the red nam-kha on the right will repel all the hosts of *b*tsan; the yellow one on the left will repel the injuries of the-*H*byungpo demons; the *m*dah on the right will repel the injuries of the *b*dud demons; the khram-shing on the back will repel the injuries of mamo she-demons, and the *H*phang on the left the *b*dud she-demons. O! the axe will cleave the angry, enemy and all the hosts of the injuring demons!!!

Hung! the owl's feather on the right will repel the eighty unlucky signs; the rook's feather on the left will repel the drowning misery; the stick on the waist will repel the former enemies; the surroundings of swords will overcome the future enemies, and the provisions on the back will expel all desires and lusts.

Hung! O! the axe adorned with the figures of the eight planets will push away the *Grzah-bdud*, the planet demon, and the twenty-eight constellations of stars will repel the injuries of the bad stars.

Hung! the axe with the nine mewa repel as follows:—(1) The white mewa repel the The-u-brang demon; (2) the black one repel the Ro-*h*dod demon; (3) the indigo-coloured one repel the blackest misery; (4) the green repel the Nagas and the evil spirits; (5) the yellow repel the *r*gyal-po; (6) the white repel the Gongpo; (7) the red repel the Yugdor; (8) the red repel the Gyang-gral, and (9) the white repel the Hlag-chhad demon. O! the axe will tear apart the enemies and the hosts of injuring and eating demons.

Hung! Kye! Kye! the eight parkha which surround the axe repel in this way:—The Li-*d*mar riding on a fowl will repel the injuries of mamo she demons, the khon-*l*chags riding on a *s*dig-*s*brul snake will repel the sa-*b*dag, Na*g*a and *g*Nyan; the Da-*d*kar riding on a fowl will repel the injuries of swords and other cutting tools; the khen-*r*gan riding on a dragon will repel the hosts of *r*Gyalpos; the kham-nag riding on a crocodile will repel the hosts of naga; the Gyan-ri-riding on a bull will repel the injuries of *s*Ngag*s*pa sorcerers; the zin-shing riding on an ass will repel the hosts of evil spirits, and the zon-*r*lung riding on a mule will cleave all the demons of the cemetery. O! the axe will smash the enemies and the hosts of the injuring and eating demons.

Hung! oh! you tiger and vulture-headed of the shing-khams (tree-region)! I beg you to repel the enemies.

O! you snake and horse-headed of the southern me-kham*s* (fire-regions)! I beg you to repel the enemies.

O! you bird and monkey-headed of the western *l*chag*s*-kham*s* "(iron-region)! I beg you to tear the enemies.

O! you pig and rat-headed of the northern sa-kham*s* (earth-region)! I beg you to cleave the enemies.

O! you four *g*shed with the heads of bull, sheep, dog, and dragon! I beg you to push the enemies.

O! Axe! cleave the heads of the enemies and all the hosts of the injuring evil spirits.

This most powerful axe will split the hardest caves, dry up the mightiest oceans, break down the tallest trees, flatten the powerful iron knock down the strongest man, kill the biggest cattle, and destroy all the most gigantic evil spirits. Now, overtake the injuring evil spirits and the enemies.

This all-powerful axe will bring everything to complete extermination and defeat whoever challenges. Now, go on to them, tearing apart whatsoever comes in your way!

May you cause this dispenser of gifts to be separated from lust; may you not break the true commands of the '*s*ngag*s*-*h*chhang,' or the mantra-holder, and the holy orders of the three Holy Ones. Separate all injuries of enemies from the dispenser of gifts. Let my (yoga or *r*nal-*h*byorpa) desires be fulfilled. Pray carry out all the works that are here entrusted to you.

O! you three-headed one with a black body! now promise that you will comply with the orders.

Upset all the bad dreams and unlucky signs;

,,	,,	80,000	kinds of evil spirits;	
,,	,,	424	,,	bad deeds;
,,	,,	720	,,	diseases;
,,	,,	360	,,	mind-distractions;
,,	,,	8	,,	untimely deaths.

Let glory come! *Tashi-shok!*

"Sarba-mangalam!"

Other Contrivances for the Same

During the Sikkim expedition of 1888, near Mt. Paul on the Tukola ridge, where the final attack of the Tibetans was made, there was found one of the mystic contrivances for the destruction of the enemy. It consisted of an obliquely carved piece of wood, about 14 inches long, like a miniature screw-propeller of a steamer, and acted like the tan of a wind-mill. It was admittedly a charm for the destruction of the enemy. And on it was written a long, unintelligible Bon *Mantra* of the kind called *zhang-zhung,* followed by a call for the assistance of the fierce deities Tarn-din, Vajra-pani and the Garuda, and concluding with *"phat! phat"*—Break! Destroy!

And for torturing one's enemy short of death there is the same popular practice as obtains amongst occidentals, namely, of making a little clay image of the enemy and thrusting pins into it.

The Prayer Flags

The Luck-Flags, Origin of Luck-flag

Lung-ta,[152] literally "*the airy horse*" which, Pegasus-like, is supposed to carry the luck of the individual through the air in every direction wished for the most extensively used of all the so-called "prayer-flags," or *Da-cho,*[153] is that for Luck, and called . This practice has something in common with the ancient Hindu rite of "The raising of Indra's Banner" *(Dhwaja).*[154] It seems to be like "the prayer-wheel," a mystic perversion of one of the earlier symbols of Buddhist mythology. In the Buddhist scriptures there constantly occurs the metaphor of "turning the Wheel of the Law" with reference to Buddha's preaching, and this figure of have speech seems to suggested to the lamas, who are ever ready to symbolise trifles realistically, their materialistic invention of the prayer-wheel, whereby every individual may "turn the Wheel of the Law" conveniently. In like manner the "Airy Horse of Luck" seems to me to have its origin in the Jewel-Horse of the Universal Monarch, such as Buddha was to have been had he cared for worldly grandeur.

The Jewel-Horse carries its rider. Pegasus-like, through the air in whatever direction wished for, and thus it seems to have become associated with the idea of realization of material wishes, and especially wealth and jewels. This horse also forms the *Vahan* or throne-support of the mythical Dhyani Buddha named *Ratna Sambhava,* or "the *Jewel*-born One," who is often represented symbolically by a jewel. And as evidence of this identity we find in many of the *Lung-ta* flags that the picture of a jewel takes the place of the horse which is not figured. It is also notable that the mythic people of the northern continent, over whom presides Kuvera, or Vaisravana, the God of *Wealth,* are "horse-faced." The flags are printed on the unglazed tough country paper, and are obtainable on purchase from the lamas, but no lama is necessarily needed for the actual planting of the flag and its attendant rites. *Lung-ta-flag* when planted is said to be *dar-ba.*

These flags are of four sorts, viz.

Lung-ta

I. The *Lung-ta,* proper,[155] it is of almost square form, about 4 to 6 inches long contains in the centre the figure of a horse with the mystic jewel *Norbu* on its back. It is hung upon the ridges of the houses and in the vicinity of dwellings. The printed contents of this sort of flag vary somewhat in the order in which the deified lamas are addressed, some giving the first place to Guru-Rinpochhe, while others give it to Manjusri, but all have the same general form, with the horse bearing the Norbu jewel in the centre and in the four corners the names of the tiger, lion, garuda, and dragon. A translation of one of these is here given:

"Hail I *Wagishwari mum! (i.e.,* yellow
Manjuri's spell).
TIGER. Hail! to the jewel in the lotus! Hung! LION.
(*i.e.,* Avalokita's spell).
Hail! to the holder of the Dorje (or thunderbolt)! Hung! *(i.e.,*
Vajrapani's spell).
Hail! to Vajra-satwa (The Diamond Souled one!)
Hail! *Amarahnihdsiwantiye swahah.*
(The above is in Sanskrit. Here follows in Tibetan.)
Here! Let the above entire collection (of deities whose spells
have been given) prosper ...... (here is inserted the year
of birth of the individual), and also prosper—
the *Body (i.e.,* to save from sickness),
the *Speech (i.e.,* to give victory in disputations),
and the *Mind (i.e.,* to obtain all desires);
GARUDA. of this year holder (above specified) DRAGON.
and may Buddha's doctrine prosper!"

The Defensores Fidei of Lamaism

It is to be noted that herein are invoked through their spells the Rig*s*-*g*sum *m*gonpo or the three great spiritual protectors *(defensores fidei)* of lamaism, viz.

1. *Manjusri,* conveys wisdom.
2. *Avalokita,* saves from hell and all fears.
3. *Vajrapani,* saves from accident and all bodily injuries, and in addition to the above are given the spells of—
4. *Vajra Satwa,* who purifies the soul from sin; and
5. *Amitayus,* who confers long life.

The Worship for the Planting of the Luck-Flags

Worship for Luck-Flag

Planting of the Luck-flags is a ritual for which there is a lamaic worship. And it is advised to be done whenever one feels unhappy and down in luck through injury by the earth-demons, & c. It is called "The great statue of Lungta," and is as follows:—

In that place are the demons who injure the life, body, power and the airy horse. The *b*dud, who commands them, lives in the northern region; he is a yellow man with heads of solid gold, holding a yellow tapestry (ba-den) on his right and a demon's rope on his left. O! Golden-headed demon! Accept these gifts and call back all the injuring demons.

"*Kye! Kye!* In the boundary of the south-eastern horizon there is a yellow dragon-headed man; he is the injuring demon, to whom I offer this ransom. O! Dragon-headed demon! Accept this gifts and call back all the injuring demons.

"*Kye! Kye!* In the boundary of the south-western horizon there is a yellow sheep-headed woman; she is the injuring demoness to whom I offer this ransom. O! Sheep-headed demon! Accept this ransom and call back all the injuring demons.

"*Kye! Kye!* In the boundary of the north-western horizon there is a yellow dog-headed man; he is the injuring demon to whom I offer this ransom. O! Dog-headed demon! Accept this ransom and call back all the injuring demons.

"*Kye! Kye!* In the boundary of the north-eastern horizon there is a yellow bull-headed woman; she is the injuring demoness to whom I offer this ransom. O! Bull-headed demoness! Accept this ransom and call back all the injuring demons!

O! Upset all the injuring evil spirits!

O! " " disagreeable demons!

O! " " demons who injure the life, body, power and the airy horse!

O! " " wandering demons!

O! " " ill-luck of bad 'airy-horses'!

O! " " bad and frightful goblins!

O! " " unfavourable circumstances!

O! " " openings of the sky!

O! " " " " earth!

O! " " injuries of bad demons!

O! May we be separated from all kinds of injuries and be favoured with the real gift, which we earnestly seek!"

"'May virtue increase!' '*Ge-leg-phel!*'

'Glory!' '*Tashi!*' '*Swaha!*'"

The magic of lamaist Astrology is detailed in the chapter on Demonolatry, as it is always associated with the prescription of demon worship.

VI. DEMONOLATRY

Like most mountaineers, the Sikkimites and Tibetans are thorough-going demon-worshippers. In every nook, path, big tree, rock, spring, waterfall, and lake there lurks a devil; hence, there are few persons who will venture out alone after dark. The sky, the ground, the house the field, the country, have each their special demons, and sickness is always due to malign demoniacal influence.

Personal Demons

The body also of each individual is beset by a burden of spirits named the "*h*go-wa-lha," or "the personal chief gods," who are in a sense the guardians of his body. These are not only worshipped by the laity, but the lamas regularly invoke them in their oblations in the "Ser-khyem" and "Ne-sal" worship. These personal gods, some of which are of an ancestral nature, are five in number, viz.

1. *The Male Ancestral god* (Pho-lha). This god sits under the armpits. Worship of him procures long life and preservation from harm.

2. *The Mother-god* (mo-lha) or maternal uncle god *(zhang-lha)*. It is said to obtain the latter synonym; on account of the custom by which a child, shortly after birth, is taken to the mother's house, which usually is " the uncle's house." I doubt, however, this being the true maternal interpretation.[156] The worship of this god secures strength.

3. *The Life god* (Srog-lha), which resides over the heart. Instead this god is frequently enumerated the *Nor-lha.* who sits in the left armpit and whose worship brings, wealth.

4. *The Birthplace god* (Yul-lha, literally "country-god"), which resides on the crown of the head, and whose worship secures dominion and fame.

The "Da-lha" or Enemy God

5. *The Enemy god* (dgra-lha), pronounced vulgarly "*dab-lha,*" which sits on the right shoulder. In this connection it is notable that no one willingly will allow any object to rest on his right shoulder, for the reason that it injures the "*dab-lha,*" and no friend will familiarly lay his hand on his friend's right shoulder for the same reason.

This latter god, who is figured in "the Wheel of Life," is especially worshipped by soldiers, as he defends against the enemy. He is also worshipped by all the laity once at least during the year for overcoming their individual enemies. Usually the whole village in concert celebrates this worship. The men carry swords, and shields, and they dance and leap about, concluding with a great shout of victory.[157]

In addition to these so-called "personal gods" there, are the good and bad spirits already mentioned, in connection with "the Wheel of Life," who sit on the individual's shoulders and prompt him to good and evil deeds respectively, they leave him only on his arrival before the Great Judge of the dead. These are practically identical with the good and evil genius of the Romans—the *Genium Album et Nigrum* of Horace.[158]

Worship According to Season

There are demons which are worshipped when the individual is happy and in health. These are called "the pleasing spirit". But they also may be worshipped in sickness or other affliction. Each class of spirits or "gods" has a particular season for worship. Thus:

The Earth gods (sa-gzhi mi-rig-gi-lha) are worshipped in the spring.

The Ancestral gods (smra zhang chhung-gi-lha) are worshipped in the summer season.

The "Three Upper Gods" (stod-sum pau-lha) in the autumn.

The Royal Ancestor of the Sikkim King—the divine *Minyak King* (stong mi-nyag-gi-lha) in the winter.[159]

Country Gods, The "Black Father Devil"

"The Country gods" or *Yul-lha* of Sikkim, like the analogous Penates of the Romans are innumerable. The chief two are mountain-god Kang-chhen-dso-nga *(Ang.* Kanchinjingna). Who is of a mild, inactive disposition, and styled a "Protector of religion," and his subordinate Yab *b*dud, or "the Black Father Devil." This latter of an actively malignant disposition, and rides on the south wind. His especial shrine is in thẹ Tista valley near Sivok, where he is worshipped with bloody sacrifice. His respectful name as given by Lhatsun Chhembo, who composed for both him and Kang-chhen-dso-nga special manuals of service, is "ma-mgon /chain-bras."

For him is prescribed actual sacrifice of life: a black ox is to be killed, and the entrails, brain, heart of it are ordered to be set upon the skinned hide, while the flesh is consumed by the votaries. For very poor people the sacrifice of a cock, as with the ancient Greeks to the destructive Nox and his counterpart Erebus, is considered sufficient.[160] The offering of the sacrifice is in the nature of a bargain, and is indeed actually termed such, viz. "ngo-len," the demon being asked to accept the offering of flesh, &c., and in return for this gift not to trouble the donors.

The Mountain-God Kang-chhen-dso-nga

In Kang-chhen-dso-nga's worship also, flesh meat needs to be given. And although the flesh of cows and other cattle is offered on such occasions, there is a tradition that formerly human flesh was offered. And the most acceptable flesh was the human flesh of "the infidel destroyers of the religion." Kang-chhen-dso-nga was never the tutor of Sakyamuni, as has been alleged—he is only a *zhi-dak* demon. Kang-chhen-dso-nga's personality has already been referred to.[161] One of his titles is "Head Tiger," as each of the five peaks is believed to be crowned by an animal—the highest peak by a tiger, and the other peaks by a lion, elephant, horse, and a *guruda*—a bird like the fabled "roc."[162] In every village there is a recognized *zhi-dak?* or "Foundation-owner demon," who is ordinarily cither a "black devil" (*b*dud), a red devil (tsan) or a Naga (*k*lu), or some other form as detailed below.[163]

Local Gods, The Red Demons

The *zhi-dak,* demons of the monasteries and temples, are always *tsen* (tsan) or red demons, these are usually the spirits of deceased novices or ill-natured lamas. And they are especially worshipped with bloody sacrifice and *red* coloured substances:

> "Rowan tree and *red* threid.
> Gars the witches type there speid."

The Pemiongchi *tsen* is named *Da-wa senge* (zla-ba sengze) or "the Moon Lion." The Yangong Gompa *tsen* is named *Lha tsen-pa* or "the Tsen god." The Darjeeling *tsen* is named *Chho-leg nam-gyal* or "the Victorious good religion." The shrine of this latter is on Observatory Hill, and it is worshipped under the name of Mahakala by the professing Hindu hillmen with the same bloody rites as the Bhotiyas and Lepchas. For the worship of each of the Monastery or Temple *tsens* there exist special manuals of ritual.

The Owner-Demons of Ridges and Passes

It is to the *zhi-dak* that travellers offer a rag torn from their clothes and tied to a stick to the Zhi-dak on gaining the summit of a hill or pass While planting this offering on the cairn, which is called *"lap-che,"* the traveller in a meek voice calls the demon by uttering the mystic "*ki-ki! ki-ki!*," then he adds "*so-so!* so-so!" which means presentation or " offering."[164] Then he exclaims in a loud triumphant strain " *Lha-gyal-o! Lha-gyal-o!*" "God has won! God has won!"

Soothsaying and Neeromancy

Exorcising of devils in cases of sickness and misfortune is done by the regular devil-dancers—"Pa-wo" and "Nyen-jorma," and oracular deliverances are most extensively made by the professional *lha-pa*.

The Lamas and Devil-Worship

Lamas foreseen discerned and counteract the ominous machinisations of most of the devils who especially lay themselves out for this sort of work and provide certain remedies for the pacification or coercion of the demons of the air, the earth, the locality, house, the death-demon.

Lamas are the Prescribes of the Devi-Worship

The lamas prescribe of most of the demon-worship, and derive their chief means of livelihood from their conduct of this demon-worship, rendered on account of, and at the expense of, the laity, who offer it on the especial recommendation of the lamas themselves. A few of the most intelligent of the lamas become *Tsi-pa*[165] lamas or astrologers. And all the laity have been led to understand that it is absolutely necessary for each individual to have recourse to the *Tsi-pa* lama on each of the three great epochs of life, viz., birth, marriage, and death; and also at the beginning of each year to have a forecast of the year's ill-fortune and its remedies drawn out for them.[166] The astrologer-lamas are always busy. Peoplle keep on flocking to them for prescriptions as to what deities and demons require appeasing. The also prescrible and the remedies necessary to neutralize these portending evils.

The Prescriptions are Based on Chinese Astrology

The nature of these prescriptions of worship will best be illustrated by a concrete example. But to render this intelligible, it is necessary to refer, first of all, to the chronological nomenclature current in Sikkim and Tibet.

Nomenclature of the Chinese System of Chronology

The Tibetan system of reckoning time is by the twelve-year and sixty-year cycles of Jupiter. The twelve-year cycle is used for short periods, and the particular year, as in the Chinese style, bears the name of one or other of the following twelve animals:

1. Mouse.	5. Dragon,	9. Monkey.
2. Ox.	6. Serpent.	10. Bird.
3. Tiger.	7. Horse.	11. Dog.
4. Hare.	8. Sheep.	12. Hog.

In the case of the sixty-year cycle these animals are combined with the five elements, viz.—1. Wood *(shing)*, 2. Fire *(me)*, 3. Earth *(sa)*, 4. Iron *(chak)*, and 5. Water *(chhu)*; and each element is given a pair of animals, the first being considered a male and the second a female. Appended is a footnote[166a] a detailed list of the years of the current cycle as an illustration and for reference in regard to the horoscopes which are translated presently.

The Conflict of the Animals

The lama astrologers arrive at their endless variety of combinations of attraction and repulsion in regard to their casting of horoscopes and their prescriptions of the requisite worship and offerings necessary to counteract the evils thus brought to light. They do it by giving a reliable meaning to these several animals and elements after which the years are named. The animals are more or less antagonistic to each other, and their most unlucky combinations are as follows:

Mouse and Horse.
Ox and Sheep.
Tiger and Monkey.
Hare and Bird.
Dragon and Dog.
Serpent and Hog.

Relationships of the elements

But it is with the five elements that the degrees of affinity and antagonism are most fully defined, according to certain more or less obvious inter-relations of the elements. The recognised degrees of relationship are (1) *mother* or greatest affection, (2) *son* or neutrality, (3) *friend* or mediocre affection, and (4) *enemy* or repulsion. The relationships of the elements are thus stated to be the following:

MATERNAL:

Wood's *mother* is Water (for wood cannot grow without water).

Water's *mother* is Iron (for water-channels for irrigation cannot be made, and therefore water cannot come, without iron).

Iron's *mother* is Earth (for earth is the matrix in which iron is found).

Earth's *mother* is Fire (for earth is the ash-product of fire).

Fire's *mother* is Wood [for without wood (carbon) fire is not].

FILIAL:

Wood's *son* is Fire
Fire's *son* is Earth
Earth's *son* is Iron
Iron's *son* is Water
Water's *son* is Wood

This is merely a reverse way of presenting the above details.

HOSTILE:

Wood's *enemy* is Iron (as iron instruments cut down wood).

Iron's *enemy* is Fire (as fire melts iron and alters its shape).

Fire's *enemy* is Water (as water extinguishes fire).

Water's *enemy* is Earth (as earth hems in water).

Earth's *enemy* is Wood (as wood grows at the expense of and impoverishes earth).

AMICABLE:

Wood's *friend* (benefactor) is Earth (as it cannot grow without earth).

Water's *friend* is Fire (as it heats water for cooking).

Fire's *friend* is Iron (as it absorbs heat and thus assists the continuance of fire).

Iron's *friend* is Wood (as it supplies the handle to iron weapons and is its non-conductor).

General Nature of the Horoscope

Each of the various kinds of horoscopes[171] takes into account the conflict or otherwise of the elemental and astral influences, which were in authority at the time of the person's birth, compared with the existing influences operative at the times lama astrologies is consulted. The ordinary horoscope is usually arranged under the following six heads, viz.

1. The year of birth of the individual in its auspicious or inauspicious bearings.
2. His *Parkha* (in Chinese "*pah-kwah*"), one or other of the eight celestial figures.
3. His *Log-men* or "Reversed calculation" of age. This is evidently introduced in order to afford a further variety of conflicts.
4. "The Seizing-Rope of the Sky." This seems to refer to a popular idea of ultimate ascent to the celestial regions by means of an invisible rope.
5. The Earth-dagger. This is an invisible dagger, and is for the individual the emblem of stability and safety so long as it is reported to be fixed firmly in the earth.

6. The ***Mewa*** or "blots." One or other of the nine geomantic figures, evidently of Chinese origin.

Each of these several heads is separately considered in detail with reference to its conflicts in regard to:

(a) the life or "srog"—pronounced *sok;*

(b) the body or *lus;*

(c) the power or capability, "*d*hang-thang"—pronounced "*wang-thang";*

(d) the luck ("wind horse") or "*r*lung-*r*ta"—pronounced *lungta;*

(e) the intelligence or *b*la.

The particular Parkha and Mewa for the several times are found by reference to the almanac; but the other details are elicited by divers calculations made upon the astrologer's board. Various manuals dealing with the subject are also consulted.

The Astrologer's Board

The astrologer's board consists of a large napkin. On that bard are drawn squares and the other necessary geomantic figures, all in a definite and convenient relation to each other. This napkin is spread on a table, and the calculations are made with coloured buttons as counters. These are kept in a bag—the several elements having each a recognized colour thus wood is *green,* fire is *red,* earth is *yellow,* iron is *white,* and water is *blue.* These counters are placed on the coloured squares as in a chess board, and are moved according to rule, either transversely from right to left or vice versa, or longitudinally over the requisite number of squares; and in addition are kept handy a heap of numerous small white and black counters to register the total results. In the top row of the board are the 60 squares of the 60-year cycle, all named and in the proper colour of their elements.

And the succeeding rows of squares are those of the sok, lus, wang-thang, lungta, and *b*la series, each with its appropriate succession of coloured elements. The other divisions relate to the Parkhas and Mewas.

The Calculations

The calculations are made according to rule backwards or forwards a certain number of years in the row of the 60 year cycle squares, and the secondary results come out of the vertical columns of the sok, lus, series according to the conflict of their respective elements as therein found; the results are noted by white or black seeds or buttons, which have the following values:

Symbols of Degrees of Relationship

The seven recognized degrees of affinity or repulsion are expressed in the astrological accounts by the following signs of circles, and crosses, and during the calculation, the circles are represented by white buttons, and the crosses by black buttons or seeds:

When the conflict of the elements comes out—

		Mother, i.e., the *best* degree		=	OOO
Ditto	ditto	*Friend, i.e.,* the *better* „		=	OO
Ditto	ditto	*Water + Water*	*i.e., a harmlesss mix*	=1	
		Earth + Earth	*ture & ∴ good*	=	O
Ditto	ditto	*Son, i.e., neutral*		=	OX
		Wood + Wood	*i.e., unmiscibility*		
Ditto	ditto	*Fire + Fire*	*& ∴ opposition*		
		Iron + Iron)	*& bad*	=	X
Ditto	ditto	*Enemy, i.e., worse*		=	XX
Ditto	ditto	*deadly hate, i.e., worst*		=	XXX

Water meeting iron, *i.e.,* its "*mother,*" is the very best and ∴ = OOO, and the same would be true of fire meeting wood. But wood meeting earth would = "*friend,*" and therefore = OO; but should earth meet wood, then it would be "*enemy,*" and therefore = X X; and water meeting wood = "*neutrality*" or OX. While fire meeting water = "*deadly hate,*" and therefore = X X X. Then the average of the total is taken as the average result of the conflict. And the several remedies necessary to avoid each and all of the calamities thus foretold are specified categorically in the astrologer's books.

Prescription for Worship on Account of One Year's Ill-luck. An Annual Horoscope

With this explanation prescription of worship is given a sample copy of demoniacal and otherwise, for one family for one year's ill-luck, in which the prescribed worship is italicised. Some further explanations have been added in footnotes which may be consulted by those interested in knowing in more detail the methods by which the lama-astrologer makes his calculations.

"The MISFORTUNE ACCOUNT of the Family of——for The EARTH-MOUSE YEAR (i.e., 1888 A.D.)

Salutation to Manju Sri![172]

A. FOR THE FATHER OF THE FAMILY

I. According to the BIRTH CONFLICT—

This male, aged 26 years, being born in the Water-Hog year, that year conflicts with the Earth-Mouse year (the present year) as follows:

srok or life	=	O,	or *good.*[173]
lus or body	=	OO,	or *better.*[174]
wang thang or power	=	X X,	or *worse.*
lung-ta or wind-horse	=	OOO,	or *best.*
la or intelligence	=	X,	or *bad.*

"1. *As modified by 'Parkha.'*—His *Parkha* for the year is *Khon,* which gives the Earth-Sheep year and the following conflict.

life	=	worse.
body	=	better.
power	=	worse than bad.
wind-horse	=	bad.
intelligence	=	worse.

2. *As modified by 'Reversed Age Calculation'.* This gives a 'good' result,[175] therefore = O.

3. *As modified by 'The Seizing-Rope of the Sky.'*—This gives a 'good' result,[176] therefore = O. [If it were bad, '*Nam-go*' is prescribed 'to close the door of the sky' (spirits).][177]

4. *As modified by 'The Earth dagger.'*—This gives a medium average. [If it were bad would have to do '*Sa-go*' or closure of the door of the earth (spirits).][178]

The summary of the year's conflict as to birth together with its prescribed remedies are therefore:—

'Life' has black in excess; therefore to procure long life *the 'Tshe-do' and Tshe zung* or *The Sutra and Dharanis for Long Life, have to be read repeatedly.*

'Body' has white in excess; therefore the body will be free from sickness (*i.e.*, only as regards this one head of calculation).

'Power' has black in excess; therefore food will be scanty: therefore crops will suffer, and cattle will die or be lost.

For this—

(a) *have read very much* 'Yang-gug' *or the Luck-Bestowing and* 'Nor-zang' *(the Best Wealth);*

(b) *offer Torma or holy food;*

(c) *also give food and sweets to monks and children.*

'Luck' has black in excess; therefore be careful not to provoke a law suit or go on a long journey.

For this—

(a) *do 'Du-kar'* 100 *times;*

(b) *plant as many 'Lung-ta' flags*[179] *as years of your age;*

(c) *offer in the temple* 13 *lamps with incense, &c.;*

(d) *have read the 'mDo-mang' very much;*

(e) *make an image of yourself (of cooked barley or rice) and throw it towards your enemy;*

(f) *also make an earthen chaitya.*

'Intelligence' has black in excess; therefore *have read the 'La-guk' or worship for recalling the intelligence.*

II. According to PARKHA—

His parkha for the year being '*khon*,' during the year he cannot excavate earth or remove stones. The Nagas and the Earth-owning demons are opposed to him. He is especially liable to the diseases of stiffened joints and skin disorders. In the second month, he is especially subject to danger. The N. and E. and S. directions are bad for him; he must not go there. *For removing these evils (a) have read the 'Gyetong-ba' and (b) do the worship of 'Gya-zhi-tong'* [= 'The 400,' i.e., 100 *torma* or holy cakes, 100 *lamps and* 100 *rice and* 100 *water offerings*] *and (c) offer a lamp daily in worship.*

III. According to MEWA—

His mewa is *Dun-mar* (= the 7 reds); therefore the Tsen and Gyalpo demons give trouble. Dreams are be bad. The gods are displeased. Head, Liver, and Heart will give pain, and Boils will ensue. To prevent these evils—

(a) *make a 'Tsen mdos' and a 'Gyal mdos' (This is somewhat like the Sa-go,*[180] *but without the ram's head);*

(b) *The favourite gods and guardians (srung-ma) of individual: Do their worship energetically;* and

(c) *ransom a sheep from the butchers.*

B. FOR THE WIFE

I. *According to BIRTH CONFLICT—*

This female born in Iron-Monkey year *(i.e.,* 29 years ago). That year compared with the Earth-Mouse year *(i.e.,* 1888 A.D.) gives:

sok	= O X
lu	= O X
wang-thang	= OOO
lungta	= X
la	= O X

1. *As modified by her Parkha,* which is *Li—*

sok	= XX
lu	= OO
wang-thang	= X X
lungta	= O
la	= X X

2. *As modified by 'Reversed Age Calculation'* = X
3. *As modified by 'The Sky-rope'* = O X
4. *As modified by 'The Earth-dagger'* = OOO

The Total of the year's conflict is therefore:

Sok and *Lu* are *bad* like No. 1, and must be treated accordingly in addition to No. 1.

Lus and *Wang-thang* are good.

Lungta is neutral; therefore the good people will be kind to you; the bad people will be trouble; therefore it is necessary *to do very much 'Mikha ta dok,'* literally to drive away scandal (literally = *men's mouth).*

The Sky-seizing Rope is interrupted *(i.e.* cut); therefore—

(1) *do very much 'te-gyed,' and 'ser-khyem'* (or oblation of wine to the gods);

(2) *prepare a 'nam-go' to close breach in the sky-connection.*

" The conjunction of her year (Monkey with Mouse) is not good; therefore she cannot journey far. If she does any business, she will suffer; therefore *have read 'Tashi tsig-pa.'*

II. According to PARKHA—

The Parkha being *Li,* she must not try to build or repair a house or allow any marriage in her house or spill any water on the hearth. The devil-spirit of a dead person is offended with her. Headache and eyeache will occur; therefore—

(a) do not look at fresh flesh meat or blood;

(b) in the 8th month will be especially bad;

(c) must not go W. or N.W.;

(d) *have read the 'Do-mang' and 'Gye-tong';*

(e) be careful not to provoke quarrels.

III. According to MEWA—

Her Mewa is '*some thing*'; therefore will occur sudden domestic quarrels of great seriousness, lying reports of infidelity, also grief among relatives, and dropsy. To prevent these do—

(a) *Gya zhi* (i.e., 100 *lamps,* 100 *rice,* 100 *water, and* 100 *torma).*

(b) *Lu-tor,* or offering of cake to the *Nagas* and *Dug-kar* (= white umbrella god with 1,000 heads).

(c) *Also ransom a goat.*

C. *FOR THE DAUGHTER, AGED 7.*

I. According to BIRTH CONFLICT—

This female, born in the Water-Horse year, 7 years ago. That year conflicted with the Earth-Mouse year as follows:

sok	= X X
lu	= OX
wang-thang	= X X
lungta	= OO
la	= X X

1. *As modified by her 'Parkha,'* which is *zin.* Its—

sok	= OOO
lu	= OOO
wang-thang	= OX
lungta	= XX
la	= OOO

2. *As modified by her 'Reversed Age Calculation'* = O
3. *As* per *'Sky-rope'* = OX
4. *As* per *'The Earth dagger'* = OX

"The Total of the year's conflict therefore is—

Sok, La, Lu, and *Lung-ta* are good of 2nd degree, *Wang-thang* is bad; therefore *do as for her father* No. 1, *above noted.*

'Sky-seizing Rope' and 'Earth-dagger' are neutral. For evil Sky-seizing Rope, *have read the Sutra 'Nam-mkha-i snying-poi mdo.' And for Earth-dagger have read 'Sa-yi snying-po-i mdo,' and repeat as frequently as years of age,* i.e., 7 *times.*

The conjunction of her birth year, the Horse, with that of the present year, the Mouse, is very bad, as these two are enemies; *for this have read* rgya nag sky zlong-gangmang.

II. *According to PARKHA—*

Her Parkha is *zin.* Be careful not to break a twig or demolish any tree sacred to the Nagas or other deities (gnyan); don't handle a carpenter's tool for the same reason. In second month when buds come out, it is somewhat bad for you, as the Nagas are then preeminent. The West and N.W. directions are bad and have to be avoided. *For these evils have read the 'Do-mang.'*

III. According to MEWA—

Her Mewa is *like her father's (No.* 1), *and therefore do accordingly.*

D. *FOR THE SON, AGED 5.*

According to BIRTH CONFLICT—

This male (son), born in the Wood-Ape year, 5 year ago. That year compared with the Earth-Mouse year gives—

sok	= OX
lu	= OO
w.	= OO
l	= X
la	= OX

1. *As modified by his 'Parkha,'* which is *kham.* Its

sok	= OX
lu	= O
w.	= OOO
l.	= OOO
la	= OOO

2. *As* per *'Reversed Age Calculation'*	= X
3. *As* per *'Sky-rope'*	= OO
4. *As* per *'Earth-dagger'*	= XX

"The Total of the year's conflict therefore is—

Lu, Wang-thang, and Lung-ta are good.

La and Sok are neutral or middling.

The Sky-rope is *not broken,* and therefore good.

The Earth-dagger is withdrawn, and therefore bad.

For the latter:—

(*a*) *make as many clay Chaityas as possible;*

(*b*) *the torma-cake of the earth-goddess (Sa-gi-tha-mo); and*

(*c*) *give also torma-cake to the Lu (Naga).*

II. According to 'PARKHA'—

He must not go to a large river, because his parkha is *kham*, and to pools and other waters reputed to be the abode of water-spirits. Don't stir or *disturb* the water. Don't go out at night. Don't eat fish. The *tsen* kind of Nagas are ill disposed to you. These spirits are especially malevolent to you in the 6th month; therefore be careful. Don't go in a S.W. and N.E. direction. *Have read* (1) *klu hbum and* (2) *Ser-hod dampa hdon.*

III. According to MEWA—

This Mewa is *ku-mar* (or 'the red 9'). The Mamo and Tsen are ill disposed to you.

For these two—

(*a*) *make 'de-gnyis kyi mdos gtong?* which is like the *Sa-go* and 'Sky-door' with threads and masts, and

(*b*) *have read well 'gser-hod gyang skyabs.'*

General Note on the Grand Average of the above.

The *Mewa* is excessively red. It thus betokens shedding of blood by accident.

Therefore must make 'Tsan mdos' and 'Mamo bloody *mdos.'*

Are like the '*Sa-go*' mast.

And have read as much as possible—(1) *stobs po-chhe-i-gzungs,* (2) *gzah-i yum,* (3) *nor-rgyun-ma-i gzungs gang-many sgrogs."*

The Enormous Amount of Lamaic Worship Prescribed

The above is a fair sample of a prescription of worship to be done by one family on account of the current year's demoniacal influences. In addition to the worship therein prescribed a special worship must be done for *each* individual according to his or her own life's horoscope as taken at birth.

His movements thus bear a certain relation to the season, as he is outside in the hottest weather and at the fire in the coldest.

Old Fashion

Formerly, his movements were somewhat different. According to the ancient tradition, he used to circulate much more extensively and frequently as follows:—

In 1st month he dwelt	on the roof for the first half of the month and for latter half on the floor. To repair the roof at such a time means the death of the head of the family.
In 2nd „ „	at top of stairway. The stair during this month cannot be mended, otherwise one of the family will die.
In 3rd „ „	in the granary. Cannot make any alterations there during this month, otherwise all the grain will be bewitched and spoiled.
In 4th „ „	on the doorway. Then cannot mend doorway, otherwise that member of the family absent on a journey will die.
In 5th „ „	in the hand corn-mill and the water-mill. Then cannot mend these, otherwise all luck will depart.
In 6th „ „	in any foxes' or rats' holes near the house. Then cannot interfere with these holes, otherwise a child will die.
In 7th „ „	on roof. Then cannot repair, otherwise the husband will die.
In 8th „ „	in the wall foundation. Then cannot repair, otherwise a child will die.
In 9th „ „	up the chimney. Then must not repair, otherwise house will be transferred to a new owner.
In 10th „ „	in the beams or standard posts. Then cannot repair, otherwise the house will collapse.
In 11th „ „	underneath fire-place. Then cannot repair,

	otherwise the housewife will die of hiccup or vomitting.
In 12th ,, ,,	in the stable. Then cannot repair or disturb it, otherwise the cattle will die or be lost.

His Prohibitions Indicted

The following precautions must be taken:—In the 1st and 2nd month when the god is in the middle of the house, the fire-grate must not be placed there, but in a corner of the house, and no dead body must be placed there.

No bride or bridegroom can come or go, nor any corpse through the door. Should there, however, be no other way of exit by a window or otherwise, and there be urgency in the matter of the passage of a bride, bridegroom, or corpse, then must be make with wheaten flour the images of a horse and a yak placing on each image respectively some skin and hair of each of these animals. Then tea and beer are also offered to the spirit, who is then invited to sit on these images. Then it is necessary that the door is removed from the hinges. This door is then placed outside. After the corpse is out, or after the bride or bride groom have either entered or coated the door is again fixed in its proper place.

No part of the fire-place can be removed or mended at that time, and no corpse can go there, nor must any marriage then take place. Should any visitor arrive not go near the fire-place. He must be screened off from the fire-place by a blanket and the "chhos-mge-khri" scripture read.

There is not much to be done in the verandah. Only the outside of the house must not be whitewashed nor repaired or disturbed in any way.

In case it is thought that he has been slightly offended, and in every case so as to err on the safe side, it is recommended that the worship of "*s*pang-kong-*s*nang-*b*rgyad chhab-*g*tor-*b*chos," or "the water sacrifice of the 8 Injurers," should be performed.

The Demons of the Earth

Earth Demons

The local earth demons are named *Sab-dak* or *Sa-dak-po* (sa-*b*dag-po) or "Earth owners." The most malignant are the "gnyan."

These infest certain trees and rocks, which are always studiously shunned and respected, and usually daubed with paint in adoration. The earth demons are very numerous, but they are all under the authority of "Old mother *Khonma"* She rides upon a ram, and is dressed in golden-yellow robes, and her personal attendant is "sa-thel-ngag-po." In her hand she holds a golden noose. Her face is full of wrinkles which are 80 in number.

Their Worship

The ceremony of *Sa-go,* so frequently referred to in the lamaic prescriptions, is addressed to her. It literally means "the closing of the open doors of the earth" to the earth spirits, and it is very similar to the worship of the *Lares* by the Romans.

In this rite is prepared the magical emblem consisting of an elaborate arrangement of masts and strings and a variety of mystic objects. Most prominent among then is a ram's skull with attached horns, which is directed *downwards* towards the earth.

Inside the ram's skull is put some gold leaf, silver, turquoise, and portions of every precious object available. Also added are portions of dry eatables, rice, wheat, pulses.

The mystic celestial (Parkha) sign of Khon is painted in ochre-colour[181] on the forehead, on the right jaw the sun, on the left jaw the moon, and above it is adorned with (1) "namka" masts, *i.e.,* masts to which diamond-shaped and square figures made by winding coloured threads in geometric patterns are attached; (2) *tar-zab* or pieces of silk rag, and (3) *tong-tse* or Chinese pice (Ang. "cash") and several wool-knobbed sticks of *phang-khra.*

Along the base are inserted on separate slips of wood the following images, &c.:

1. A man's picture *(pho-dong).*
2. A woman's do. *(mo-dong)* with a spindle in her hand.
3. A house do.
4. A tree do. [*tam-shing* (khram-shing)].
5. Figures of the mystic 8 *Parkha* and the 9 Mewa.

The whole arrangement is now fixed to the outside of the house above the door; the object of these figures of a man, wife, and house is to deceive the demons should they still come in spite of this offering, and to mislead them into the belief that the foregoing pictures are the inmates of the house, so that they may wreak their wrath on these bits of wood and so save the real human occupants. Then when all is ready and fixed, the lama turns to the south-west and chants—

O! O! *ke! ke!* Through the nine series of earths you are known as Old Mother Khon-ma, the mother of all the Sa-dak-po. You are the guardian of the earth's doors. The dainty things which you especially desire we herewith offer, *viz.*, a couch-white skull of a ram, on whose right cheek the sun is shining like burnished gold, and on the left cheek the moon gleams dimly like a conch-shell. The forehead bears the sign of Khon, and the whole is adorned with every sort of silk, wool and colour and precious substances, and it is also given the spell of Khon (here the lama breathes upon it). All these good things are here offered to you, so please close the open doors of the earth to the family who here has offered you these things, and do not let your servant Sa-thel ngag-po and the rest of the earth spirits do harm to this family. By this offering let all the doors of the earth be shut. O! O! *ke! ke!* Do not let your servants injure us when we build a house or repair this one, nor when we are engaged in marriage matters, and let everything happen to this family according to their wishes. Do not be angry with us, but do us the favours we ask.

"*Om kharal dok!*[182] (here clap hands)
Om khamrhil dok! (do. do.)
Benneu swaha!"

The Demons of the Sky

Sky Demons and Their Worship

The local demons of the sky are under the control of the grandfather of the three worlds—Old Father Khen-pa, who is an old man with snow-white hair, dressed in white, and riding on the white dog of the sky, and in his hand he carries a crystal wand. He is the owner of the sky. The ceremony called *nam-go*, or "the closing of the doors of the sky," so frequently prescribed by the *tsi-pa* lamas, is addressed to him. An arrangement of masts, threads, images, exactly similar to that used in the above-noted *sa-go* ceremony, is constructed, the only difference being that in this case a dog's skull is used (the Dog was especially associated with the analogous Lares worship of the Romans, *vide* foot-note[183]), and it is directed upwards, pointing to the sky; and the sign of the *parkha* painted on the forehead is that of *Khen,* and is in blue colours. And the ceremony is the same except in its introduction and in the name of the chief servants:—

"O! O! we turn towards the Western sun, to the celestial mansion where the sky is of turquoise, to the grandfather of the three worlds—Old Khen-pa, the owner of the sky. Pray, cause your servant, the white Nam-tel, to work for our benefit, and send the great planet Pemba (Saturn) as a friendly messenger."

Prevention from Injury by the Eight Classes (or Demons)

Om-swa-ti! The means of preventing the injuries of the eight classes (of demons).

The Offerings

First of all prepare offerings of blood, milk, curdled milk, tea, beer, and clean water, which must be arranged properly, and the mantras or spells of "the Vast sky-like Treasury" or *Om-a hung-bajra-sparnakham* must be repeated. Then chant:—

The Prayer

I beg you O! all guardians and evil spirits (of the under-noted places) to attend to this invitation, viz. the dwellers of the vast extending ocean of the Upper-Ngari khorsum (stod-*m*ngah-ri-*s*kor-*g*sum), the Intermediate, Central Western the four divisions of Tibet (bar-*d*bus *g*tsang-rau-*b*zhil) Amdo "Kham and Gango of Eastern Tibet and Bhotan (*s*mad-*m*do-khams-*s*gang-drug),[184] India (the white plain), China (the black plain), Li-bal[185] "Mongolia (the yellow plain), Upper and Lower Turkistan, and all the kingdom of this continent (*h*jsambu-*g*ling), the other three great continents and the eight island, and also the spirits of all retired nooks, deserts, rocky places, caves, cemetery, fire-hearths, fortresses, streams, oceans, ponds, fountains, forests, roads, empty and uninhabited places, farms and other important places; and also those who always attend the congregation of priests, parties of women, festivals of births, singing parties and the learners of arts, and also all the dwellers from the highest to the lowest regions of hell.

I beg you, O! ye guardians of the different kinds of *r*gyu*d*, to "attend this invitation.

I beg you, O! Pho-hla, mo-lha, zhang-lha, srog-lha, and yul-lha, "to attend this invitation.

I beg you, O! *d*gra-lha of noble and ancient generations, to "attend this invitation.

I beg you, O! all ye gods of the white party who give refuge, to "attend this invitation.

I beg you, O! all ye demons of the black party who are averse to "the true path, to attend this invitation.

I beg you, O! all ye goblins and demons from the highest order to the lowest, counting from *btsan* down to shin-*h*dre (life-taking demon), *g*son-*h*dre (the demon-eater of living animals), and all the inferior classes of divinities, to attend this invitation; *viz.*, lha (gods), naga, *b*dud, *b*tsan, yamantaka (*g*shin-*r*je), mamo, *g*zah (planets), *r*gyal-po *d*Mu, the-u-rang, sa-*b*dag, *g*nyan, srin-po and the injurers of all the regions.

O! I give to you all these offerings Pray accept them. They are of red blood, of sweet tea, of clean water, of intoxicating drink, and of white butter:

Those who prefer beer, please take beer!

,,	,,	tea	,,	,,	tea!
,,	,,	blood	,,	,,	blood!
,,	,,	water	,,	,,	water!
,,	,,	milk	,,	,,	milk!

Pray accept these food offerings and do us no further injury!

Pray do not injure the human beings of the upper regions!

,,	,,	lower animals of the lower regions!
,,	,,	crops of the fields!
,,	,,	moisture of the plants!
,,	,,	essence of wealth!
,,	,,	good qualities of the kingdom!
,,	,,	wealth and riches!

" " good repute and influence!

" " life and soul!

" " breath and prosperity!

O! may we all be possessed of perfect minds!

O! may we all be happy and useful to each other!

O! may we all obtain the highest power of Tathagatas!

O! may we all obtain the sphere of piety, and having obtained it, may all our wishes be fulfilled and reach the supreme end!

Bajra mu! Now I beg you all to depart to your respective dwellings!

"Let Glory come!" "*Tashi shok!*"
"Virtue!" "*dGe-o!*"

Exorcising the Disease-Producing Demons—The "She"

The Disease-Demon is Exorcised by Threats

There are certain demons who produce disease, short of actual death. They are called gshed (pronounced *she).* These are exorcised by an elaborate ceremony in which a variety of images and offerings are made. The officiating lama invoking his tutelary demon thereby assumes spiritually the dread guise of his favourite demon, and orders out the disease-demon under threat of being himself eaten up by the awful tutelary demon, which now possesses the lama.

The directions for this exorcism are the following:

The Offerings, and Effigies

On the five terraces of the magic circle of Rirab make the image of a yellow frog with a nam-kha, having its belly and face yellow, and on the east, a two-headed figure with heads of a tiger and a vulture, riding on an ass and holding the eight *parkhas;* on the south a two-headed figure with heads of a horse and a snake, riding on a red horse and holding a lamp; on the west a two-headed figure with heads of a bird and a monkey, holding a sword and riding on a goat; and on the north a two-headed youth with heads of a rat and a pig, riding on a blue pig and holding a water-bag. On the south-east, a dragon-headed woman riding on a *m*dso (half-breed yak); on the south-west a sheep-headed woman riding on a bull; on the north-west a dog-headed woman riding on a wolf; and on the north-east a bull-headed woman riding on a buffalo. Thirteen *h*phang,[186] *m*dah, rgyang-bu, and nam-kha. Iron on the east, water on the south, fire on the west, and gold on the north with a *s*lud, literally *"ransom"* of dough-cake of wheaten flour, in their front, and a lamp and a piece of flesh on each corner. Then bless it with the six mantras and mudras each.

The Exorcism

Then assuming the guise of one's own tutelary deity or *yidam,* chant the following:

Salutation to (the Chinese King) Kong-*r*tse-*h*phrul-*r*gyal, an incarnation of Manjusri!

Hung! Hear me, O! you collection of *g*she*d* demons! Hear me, O! all you *g*she*d* that cause injury! Listen to my orders and come to receive my presents with great reverence!

I am the representative of the King of the Angry Demons "(Khro*r*gyal)!

I am a great demon-eater!!!

I am The All-terrifying and Injuring One! There is no one who dare disobey my commands!

There is nothing which is not composed of the five elements, and there is nothing to obstruct the communication of my words to your ear. So then, come to receive this ransom!

Ja-hung-bi-ho! O! all you evil spirits and the ghosts of the dead! listen to me and come to receive this present. Through the power of the element of Iron, O! eating-demons, ghosts and evil spirits! come to receive this present with mild hearts. O! you *g*she*d* of the four directions, eating-demons, ghosts and evil spirits! come and receive it with mild hearts.

Om mama khamkham chhuye swahah! Hung! The *g*she*d* of the eastern direction is the woman with the heads of a tiger and vulture, riding on a red ass. She is surrounded by a thousand attendant *g*she*d.* O! you! having received this ransom, do not injure the dispenser of gifts, and expel all the eating-demons, ghosts and evil spirits of the east. I here drive away all the *g*she*d* by this burning thunderbolt through the force of truth. O! eating-demons, life-cutters, breath-takers, death-causers, and all the evil spirits! I drive you all away. If you remain here any longer, I, 'Yeshes-khro-wo-chhen-po,' or 'the Great Angry One of Fore-knowledge,' will break your heads into a hundred bits and cut "up your body into a thousand pieces. Therefore, without disobeying my commands, begone instantly.

Om mama ramramye hung phat! Hung! The gsh*e*d of the southern direction has the heads of a horse and a snake, and rides on a red horse, and he is surrounded by a thousand attendant *g*she*d*. O! you! having received this ransom, do not injure the dispenser of these gifts, and expel all the eating-demons, ghosts and evil spirits of the south. I here drive away all you *g*she*d* by this burning brand through the force of truth. O! you injurers of me and the dispenser of these gifts, you eating-demons, life-cutters, breath-takers, death-causers, and all you evil spirits! I drive you all away. If you do not depart instantly, I, 'the Great Angry One of Fore knowledge,' will smash your head into a hundred bits and cut up your body into a thousand pieces. Begone immediately and do not disobey my commands.

Om mama karakaraye hung phat! Hung! The *g*she*d* of the western direction has two heads of a bird and a monkey, and rides on a grey goat, and he is surrounded by a thousand attendant *gshed.* O! you! having received this ransom, do not approach the dispenser of these gifts, and expel all the eating-demons, ghosts and the evil spirits of the west. I here drive away all these *g*she*d* by the burning sword through the force of truth. O! you injurers of me and this dispenser of gifts, you eating-demons, life- cutters, breath-takers, death-causers, and all you evil spirits! I drive you all away. If you stay without, I, 'the Great Angry One of Fore-knowledge,' will smash your head into a hundred bits and cut up your body into a thousand pieces. Begone immediately and obey my commands.

Om mama khamkham chhueye swahah! Hung! The *gshed* of the northern direction has the heads of a rat and a pig, and rides on a blue pig, and he is surrounded by a thousand attendant *gshed.* O! you! having received this ransom, do not injure the dispenser of these gifts, and expel all the eating-demons, ghosts and the evil spirits of the north. I here drive away all you *g*she*d* by the golden rod through the force of truth. O! you injurers of me and this dispenser of gifts, you eating-demons, life-cutters, breath-takers, death-causers, and all you evil spirits! I drive you all away. If you remain here, I, 'the Great Angry One of Foreknowledge,' will smash your heads into a hundred bits and cut up your body into a thousand pieces. So depart instantly and obey my commands.

Hung! The g*shed* of the south-east is the dragon-headed woman, riding on a *m*dso-yak. She is surrounded by thousands of *g*shed as her attendants. O! you! having received this ransom, do not injure the dispenser of these gifts, and expel all the eating-demons, ghosts of the dead, and all the evil spirits towards the boundary of the south-east.

Hung! The g*shed* of the south-west is the sheep-headed women riding on a bull. She is surrounded with attendants of thousands of *gshed.* O! you! having received this offering, do not injure the dispenser of these gifts, and expel all the eating-demons, ghosts and the evil spirits towards the boundary of the south-west.

Hung! The g*shed* of the north-west is the dog-headed woman, riding on a pig. She is surrounded by thousands of her attendants. O! you! having received this offering, do not injure the dispenser of these gifts, and expel all the eating-demons, ghosts and all the evil spirits towards the boundary of the north-west.

Hung! The g*shed* of the north-east is the bull-headed woman, riding on a buffalo. She is surrounded by thousands of her attendants. O! you! having received this ransom, do not injure the dispenser of these gifts, and expel the eating-demons, ghosts and all the evil spirits towards the boundary of the north-east.

Om "mama khamkham chhuye swahah! O! you flesh-eating demons, ghosts of the dead, life-cutting demons, breath-taking demons, death-causing demons, and all kinds of-evil spirits! I here drive you all away. If you don't go instantly, I, 'the Great One of Foreknowledge,' will smash your head into a hundred bits and cut up your body into a thousand pieces. So you had better go away instantly and not disobey my commands.

Now they are all driven away to the extreme boundaries of the four directions. *Om su su ta ta ye swahah!* (Here the people shout joyously ' *God has won !' 'The demons are defeated!'*).

Kye! Kye! O! you! frog of precious gold, made from the thunder-bolt of 'Byam-*m*gon' (pronounced Cham-gon), or 'The loving protector,' please remain in the south and there become the king of all the evil spirits.

We pray you remain also in the vast ocean, where the rains are deposited and the clouds originate, and there become the overruling emperor of 'the land-owning demons' and of 'the kings.'

Upset also all the g*shed* of the bad planets, of the stars, mewa, time, day, month and year; upset all the *g*she*d* of bad luck; I give you from the depths of my heart the offerings of the five sublime namkha-masts, the *r*gyang-bu, etc.

Let glory come! *Tashi-shok!*

Let virtue increase! *Ge-leg-phel!*"

DEATH CEREMONIES

The rites in connection with a death include a considerable amount of devil worship.

Death Ceremonies

If a death occurs, the body is not disturbed in any way until the "*h*pho-bo" (pronounced "pho-o") lama has extracted the soul in the orthodox manner. It is believed that any movement of the corpse might eject the soul, which would then wander about in an irregular manner and get seized by some demon. Immediately on death, therefore, a white cloth is thrown over the face of the corpse, and the "*h*pho-bo," or Soul-extracting Lama, is sent for. On the arrival of this lama all *weeping* relatives are excluded from the death chamber, so as to secure solemn silence, and the doors and windows closed, and the lama sits down on a mat near the head of the corpse, and commences to chant the *h*pho-bo service, which contains directions for the soul to find its way to the Western Paradise (dewa-chen) of the mythical Buddha—Amitabha. After advising the spirit to quit the body and its old associations and attachment to property, the Lama seizes with the forefinger and thumb a few hairs of the crown of deceased's head, and plucking it forcibly is supposed to give vent to the spirit through the roots of these hairs.

It is generally believed that if the "*h*pho-bo" is, as he should be, a lama of exceptional virtue, an actual perforation of the skull occurs at this instant through which passes the liberated spirit. The spirit is then directed how to avoid the dangers, which beset the road to the Western Paradise, and instructed as to the appearance of the demons and other personages who are to be met with *en route*, and it is then bid God-speed. This ceremony lasts about an hour. This is the way the soul is extracted in the orthodex on annes. In cases where, through accident or otherwise, the body of deceased is not forthcoming, this operation for the extraction of the soul is done by the lama spiritually while engaged in deep meditation.

Death-Horoscope

In order to ascertain what is for age and birth year of those persons who may approach and touch the corpse, and the necessary particulars as to the *date* and mode of burial, and the necessary worship to be done for the welfare of the surviving relatives. The *Tsi-pa,* or astrologer-lama has been requisitioned for a death-horoscope.

The nature of this horoscope will best be understood by an actual example, of the death-horoscope of a little girl of two years of age, who died at Darjeeling in 1890.

"Hail to Lama Manjusri!

Death Horoscope of a Girl

This girl was born in a Bull-year, with which the Snake and the Sheep are in conflict; therefore those individuals born in the Snake and the Sheep-year cannot approach the corpse. The death-demon was hiding in the house inside certain coloured articles, and he now has gone to a neighbouring house where there is a family of 5 with cattle and dogs (therefore that other family needs to do the necessary worship). The death-demon will return to the house of the deceased within three months; therefore the 'za-de-kha-gyur' service must be done before that time.

Her Parkha being *Dva* in relation to her death, it is found that her spirit on quitting her body entered her loin girdle and a sword. [In this case the affected girdle was cast away and the sword was handed over to the lama.] Her life was taken to the east by Tsan and King (gyalpo) demons, and her body died in the west; therefore small girls, cousins, sisters and brothers in that house will be harmed. The death was due to Iron. The death-demon came from the south and has gone to the east.

Her Mewa gives the '3rd Indigo blue.' Thus, it was the death-demon of the deceased's paternal grandfather and grandmother who caused her death; therefore take (1) a Sat*s*-*t*sha (a miniature earthen chaitya), and (2) a sheep's head, and (3) earth from a variety of sites, and place these upon the body of the deceased, this evil thus will be corrected.

The Day of her Death was Friday. Take to the north-west a leather bag or earthen pot in which have been placed four or, five coloured articles, and throw it away as the death-demon goes there. The death having so happened, it is very bad for old men and women, On this account take a horse's skull[187] or a serpent's skull[188] and place it upon the corpse.

Her Death Star is 'Gre.' Her brother and sister who went near to her are harmed by the death-messenger (shin-je). Therefore, an ass's skull and a goat's skull must be placed on the corpse.

Her death Hour was soon after sunset. And in the 12th month her life was cut. The death-demon therefore arrived in the earthen cooking pot and bowl of a man and woman visitor dressed in red who came from the south. Thus, the deceased's father and mother are harmed, and especially so if either is born in the Sheep-year.

"*Precautions to secure a Good Rebirth.* It is necessary to prepare an image of Vajrapani, Vajra-satwa, and before these to have prayer[189] done for the good rebirth of the girl's spirit. If this be done, then she will be reborn in the house of a rich man in the west.

For deceased's Spirit. It is necessary to get the lamas to read the service (smon-lam) praying for rebirth in The Paradise of Deva-chhen.

For Survivors of family. It is necessary to have read the prayers for, Long Life, *viz.*, '*tshe-mdo*' and 'tshe-*gzungs*.'

Directions for Removal of Corpse. Those who remove the corpse must have been born in the *Dog* or the *Dragon* year. The body must be taken outside of the house on the morning of the third day following the death and it must be carried to the south-west and be *buried* (not burned, or given to birds or dogs)".

Location of Corpse

On obtaining the Death Horoscope, the body is then tied up in a sitting posture by the auspicious person indicated by the horoscope, and placed in a corner of the room which it has been confirmed by the lama, is not occupied by the house-demon.

Invitation and Entertainment of Friends

Notice is sent to all relatives and friends within reach, and those invited collect within two or three days they are entertained with food of rice, vegetables, and a copious supply of *murwa* beer and tea. This company of visitors remain loitering in and around the house, doing great execution with hand-prayer-wheels and muttering the "*Om-mani-padme-hung;*" until the expulsion of the "*shen,*" or death-demon[190] which follows the removal of the body, in which ceremony they all have to join. The expense of the entertainment of so large a company is very considerable.

Feasting the Deceased

During this feasting the deceased is always, at every meal, offered his share of what is going including tobacco. His own bowl is kept filled with beer and tea and set down beside the corpse, and a portion of all the other eatables is always offered to him at meal times; and after the meal is over his portion is thrown away, as his spirit is supposed to have extracted all the essence of the food, which then no longer contains nutriment, and is fit only to be thrown away. After the corpse has been removed, till the 49th day of his death his cup is regularly filled with or beer. It is thought that his spirit. His spirit is free to roams about for a maximum period of 49 days subsequent to death.

The Litanies—For "The Western Paradise"

For sending the soul of the deceased direct to the lamas chant by relays all might and day. The lamas chant by relays all night and day the *De-wa-chan kyi monlam,* or the service. "The Western Paradise" of the mythic Dhyani Buddha—Amitabha. According to the means of the deceased two or more lamas are entertained to read this service in chorus, as the more frequently it is repeated the better for the deceased. A special reading of this service by the assembled monks in the Grompa is also arranged for by those who can afford the expense.

For "The Valley of the Shadow of Death"

Lamas also read at the house of the deceased the "thos-grol" (pronounced "*tho-dol*"), or guide for the spirit's passage through the valley of horrors intervening between death and a new rebirth. This passage is somewhat suggestive of Bunyan's "Pilgrim's Progress," only the demons and dangers which beset the way are much more numerous and awful. But full directions are read out for the benefit of the deceased as to how to avoid these pitfalls and ogres, and how to find the proper white-coloured path which will lead to a good rebirth. It is, however, rather incongruous to find that while the lama reading this service is urging the spirit to bestir itself to the necessary exertions for a good rebirth, the other lama by his side in the *De-wa-chan* service is sending the spirit direct to the Western Paradise. This ritual which is out the rituals of rebirth. It is non-Buddhist rituals which done the ages has been absorbed into Buddhism.

Litanies for Extraction from Hell

Though it is scarcely considered orthodox, many of the lamas find, by consulting their lottery books, that the spirit of the deceased has been sent to hell, and the exact compartment in hell is specified. Then must be done a most expensive service by a very large number of lamas. First of all is done "*d*ge-ba" or "virtue" on behalf of the deceased; this consists in offerings to The Three Collections, viz.—

1st. Offerings to the *Gods* of sacred food, lamps, &c.

2nd. „ „ *Lamas* of food and presents.

3rd. „ „ *Poor* of food, clothes, beer, &c.

The offering for the well being of the deceased who is supposed to in hell by that time.

Then many more expensive services must be performed, and especially the propitiation of *Thuk-je-chhen.po,* or "The Great Pitier," for his intercession with the king of hell (an offshoot of his own self) for the release of this particular spirit. Even the most learned and orthodox lamas believe that by such a service may be secured the release of a few of the spirits actually in hell. But in practice every spirit in hell for whom its relatives pay sufficiently may be released by the aid of the lamas.

Sometimes a full course of the necessary service is declared insufficient, as the spirit has only got a short way out of hell—very suggestive of the story of the priest and his client in Lever's story, and then additional expense must be incurred to secure its complete extraction. Before removing the corpse from the house, an especial feast of delicacies, including cooked pork and drink of sorts, are set before the body of the deceased.

A lama presenting a "scarf of honour " to the corpse thus addresses it:—You! (and here the deceased's name is stated) now have received from your relatives all this good food and drink, partake freely of its essence, as you won't have any more chances! For you must under-

"stand that you have died, and your spirit must be gone from here, and never come back again to trouble or injure your relatives. Remember the name of your spiritual lama-teacher (rtsa-wa Mama), "which is ..... and by his aid take the right path—the white one. "Come this way here again the name of deceaed is taken)!"

The Funeral Procession

The lama precedes the carrier of the corpse. He holds the end a white scarf, the other end of the scarf is tied to the corpse. At the same time, he has a thigh bone trumpet in his one hand and a hand-drum in the other. He has blowing his trumpet and beating the drum and chanting a liturgy. He frequently looks back to invite the Spirit to accompany the body, which he assures it is being led in the right direction. And the corpse-bearer is followed by the rest of the procession, some bearing refreshments, and last of all come the weeping relatives. The ceremony of guiding the deceased's spirit is only done for the laity—the spirits of deceased lamas are credited with a knowledge of the proper path, and need no such instruction. The body is usually carried to the top of a hillock for burial or cremation. The scarf used in the funereal procession is carried before the coffin in China, it may probably represent the Chinese *hurin-fan,* or "soul's banner."

Expelling the Death-Demon

Exorcising the Death-Demon

The exorcising of the death-demon is entitled Za-de-kha-gyur,[191] or "The turning away of the face of the eating devil," *i.e.,* "The expulsion of the Eating or Death-demon." It is one of the most common lamaic ceremonies. It is always done after a death, within two days after the removal of the corpse, in order to expel from the house and locality the demon who caused the death. This ceremony, which requires the presence of four or five lamas, is as follows:

The Images of Himself and Attendants

On a small wooden platform is made the image of a tiger by means of the grass and mud plaster; it is fashioned in a walking attitude, with mouth wide open. The mouth and tusks made of a dough and the body is coloured with yellow and brown stripes, in imitation of a tiger's markings, and around its neck is tied a rope of threads of five colours. Then a small image of a man is made by kneaded dough in which are incorporated filings from the alloy known as the Rin-chhen sna-nga *r*dar, or the five precious things, viz., gold, silver, copper, iron, and tin. Into the belly of this image, which is called "the eating-demon," is inserted a piece of paper, on which is written the following banishing spell[192]:—"Go, thou eating devil, having your face turned to the enemy!"[193] It is then clad in pieces of silk, and is placed sitting astride the tiger's back.

Another figure is made the head of a bird is placed on it. It is thus a human body with the head of a bird. Its face is painted red; in its belly is inserted paper on which is written "You eating devil, don't remain in this village, but go to the enemy's country." It is then placed in front of the tiger, and is made to hold the free end of the rope attached to the tiger's neck, as a groom.

Another figure of human shape, but with an ape's head, is placed behind as driver.

Then with a piece of "father" tree[194] shape a label containing the spell therein inscribed, which is an order to take away the "Eating-demon," and plant this in the shoulder of the bird-faced[195] figure. And Making a similar stick out of a "son" tree[196] and inscribed with another spell,[197] plant it in the shoulder of the tiger-riding figure, i.e., the death-demon himself. With black thread make a geometrical figure *nam-jang nak-po,* as figured in the nam-go mast already described. Make four arrows of wood with red painted shafts named "*m*dah khra," and place one on each shoulder of the tiger-seated demon-figure and of the bird-faced figure.

Food and Drink Offerings

After that around these figures morsels of every kind of eatables, grains, fruits, spices, including raw meat and spirits are strewn a few small coins of silver and copper are also placed.

Enchanted Weapons

The following weapons are then enchanted for the conflict, viz. pieces of iron, copper, small stones, preferably of white and black colours, grams, the root of ram-pu[198] for the use of the lamas. For the lay army of the household and neighbours, a sword, knives, reaping hook, yak's tail, a rope of yak's hair with hook at end as figured with the Fierce *Gonpa*-demons.

The Act of Exorcism

When these preparations are completed *and the sun has set*—for demons can only move in the darkness—then the ceremony begins, The head lama invokes his tutelary deity to assist him in the expulsion of the death-demon. He then chants the following Sanskrit spell:—

> "Om! dudtri maraya srogla bhyo! bhyo!
> Raja dudtri maraya srogla bhyo! bhyo!
> Nagpo dudtri maraya srogla bhyo! bhyo!
> Yama dudtri maraya srogla bhyo! bhyo!"

When this spell is concluded, the lama with an imprecatory gesture blows his breath spiritualized by his tutelary deity upon the images. The other lamas loudly beat a large drum, cymbals, and a pair of *kang-ling* thigh-bone trumpets. The laymen armed with the afore-mentioned weapons loudly shout and wildly cut the air with their weapons.

On silence being restored the lama chants the following:

Hung! Hear you eighty thousand demons![199] In olden time in the country of India the King Chakra . . . .[200] was taken ill, being attacked by all the host of gods, devils, 'eating-demons,' and the accident-causing[201] demons. But, learned and revered Manjusri by doing the following worship reversed the devils and cared the king. With the five precious things he made a shapely image of the eating-demon, and on it planted 'nam-*m*kha *r*gyang-bu, *m*dah-khra and phang-khra,' and writing on slips of wood the *gyur-yik* spells, he stuck them into the demon's image, and he heaped around it the nine sorts of catables as a ransom from the householder, the dispenser of gifts, and he said, 'Now O! devil! the sun has gone. Your time too for going-has arrived in the black darkness, and the road is good. BEGONE! "Begone to the country of our enemies and work your wicked will "there! Quickly begone! Jump! Turn about (reverse)!' And thus the devil was turned away and the king was cured. Again in the Indra country in the south of India was a king named Dana-aso. Several additional examples of the efficacy of this rite are cited below).

Hung! O! Yamantaka. Thou greatest of the gods, the Destroyer, the King of the dead! Let the death-demon be sent off to our enemy!

O! Ekajati, thou chief of the Ma-mo fiendesses, let the death-demon be sent off to our enemy!

O! one-eyed white devil! let the death-demon be sent off to our enemy!

O! Hanubhati, flesh-eating demon, chief of all the demons, let the death-demon be sent off to our enemy!

O! Nanda and Takshaka, chiefs of the Nagas, let the death-demon be sent off to our angry enemy!

O! Red Father Shu,[202] chief of all the Tsen, let the death-demon be sent off to our enemy!

O! 'The well-filled One,'[203] chief of all the Yakshas,[204] let the death-demon be sent off to our enemy!

O! Eastern King,[205] the chief of all the Gandharva, let the death-demon be sent off to our enemy!

O! Western King, the chief of all the powerful Nagas, let the death-demon be sent off to our enemy!

O! Northern King, the chief of all the givers, let the death-demon be sent off to our enemy!

O! Guardians of the ten directions and your retinue, let the death-demon be sent off to our enemy!

O! all you Tsen, Ma-mo from the grassy valleys and all Men-mo, let the death-demon be sent off to our enemy!

O! all male and female Gong-po, who abstract the essence of food and your retinue! let the death-demon be sent off to our enemy!

"O! Death-demon, do thou now leave this house and go and 'oppress our enemies. We have given you food, fine clothes, and money. Begone to the country of our enemies!! Begone Begone Now be off far from herd!!!"

The Ejection of the Effigy of Death-Demon

At this, the lama smites his palms together, and all the lamas beat their drums, clamourously; the laymen wield their weapons, shouting "Begone! Begone!" Amid all this uproar the platform containing the image and its attendants is lifted up by a layman, one of the relatives, selected according to the astrologer's indications, who holding it breast high, at arm's length, carries it outside, attended by the lamas and laity, shouting 'Begone!' and flourishing their weapons. It is carried off for about half a mile in the direction prescribed by the astrologer lama, and deposited, if possible, at a site where four roads meet.

Subsequent Ceremonies

After the procession carrying the platform and images comers, to make sure that the demon is not yet lurking in some corner of the room, the sorcerer-lama[206] remains behind, with a *dorje* in his right hand and a bell in his left. With the *dorje* he makes frantic and thumb of the right hand, without relinquishing the *dorje,* he throws in all directions hot pebbles, which have been toasted in the fire, muttering his charms, and concludes:

Dispel from this family all the sorceric injury of Pandits and Bons!!

Dispel all strife. Dispel all the mischief of inauspicious, planets, and the conjunction of the red and black *Mewa.* Dispel all the evil of the 8 'parkha.'

Turn to the enemy all the misfortune.

Turn to the enemy all plagues, loss, accidents, bad dreams, the 81 bad omens, unlucky years, months, and days, the 424 diseases, the 360 causes of plagues, the 720 causes of sudden death, the 80,000 most malignant demons.

"Turn all these to our enemy! *Bhyo! Bhyo! Bhyo!* Begone!" And the lama adds—"Now by these angry spells the demon is expelled! *O! Happiness!*"

Then all the people triumphantly shout:

"*Lha-gyal-o-o!*　　*Lha-gyal-o-o!!*

God has won!!

Du pam-bo!!　　*Du pam-bo!!!*

THE DEMONS ARE DEFEATED!!!!"

The Lay figure of the Deceased, and its Rites

Effigy of Deceased, The Face Paper

Cremation of corpse take place according to instructions. But the rites do not terminate. Disposal of the soul remains. That same day, after the removal of the corpse, a lay figure of the deceased is made by dressing a stool or block of wood in the clothes of the deceased, and for a face is inserted the printed paper called *m*tshan spyang or "spyang-pu"—pronounced *chang-ku.*

The Burning of the Paper

On the conclusion of the full series of services, this paper is ceremoniously burned in the flame of a butter-lamp and the spirit is thus given its final *conge.* According to the colour and quality of the flame and mode of burning the fate of the spirit of deceased is determined. This process usually discovers the necessity for further courses of worship.

The directions for noting and interpreting the signs of this burning paper are contained in a small pamphlet which is translated here entitled:

> *The mode of Divining the signs of The Flames during the Burning of the 'Chang' paper.*

Salutation to 'Chhe-*m*chhog, Heruka,' or 'The most Supremo Heruka!' The marking of the five colours of the flames is as follows:

Divination by the Fire

If the flames be white and shining, then he has become perfect and is born in the highest region of Ok-min *(i.e.,* The Supreme).

If the flames be white and burn actively with round tops, then he has become pious and is born in the Eastern '*m*ngon-*d*gah,' or 'The Paradise of Real Happiness.'

If they burn in an expanded form, resembling a lotus (*padma*), then he has finished his highest deeds and has become religious.

If they bo yellow in colour and burn in the shape of '*r*gyal-*m*tshan,' or 'Banner of Victory,' then he has become religious nobly.

If they be red in colour and in form like a lotus, then he has become religious and is born in bde-wa-chan, or 'The Paradise of Happiness.'

If they be yellow in colour and burn actively with great masses of smoke, then he is born in the region of the lower animals, for counteracting which a *g*ytsug-lag-khang, or 'An Academy,' and an image of the powerful and able Dhyani Buddha (*s*nang-par-*s*nang-*m*dsad) should be made; then he will be born as a chief in the middle country *(i.e.,* The Buddhist Holy Land in India).

If the fire burns with masses of dense smoke, then he has gone to hell. For counteracting this images of Vajra .... (Dorje-*r*nam-*hjoms*) and Vajra-pani should be made; then he will be born as a second daughter of a wealthy parent near his own country, and after his death in that existence he will be born in the fairy land.

If the fire burns fiercely, with great noise and crackling, then he will be born in hell. For preventing this, images of Mi-*h*khug-pa and Vajra-Satwa and Avalokita should be made, and 'the hell confession of the hundred letters' (yig *r*gya-na-rag *s*kang-*b*shags) should be repeated. Then he will be born as a son of a wealthy parent towards the east.

If the flames be blue in colour and burn furiously, he is born in hell. To prevent birth in hell, have read Yige-*br*gya-pa ki-ka-ni dri-med-*b*shags-*r*gyud, *m*do-thar-chhen-tshe-*h*bar, *s*dig-*b*shag*s*, *l*ung-*b*shag*s*, mani-*b*kah-*h*bum, and *s*pyan-*h*byed must be repeated; then he will either be born as a son of a carpenter towards the east or again born in this late mother's womb. But of this is not done, then he well again be born as a dog, who will become mad and harm everybody and then he will be born in the ngu-hbod compartment of hell.

If the flames burn *yellow, without any mixture of other colours,* will be born in the region of the Yidags. For preventing this make images of the Dhyani Buddha Ratna Sambhava surrounded by the Nye-sra*s*, also images of Manjusri and of Shakyamuni surrounded by his disciples; then he will be born as a Lama towards the south and will devote himself to religious purposes.

If the flames are *yellow in colour and burn furiously,* then make *g*torma-*br*gya-tsa and offer extensive charity to the poor; then he will be born again in his own family. Failing to do this, he will be born in the region of the Yidags.

If the fire flames be *white and burn furiously,* he well be born as a Lha-ma yin. Then image of Mahamaya (Yum-chhen-mo) and Amitayus should be made. Then he will be born in the Happy Paradise of Dewa-chan. If only Tshogs-*r*gya be done then he well be born as a son of wealthy parents.

"If the fire burns furiously in *red, emitting sparks,* he will be born as Lha-ma-yin for preventing which do *d*kon-*br*tseg*s*, and thos-grol must be read, and then he will be born as a son of a blacksmith.

If the fire burns furiously without any colour then he will be born as a Garuda towards the north, for preventing which make images of Don-yod grub-pa (Dhyani Buddha *Amogha Siddhi*), *r*Nam-*h*joms, *s*grolma-*h*jigs-pa *b*rgyad-*s*kyobs (Dolma—The Defender from The Eight Dreads[208]). *s*Man-lha (The God of Medicine), and the worship of Maitreya must be repeated; then he will be born as a son of a famous chief, or he will be born again in his own family.

If the fire burns of a *bluish-black* colour, then repeat *g*zung-*h*dus (*i.e.*, The *'Do-Mang')*, *m*tshan-*b*rjod, Sangs-*r*gyas-*m*tshan-*h*bum (The Hundred Thousand Holy Names of Buddha); then he will be born as a chief. By doing these services here prescribed his birth will be good in every case. 'O! Glorious results! *Sarba mangalam!* All happiness!"

Miniature Chaityas Made from the Ashes

The ashes of this burned paper are carefully collected in a plate, then they are mixed with clay to form one or more miniature Chaityas named Sa-tschha. One of these is retained for the household altar and the rest are carried to any hill near by where they are deposited under a projecting ledge of a rock, to shelter them from the distintegrating rain.

On the burning of this paper, the lay figure of the deceased is dismantled, and the clothes are presented to the lamas, who carry them off and sell them to any purchasers available. Money thus got is considered an offering to the lama.

After the lapse of one year from death it is usual to give a feast in honour of the deceased and to have repeated the *s*man-hla service of the Medical Buddhas. When all the ceremonies are over, to the best satisfaction of the lamas the widower or the widow can re-marry.

The Exorcise Ghosts

A Ghost is Always Noxious

Some ghost are in wicked and they return. Some ghosts are those of dead rich men which come back to see how the money left by them is being utilized. In either case its presence is noxious. It makes its presence felt in dreams or by making some individual delirious or temporarily insane.

How Exorcised

If the lama decides that there is such a ghost, then he must be burnt. For this purpose a very large gathering of lamas is necessary, not less than eight and the service of "byin sreg*s*," "burnt offering," is done. On a platform of mud and stone ouside the house is made, with the usual rites, a magic circle or "kyil-*h*k*h*or," and inside this is drawn a triangle names "hung-hung," as in the diagram here annexed. Small sticks are then laid along the outline of the triangle, one piled above the other, so as to make a hollow three-sided pyramid, and around this are piled up fragments of every available kind of food, stone, tree-twigs, leaves, poison, bits of dress, money, &c., to the number of over 100 sorts. Then oil is poured over the mass, and the pile set on fire. During its combustion additional fragments of the miscellaneous ingredients reserved for the purpose are thrown in, from time to time, by the lamas, accompanied by a muttering of spells. And ultimately is thrown into the flames a piece of paper on which is written the name of the deceased person—always a relative—whose ghost is to be suppressed. When this paper is consumed the ghost has received its quietus, and never gives trouble again. If still there is trouble, it means some other ghost is there. Or some demon is present there, for which fresh creatives measures are necessary.

References

1. The Hinduized Nepalese lately settled in Eastern Sikkim are not natives of Sikkim.
2. For general notes on Sikkim Lama-ism after Schlagintweit, the chief writers are Sir John Edgar, Mr. A.W. Paul, C.I.E., who afforded me many facilities for acquiring information, Sir Joseph Hooker and Sir Richard Temple.
3. Koppen: *Die lamaische Hierarchie und Kirche*, Berlin, 1859.
4. *b*kah-dam-pa.
5. *Tsongkhapa* means "Of Tsongkha or the Onion Country," the district of his birth in Western China near the eastern confines of Tibet. His proper name is *b*Lo-bzang-tak-pa; but he is best known to Europeana by his territorial title.
6. *m*gon-po bar-nak.
7. *b*de-mchhog.
8. phyag-rgya-chhew-pa.
9. *r*do-*r*je hchhang.
10. Sa-*s*kya-pa.
11. Sems-*d*pah chhen-po.
12. Rig-*h*dsin chhon-po, or 'the great Sage.'
13. *s*byin-dak.

14. Phun tshog*s*.
15. *k*long-chhen rab h*b*yani.
16. *s*grub-pa-*b*kah brged.
17. gu-ru pad-ma *h*byung-gynas.
18. gu-ru *r*do-*r*je gro-lod.
19. gu-ru pvi-ma *h*od zer.
20. gu-ru Seng-ge *s*gra *s*grogs.
21. gu-ru *b*lo-ldan mehhog Sred.
22. brag-phug.
23. *d*yon-pa.
24. *m*khah *h*gro gsang.
25. *s*bas.
26. *b*de chhen.
27. *r*gyab ri brag dang, *m*dun ri *m*tsho.
28. *m*chhod *r*ten.
29. *Da-garbha* (Pali Da-goba) = relic receptacle. *Chaitya* (= *chi* +styai = to heap together, a mound) came afterwards to be called *stupa* and in Pali *Thupa* or vulgarly *Tope*, but especialy applied to a relic-holder in an Assembly Hall, while *stupa* denoted the larger one in the open air.
30. *Himalayan Jours.*, Vol. I, p. 320.
31. *m*thong wa rang grol.
32. It is believed by the lamas that on the burning of the body of a Buddha no mere ash results, but two varieties of nodules which are named: (a) *phe-dung*, small white seed-like granules; (b) *ring-srel*, yellowishh larger nodules from the bones, and of these an enormous quantity are forthcoming. It is the former which are said to be preserved in the great Tashiding Chaitya.
33. *h*od srung.
34. *The Oriental*, p. 13.
35. *h*du-khang.
36. gtsug-lag-khang.
37. *k*n*y*jira.
38. *r*gyal-*m*tshan.
39. Pemiongchi the balcony doors contain painted representation of the seven precious things of a universal emperor (*Chakravarta raja*), such as Shakya was to have been had he become a Buddha: viz.-(1) the precious wheel; (2) the precious white elephant; (3) the precious flying horse; (4) the precious gem; (5) the precious general; (6) the precious minister; and (7) the precious wife. These objects are frequently figured in the base of images and pictures of Buddha. *See* also Chapter V, p. 323.
40. ki-kong *d* mar nag.
41. yul *h* khor *b* srung.
42. *h*phags *s*keys-pa

43. The title "Chief of Rarity" seems to have been the name of an indigenous Tibetan god.
44. This is a staff (Tib. *Khar-sil*, Skt. *hi-ki-lo*) surmounted by 9 to 12 jingling rings, carried in the hand of the Indian Buddhist monk, to warn the villagers of his approach when he went a-begging, bowl in hand.
45. *s*pyan-ras-*g*zigs.
46. *Buddhism*, p. 490.
47. Campbell, *J.A.S.R.*, 1849; Hooker Sir R, Temple, *Jour.*, p. 212 : *Him. Jours*. I.
48. *r*do-rje *s*lob-*d*pon.
49. *d*hu-mdsad.
50. chho*s* khrim*s*-pa.
51. hphan.
52. Sri*d*-pa-hi *h*khor-lo.
53. Kindly supplied by Mr. White.
54. These sins are thus depicted by Sir E. Arnold in *The Light of Asia*, p. 164:—

    "Patigha—*Hate*—
    With serpents coiled about her waist, which suck
    Poisonous milk from both her hanging dugs,
    And with her curses mix their angry hiss.
    Then followed Ruparaga—*Lust* of Days—
    That sensual sin which out of greed for life
    Forgets to live; and Lust of Fame * * * (and) Fiend of Pride
    * * * * * * and—*Ignorance*—the Dam
    Of Fear and Wrong, Avidya, hideous hag
    Whose footsteps left the midnight darker."
55. Sir E. Arnold (*loc. cit.*, p. 165) thus expresses the Nidanas:—

    "Whirling on the Wheel,
    Avidya—Delusion—Sets those snares,
    Delusion breeds *Sankhara*, Tendency
    Perverse; Tendency Energy—*Vidnnan*—
    Whereby comes *Namarupa*, local form
    And name and bodiment, bringing the man
    With senses naked to the sensible,
    A helpless mirror of all shows which pass
    Across his heart, and so *Vedana* grows
    'Sense-life'—false in its gladness, fell in sadness;
    But sad or glad, the Mother of Desire,
    Trishna, that thirst which makes the living drink
    Deeper and deeper of the false salt waves
    Whereon they float, pleasures, ambitions, wealth,

Praise, fame, or domination, conquest, love;
Rich meats and robes and fair abodes and pride
Of ancient lines, and lust of days and strife
To live, and sins that flow from strife, some sweet,
Some bitter. Thus Life's thirst quenches itself
With draughts which double thirst."

56. In the older pictures a man, who represents Buddha, is guiding the blind woman. But the Ajanta painting shows this man leading a (blind) camel, it is mident that the Lamas constructed their picture from a written description, and interpreted the word *nga-mo* (*r*nga-mo), a camel—an animal practically unknown in Central Tibet—as *ga-mo* (*r*gad-mo) "and old woman."

57. The newer style has a boat being ferried across the ocean of life with human passengers.
Another form is a pair of caressing lovers.

58. "heaved up."

59. *m*chhod sham.

60. chhab-bum.

61. nas bzed.

62. spos-*h*dsin.

63. *m*chhod ting.

64. *m*chhod *s*kong.

65. nyer-*s*pyod *m*chhod-pa.

66. mchhod yon.

67. zhabs sel.

68. me-tog.

69. pdug-spos.

70. mar-me.

71. dri-chhab.

72. zhal-zas.

73. rol-mo.

74. In the Hindu worship of a deity, there are 16 stages of ceremonial adoration following the Invocation to come (*avahan*), and the Invitation to be seated (*asan*), and in each stage *mantras* are chanted. I have italicised those stages which are found in the above lamaic ritual :—

    1. *Padya*, washing the idol's feet.
    2. Azgha, washing the idol's hands.
    3. Achmana, offering water to rinse mouth.
    *4. Snana, bathing the idol.
    *5. Vastra, dressing the idol.
    6. Chandan, offering sandal wood, saffron, or holi powder.
    7. Akshat, offering rice.
    8. *Pushpa*, offering flowers.

9. *Dhupa*, offering incense.
10. *Dipa*, offering lamp.
11. *Naivedya*, offering food.
12. Achmana, second offering of water to rinse mouth.
13. Tambula, offering betel.
14. Supari or puga, offering Arcca nuts.
15. Dakshna, offering money.
16. Nizajan, waving lights or camphor.

75. *b*skang-*g*so.
76. In the room in which worship is done there must be present these three essential objects representing the *s*ku-*g*sum (Skt. *Tri-kaya*): (a) an image, (b) a chhorten, and (c) a holy book, which are symbolic of "The Three Holy Ones." In the early Indian Caves this Triad was represented by a *Chaitya* (= Buddha), *Wheel* (= Dharma), and a Lion (= the Assembly).
77. dril-bu.
78. kluu*s*-bum.
79. *m*dah-dar.
80. ils-*s*myan.
81. dung.
82. *r*gye-gling
83. rag-dung.
84. *r*kang-*g*ling.
85. *s*tag-dung.
86. *r*nga-chhung.
87. chhos-*r*nga.
88. *m*dum-*l*chog.
89. Note on Buddhist Rosaries in Japan. By J.M. James, Trans. Jap. As. Soc., p. 173, 1881.
90. *The Burman : His Life and Notions*, I., p. 201.
91. *The Burman : His Life and Notions*, I, p. 201.
92. *r*dog-*h*dsin.
93. *r*tsa-wahi *b*la-ma.
94. grang-*h*dsin.
95. *l*chu-bshad.
96. *Trarels in Tartary, Tibet and China*. By M. Huc and Gabet. Hazlitt's trans. I, p. 79.
97. po-dhi-tse.
98. dung-phreng.
99. tsanden.
100. pyi-ru.
101. thod-phreng.
102. *g*lnag-chhen grod-pa

103. rag sha.
104. *r*do-rje-*h*jigs-byed.
105. phyag-na *r*do-rje.
106. *r*ta-mgrin.
107. grugs-*r*je chhen-po.
108. *s*grol-ma *l*jang-khu.
109. *s*grol-*d*kar.
110. do-rje phag-mo.
111. *h*od-zer-chan-ma.
112. *m*gon-po nag-po.
113. *r*nam-sras.
114. dsam-bha-la.
115. Seng-ge-*s*gra.
116. *h*jam-*db*yangs.
117. *b*de-mchhog.
118. pad-ma *h*byung-*g*nas.
119. Since the above was in type, I find that Rockhill in *The Land of the Lamas*, London, 1891, p. 326, notes that Wilhelm de Rubruk, writing in the second half of the 13th century, A.D. (Soc. de Geog. de Paris, IV, p. 283) states regarding the Buddhist monks of Karakorum: "Habent etiam quocumque vadunt semper in manibus quandaun testem centum vel ducentorum nucleorum sicut nos portamus paternoster et dicunt semper hec verba, on man baccam hoc est *Dcus, tu nosti,* secundum quod quidam corum interpretatus est michi, et totiens exspectat, remuneratonemaa Deo quotiens hoc dicendo memomchi, et totiens exspectat, remuneratonem a Deo quotiens hos dicendo memoratur."
120. *h*bag.
121. *s*ku.
122. Ye-she *m*gon-po.
123. glang.
124. *s*tag.
125. *s*pre-u.
126. *b*kah-*h*gyur.
127. *b*stan-*h*gyur.
128. This is the "*Chebu* Lama" of Hooker's *Himalayan Journals*.
129. "Bhotiya" menas an inhabitant of "Bhot" or Tibet, and is thus synonymous with "Tibetan."
130. Such small manuals are about eight or ten inches long by two to three inches broad and usually have the leaves stitched together.
131. The alleged reason for this being the pre-eminence of the father, from whom comes the bone and structure of the child, while from the mother only came "the flesh." It is notable that the Tibetans habitually say "apo-ame" *i.e.*, father and mother, and not like the Indians "*ma-bap*," *i.e.*, mother and father.

132. For description, vide Chapter V, p. 320.
133. Or "Banquet to the whole assembly of the Gods and Demons"—*vide* p. 276.
134. Mt. Thang-lha with its spirit "Kiting" is a northern guardian of Sikkim.
135. The Ten Precepts (Skt. *Dasasila*) Mi-*dge*-*b*chu—literally "The Ten Virtuous Deeds," according to the Lamas, are (1) Not to kill any living being, (2) Not to steal, (3) Not to commit adultery, (4) Not to lie, (5) Not to drink wine (this is not observed), (6) Not to sit on a lofty seat or have a large bed, (7) Not to wear flowers or ribbons, (8) Not to be fond of songs or dances, (9) Not to wear ornaments of gold or silver, (10) Not to catch flesh food after noon.
136. Not ayman is allowed to serve out the monks' food.
137. The first Bhotiya King of Sikkim, *vide* p. 249.
138. This may be a reference to the great Emperor Ashoka or his confessor—Upagupta, the Thirteenth Patriarch of the early Buddhist Church in India.
139. *Pardo*, the ghostly interval death and judgment—*vide* article "Wheel of Life," in chapter on "Temple," p. 266.
140. Each stanza refers to a different form of the goddess between as noted in the foregoing text.
141. The allusion here is that Avalokita—"The Storehouse of Pity"—on looking down upon the world shed tears out of pity for the misery of humanity. The tear from the left eye on falling to the earth formed a lake, on which instantly, like a lightning-flash, appeared, floating on a lotus flower, the goddess Dolma, who was then commissioned by Avalokita to soothe human suffering.
142. In this form of Dolma's image a figure of Tathagatha Amitabha Buddha is seated on her hair.
143. Part of Dolma's spell or *mantra* already given under head of "Rosaries." *vide* p. 288.
144. *Ibid.*
145. The Tibetan measure is a "dpag-tshad" which according to Csoma deKoros, equals 4,000 fathoms, and hence a geographical mile. But it seems to correspond to the same Indian unit of measure which is translated in the Ceylonese seriptures as a Yojana, *i.e.*, a unit of about 4 *kos*, and therefore over five or six geographical miles.
146. Vide p. 261 for particulars of the Four Guardian Kings of the Quarters. Another arrangement gives guardian deities for each of "the ten directions." viz., Indra on the East; Agni (the fire god) on the South-East; Yama (the death god) on the South; Rakshas (?Sura) on the South-West; Varuna (the water god) on the West; Vayu (the wind god) on the North-West; Yakhas on the North; Soma (the moon) on the North-East; Brahma, above; Bhupati (sa-*b*dag or Earth Spirit) below.
147. rin-po-chhe *s*na *b*dun.
148. The seven Banners—"Gyaltshen sna bdun"—are:

1. Kangsang Rimpochhe or The precious House.
2. Gos " " " Royal Vestments.
3. Hlam " " " Boot.
4. Lang chhen chem " " " Elphant's tusk.
5. Tsunmo na-ja " " " Queen's Ear-ring.
6. Gyalpo " " " King's "
7. Norbu Rimpochh " " " Jewel.

149. This "Buddhist Creed," which is carved on most of the later Buddhist votive images in India, Hodgson translates (J.A.S. No. 40,1835):—"The cause or causes of all sentient existence in the versatile world the Tathagata has explained. The Great Sramana (*i.e.,* Buddha) hath likewise explained the cause or causes of the cessation of all such existence." This stanza is complete in itself, but a second is occasionally added, namely:—

"Sarba papasya akaranam
Kusalasyopasapradam
Swachittam pariyodapanam
Otan Buddhanusasanam,"
which Csoma deKoros has translated:—
"No vice is to be committed;
Every virtue must be perfectly practised;
The mind must be brought under entire subjection;
This is the commandment of Buddha."

150. Birch-bark, though not used in Tibet, was used in ancient India and Persia as a writing material. The rituals of the Magi in the most ancient Persian were written on birch-bark. See also Q. Curtius, VIII, 9, 15, *Ariana Antiqua*, pp. 60, 84; Prinsep's *Essays. H.Tsiang's.*

151. *Blue* is the contemptuous colour in which any offensive dog is to be regarded.

152. *r*Lung-*r*ta.

153. Dar-*l*chog.

154. And the votive pillars of the earlier Buddhists offered for railings to stupas were called.

155. Schlagintweit's figure, in addition to being printed in reversed fashion, is so mutilated and indistinct that I give another illustration.

156. Zhang-lha is usually interpreted "maternal uncle god," but it may also mean "uterine god."

157. The story of his acquiring from the *sea* the banner of victory is suggestive of Indra's victorious banner, also procured from the sea.—*Brihat Sanhita*, translated by Dr. Kern, *J. Roy, As. Socy.* (new series), VI, page 44.

158. *Horat.* 2, *Epist.*

159. The Sikkim King is descended from the Mi-nyak dynasty of Kham in Eastern Tibet—a dynasty which once held sway over Western China, and regarded, as semi-divine by the Tibetans. It is said to have been founded

by a son of Thi-srong-de-tsan, the Tibetan King who was associated with Padma-Sambhava in the foundation of Lamaism.

160. Most Sikkimites before sowing a field sacrifice a cock to the demons.

161. *Vide* p. 263.

162. *Vide* also p. 342.

163. If a man's sins are insufficient to procure rebirth even in the hells, he is reborn as a zhi-dak—say the Sikkim Lamas. The zhi-dak may be one or other of the eight classes, viz.

   1. "lha" or "spirits" (all male) of a white colour and fairly good disposition; but they must suffer many indignities in order to procure a higher rebirth.
   2. "*k*lu" or Nagas, mostly green in colour and frequenting lakes or springs.
   3. gnad-*s*byan, or "disease-givers," are also red in colour.
   4. *b*dud (or black devils). All are male and are extremely wicked.They are the spirits of those who opposed in life the true religion. They eat flesh and are not to be appeased without a pig—the most luscious morsel to a hillman's palate. Their wives are called *b*dud-mo.
   5. "tsan," or red demons (all male). They are usually the spirits of deceased novices, and are therefore especially associated with Gompas.
   6. "*r*gyal-po," or "Victors," are white in colour, and are spirits of kings and deceased lamas who fail to reach Nirvana.
   7. "ma-mo" are all female, and black in colour. It includes *Mak-sor rgyul ma*, called also *Maharani*, or "the Great Queen," the disease-producing form of the Hindu Durga.
   8. "gzah" or "planets"—Rahula, & c.

164. This exclamation *gsol-gsol* may also mean "worship" or "entreaty."

165. *r*tsis-pa—the *Chebu of Hooker's Himalayan Jours.*

166. The horoscope for birth is name *s*kyes-rtsis, that for the whole life is tshe-rabs las *r*tsis. he annual horoscope is *s*kag-rtsis, hat for marriage is pag-*r*tsis, and for death *g*shin-rtsi*s*.

166a. The Tibetan Chronological Table here given differs from that of Schlagintweit *(op. cit.*, p. 282) in making the initial year of the current sixty-year cycle, viz., the fifteenth *Rabjung*,coincide with the year 1807 A.D., as this is alleged by the learned *Tsipa* Lama of Darjeeling to be the true epoch, and not the year 1866 as given by Schlagintweit.

Year A.D.	*Tibetan Era*			*Year A.D.*	*Tibetan Era*		
	Cycle No.	*Cyclical year*	*Year name*		*Cycle No.*	*Cyclical year*	*Year name*
1858	XIV	52	Earth -Horse.	1890	XV	24	Iron -Tiger
1859	,	53	,, -Sheep.	1891	,,	25	,, -Hare.
1860	,,	54	Iron -Ape.	1892	,,	26	Water-Dragon.

1861	,,	55	,, -Brid.	1893	,,	27	,, -Serpent.
1862	,,	56	Water-Dog.	1894	,,	28	Wood-Horse.
1863	,,	57	,, -Hog.	1895	,,	29	,, -Sheep
1864	,,	58	Wood-Mouse.	1896	,,	30	Fire -Ape.
1865	,,	59	,, -Ox.	1897	,,	31	,, -Bird.
1866	,,	60	Fire -Tiger.	1898	,,	32	Earth -Dog.
1867	XV	1	,, -Hare.	1899	,,	33	,, -Hog
1868	,,	2	Earth -Dargon.	1900	,,	34	Iron -Mouse.
1869	,,	3	,, -Serpent.	1901	,,	35	,, -Ox.
1870	,,	4	Iron -Horse.	1902	,,	36	Water-Tiger.
1871	,,	5	,, -Sheep.	1903	,,	37	,, -Hare.
1872	,,	6	Water-Ape.	1904	,,	38	Wood -Dragon
1873	,,	7	,, -Bird	1905	,,	39	,, -Serpent.
1874	,,	8	Wood-Dog.	1906	,,	40	Fire -Horse.
1875	,,	9	,, -Hog	1907	,,	41	,, - Sheep.
1876	,,	10	Fire -Mouse	1908	,,	42	Earth - Ape.
1877	,,	11	,, -Ox	1909	,,	43	,, -Bird.
1878	,,	12	Earth -Tiger.	1910	,,	44	Iron -Dog.
1879	,,	13	,, -Hare.	1911	,,	45	,, -Hog.
1880	,,	14	Iron -Dragon.	1912	,,	46	Water-Mouse
1881	,,	15	,, -Serpent.	1913	,,	47	,, -Ox
1882	,,	16	Water-Horse.	1914	,,	48	Wood-Tiger.
1883	,,	17	,, -Sheep.	1915	,,	49	,, -Hare.
1884	,,	18	Wood-Ape.	1916	,,	50	Fire -Dragon.
1885	,,	19	,, -Bird.	1917	,,	51	,, -Serpent.
1886	,,	20	Fire -Dog.	1918	,,	52	Earth -Horse.
1887	,,	21	,, -Hog	1919	,,	53	,, -Sheep.
1888	,,	22	Earth -House	1920	,,	54	Iron -Ape.
1889	,,	23	,, -Ox	1921	,,	55	,, -Bird

167. If a man's sins are insufficient to procure rebirth even in the hells, he is reborn as a zhi-dak—say the Sikhim Lamas. The zhi-dak may be one or other of the eight classes, viz.—

(1) "lha" or "spirits" (all male of a white colour and a fairly good disposition; but they must suffer many indignities in order to procure a higher rebirth.

(2) "*k*lu," or Nagas, mostly green in colour and frequenting lakes or springs.

(3) *g*nad-*s*byan, or "disease-givers," are also red in colour.

(4) *b*dud (r black devils). All are male and are extremely wicked. They are the spirits of those who opposed in life the true religion. They eat

flesh and are not to be appeased without a pig—the most luscious morsel to a hillman's palate. Their wives are called *b*dud-mo.

(5) "tsan," or red demons (all male). They are usually the spirits of deceased novices, and are therefore especially associated with Gompas.

(6) "*r*gyal-po," or "Victors," are white in colour, and are spirits of kings and deceased lamas who fail to reach Nirvana.

(7) "ma-mo" are all female, and black in colour. It includes *Mak-sor rgyal ma,* called also *Maharani,* or "the Great Queen," the disease-producing form of the Hindu Durga.

(8) "*g*zah" or "planets"—Rahula, &c.

168. This exclamation *gsol-gsol* may also mean "worship" or "entreaty."

169. *r*tsis-pa—the *Chebu of Hooker's Himalayan Jours.*

170. The horoscope for birth is named *s*kye*s*-rtsis, that for the whole life is tshe-rabs la*s r*tsis. The annual horoscope is *s*kag-*r*tsi*s*, that for marriage is pag-*r*tsi*s*, and for death *g*shin-*r*tsi*s*.

171. The horoscope for birth is named *s*kye*s*-rtsis, that for the whole life is tshe-rabs las *r*tsi*s*. The annual horoscope is *s*kag-rtsis, that for marriage is pag-*r*tsi*s*, and for death *g*shin-*r*tsi*s*.

172. The Bodhisat Manjusri is the presiding divinity of the astrologers, and he is always invoked at the head of astrologic prescriptions.

173. The year of his birth being the Water-Hog gives, according to the astrologic table, Water as the *srog* for that year, and the present year being the Earth-Mouse year its *srog* according to the table, is also Water. Therefore Water meeting Water = *0*, *i.e.*, "good."

174. The *lus* of these two years are found by the table to give the elements respectively of Water and Fire. Therefore Water meeting its friend Fire = *00* or "better" i.e., good of the second degree.

175. This *Log-men* or "Reversed + downwards" is a more abstruse calculation according to the saying :—

"skyes-pa pu-yi stag thog nas lo grangs thur,"

bud-med ma-yi sprel-thog nas lo grangs gyen.

For *males*—the *sons* of elements—begin from *Tiger* and count age *downwards*.

For *females*—the *mothers*—begin from *Ape* and count age *upwards*. Thus the birth year of this individual being Water-Hog, and he being a male, and the *son* of Water being gives us for his *Log-men* the Wood-Tiger year (which = 1854 A.D.). And as he is a male, on counting *downwards* from the Wood-Tiger the number of years of his age (*i.e.*, 26), we get the year Earth-Hare (*i.e.*, 1879 A.D.). And according to the Log-men Manual, the Earth-Hare year is "*h*byor-pa," or *Riches*, which is given the value of "good," i.e. = *0*.

176. This is calculated on the srog of the *Log-men* year, minus five years. In this case we have seen the *Log-men* year is the Earth-Hare year. Counting back to the fifth year gives the Wood-Hog, which has as its *srog* the

element water, and the *srog* of the present1888 A.D. year, viz., Earth-Mouse, being also Water, therefore = 0 or good for the "sky-seizing Rope."

177. *Vide* p. 373.
178. *Vide* p. 371.
179. *Vide ante*, p. 318.
180. Page 363.
181. The symbolic colour of the earth.
182. The meaning of the "*dok*" *is* "let all evils be annihilated!"
183. "The images of men and women made of wool were hung in the streets, and so many balls made of wool as there were servants in the family, and so many complete images as there were children (*Festus apud Lil. Gyr*). The meaning of which custom was this : These feasts were dedicated to the Lares,who were esteemed infernal gods; the people desiring hereby that these gods would be contented with these woollen images and spare the persons represented by them. These Lares sometimes were clothed in the skins of *dogs* (*Plutarch. in Prob.*) and were sometimes fashioned in the shape of dogs (*Plautus*), whence that creature was consecrated to them."—*Tooke's Pantheon*, page 280.
184. *i.e.*, the Lower Do (or Amdo), Kham, and "The Six Ridges"—provinces of Eastern Tibet.
185. *Li*-yul or Khoten, and *Pal*-yul or Nepal.
186. *Vide ante* article "Nam-go."
187. A fragment of such a skull or its image made of dough is usually all that is used.
188. Dough also will do.
189. It has frequently been asserted that no prayer is practised in lamaism. This is not true: real prayer is frequently done; the word used here is *g*sol-wa-*g*tab.
190. Fully described hereafter, *vide* p. 383.
191. Za-*h*dre-kha sgyur.
192. gzlog-pa-hi *s*nag*s*.
193. za-hdre-kha *s*gyur *d*gra phyog*s*.
194. pho shing is interpreted "male" tree, but might possibly be intended for "bamboo".
195. Za hdre dgra phyogs Su-kha sgyur ro.
196. pu shing.
197. Za hdre kha Sgyar ro
198. Sweet *Calamus*.
199. *b*gag*s*.
200. lkhor-lo-tuk-pa. "the noisy wheel."
201. *Sri*.
202. Shu*d* = "active."

203. kang-wa bzang-po.
204. gnod-*s*byin.
205. *r*gyal-po.
206. Ngag-pa
207. *b*gegs.
208. "The Eight Dreads" are dread of Fire, Prison, Plunder, Water, Enemy, Elephants, Lions and Snakes:—*Vide* my article "On some Ajanta paintings" in *Indian Antiquary* for the current year (1892).

5

Monasteries in Sikkim: A Geographical Study

Establishment of a *Gompa* or Monastery is one of the characteristic features of Tibetan Buddhism where religious professionals, students, teachers and others, reside together within a framework of social organizational.[1] A monastery in Tibetan Buddhism, has its own hierarchy of monastic grades. It is virtually a residential college for religious studies and teaching centre for craft, script, art, etc. At present, there are 77 monasteries in Sikkim.[2]

1. Origin and Development of Monasteries

Tibet, Bhutan and Sikkim—religious are Buddhist states. Their religious unification happened in early seventeenth Century. Both in Tibet and Bhutan the monastery and *Dzong*[3] played a dominating role during the period of unification under particular Buddhist sects: *Gelugpa* in Tibet and *Drugpa* in Bhutan. The state of Sikkim on the other hand, emerged overnight under the guidance of three lamas from Tibet and Buddhism became the state religion after this. Three Nyingmapa lamas from Tibet installed Phuntsong Namgyal, a Tibetan colonist, as the *Chogyal* (a fountain head of both secular and spiritual power) in 1642. While both in Tibet and Bhutan successive heads of the state were the reincarnations of the previous heads, in Sikkim religion was never given such a top priority in the selection of the head of the state. It maintained a hereditary ruling system. Sometimes, the hereditary head was rather accepted as the reincarnation of some important religious personality. Therefore, even though the head of religion never acted automatically as the head of the state in Sikkim, a "priest-client"[4] relationship prevailed within the fold of this hereditary ruling system. The system of reincarnation under the fold of hereditary succession was not uncommon in Sikkim e.g., the last king was the reincarnation of the famous Karmapa lama of Kham (Tibet). He was also recognized as the spiritual head of the Rumtek and Phudong monasteries.[5]

The three lamas of Nyingmapa sect,[6] the oldest school of Buddhism from Tibet met together at Yaksum to install the first Chogyal in the unruly territory of Sikkim. This as per records available to those who want to do research. The territory extended between Arun river (in Nepal) on the west to the Ha valley (Bhutan) on the east and Khamba Dzong (Tibet) on the north to Phulbari—Kisanganj (West Bengal and Bihar). The territory was settled by three major communities—the Lepchas, the Limbus (*Tsong*), and the Mangars besides the Bhutias or the early Tibetan colonists. Probably there we: some other groups as well but they seem to have been numerically very insignificant and there is no specific record of any other community of this period.[7]

The Limbus were mainly settled in the area between Rangit river on the east to the Arun river on the west. They occupied the easternmost part of Nepal, western Sikkim and Darjeeling District (Darjeeling and Kurseong Sub-division of West Bengal).[8] Majority of the Limbus never accepted Buddhism although some cases of conversion did take place in the early phase. During the regime of the fourth Chogyal the relation between the Bhutia Chogyal and the Limbus sharply deteriorated. Finally they formed a separate territory—Limbuana, covering the area between Singila on the east and Arun river on the west. Thus, Sikkim lost the western front permanently.

The Mangars were mainly settled in the lower part of the Rangit river system and were loosely consolidated in the unruly territory.[9] Although they took in the various military expeditions of Sikkim,[10] their relation with the ruler was never very good and they never followed Buddhism. The Lepchas formed the most important community both in terms of number and power and they were also consolidated under different chiefs.[11] They were mainly settled in lower part of the Tista-Rangit river valley system. They were converted to Buddhism in course of time. The Bhutias were mainly settled over the valleys and ridges on the northern and eastern parts of the country which offered similar ecological condition as their homeland—Tibet and was also easily accessible to it. Actually, the entire land east of Tista including upper catchment area (Lachen-Lachung) were known to the Tibetan traders, graziers, herders and Buddhist missonaries.[12] The ancestors of the first Chogyal had settled there long before 1642.

With the installation of the Bhutia Chogyal Phuntsong Namgyal in 1642, Buddhism got a boost in Sikkim with the patronage of the Chogyal, it became the state religion. Thereafter it was propagated by the lamas with all the zeal and enthusiasm. Immediately after the installation of the Chogyal they started either building or at least selecting site for a number of monasteries around Yaksum. A *Stupa* Chorten-Tashi Wod-hBor was built at the site of coronation at Yaksum during the time of consecration. This stupa is the first religious structure of any kind in Sikkim. On that occasion of coronation all the Lamas as well as the Chogyal requested lama Lhatsum to select a spot for a monastery. The monastery at Dubdi was said to have been built by lama Lhatsum.[13]

Lama Lhatsum also selècted site for Pemayangtse monastery and Rabdanse palace and also marked Pemayangtse as a proper site for a monastery for *Tasongs* or pure monks.[14] At this time, lama mNga-bDag also built/selected site for two monasteries at Tashiding, one at the junction of Barbong and Karma, and the other at Rinchenpong. Kathog, lama built/selected site for Kathog monastery, i.e., Kartok in East Sikkim. In course of time monasteries were built in those selected sites. Lama Jig-med Gyatsho, incarnation of Lama Lhatsum Chenpo, came from Tibet during the regime of second Chogyal Tensung Namgyal and was engaged in monastery building activities.[15]

During the period of the third Chogyal Chakdo Namgyal (1700-17), Bhutan invaded Sikkim[16] and the king took refuge under the 6th Dalai Lama in Lhasa (Tibet). There he attended monastic school and became a learned scholar. During his tenure Buddhism got strong footing in the soil of Sikkim. Lama Jig-med Poa came into Sikkim in 1709 under the request of Chogyal and under his guidance Buddhism and the monastic establishment further spread and rituals were systematized. The King not only granted land to the Pemayangtse monastery but also introduced the custom that every second son of a three child Bhutia family should join the monastery. This resulted, not only in the increase of the number of lamas but also generated a demand for more monasteries.

During this period, the three monasteries of Senon, Chogyel Lakhang of Tashiding and Sanga Cholling were established. Lama Jig-med Poa also organised the Pemayangtse monastery on the model of the Mindoling monastery of Tibet.[17] Thus, though founded later than Dubdi, Pemayangtse became the first monastery in Sikkim to be systematized. In course of time, it became the Royal monastery in Sikkim and served as the head monastery of the Nyingma sect. Lama Jig-med Poa also played active role in the state affairs after the death of the third Chogyal (1717) as the fourth Chogyal Gurmed Namgyal ascended at the infant age of only 10. After the death of the great lama Jig-med Poa, the Chogyal became depressed and went to Tibet on a pilgrimage where he met the famous Karmapa lama-Chang Chuti-Dorjee. To him he promised to build a Karmapa monastery in Sikkim. Thus the Ralong monastery was founded in 1730 with landed estate for its support.[18]

In this way, the Karmapa sect received royal patronage for the first time in Sikkim. The King also founded two important Karmapa monasteries at Phudong and Rumtek. Interestingly, these two monasteries were established for the first time outside the monastery cluster around the capital, Yaksum-Rabdanse. He also granted more land to Pemayangtse monastery. During the period of the successive rulers most of the monasteries were established on the north and eastern part of the country. The following reasons may be responsible for the shifts of location—(i) the southern part of the state was almost uninhabited during that period and in the later part of the 19th century the land was occupied by the migrant Nepalese; (ii) the formation of Limbuana restricted the establishment of monasteries on the western part; also, (iii) the old capital region had already become overcrowded by monasteries. Sikkim faced internal trouble on the issue of succession of the fifth Chogyal Namgyal Phuntsong because a group of influencial Lepcha opposed his nomination.[19]

There was every of danger of internal strife. The Tibetan authority deputed one administrator—Rabden Sharpa—to look after the state affairs on behalf of the infant king (born and succeeding in 1733). During the tenure of this Chogyal (1733-80), two monasteries were established— those of Rishihat and Wangdu Dorjiling in Darjeeling.[20] Bhutan and Nepal attacked Sikkim during the later part of his regime in 1770 and 1775 respectively. The King was succeeded by his son Tenzing Namgyal in 1780. Nepal made a fresh attack against Sikkim in 1788. The Raja fled to Tibet with his family and was succeeded nominally by his son Cho-Phoe Namgyal in 1790. After the British-Nepal treaty of Titalia in 1817, Raja returned to the new capital—Tumlong. In this period of political uncertainty monastery building activities were limited and confined to the northern part of Sikkim as the entire southern part was occupied by Nepal (west of Tista) and Bhutan (east of Tista).

Only a few monasteries at Lachung, Chungthang, Tolung and Lachen were established during this period (Table 5.1). In fact, the Hindu Gorkhas even destroyed a number of monasteries during their 26 years (1788-1814) stay in Sikkim. Monastery building activities started again after the 1817 treaty and 13 monasteries were established between 1840 to 1860[21] (Table 5.1). Some fundamental changes were initiated in the course of the history of Sikkim after this period. Firstly, this treaty brought an end to Tibet's political control over Sikkim although cultural as well as religious influence remained constant atleast till the end of the 19th century. Sikkim also faced internal trouble on the question of Nepalese immigration since the 1861 treaty of Tumlong.[22] With the direct encouragement from the British authority, the number of Nepalese settlers in increased very rapidly.

TABLE 5.1

Monasteries in Sikkim

Name	*Sect*	*Year of Establishment*
West:		
1. Dubdi Sangha	Ny.	1701
2. Khecshopheri	Ny.	1788
3. Pau Hungri	Ny.	1860
4. Melli Asing	Ny.	1740
5. Pemayangtse	Ny.	1705
6. Sinen Ngadak	Ny.	1716
7. Tashiding Chogyel	Ny.	1716
8. Sangha Choling	Ny.	1714
9. Luntse	NA.	1850
10. Rinchenpong	Ny.	1730
11. Chakung	NA.	NA.
12. Anden Wolung	NA.	NA.
13. Nupling/Nobling	NA.	1884/1875
East:		
14. Sumin	NA.	1924
15. Linkey Machong Chonkar	NA.	1860

16.	Rhenock Bora Kagyud	Kr.	1841
17.	Amba Mamring	NA.	NA.
18.	Changey	NA.	1988
19.	Kartok Dojiden	Ny.	1840
20.	Simik Dahduling	Ny.	1850
21.	Rakdong Tintek	NA	1941
22.	Samdong Mintok	Ny.	1913
23.	Tumin Karmacholing	Kr.	1915
24.	Song Kagyud	Kr.	1912
25.	Martam Chenkar	NA.	1947
26.	Rumtek Kagyud	Kr.	1740
27.	Rumtek Dharma Chakra Centre	Kr.	1960s
28.	Sang-Ngor Choi-Tshog Centre (Ranka)	Kr.	1990s
29.	Pabyuk Bora Kagyud	Kr.	NA.
30.	Enchey Sangacholing	Ny.	1840
31.	Ugen Dongak Cholling (Gangtok)	NA.	NA.
32.	Tsuklakhang (Gangtok)	NA.	NA.
33.	Lingdok Chonkar	NA.	1875
34.	Pendam	NA.	1954
35.	Chandmari Kagyud (Gangtok)	Kr.	NA.
North:			
36.	Tolung	Ny.	1789
37.	Lingthem Chophel Targeiling	Ny.	1857
38.	Gor Taryang	NA.	NA.
39.	Ship Kinza Choling	Ny.	1944
40.	Lachen Gnedupcholing	Ny.	1806/58
41.	Lachung Samtencholing	Ny.	1788
42.	Lachung	NA.	1850
43.	Chungthang Chimorinchen	NA.	1768
44.	Singchit Nadak	Ny.	1923
45.	Santong Tinsing	NA.	NA.
46.	Ringong Rikzincholing	Ny.	1860
47.	Phodong Kagyud	Kr.	1740
48.	Labrong	NA.	1844
49.	Phensong	Ny.	1840

Contd ...

50. Chewang Ani	Ny.	1936
51. Hee-Gyathang (Tashiling)	Ny.	1935
52. Santam	Ny.	NA.
53. Tingbong	Ny.	NA.
54. Lingden	NA.	NA.
55. Barphok	NA.	1939
56. Seyem	Ny.	NA.
57. Shagyong (L. Dzongu)	NA.	NA.
58. Silim Phagyal	NA.	NA.
South:		
59. Kitam Nyangma	Ny.	NA.
60. Ralong Kagyud	Kr.	1730
61. Gyaltshe Rimpoche Centre (Ralong)	Kr.	1980s
62. Dolling Rikzin Lonoyang	Ny.	1840
63. Kewzing	NA.	NA.
64. Khyosing Mangbro (Kewzing)	NA.	1874
65. Wak Samtencholing	NA.	1927
66. Namchi Boomtar	Ny.	NA.
67. Namchi Ngadak	Ny.	1836
68. Namchi—(Tamang)	Ny.	1929
69. Sendop Cholong, Namchi	NA.	NA.
70. Melli Tashi Chodarling	NA.	NA.
71. Namthang Norbucholing	NA.	1933
72. Barmiok Woselcholing	Ny.	1952
73. Parbing Karma Tashi	Ny.	1934
74. Yangang Tashi Palding	Ny.	1841
75. Lingi Phagyal	Ny.	NA.
76. Ben	Kr.	1905
77. Shar-Chok Bey-phuk, Samgmo	NA.	NA.

Ny. Nyingmapa sect. Kr. Karmapa sect:. NA. Not available.

Source: Ecclesiastical Dept. Govt. of Sikkim 1995; Waddell, L.A. (1894); and Maharaja Thutob Namgyal and Maharani Yissey Dolma, *History of Sikkim* (1908).

One Political Officer to Gangtok in 1889 and capital shifted from Tumlong to Gangtok. During this period only two monasteries were established in Sikkim (Table 5.1). Monastery building activities started once again from the first decade of the 20th century. About 16 monasteries came up between 1912 to 1947. These monasteries are mainly small village monasteries. In the post-British period very few monasteries have been established with exception to the Dharma Chakra Centre at Rumtek, Gyaltshe Rimpoche Centre at Ralong and Sang-Ngor Choi-Tshog Centre at Rankha (East Sikkim). At present, these three Karma monasteries with their huge structure and large number of students are functioning properly. The expenditure for running these monasteries is also very huge. It is being borne mainly by devotees from all over the world.

2. Classification of Monasteries

It is very difficult to classify the monasteries on the basis of a single criterion. These have been classified in terms of their size, number of monks, sect and community.

TABLE 5.2

Monastery-wise Distribution of Lama in Sikkim: 1894, 1993 and 1995

Name of the Monastery	*No. of Lamas 1894(2)*	*Number of Electoral 1993*	*1995*
West:			
Dubdi Sangha	30	27	34
Khecshopheri	11	41	51
Pau Hungri	NA	07	08
Melli	15	59	30
Pemayangtse	108	102	125
Tashiding	20	59	63*
Sinen Ngadak	08	60	65
Sanghacholing	25	49	52
Luntse	15	20	45
Rinchenpong	98	26	20
Chakung	NA	11	12
Anden Wolung	NA	16	15
Nupling/Nobling	08		
East:			
Sumin	NA	26	22
Linkey Maching Chonkar	20	79	132

Contd ...

Rhenock Bora Kagyud	NA	34	38
Amba Mamring	NA	10	09
Changey	NA	26	29
Kartok Dojiden	20	26	26
Rakdong Tintek	NA	50	40
Samdong Mintok	NA	38	21
Tumin Karmacholing	NA	43	46
Song Kagyud	NA	31	46
Martam Chenkar	NA	28	23
Rumtek Kagyud	80	189	137
Pabyuk Bora Kagyud	20	35	24
Enchey Sangacholing	15	91	70
Simik	20	86	NA
North:			
Tolung	90	88	88
Lingthem Chophel Targeiling	20	21	13
Hee-Gyathang (Tashiling)	NA	20	07
Gor Taryang	NA	47	35
Ship Kinzacholing	NA	65	15
Lac hen Gnedupcholing	08	90	51
Lachung Samtencholing	08	48	48
Chungthang Chimorinchen	08	41	31
Singchit Nadak	NA	28	28
Santong Tinsing	06	33	39
Ringong Rikzincholing	30	45	41
Phodong Kagyud	100	333	314
Labrong	30	39	41
Phensong	100	188	225
Chewang Ani	NA	36	46
Lingi Phagyal	NA	46	15
Kitam Nyangma	NA	12	08
Ralong Kagyud	80	121	101
Dolling Rikzin Lonoyang	08	2.8	33
Khyosing Mangbro (Kewzing)	NA	14	15
wak Samtencholing	NA	07	05
Namchi Boomtar	NA	15	21

Namchi Ngadak	06	14	22
Melli Tashi Chodarling	NA	25	09
Namthang Norbucholing	NA	16	08
Barmiok Woselcholing	NA	23	36
Parbing Karma Tashi	NA	107	21
Yangang Tashi Palding	10	46	59

Sources: (1) Electoral Roll 1993 and 1995. Election Commission. Govt. of Sikkim; (2) Waddell, L.A. 1894. *op.cit.*, p. 257-58.

Note:— Of the 77 monasteries mentioned in Table 5.1, only 5 are enlisted in the Sangha constituency, consisting of the Buddhist monks, which is a speciality in the case of Sikkim politics; as such, those 5, 6 are only included in Table 5.2.

NA = not available;
1994.

The monasteries of Sikkim may be grouped into two major categories (i) The first is the Gompa founded in or around the village serving mainly as a chapel for the community (ii) The proper monastery—a residential college for religious study where religious professionals reside together within a framework of social organization. Most of the Gompa or village monasteries belong to the first category and they consist of merely a *Lhakang* or temple with one or more priests engaged in ministering the rituals to the surrounding villages.[23] Most of them are also single storied, with a few stupa or chorten (tomb).[24] Some of these monasteries have separate *Mani Lakhang*—(places of worship for women). They are mainly maintained from the donation of the local people or grant received from Government. In many village some powerful communities or group dominate the monasteries. The lamas are also favourites of those communities who are inevitably chosen the dominant section.

The important and the premier monasteries of Pemayangtse, Tashiding, Phensong, Rumtek, Ralong and Phudong come under the second group. All of these have much landed estates for their maintenance. A large number of lamas are attached to these. (Table 5.2). In addition, the Buddhist community of Sikkim also consider the monasteries of Tolung, Enchy, Kartok, etc. as equally important. These monasteries were either built or the sites were selected by the first three famous lamas or some reputed lamas in the later period. These monasteries also have large number of lamas. In these major monasteries, the monastery establishment usually consists of a Lhakhang, Mani-Lhakhang, school, library, residence for students and monks and a number of Stupas or Chortens. The main structure is usually a two-storeyed building where the lower story houses the Lhakang and the other buildings cluster around it.

During the regime of the third Chogyal, Lama Jeg-med-Pao introduced monastic order in Pemayangtse and also appointed a batch of 108 monks to perform the monastic functions.[25] It must be seen that the number 108 is very important in Buddhist order. It has been mentioned earlier that the third Chogyal also introduced the custom that one son from every Bhutia family should join a monastery. This resulted in the growth of lama population in course of time. According to Trevor Ling,[26] there was a rise of 742 lamas during the period between 1720 and 1890 and the changes were noticeable among the districts (Table 5.3). In this period the lama population was mainly concentrated in the east whereas the number of lama population remained almost static in the west.[27] This may be correlated with the limited growth of monastery on the western part during the said period (Table 5.1). In 1894, there were 6 big monasteries in Sikkim in terms of the size of the lama population.[28] Each monastery increased the number of lamas (Table 5.2). During the period of hundred years from 1894-1995 lama population didn't increase much. Looked at demographically the increase is less what it should have been. It increased by about 170 per cent in about a hundred years.

TABLE 5.3

District-wise Distribution of Lamas in Sikkim 1720-1995

Year	*West*	*East*	*North*	*South*	*Total*
1720	191	03	—	—	194
1730	206	03	—	80	289
1740	221	183	—	80	484
1790	232	183	103	80	598
1840	232	318	103	80	733
1850	232	378	111	104	825
1860	232	428	147	104	911
1890	237	448	147	104	936
1894*	248	185	405	104	942
1993**	477	792	1168	428	2866
1995**	520	663	1037	338	2558

Source: Trevor Ling (1991) ** Number of Lama in the Electorate List. * Waddell, L.A. 1894, *op. cit.*

In addition, the three large monasteries of Karma-Kagyudpa sect at Rumtek, Ralong and Rankha have recently started functioning as mentioned earlier. At present, two of these monasteries are functioning as proper residential college and large number of lamas are attached to these. However, due to their different style of functioning, it is difficult to compare them with the major old monasteries of Sikkim.

The monasteries in Sikkim belong to two major sects of Tibetan Buddhism—Nyingmapa and Karma-Kagyudpa. It is mentioned earlier that the three lamas belonged to three different sub-sects of Nyingmapa sect from Tibet who installed Phuntsong Namgyal as the first Chogyal. Buddhism became the state religion of Sikkim after this. During the same period Tibet unified under the fold of Gelugpa sect and Bhutan under the Drugpa sect. Both Tibet and Bhutan witnessed several inter-sect clashes during their processes of unification. Gelugpa Tibet also made several attacks against Bhutan during the process of its unification. Interestingly, there is no such record on Sikkim. One of the possible reasons is that the relation between old Nyingmapa and the reformed Gelugpa and Drugpa sects etc. remained friendly both in Tibet[29] and Bhutan. The then Dalai Lama of Tibet recognised Sikkim's ruler and even gifts to him and "... in the context of Tibet, Sikkim was like a small feudal unit."[30]

The relation between Tibet and Sikkim remained friendly, atleast in religious matter till the closure of the border with Sikkim following the Indo-China war. Sikkim was actually under Tibet's protection till the penetration of the British power following the Treaty of Titalia. Actually, a 'patron-supplicant' relationship existed between Tibet and Sikkim before this treaty.[31] On the other hand, Bhutan attacked Sikkim twice in 1700 and 1777 and after the first attack even occupied the then capital of Sikkim for about eight years. However, during their stay they never destroyed any monastery. In fact, throughout the history of Sikkim there is no record of any intern-sect dispute among the Buddhists.

The Chogyal also did not differentiate among the sects. The fourth Chogyal established the first Kagyudpa monastery at Ralong and alloted landed estate to it and at the same time he also alloted more land to the Pemayangtse monastery belonging to the Nyingma sect. In fact, among the Buddhist communities in Sikkim there is hardly any distinction among the sects and the subsects. "The common feature of these is the worship of Padmasambhava, known as the central deity"[32]. The monasteries established during the first three successive Chogyals[33] belong to the Nyingmapa sub-sect.[34] Among these monasteries, Pemayangtse received landed estate from the third Chogyal and served as the head of the Nyingmapa group of monasteries and was also recognized as the Royal monastery of Sikkim.[35] Two other monasteries—Phensong and Tashiding also received landed estate in course of time.[36] Besides these three premier monasteries a few other monasteries of this sect viz Enchey, Tolung etc. also hold important position. Rest of the monasteries of this sect are very small.

Among the monasteries of the Kagyudpa sect, Ralong is the most important. It was founded by the Fourth Chogyal-Gyurmed Namgyal, in 1730 with landed estate for its maintenance. The same Chogyal also founded the monasteries of Rumtek and Phudong. All of these three monasteries received landed estates in course of time.[37] Ralong serves as the head of the Kargyupa group of monastery. The other monasteries of this sect are very small. They either receive grant from the Government or totally depend upon donation. Recently, three big monasteries of this sect-Dharma Chakra Centre at Rumtek (1960), Gyaltshe Rimpoche Centre at Ralong and another at Rankha (near Gangtok) have been established with the support of Tibetan refugees and other Buddhist devotees from all over the world. These three monasteries are quite different from the existing, old monasteries of Sikkim. The facilities provided at these monasteries are very good. There are residential facilities, there are study centres. There scholars from over the Buddhist word come here for studies and research.

They receive either small grants from government for maintenance or depend totally upon the donations from the local inhabitants. Therefore, their means of livelihood are limited.

In addition to the Bhutias, who were the first to embrace Buddhism the Lepchas, the Sherpas, the Tamangs and the Tibetan follow Buddhism in Sikkim.[38] At present, there is no restriction on entry to any monastery of any community in Sikkim. Initially, however there were some restrictions of entrance in Pemayangtse monastery which used to be open only to those of pure Bhutia blood and few Lepchas of high position. Monkhood also was totally restricted to those of pure Bhutia blood. Such restrictions are done away with at present.[39] Interestingly, a number of monasteries are earmarked for some particular communities like Parbing for the Sherpas, Bumter for the Tamangs, Lingthem for the

Lepchas etc. These are mainly village monasteries, but such monasteries are well known throughout Sikkim. These monasteries are located in areas settled mainly by certain dominant communities, e.g., the Lepcha monastery in the Dzongu area of North Sikkim. In such cases the lamas are placed in that monestry from that particular community.

3. Distribution

A place on a high ground is selected for constructing a monastery. The selection of the site follows two essential conditions[40] —(i) monastery be built in the long axis of the hill and (ii) it is desirable to have a lake in front of the premises, even at a long distance. The site infront of a waterfall is considered ideal but it is bad in front of a river.[41] In the regional context, the monasteries are located over the ridge top and higher slope of the ridges.

The distribution of the monasteries in Sikkim is uneven as we find there in every aspects of habitation over the dissected topography. Besides topography, spatial distribution of community and political factors also play vital roles in the distribution pattern. In general, the monasteries are located in the Buddhist dominated areas. Of course the cosmopolitan town like Gangtok is an exception. But Gangtok served as the capital of the Buddhist state for about 86 years (1889-1975). About half of the monasteries in Sikkim are located in some particular localities of political importance. The first capital, Yaksum-Rabdanse, for example used to be one such area where seven monasteries are located within a radius of 9 km. Monastery building activities were confined within this area till the regime of the third Chogyal. The capital of the state shifted from Rabdanse to Tumlong in 1814 and consequently a number of monasteries were established around this new capital.[42] About 6 monasteries are located within a radius of 3 km. In 1889, the capital shifted to Gangtok. Therefore and monasteries had to constructed. Besides these three capitals there are small clusters or chains of monasteries located in areas dominated by Buddhists, sometimes of a certain particular community. For example, there are about six monasteries located within a short distance from each other in the Dzongu area, at present the reserved homeland of the Lepchas. A number of monasteries, about 5 in number, are located over the ridge between the Rongpo chu and Rongni chu in East Sikkim, which is traditionally inhabited by the Buddhist Bhutias and the Lepchas. The distribution of village monasteries depends upon the concentration/

segregation of Buddhist communities viz the Bhutias, the Sherpas, the Lepchas, and the Tamangs.

Concentration or sparseness of the Buddhist Communications in any particular area also had a hearing, when a monastery was to be located. The introduction of British administrative system, produced three distinct type of landed estates—Raja's Private Estate, Monastery Estate and Regular Estate. The British land management system continued till the abolition of landlordism in 1949 but the Private and Monastery Estates more or less followed the system till the merger of the state with India in 1975. Thus, a parallel government existed in those estates till the end of the hereditary ruling system where Buddhist ethos prevailed under the state patronage even though the Buddhist communities were outnumbered by the Hindu Nepalese at the end of 19th century. The Nepalese were not allowed to settle in the Private estates,[44] particularly in the North Sikkim (Dzongu area). The area was totally reserved for the Lepcha-Bhutia communities.[45] According to the first Cadastral Survey (1985), there were 389 revenue blocks[46] in Sikkim. Of these 62 revenue blocks were under the Private Estate and 38 under the six monastery Estates.[47]

The revenue block of the monastery estates were located surrounding the respective monastery. In case of Private estate they were mainly located in some few pockets like around the capitals (Yaksum-Rabdanse, Tumlong and Gangtok) and in Dzongu area. About half of the total monasteries in Sikkim were located in these two categories of landed estate. These estates offered ideal condition for the establishment of monasteries as majority of the settlers followed the religion of the ruler. In the Private estate most of the monasteries were very small and most of them are recognized for a particular community like the Lepcha monasteries in the Dzongu area. At present, there are 77 monasteries distributed over four districts of Sikkim. North district accommodates highest number of monasteries (23) which is followed by East (22), South (19) and West district (13).

4. Monks

Since lama carryout a very important at the monastery, it essential that a look is given to their activities and duties. The following hierarchical order is followed in the Pemayangtse monastery,[48] whose model is more or less followed by all the big monasteries of Sikkim. The monastic discipline starts as soon as the students pass the entrance to the noviciate and are formally admitted to monkhood. After passing two professional examinations which normally take two to three years, the noviciate becomes a junior monk. The promotion of the junior monk to higher ranks depends upon the hierarchy pattern of the monastery and not on any further examination.

Junior Monk—Thungpo—Chapdip—Konyer—U-Chho— { Umdza / Dorjee-lopon }

There is Thungo and Chapdip; these jobs are junior monks. They are appointed for one year. Then there is Konyer, who is appointed for three years. With the completion of the duties of Konyer the stage of learner or *trapa* is over and he becomes an U-Chho or elder monk. Dorjee–Lopon and Umdza are the two highest posts of equal rank and privileges. Dorje-Lopon is responsible for all the spiritual aspects while Umdza looks after the secular/temporal matter and supervises the monastic establishment and exercises all discretions. These two posts are time bound.

Adda and Thwimi monks are selected from among the elder monks. *Adda* monk is incharge of the office record and their maintenance while the *Thwimi* monk looks after the economic administration of the monastery. *Chinyer* monk is storekeeper and incharge of the menials of the monastery.

Two monks are appointed to this post for three years. *Chotinpa* is not only the librarian maintaining discipline among the monks but is also the spokesman of the monks. He is selected from among the senior monks by voting. Previously he was appointed by the king but at present the Eccelesiastical Department issues the appointment for one or more terms. *Uchunpa* is responsible for playing the cymbals and looking after the service of Umdza during his absence. *Kanqsapa* is responsible for arrangement of rituals in the monastery. These two posts do not fall in hierarchical order although they are selected from among the elder U-Chhos. At present, very few monks reside the major monasteries and most of them reside in nearby village/town. They look after their families[49] and are engaged is various occupations starting from cultivation to other tertiary works.

5. Function

In Tibet, monks and monasteries used to take active part in the processes of political unification and administration of the state and this model was followed by Bhutan as well. In contrast, even though Sikkim followed Buddhism and remained under Tibet's tutelage for long period, the monasteries played a different though no less important role in the hereditary ruling system where the monks did exert considerable influence on the administration of the state. As a result, there evolved a priest-client relation between the clergy and the Ruler.[50] The heads of the major monasteries were chosen from Bhutia aristocracy including Kazi[51] and they held high positions in the state council till the penetration of British administration, after the appointment of the Political Officer at Gangtok in 1889. The functions of these religious institutions may be grouped into two categories (i) Religious and (ii) Secular. This distinction was also noticed in functional activities of the monks. .Both these functions have gone through changes with the passage of time. After the initial stage of the spread of Buddhism, imparting monastic education was the key function of these monasteries.

In addition, the monks also served as doctors, judges, bankers, traders and crisis managers in their localities in addition to performing ritualistic functions. The monasteries which were basically places of worship and rituals also functioned as monastic schools, trade centres[52] and grannaries.[53] The political role of the monks gradually diminished with the penetration of British power with the Treaty of Titaliya in 1817. The monk, both from Sikkim and Tibet, used to take active part in the politics of Sikkim. They served as ambassador, negotiator and other international policy makers. In the administrative affairs they lost these privilege after the appointment of Political Officer in 1889. Under the guidance of British administration Sikkim witnessed several administrative changes and in the new setup the secular role of the monks became restricted, and they became confined mainly to their estates, although representatives from important monasteries of Pemayangtse and Phudong continued to be included in the state administrative council for some more time.

In the post-British period, the Sangha seat in the State Council was introduced in 1958, where lamas from selected monasteries could elect one candidate through secret ballot. Normally, the Sangha seat is contested by the monks and the elected member looks after the Ecclesiastical Affairs. But during the last two Assembly elections they elected member from outside the monk communities and Ecclesiastical Affairs is no longer under his jurisdiction. At present there are 2588 voters in 56 monasteries in Sikkim (Table 5.2).[54] After the merger of state under secular India the role of monk and monastery in the state affairs totally became insignificant but they are very concern about their heritage. Recently, monk body strongly protested against the establishment of a Hydel Project in the Rathang chu (river) basin in West Sikkim. In fact, Rathang chu basin is the homeland of old capitals (Yaksum and Rabdanse) and old monasteries including Pemayangtse and Tashiding.

It will be worthwhile to discuss here in more detail the two most important function of the monastery—Education and Estate management- which also have evolved through the centuries.

Education: The third Chogyal introduced the custom of joining the monastery by one child from every Bhutia family, which was followed by the other Buddhist communities also. In the past, boys from any Buddhist family could get admission to the monastery[55] from the age of seven or eight and each student was placed under one monk. The young student first learnt preliminaries of reading and writing which took atleast two to three years. After that he could be admitted in noviciate. Monastic discipline started after the entrance to the noviciate and lasted for another two to three years.

The second part of the training included blowing copper trumpets, performing religious dances, playing cymbals and the art of making *torma* (votive offering to the gods in the shape of conical cakes).[56] After this they could undertake other specialized training like Medicine, Astrology, Painting, etc. The establishment of monastic schools changed the old monastic education system. One of the main reason for such change is the declining number of monks[57] for teaching as in the traditional system each student had to be assigned under one monk. In Sikkim the first monastery school opened at Enchy and Pemayangtse in the early 1950s and gradually other monasteries also opened such schools. In 1986, there were 15 such schools and the number increased to 31 in 1990.[58]

These schools are financed by the Education Department through the Eccelesiastical Department. The concerned monasteries have to provide the class rooms and accommodation for students. In such school the course extends to a period of five to six years covering more or less the first two phases of the previous system. After the successful completion one can join the 'Sikkim Institute for Higher Nyingma

Studies, Gangtok, which offers courses from intermediate to post-graduate level.[59] Most of the schools do not have any accommodation facilities. The students from nearby villages attend school as day scholars and the number of dropout is high. On the contrary, Dharma Chakra Centre at Rumtek and Gyaltshe Rimpoche Centre at Ralong still offer, more or less, the old monastic education system.[60] A huge number of students are attached to these centres and they are provided with accommodation on the premises.

Estate: Making of grants of land for religion by the devotees and the crown everywhere in the world. The same practice was automatically followed in Sikkim. Each of the five major monasteries have thus accumulated huge tracts of land around the monastery over which the monks and monasteries enjoyed supreme authority.[61] Sikkim witnessed a sharp change in the land management system with the introduction of lease out system of land by the British Administrator in the beginning of the 20th century.[62] Following the implementation of lease out system of cultivated land, it was felt essential to legalize the huge tracts of land under the monk and monastery. In view of this, Chogyal Sidkeong Tulku made a grant of certain legal rights to Pemayangtse monastery in 1901 and also demarcated the estate, comprising of twelve revenue blocks and two bazars.[63] In course of time, this system was also implemented in the other monasteries.

In this new system the monastery or monk became the primary holder of the land who could directly lease out the land to the share cropper[64] or the *bustiwallas*.[65] The bustiwallas again leased their land out, fixed terms and conditions of crops share, to the share cropper (*Adhia* or *Kut*). Besides these, rent-free land was given to the *Chakareys*, the servant of the monastery, in lieu of their menial services. The monastery estates held not only cultivable land but a large tract of non-cultivable land including forest and barren land. Though landlordism was abolished in Sikkim in 1949, exemption was granted to the five monasteries and the Raja's private estate. Interestingly, Tashiding received landed estate (Tashiding revenue block) for the first time in the same year.

The recommendation of the Land Reform Committee (1975), expressed the need for abolition of monastic estate and thus made significant impact on the age-old status of the monastery estates and the economy of the monastery. The detailed picture of the landed estates and their management appeared in the first survey report, 1950-58 (Table 5.4). The income of these estates varies from monastery to monastery and it depends on their areas of cultivable and cardamom land, number of bazars and forest resources (Table 5.5). In the post-merger period, the monasteries have gradually lost their control on these lands. The Sikkim Agricultural Land Ceiling and Reform Act of 1977 has limited the holding size of the monastery land to sixty standard acres of land.[66]

Before 1973, there were two categories of monastery estates in terms of their management. The monastery estates were either managed by the monastery wing of the Raja's Private Estate (Rumtek and Phudong) or by the *Udor-Tsosum*, managing body of the monastery (Pemayangtse, Tashiding, Phensong and Ralong).[67] In both cases, block mandal collected the land and other taxes.[68] The Survey and Settlement Report of the 1980-82 shows a drastic reduction in the size of the monastery estates as compared to the 1958 report. There are mainly two reasons for such reduction of the monastery land[69] (i) The Government acquired the monastery land for different developmental works (including afforestation programme). (ii) During the survey and settlement of 1980-82, the lease out lands were recorded in the names of bustiwallas as primary holders. In the survey report of 1980-82, the land recorded under the monastery covers, only those land which the monasteries held as primary holders (major part of this land are under forest, monastery building and negative land like steep slope, bare rock etc.)

At Present, all the monastery estates are managed by the respective Government departments.[70] On the recommendation of Sikkim Agricultural Land Ceiling and Reform Act, 1977 each monastery estate receive Rs. 2500 to meet the expenses of daily and periodic religious rites.[71] This amount is not sufficient for any of these monasteries and each monastery depends on the donation from the devotees.

TABLE 5.4

Area of the Monastery Estate in Sikkim: 1958

(Area in Acre)

Monastery Estate	*Cultivated Area*	*Khasland*	*Total*	*No. of Revenue Block*
Pemayangtse	7782.36	1759.49	9541.85	12
Phensong	2849.97	2377.21	5227.18	5

Contd ...

Tashiding	917.57	762.09	1678.66	1
Phudong	4317.43	5217.69	9535.03	9
Rumtek	1853.87	779.48	2633.35	5
Ralong	4275.32	2153.50	6428.82	6

Source: Survey and Settlement Report 1958.

In conclusion, it may be said that the monastery is the first and foremost among any kind of institutions in Sikkim. They performed as the pivot of many functions, both religious and temporal, for a long period. But, interestingly enough, there has been not a single monastery-based big settlement in Sikkim. It requires further study as to why these monasteries never acted as a growth centre for the neighbour-hood.

TABLE 5.5

Income of the Monastery Estate: 1973

(In Rs.)

Source of Income	*Pemay-angtse*	*Phens-song*	*Tashi-ding*	*Phudong*	*Rumtek*	*Ralong*
Land rent and Local Rate	7428	2074	947	5172	9700	5000
Forest Royalty	8000	1000	—	2732	13700	7000
Cardamom Damthey Khazana	8000	2728	200	5748	—	7000
Bazar	3200	—	—	2402	—	6500

Source: Dhamala, R.R. *Monasteries of Sikkim with specific reference to the Economic Structure*. Occasional Paper-8. Centre for Himalayan Studies, 1993, *op. cit.*, pp. 25-29.

Notes and References

1. Trevor Ling. Sikkimese Buddhism in the Nineteenth Century. In (Subba, T.B. and Datta, K. ed. *Religion and Society in the Himalayas*. New Delhi, Gian. 1991, p. 49.
2. Ecclesiastical Department, Government of Sikkim, 1995.
3. Tibetan term for a district and also a fortified monastery that housed the district headquarters. In Sikkim districts were known as Dzong.
4. Sinha, A.C. *Politics of Sikkim: A Sociological Study*. Faridabad. Thomson, 1975, p. 40.
5. *Ibid.*, p. 39.
6. Lama Lhatsum Chenpo of Lhasumpa, Lama Sempah Chenpo of Kartokpa and Lama Rigdsim Chenpo of Ngadakpa sect.

7. Maharaja Thutob Namgyal and Maharani Yissey Dolma. *History of Sikkim*, 1908 (Manuscript).
8. Subba, T.B. Limbu Ethnicity at Crossroads. *The Himalayan Mischellany*, V. 4, March 1990, p. 42.
9. There was Mangar Raja Hindupati across the Illam pass and mNga-bDag Lama, one of the three lama, visited Mangar Raja along with Gorkha and Newar Raja soon after the consecration of the first Raja of Sikkim in 1642 (Maharaja Thutob Namgyal and Maharani. Yissey Dolma, 1908, *op. cit.*).
10. Maharaja Thutob Namgyal and Maharani Yissey Dolma, 1908, *op. cit.*
11. First Chogyal divided the country into 12 Dzongs and appointed 12 Dzongpen (territorial Governor) from influencial Lepcha chiefs. (Sinha, A.C. 1975, *op. cit.*).
12. Be-Yul Denzong or the hidden valley of rice. Perhaps the rice growing hidden valleys are Lachen and Lachung valleys—the high altitude valleys like Paro and Thimphu in Bhutan.
13. As per Maharaja Thutob Namgyal and Maharani Yissey Dolma. (History of Sikkim, 1908) Dubdi was established first but as per Waddell. L.A (*Lamaism in Sikkim, 1894)* Sangha Choling and Pemayangtse were built first.
14. Risley, H.H. History of Sikkim and its Ruler, In (*Gazetteer of Sikkim 1894*. Delhi B.R. Publisher, 1985, p. 11).
15. *Ibid.*
16. Bhutanese occupied Rabdange palace for about 8 years, They built a number of Dzongs and one monastery—Paro-gon, near Pemayangtse.
17. Maharaja Thutob Namgyal and Maharani Yissey Dolma. 1908, *op. cit.*
18. *Ibid.*
19. Risley, H.H. 1894, *op. cit.*, pp. 15-16.
20. Phodong monastery in the Bhutia Busty of Darjeeling (Waddell, L.A. *op. cit.*, p. 252). Rishihat was founded by the Pemayangtse monastery.
21. Between 1819 and 1826 Chogyal Cho-Phoe Namgyel faces series of disputes with his minister. (Risley, H.H. 1894, *op cit.*).
22. Sikkim became British dependency after this treaty.
23. Waddell, L.A. Lamaism in Sikkim. In *Gazetteer of Sikkim, 1894*. Delhi, B.R. Pub., p. 253.
24. The structure preserves the relics of Saints.
25. Maharaj Thutob Namgyal and Maharani Yissey Dolma. *History of Sikkim*, 1908 (Manuscript).
26. Trevor Ling, 1991, *op. cit.*, p. 53.
27. Trevor Ling misrepresents the size of lama population in the North and south district. Perhaps he counted some of the monasteries of North district under East district.
28. Pemayangtse (108), Phudong, (100), Phensong (100), Tolung (90), Ralong (80), Rumtek (80). (Waddell, L.A. 1894, *op. cit.*).

29. Except in 1717, the Dzungar troops of the Mongols caused severe damage to the Nyingma tradition and its monastery. (Dudjom Rimpoche. A Brief Analysis of Some Important Chronological Events in the History of Buddhism and Tibet (translated by Ringzin Tsepak. *The Tibet Journal,* V. 12 (3) Autumn 1987, p. 13).
30. Sinha, A.C. Frontier Feudalism and State Formation in Sikkim. In (Sinha, S. ed. *Tribal Politics, and State Systems in Pre-Colonial Eastern and North-Eastern India.* Calcutta K.P. Bagchi, 1987, p. 349).
31. *Ibid.*, p. 360.
32. Dhamala, R.R. Monasteries of Sikkim with specific reference to the economic structure. *Occasional Paper No. 8.* Centre for Himalayan Studies. University of North Bengal, 1992, pp. 21-22.
33. Dubdi, Pemayangtse, Silen Tashiding and Sangha Cholling.
34. Majority of the Nyingma monasteries belong to the sub-sect of Lhatsunpa. Namchi, Tashiding, Sinon and Lachung Thangmuche belong to Ngadakpa and Doling and Kartok monastery to the sub-sect of Kartokpa (Waddell, L.A., 1894, *op. cit.*, p. 258).
35. According to Waddell, L.A. Pemayangtse exercises supervision over the Lepcha monastery of Lingthem, Zimik and Phaggye (Fadie).
    Dubdi, Sangha Cholling, Linche and Pathing and Ging of Darjeeling are directly controlled by the Pemayangtse (Dhamal, R.R. A Socio-Economic Study of the Pemayangtse Monastery of Sikkim, 1991, *op. cit.*, p. 59).
36. Tashiding received landed estate in 1949. There is no past record about Phenson. Its name appeared for the first time in the Administrative Report of 1933-34.
37. The name of Phudong and Rumtek appeared for the first time in the Administrative Report of 1933-34.
38. According to 1981 Census, 28.7 per cent of the total population follow Buddhism, Among the district, East district constitute highest number (42%) which is followed by South (20.8%), West (19.3%) and North (17.9%) district.
39. Except Laprong communities, mainly settled around Ralong block of South Sikkim.
40. "Back to the hill-rock. And front to the tarn" (rgyab ri brag dang, mdun ri mtsho). Waddell, L.A. *Lamaism in Sikkim, 1894, op. cit.*, p. 254.
41. Waddell, L.A. 1894, *op cit.*, p. 254.
42. Except Phudong, established in 1740.
43. Enchy monastery was established in 1840.
44. If the Nepalese were allowed to settle, they have to pay more tax than the Lepchas and the Bhutias. (Sinha, A.C. *Politics in Sikkim.* 1975, *op. cit.*, p. 45).
45. Sinha, A.C. Politics in Sikkim. 1975, *op. cit.*, p. 45.
46. In Sikkim, the distribution of population is sparse on the slope without forming any village in true sense. The Revenue Blocks are aggregate of

Bustee (hamlet) and sometimes 5/6 houses forming such a *bustee.* In many cases, each *bustee* is occupied by a particular community.

47. Govt. of Sikkim. Report on Sikkim Settlement, 1958.
48. Dhamala, R.R. A Socio-Economic study of the Pemayangtse Monastery of Sikkim, 1991, *op. cit.*, pp. 58-76. For more details please consult this article.
49. Celibacy is not maintained among the monks in Sikkim.
50. Sinha, A.C. Politics of Sikkim. 1975, *op. cit.*, p. 40.
51. Hereditary Landlord belongs to both Bhuũa and Lepcha.
52. There is no such record in the British Report but it may be expected that they took active part in the trade like the monks of Tibet.
53. Monastery lands were leased out in terms of grains so there had to be provision for storage in the monastery.
54. Voter List of 1995, Election Commission, Sikkim.
55. Admission was open only for pure Bhutia family in Pemayangtse.
56. Dhamala, R.R. The Monastic Education System in Sikkim. *The Himalayan Miscellany,* V. 4, March 1990, p. 61.
57. *Ibid.*
58. *Ibid.*, p. 62.
59. Madhyama (intermediate)—four year, Shastri (graduate)—two year and Acharya (post-graduate)—three year.
60. They also offer English language.
61. White, J.G. *Sikkim and Bhutan: Twenty-one years on the North-East Frontier, 1887-1908.* New Delhi, Manas, 1986, p. 28.
62. J.C. White, the first Political Officer, introduced the lease system of land tenure.
63. Dhamala, R.R. A Socio-economic Study of the Pemayangtse Monastery of Sikkim, 1991, *op. cit.*, p. 68.
64. Locally known as *Adhia* or *Kut* depends on the condition of the crop share.
65. The Bustiwala, owner of the holding, which is heritable and transferable, pays land revenue and other local taxes to the Govt. or the monastery estates following the prescribed land revenue rates (Survey and Settlement Report, 1958). The *Bustiwala* also recorded as primary holder. They belong to different communities; like the Nepalis, the Lepchas, the Bhutias etc. including monks of that monastery.
66. Land classified into three circles, based on locality, productivity of the soil and access to the market. Each circle divided into three classes according to attitude (Notification No. 615/LR 1957).

    The following table showing the standard acre in different class and circles.

Standard Acres
(Area Equivalent to One Standard Acre)

Circle	*Landuse category*	*CLASS*		
		I (*below 3500'*)	*II* (*3500-4500'*)	*III* (*above 4500'*)
A	Paddy and cardamom	1.00	1.25	1.50
	Dry	2.00	2.50	3.00
	Banjo*	3.00	3.00	3.00
B	Paddy and cardamom	1.10	1.37	1.65
	Dry	2.20	2.75	3.30
	Banjo*	3.30	3.30	3.30
C	Paddy and cardamom	1.30	1.50	2.00
	Dry	2.60	3.00	4.00
	Banjo*	4.00	4.00	4.00

*Uncultivated land

Source: Agricultural Land Ceiling and Land Reform Act, 1977.

67. Dhamala, R.R. Monasteries of Sikkim with specific reference to the economic structure, *op. cit.*, pp. 21-22.
68. House tax, bazar tax, forest royalty etc.
69. Dhamala, R.R. Monasteries of Sikkim with specific reference to the Economic Structure, *op. cit.*, p. 21.
70. *Ibid.*, pp. 21-22.
71. *Ibid.*

6

Monasteries of Sikkim with Specific Reference to the Economic Structure

I

Introduction of Buddhism in Sikkim

Buddhism was first introduced in Sikkim sometime in the mid-17th century. Some believe that Padmasambhava on his way to Tibet had visited Sikkim and sown the seeds of Buddhism. There is however no doubt that the introduction and spread in Sikkim is very much the work of Tibetan monks. In the History of Sikkim compiled by Maharaja Thutob Namgyal and Maharani Yishey Dolma, they have identified three periods regarding the introduction and spread of Buddhism in Sikkim: (1) introduction (2) development (3) final spread. These are expressed as "the earliest, the middle and the latter triumphs:"[1] The first period coincides with Padmasambhava's visit to Tibet during the reign of Thi-Srong-Deu-tSan in the mid-8th century. It is believed that the Guru on his arrival in Sikkim exorcised the land of all evil spirits and got rid of every obstacle that would tend to obstruct or disturb the course of development practices. He then compiled several works which were kept hidden under rocks.[2] The gtar-ston-Tig-dzin-rGod-Kyi-LDan-Phree Chan came miraculously and got the image of Guru Dral Po and Thing-Ka. He spent long periods in devotion and mediation in western and northern passes, and constructed monastery.[3]

The above accounts have been compiled from the Tibetan sources. It is probably that this is however shrouded in mythology certain monks might have visited Sikkim and preached Buddhism even prior to 1642. According to the available sources of information, the spread of Buddhism to Sikkim started after the arrival of three monks from Tibet and consecration of the first king of Sikkim in 1642. It is said the three monks, Lhatsun-Namkha-Jiored better known Lhatsun Chenpo, Kathok-

Kuntu Zangpo or Kathokpa Lama and Ngadak Sinpa Phuntshog Rinzing or Ngadakpa Lama came to Sikkim from three different directions, Lhatsun Chenpo came from north via Dzongri, the Kathokpa Lama from west by way of Singlela and Ngadakpa Lama came from south via Darjeeling and Mamchi.[4]

These three monks met at Yuksom and there they consecrated the first king of Sikkim Phuntshog Namgyal in 1642. The king was given the title of *Chhogyal*, a fountain-head of both secular and spiritual power. The king proclaimed Buddhism as the state religion and built the first stupa Chortan Tashi Wodber near the site of coronation.[5] During the reign of first Chhogyal Phuntshog Namgyal a number of monasteries were either constructed by these monks or the auspicious sites were selected for the future construction of monasteries. Slowly and steadily Buddhism spread throughout Sikkim. The two sects of Tibetan Buddhism prevalent in Sikkim are the Nyingmapa and the Karma-Kargyupa. The Nyingmapa or the old school was introduced by the first three monks visiting Sikkim. As these monks belonged to the three sub-sect of Nyingmapa school, i.e., Lhatsunse, Kathokpa and Ngadakpa, the monasteries in Sikkim also belonged to these sub-sects.

At present for the majority of people who profess Buddhism, the distinction among the sub-sects carry little meaning. The common feature of these is the worship of Padmasambhva, known in Sikkim as Guru Rimpochey as the central deity. Another sect prevalent in Sikkim is the Karma-Kargyupa. The introduction of Karma-Kargyupa sect in Sikkim has a very interesting story.

The fourth Chogyal Gyurmed Namgyal (r. 1717-1733) depressed by the events in the state such as of frequent raids by the Bhutanese and Nepalese forces and some problems in the family, started forth on a pilgrimage into Tibet, disguising himself as a common man. On arriving at the Tsurphug monastery of Karma-Kargyupa, the Hierarch of the Sect, the 12th reincarnation of Gyalwa Karmapa could recognise the king and offered him suitable honours. The king, in return promised to construct a monastery of Karma-Kargyupa sect in Sikkim with a suitable estate around it for its maintenance. As per the king's dictiron these monasteries of this sect were constructed at Humtek and Phedong.

Monasteries of Sikkim

The oldest monastery of Sikkim is at Dubdi. It was constructed by

Lhatsun Chenpo, to commemorate the consecration of the first king of Sikkim. He also constructed the monasteries at Sangacholing and Pemayengtse. The Ngadakpa Lama constructed the Lhakhang Marpo, the monastery of Tasi-ga-legs at Tashiding and the Rinchenpong monastery. The Kathokpa Lama constructed the Kathok monastery. Great attention was paid to the construction, renovation and the furnishing of the monasteries by the third Chogyal Chagdor Namgyal (r. 1700-1716). He was greatly assisted in this work by a monk Jigmed Pao who was believed to be the reincarnation of Lhatsun Chenpo. The most important monastery constructed by them was the Guru Lhakhang at Tashiding. With the passage of time the number of monasteries increased.

At present there are sixty-seven monasteries. In addition, there are one hundred and thirty-two Manlthakhang (Place of worship for ladies). Lhakhang or Tsankhang (hermitage or place of meditation).[7] Among these/six monasteries, i.e., Tashiding, Pemayangtse, Phensang Ralang. Phodong and Rumtek are considered the most important. Of these first three monasteries belong to the Nyingmapa sect and the latter monasteries belong to the Karma Kargyupa sect.

A Brief Description of Important Monasteries

1. *Tashiding*: Tashiding Gompa, is situated on top of a hill between Ralong and Rangit river in the West district of Sikkim. As is commonly known, it is considered the hottest of all the monasteries in Sikkim. A number of legends is associated with the site where the present monastery stands. Padmasambhava is believed to have stayed here for meditation. Legend has it that he shot an arrow vowing to meditate at the place where it fell. It dropped on the place where the present monastery is located. It is also believed that the site at Tashiding was accepted as the most sacred in Sikkim by the first three monks following the observance of occurrence of a divine phenomenon. A bright streak of light issuing from the top of Mount Khangchendzonga shone right upon a spot at Tashiding, at the same time a most delicious fragrance of license and sounds of melodious musical instruments filled the air. The monks along with the king Phuntshog Namgyal visited the spot and built the Chorten named Thongwa-Rang-Grol which means the stupa, the sight of which confers self-emancipation.[8]

The Ngadak Lama built the monastery of Tashi-ga-legs and also a Maitreya temple at the site. The Chogyal Lhakhang was build by Peda Wangmo, elder sister of king Chagdor Namgyal, in the first half of the

18th century. Jigmed Pao himself performed the consecration ceremony of all Lhakhangs and Chortens at Tashiding. The main festival of the monastery is *Bumchu*, which falls on the 15th day of the first month of the Tibetan calendar corresponding to February-March.

The ceremony is conducted to open the urn of holy water for the audience of the devotees. The holy water which is believe to have been consecrated by founder of the monastery, the Ngadakpa Lama, has remained clear till this day and has dried up. The devotees deeply believe in the miraculous power of the holy water. Thousands of devotees both from Sikkim and outside visit the place during this festival. Some come from as far as Japan.

2. *Pemayangtse*: This monastery is located near Gyalshing the headquarter of the West district. Pemayangtse means a perfect sublime lotus, i.e., the monastery of perfect sublime lotus or Padmasambhava.[9] Regarding the construction and organization of this monastery two phases could be traced:

I. The site for the monastery was selected by Lhatsun Chempo and a shrine there was constructed there. When Jigmed Pao visited Sikkim in 1709, he instructed the monks of the monastery about the mode of chanting prayers.

II. King Chagdon Namgyal along with Kanchan Rolpai Dorjee constructed the present building of the Monastery. Pure Bhutia blood, good parentage, absence of physical blemishes became the chief qualifications for admission to the monastery for monkhood, and celebacy was strictly maintained. No converts were admitted. The king conferred on importance upon 108 monks and appointed 108 families as chief laymen for supporting these monks.

He also declared that the monks of the Pemayangtse were to be the chief spiritual guides of every succeeding king. They have the customary right of performing all the religious functions of royalty. Its head lama alone had the right to anoint the Chogyal. The Pamayangtse is considered the premier monastery of Sikkim. All the Nyingmapa monasteries in Sikkim are subordinate to it. Certain monasteries viz., Dubdi, Sangacholling, Linche and Pathing in Sikkim and Ging in Darjeeling are directly under its control and they follow the rites and rituals according to its conventions. The head lama of these monasteries are sent from the Pemayangtse. The historical account of the monastery shows that its monks participated actively in secular activities too. They acted as royal advisers, fought in wars against Nepal and Bhutan, represented the State in various negotiations and treaties. Thus, from its inception the monastery and its monks enjoyed privileged position in Sikkim. To meet the expanses of religious performances, a vast tract of land was granted to it by king Chagdor Namgyal and in 1901, king Sidkeong Tniku made a grant of certain legal rights in perpetuity, for the maintenance of the monastery.

3. *Phensang*: Another important monastery of Nyingmapa sect is Phensang. It is located in the North district about twenty km. north of Gangtok. The Phensang monastery's religious name is Sang Ngak Choling Gumpa. The site for the construction of monastery was selected by Lhatsun Chempo and the building was constructed by the third Chogyal Chagdor Namgyal and Jigmed Pao. In 1902, the Prince Chuni Ongmu (later Rani Chuni Ongmu of Bhutan) became a nun and took charge of the monastery including its estate. The main festival of the monastery falls on the 28th and 29th days of the 10th month of the Tibetan calendar.

4. *Ralang*: The oldest monastery of Karam-Kagya sect in Sikkim is located at Ralang in the South district. The monastery was constructed in 1718 by the fourth Chogyal of Sikkim Chogyal Gyurmed Namgyal (r. 1717-1733), on his return from pilgrimage to Tibet. The monastery was reconstructed on a larger scale and the number of the novice admitted to the monastery increased considerably during the abbotship of Bereiok Lama Farma Tenzing Rabgay. It is said that when the consecration ceremony of the monastery, i.e., *Rabney* was being performed by the hierarch of the sect viz., Gyalwa Karmapa of Tsurphug in Tibet, the monks and the people of Ralang notice many auspicious signs.

5. *Phodong*: Another important monastery of Karma-Kargyu sect is Phodong, in the North district. The religious name of the monastery is Karma-Tashi-Cho-Khorling Gumpa. Originally there was a meditation hermitage, *Tsamkhang*. In 1723, during the reign of Chogyal Gyurmed Namgyal a monastery was constructed at the spot. The Gyalad Karmapa sent a monk Karma Tsundu from his monastery in Tsurphug, to take charge of the monastery.

During the reign of Chogyal Tsugphud Namgyal (r. 1793-1863) the old monastery was dismantled and a new one constructed in its place. It was reconstructed by the Chogyal Sidkeong Tulku. The present monastery was constructed in 1977.

Like the monks of Pemayangtse, the monks of the Phodong monastery participated actively in the secular affairs of the State as is evident from the account of J.C. White,[10] the first British Political Officer in Sikkim. It is the only monastery in Sidkeong Tulku and Ralden Thondup Namgyal as its spiritual patron. Sidkeong Tulku was recognised as the reincarnation of a great monk of a Karma-Kargyu sect, whereas the Chogyal Parden Thundup Namgyal was recognised as the reincarnation of Sidkeong Tulku. The main festival of the monastery falls on the 28th and 29th days of the 10th months of the Tibetan calendar when religious dances are performed.

6. *Rumtek*: The religious name of the Rumtek monastery is Karma Thupten—Choi—Khorling. It is located in the East district, about 15 miles away from Gangtok. The monastery constructed during the reign of Chogyal Gyurmed Namgyal was destroyed by an earthquake and another one was constructed on the site in 1740. It is believed that the first Chogyal Phuntshog Namgyal on his way to Yoksom had stayed at the place where a monastery was constructed later on. In 1960 when the head of Karma-Kargyu sect, the Gyalwa Karmapa, came to settle in Sikkim, he stayed at this monastery till the construction of the second Rumtek monastery, the Dharma-Chakra Centre, was completed.

The main festival of the monastery is the annual dance held on the 20th and 29th day of the 10th month of Tibetan calendar. A study centre of Kargyu sect known as Karma Shri Nalanda Institute for Buddhist Higher studies was established in 1981, which attracts a large number of Buddhist scholars not only from Sikkim but also from neighbouring countries.

II

In order to understand the socio-political environment of Sikkim, it is deemed essential to outline, in short, the history of the state. The objective of this paper is not only to state the fiscal management pattern of monasteries of Sikkim but also to delineate the change in the economic structure due to the change in the socio-political environment of Sikkim.

Socio-Political History

The history of Sikkim can be authentically traced back to 1642 when Phuntsog Namgyal was consecrated as the first king of the state by the three Tibetan monks of the Nyingmapa sect, from Tibet. Its political history can be broadly divided into four phases of development: (I) 1642-1817, period of Tibetan influence, (II) 1817-1947, period of British Indian influence, (III) 1947-1973, period of Indian influence, (IV) 1975 onwards, when Sikkim became the twenty-second state of the Indian Union.

I. 1642-1817

During this period, Buddhism was propagated among the non-Buddhist population of the state and number of monasteries as were constructed. It is also to be noted that during this period the State was engulfed in a series of war. The first attack came from Bhutan in 1706, during the reign of third Chogyal Chandor Namgya Tibet helped the king against the Bhutanese menace. Next war was waged by Nepal in 1786 and it conquered the whole of Sikkim, west of river Teesta. Consequently, Sikkim was compelled to pay tribute to Nepal till 1813. The lost territory was restored to Sikkim by the British in 1817 following the signing of Treaty of Titaliya. After this, the political influence of Tibet on Sikkim started waning and the State gradually came under the British influence.

II. 1817-1947

The Treaty of Titaliya (1817) granted Sikkim not only a protection against the Gorkha invasion but it marked the beginning of the end of Sikkim's independence and initiated British penetration. By the Treaty of Tumlong (1801) Sikkim lost all freedom of action and become defacto protectorate of the British government in India.

Beside the signing of these two treaties, the other landmarks of this period were (i) Darjeeling district to the British by the Sikkim King (ii) large scale migration of the Nepalese thereby changing not only the economy, but also the demographic pattern of the State.

Under the British influence the king had little choice to run the administration of the State. Wherever any king showed tendencies of which the British Government of India did not approve, the latter took quick action either to make him refrain from showing such tendencies.[11] It was the ability of Maharaja Tashi Namgyal (1914-68) that the sphere of autonomous administration was enlarged. It was his ability that he worded according to the dictate of British. But at some time he did what was the best for his country. The king was under threat of being replaced if he did not do the beloling of the British.

III. 1947-1974

When the British departed from India. They had to bare Sikkim too, the plitical scene in Sikkim changed radically. On the one hand, the free Indian Government signed a Standstill Agreement with Sikkim in 1948 in order to remove all confusion regarding their positions and to retain their respective rights and obligations evolved through earlier treaties and conventions, on the other hand, the educated elites of the State, while drawing inspiration from the freedom movement in India, started various political parties. The two political parties which influenced Sikkim's politics and administration were the Sikkim State Congress and the National Party. While the former stand for such ideals like abolition of landlordism, starting of a responsible government and accession with India, the latter emerged to counter the demands made by the former. It considered democracy as unfit for Sikkim and merger as a move to abolish the identity of Sikkimese culture and tradition.

The period between 1947 and 1949 was marked by a number of mass demonstration and agitation organised by the Sikkim State Congress. To press its demands for the democratic reforms, it also organised state-wide 'No Rent' compaign resulting in a political impasse. Consequently, the Indian Government took over the administration and appointed J.S. Lall as the Dewan of the state. During his tenure, house tax and forced labour were abolished in order to facilitate the withdrawal of 'No Rent', campaign.

The 1950 Treaty signed between India and Sikkim affirmed the protectorate status of Sikkim under India. India undertook the responsibility of Sikkim's defence, territorial integrity and external relations, whether political, economic or financial. This Treaty spoke of Sikkim's autonomy with regard to its internal affairs subject to the provisions of the Treaty. The intervening period between 1950 and 1973 was dotted with internal strife between the Durbar and the people which eventually culminated in the revolution of 1973, installation of elected ministry for the first time and the signing of the Tripartite Agreement. Finally, the State was merged with the Indian Union in May 1975.

IV. 1973 and onwards

The merger of the state with India led to the abolition of the hereditary rule of the Chogyal. The power to rule the state was thus passed on to the popularly elected legislative assembly. In the post-merger period the Government of Sikkim has been paying attention to remodell the administrative apparatus to suit the process of modernisation and an increased investment in different sectors aimed at socio-economic transformation of the society from a traditional and feudal to a progressive and modern one. Speaking of the social history of Sikkim, the Lepchas are believed to be the original inhabitants of Sikkim. They were animists and politically unorganized.

After the establishment of political order in 1642 with the blessings of the Tibetan monks, Sikkim reflected more of Tibetan characteristics in terms of religion, language and customs. The Tibetan form of Buddhism[12] was the State religion. As it was the religion of the royalty, it was quite natural for the subjects to follow the religion of the ruler. Although there were a few instances of conflicts between the Lepchas and Bhutias,[13] on the whole, Sikkimese society presented a uniform character. Another dimension to the otherwise uniform character was added once the British influence started permeating through Sikkim administration, viz., the steady migration of Nepalese who were predominantly Hindus. However, owing to the fact that the Buddhism was the religion of the kingdom where the king was the fountain-head of both temporal and spiritual power (Chogyal), the presence of Hindu subjects did little to alter the social character of the state. The majority of immigrant Nepalese were peasants; land since long has remained a prime factor in the economic structure of Sikkim. The influence of the presence of Nepali-Hindu was in the financial field.

Theoretically, all land belonged to the king over time, various landlords were granted land by the king either in lieu of services or as special inducements. Writing in 1872, J.W. Edger spoke of twelve Kazis and several other officers who exercised jurisdiction over a specific tracts of lands (*illakas*) ...... The Kazis and other officers exercised limited civil and criminal jurisdiction within the lands and revenue of which they collected.[14]Following the British influence in the administration attempt was made to codify the land-revenue system and the powers of landlords defined. There were mainly three kinds of estates: (I) Private Estates (II) Monastery Estates (III) Lessee-Landlord

Estate. The third type of estates were given to various individual landlords on lease. The lessee landlords had again, settled the land with secondary holders. The lessees acted as the intermediary for the collection of land revenue and exercised some judicial powers as well within the jurisdiction of the their estates.

The revenue collected from the Monastery Estate was kept with the respective monasteries. However, this system of landlordism came under attack in the late 40s. Peasants, majority of whom were Nepalese, were in the forefront of the movement for the abolition of landlordism. The demand of the people was partially fulfilled when the Government issued a notification in August 1949[16] thereby abolishing the intermediary róle of landlord as revenue collector. Whereas earlier *Mandal* (revenue collector) used to be appointed by respective landlord, after 1949 he was in the service of the State revenue administration. With this step revenue collection came to be considered as state function. However, this Private Estates and the Monastery Estates were kept outside the purview of this notification.

It may also to be noted that this notification did not usher in any agrarian reform nor did it seek to abolish the system of landlordism though, it certainly curtailed the powers of landlords to some extent. The first attempt towards land reform was made in 1975 when the Land Reform Committee was constituted under the Chairmanship of N.B. Khariwada to study the various aspects of agrarian reforms including the system of land management and cultivation regarding the Monastery and Private Estates.[17]

After 1975, following its merger with the Indian Union, the socio-political and economic character of the State has undergone many changes. The society is fast accruing a cosmopolitan character. Though agriculture still remains the main occupation in rural Sikkim, more industries are coming up in the semi-urban and urban areas. Politically too, democratic processes have replaced the monarchical system. Adaptation to the new political process was quite first.

III

Monastery Estates

Among the six important monasteries Impact of changes on the economic structure of Monasteries in Sikkim, five were granted lands adjoining the monasteries for their maintenance and performance of daily, periodic and annual religious ceremonies. For same reason Tashiding monastery was left out. The Tashiding monastery was granted land in 1949 by settling the adjoining areas with the monastery. Before 1949, it was dependent on the Government's subsidy and public contribution. The practice of making grants of lands by the kings or devotees either to the monastery or to the monks of these monasteries increased the size of these estates considerably. Generally, only a small portion of land is held by the monastery as the primary holders and the rest are leased out to the secondary holders, known as *bustiwallas*. The following are different categories of land holding in the monastery estates:

1. Land held by the monastery in its own name or in the name of its monks. They are known as primary holders.
2. Land given by the primary holders to the share croppers on fixed terms and conditions of crop sharing, i.e., land given on *Adhia* or *Kut*.
3. Land given to *Chakareys*. The *Chakarays* are the servants of the monastery who are given rent-free land in lieu of menial services they render to the monastery or its monks.
4. Non-agricultural land, i.e., forest and bazar area.

Area of Monastery Estates

Monastery Estates were surveyed and the Survey Report on Sikkim Settlement 1950-55[18] was submitted. This survey report was the first of its kind in Sikkim. According to it, the Monastery Estates constituted 8 per cent of the total number of holdings surveyed. The total area of the estate under different monasteries were as follows:

TABLE 6.1

Area of Monastery Estates

(In acres)

Name of the Monastery	*Cultivated land*	*Khasland*	*Total*
Tashiding	916	762.09	1678.68
Pemayangtse	7782.36	1759.49	9541.85
Ralang	4275.32	2153.50	6428.62
Rumtek	1853.87	779.48	2633.30
Phodong	4517.34	5217.69	9535.03
Phensang	2849.97	2377.21	5227.18

Source: The Survey and Settlement Report, 1958.

Besides Pemayangtse, Ralang and Rumtek monasteries had cultivated and khasland. Besides these land there were market areas under it. The markets of Gyalshing and Legship were under Pemayangtse, a part of Ravang market under Ralang monastery and the market area at the Middle Camp near Gangtok was under Rumtek monastery. The reserved forest are under the monasteries was not surveyed during this period (1950-1956). In 1980-82, another survey of settlement in Sikkim was undertaken. The Government is yet to being out its report but from the records available at the Office of Survey and Settlement, Gangtok, the area of cultivated land under each monastery is calculated as follows:

TABLE 6.2

Number of Blocks and Area of Cultivated Land Under Different Monasteries

Name of the Monasteries	*No. of Blocks*	*Area*
Tashiding	2	130.6860
Pemayangtse	5	110.7780
Ralang	4	59.6245
Rumtek	4	87.8720
Phodong	7	45.1320
Phengang	4	150.5260

Source: Deptt. of Survey and Settlement, Gangtok.

A comparison of above two Tables (I & III) shows that there is a considerable decrease in the area of monasteries estates. There are two reasons have been cited:

I. The Govt. of Sikkim has from time to time acquired the monastery land for establishing its offices or residential quarters.

II. As mentioned earlier, the monastery had leased lands to the *Bustiwallas* and they were known as the secondary holders of the land. During the Survey and Settlement Operation, 1980-1982, these lands were recorded in their individual names as most of these lands were settled with them by the Monastery after taking site salami, whereas under the Monastery, only those lands were recorded which it held as primary holders.

Management of Monastery Estates

Before 1973, the monastery estates were either managed by the monastery wing of the private estate or by the *Udor-Tsosum* of the monastery. The estates of Rumtek and Phodong monasteries fall under the former category, whereas the estates of Pemayangtse, Tashiding Phensang, Ralang monasteries under the latter groups.[19]

I. In the estates managed by the monastery wing of the private estates, the correction, transfer and mutation of the records of rights of land were solely in the hands of private estates. The Udor-Tsosum was not kept informed of the matter. The land rent, local rates and other taxes such as grazing fees, royalty from forest products, tax on cardamom (*damthay Khazana*) were collected by the private estate. Only a share of the revenue used to be given to the monastery for its maintenance and performance of religious ceremonies. The land rents were collected through block *mondals* who instead of getting commission for it received tax exemption known as *minah*, on their holdings.

II. The estates of Ralang, Tashiding, Phensang and Pemayangtse monasteries were managed by the *Udor-Tsosum* of the respective monasteries through *Twimi*. They were responsible for the maintenance of records and issue of revenue demands to the *bustiwallas*. Both land rent and local rate (*dhuri Khazana*) were collected by the *mondals* on behalf of the monastery. The revenue thus collected was utilised for the maintenance and the performance of religious ceremonies of the monastery.

At present, all the monastery estates are managed by the State Government of Sikkim through its respective departments.

Income and Expenditure Pattern of Different Monasteries

Sources of Income

The main sources of income of these monasteries are land rent, known as *dhuri khazana*, cardamom *damthey khazana*, forest royalty share and bazar tax. The *dhuri khazana* or house tax is collected annually at the rate of Re. 1/- per house. Besides these, the monasteries collect a share of agricultural products from its share-cropper.

There are three categories of employees in the monastery who are exempted from land rent payment in lieu of salaries. They are:

1. Employees who are selected by the committee of a monastery, *Duchi* for permanent period. For them, the exemption is life long.
II. Employees employed for a period up to a maximum of three years. For them the exemption is for the period of employment.
III. The *modals* are exempted from paying land revenue in lieu of their services of collecting land revenue from monastery estate. They do not get any commission or salary for their services. This practice of exempting the employees from taxation is called *Minah*.
IV. The last category of employees who enjoy tax exemption is *Chakarey*. *Chakarey* is a servant who renders menial service to the monastery or its monks and in return she is given a rent-free land.

Mode of Collection of Revenues

For the purpose of revenue collection block *modals* were appointed by the *Udor-Tsosum* or the Duchi of the monastery. That was the general practice followed all over Sikkim. These mondals were responsible for the issue of revenue demands and the collection of revenue from the *bustiwallas*. They deposited the money at the local bank or the monastery. The responsibility for collecting the cardomom *damthey khazana* was given to a person for two years by the *Duchi* of the monastery on a contract basis.

The royalty on forest product was collected by the Forest department, out of which the Department used to give to the monastery 50 per cent share on the sale of timber, and 1/6th share on other forest produce. For the collection of *Kut*, *adhia*, a person was appointed, known as grain contractor, by the *Duchi* for two years. Since 1975, the land revenue is being collected by the concerned District Officer and deposited in the Government accounts.[20] The bazar tax is collected by the department of Local Self Government. The Cardamom Khazana is included in the land revenue. The grains are collected by the monastery through its grain contractor.

Income of Different Monasteries Upto 1973

Pemayangtse: According to the Survey report, 1958, the land rent was assessed at Rs. 6,765.11. The monastery also collected local rate known as *dhuri khazana* (house tax) @ Re. 1/-per house p.a. The monastery had two markets under it, viz. Gyalshing and Legship. Before, 1956, the Durbar used to collect taxes for the sites occupied by shops, houses, stables, godowns and enclosed bazars through a contractor.

In 1956, the monastery took over the administration of these bazars. Since then the *Duchi* had been to king after the maintenance and upkeep of these with the assistance from the Bazar department. From the two bazars it collected the ground rent, bazar and stable tax. The annual collection from these were Rs. 18,000 approximately. Later, however, the Bazar department started collecting all the taxes and refunded to the monastery only the ground rent. The cardamom *demthfey khazana* was collected through a contractor. The annual collection was Rs. 6000/- approximately. The total income of the monastery from different sources in 1973 were as follows:

TABLE 6.3

Statement Showing the Income of Pemayangtse Monastery, 1973

(In Rs.)

Source of Income	*Total Receipt*
Land rent and local rate	7,428
Forest royalty share	8,000
Bazar tax etc.	3,200
Cardamom damthey khazana	8,000
Total	26,628

Source: Department of Ecclesiastical Affairs, Gangtok.

It gets 50-60 murries[22] of paddy, millet and corn as an annual share of agricultural produce from its kutdars. Besides these, the Ecclesiastical Affairs department gives Rs. 600/- as annual subsidy for meeting the expenditure on the daily rituals of the monastery.

Tashiding: Tashiding monastery did not have a income of its own till 1949. It used to depend mainly on the annual grant of Rs. 300/-from the Durbar and public contribution, after 1949, the different sources of income consisted of land rent, local rate and the cardamom *damthey khazana*. In 1958 the land rent was Rs. 798.01. In 1973, the monastery collected Rs. 875/- as land rent, Rs. 300/- towards cardamom *damthey khazana* and the local rate stood at Rs. 72/-.

Phensang: The main income of Phensang monastery was derived from land rent, forest royalty share and cardamom *damthey khazana*. In 1958, the land rent was Rs. 911.37. The total income of the monastery in 1973 were as follows:

Besides these, the monastery has a fixed fund of *Kang-cha*. The money is provided by the devotees and the monks for regular butter lamps and performance of periodic pujas. This amounts to Rs. 14,360/-. It is called *Kang-cha*. The amount is kept with a responsible person who would in turn, as interest on the *Kangycha* amount, after the expenditure for the rules regularly.

TABLE 6.4

Statement Showing the Total Income of Phensang Monastery 1973

(In Rs.)

Source of Income	*Total Receipt*
Land rent and local rate	2073.87
Forest royalty share	1000.00
Cardamom damthey khazana	2728.30
Total	5803.17

Between 1972-1975, it collected 532 mds. of grains as its share of agricultural produce from its *kutdars*.

Phodong: In 1958, the total land rent of this monastery was Rs. 3097.88. Besides the land rent, it also collected local rate, forest royalty share, bazar tax and cardamom *damthey khazana*. The total annual receipt in 1973 were as follows:

TABLE 6.5

Statement Showing the Annual Income of Phodong Monastery

(in Rs.)

Source of Income	*Total Receipt*
Land rent and local rate	5,172.00
Forest royalty share	2,732.00

Bazar tax	2,402.00
Cardamom damthey khazana	5,784.00
Total	16,090.00

Source: Department of Ecclesiastical Affairs, Gangtok.

The annual *kut* share was 271 kg. of grains (approx). However, according to the *Duchi* of the monastery generally it does not get the total share of grains from its *kutdars*.

Ralang: According to the Surevy report, 1958. The monastery used to collect bazar toll tax and ground rent from its bazar at the Middle Camp. The annual collection from it was Rs. 2500. The annual collection from cardamom *damthey khazana* was Rs. 5000. The annual *kut* share was around 140 murries of grains.

TABLE 6.6

Statement Showing the Total Income of Rumtek Monastery, 1972

(in Rs.)

Source of Income	*Total Receipt*
Land rent and local rate	9,700
Forest royalty share	13,700
Total	23,400

At present, land rent, local rate, forest royalty share and bazar tax are being collected by the respective departments of the Government. As a temporary measure the Government is giving to each of these six monasteries an annual grant of Rs. 2500 to meet the expense on performing daily and periodic religious rites pending the decision on the provisions of the Sikkim Agricultural Land Ceiling and Reforms Act, 1977 (as amended in 1978).

Expenditure

The expenditure of these monasteries towards the performing daily, monthly or annual religious rites is met out of the income from their respective estates. The annual expenditure of these monasteries are as follows:

TABLE 6.7

Statement Showing the Annual Expenditure of Six Monasteries

(in Rs.)

Monastery	*Annual Expenditure*
Pamayangtse	26,002 + grains
Palang	18,830 + grains
Phensang	9,890 + grains
Tashiding	18,762 + grains
Phodong	7,882 + grains
Rumtek	11,469 + grains

Source: Deptt. of Ecclesiastical Affairs, Gangtok.

The above expenditure includes performing puja, maintenance of the monastery and its monks, monthly salary of *Kansapa* @ Rs. 30 p.m. and two *Kunners* @ Rs.14 each. Relang monastery pays Rs. 300 p.m. to its Kunner for looking after the Ralang mani-lhakhang. For the performance of religious rites and burning perpetual lamp at Gompa, the annual expenditure of different monasteries are as follows:

TABLE 6.8

Statement Showing the Annual Expenditure for Performing Different Religious Rites in the Monastery

(in Rs.)

Monastery	*Expenditure*
Pemayangtse	14,000
Tashiding	5,000
Phensang	6,000
Phodong	6,000
Ralong	6,700
Rumtek	6,700

Source: Deptt. of Ecclesiastical Affairs, Gangtok.

Earlier, each monastery was required to pay 10 per cent of the land revenue collected and all the local tax to the panchayat unit falling within its estate. Now the government is collecting the land revenue and local tax, the monastery does not pay anything to the panchyat its area.

Monastery Estate and the Question of Land Reform

In Sikkim, the ideal of land reform was in the air since the late 1940's. At the time various political parties were formed with the avowed objective of the abolishing the system of landlordism and ameliorating of the poor and oppressed condition of the cultivators. As stated earlier, in response to the popular demand, the Government through notification dated 20th August, 1949 decided that all the land revenue previously paid to the agents of estates, i.e., mondals, would be directly paid to the State treasury. But the Private Estates and the Monastery Estates were kept outside the purview of this notification.

The absolute power of the monastery, over the tenants settled in its 1961, estate, was questioned by the Sikkim National Congress in 1961. In a meeting held on March 10, the party adopted the resolution that in the monastery estate, the monastery authority itself made the rules and regulations to be imposed on the ryots. The life of the ryots of these estates no better than that of a slave. It further demanded that such exploitation by the authority monastery should be stopped and there should be uniformity in governing all the people of Sikkim.

The working committee of Sikkim State Congress at its meeting held on 22.9.60 and on 23.3.61 expressed surprise at the continuation of monastery and private estates even after the abolition of landlordism in other parts of Sikkim. "Now it is found that there are the administrations functioning parallely in some private and monastery estates. Consequently, the people in these area are put to great difficulties and disadvantages in various matters of administration and development." It requested the Maharajah to bring every part of Sikkim under a uniform system of administration.

For the first time, the Land Reforms Committee (1975) expressed explicitly the need for the abolition of monastery estates. It maintained that the existence of private estates and the monastery estates in political and administrative parlance could be seen as a separate organisation operating largely outside the control of government. Control over agricultural and forest land, the collection of land revenue, the maintenance of land record were held to be a part of state activities in modern administration. The committee, from its visits to various monastery estates, concluded that there was a popular denabd for their abolition without paying compensation.

Accordingly, it recommended for the abolition of rights of the monasteries on their estates and income. It suggested that on the abolition of these estates entire revenue collection should be brought under the department of Land Revenue and collection agencies would have to be appointed by the government on payment of usual commission or pay and allowance.[25] As a first step towards this direction, the Government should acquire the land records hitherto held by the respective monastery for the correct assessment of land revenue and tax. It, however, maintained till the formulation of land reform legislation, the religious institutions (monastery) may be allowed to retain its homestead farm along with the appertaining buildings and structures used for the purpose of accommodating visiting monks and these may be exempted from paying land revenue and other taxes.

Impact of the Committee's Recommendation on the Economy the Monastery

The monastery used to collects the rent and taxes. They deposited them at the bank under its account. The amount accruing from such source, as had been done earlier, was spent mainly on the maintenance and performance of religious rites of the monastery. As per the recommendations of the Land Reforms Committee, the Government issued a notification by which it withdraw the power of the monastery to collect the revenue and other taxes, and authorised the District Officer of respective district to collect the same and deposit with the Government. It maintained that it would give a share of revenue to the monastery concerned after it decided on the status of monastery estate.

The Sikkim Agricultural Land Ceiling and Reforms Act was passed in 1977. According to it the six big monasteries were entitled to hold sixty standard acres of land.[26]But the Government has failed to take any step towards this direction. As a result, the monasteries are still deprived of the income from estates. In order to enable the monastery to meet the expenses, the Government decided in 1978 to pay each monastery an annual subsidy of Rs. 2500 pending the Government's decision on the implementation of the provisions of Agricultural Land Ceiling and Reforms Act 1977. The position has not changed till this date. According to some monks this has affected the monastery's economy aversely and they have to depend more on public contribution for the performance of various rites.

Summary

In its formature years the neighbouring states had a big influence on Sikkim. Internal atmosphere was peaceful and conducive. In the initial phase of its political growth, the Tibetan system of government influenced the structure and processes of the government significantly. Here too, like in Tibet, religion (Buddhism), religious institutions (monasteries) and religious teachers (monks) played important role in the state administration. However, after the British influence in the Himalayan kingdom overshadowed the political influence of Tibet, sacerdotal influence on the secular affair also relegated to the background. After the British left the country, there were significant social and political changes in the State and finally it joined the Indian Union in 1975, thereby changing the monarchical character of the Government. The monasteries performed multifarious functions which include socio-religious, political, economic and judicial. Of these, the last two functions, i.e., economic and judicial were limited within the jurisdiction of their respective estates.

As we have noted earlier, changes in the character of political structure affected the functions of these institutions, especially the temporal functions. The political movements of late 1940's, with its focus on the amelioration of poor conditions of peasants brought a political awareness among the peasants of the State and the peasants settled within the monastery estate were not immune to these changes. Although the socio-religious role of the monasteries were never challenged disgruntled voices of the peasants could be heard, for example, in 1948 the *chakareys* of the Pemayangtse monastery refused to render their service to the monastery and monks for which they were given rent-free land with the exception of house rents. They demanded equal status with other peasants of the estate (secondary holders) and showed willingness to pay the usual rent and taxes on their holdings.

Whatever decisions were taken during or after the movement none affected the position of the monasteries, nor did it interfere in their administration. Consequently, when the notification of August 1949 was issued in order to abolish the intermediary role of landlords, the monastery estates were kept outside its purview. However, after 1973, various decisions of the Government have affected the position of monasteries to a great extent. It is reported that during the 1973 political movement, the monasteries of Pemayangtse, Ralang and Tashiding became the target of mob fury. Soon after the turmoil, the *Mondals* were appointed by the respective district officers on the order of the Chief Executive in December 1973 "to collect the taxes from the Estates and deposit the same at the District Office."

The recommendations of the Land Reform Committee have not been favourable to these monastery estates either. Following the Committee's recommendations the notification of 1975[27] authorised the district officers to collect the land revenue and deposit the same in the government account. The idea was to give the monastery a share of the land revenue after the status of its estate was determined, but so far nothing has been done towards this direction. The bazar tax and forest royalty were collected by the respective departments during the pre-merger period too and the monasteries was given share of the income. The practice is continuing to this day although there are complaints by various monasteries against these department for being defaulters.

Equally noteworthy fact regarding these monasteries is that after 1975 successive Governments through the Ecclesiastical Affairs and Culture departments have been paying more attention to the renovation maintenance and smooth functioning of these monasteries.

The function undertaken and privileges enjoyed by the monasteries were unquestioned till the 1940's. However, with the changing socio-political scenario the monastery too passed through a transitional phase of confusion and doldrums. Although a degree of uncertainty still prevails regarding the status of its estate and the income there from, the fact has come to stay that the State would like to perform its own the secular functions but leave the socio-religious domain of the monastery unaffected and unchallenged.

References

1. Maharaja, Thutob Namgyal & Maharani Yashey Dolma: *History of Sikkim* (1908) (MS) Paragraph 31.
2. *Ibid.*, para. 31.
3. *Ibid.*, para. 32.
4. L.R. Waddell: *Lamaism in Sikkim*, New Delhi, Manjushri Publishing House (Reprint), 1978, pp. 12-13.
5. N. Dorjee: 'Role of Buddhist Institutions in Sikkim,' *Shunyata*, 3:1, 1989, p. 42.
6. Namgyal & Dolma, *op. cit.*, para. 156.
7. Govt. of Sikkim, *District Census Handbook*, 1981, Gangtok.

8. Namgyal & Dolma, *op. cit.*, para. 83.
9. L.A. Waddell, *op. cit.*, p. 21.
10. For details, see J.C. White, *Sikkim and Bhutan: Twenty-one years on the North East Frontier, 1897-1908*, Manas Publications, Delhi (Reprint in India), 1980.
11. The Cases of Maharaja Thutob Namgyal, Sidkeong Namgyal and Tashi Namgyal are a few examples. For detail, see, L.B. Basnet, *Sikkim: A Short Political History*, Delhi, S. Chand & Co., 1974.
12. The Tibetan form of Buddhism as distinct from Buddhism practised in India, Sri Lanka, Burma, etc. is a mixture of Buddhism with a preponderance of amount of mythology, mysticism and magic, the doctrine of incarnate lamas and the worship of canonised saints, see, L.A. Waddell, *Lamaism in Sikkim*, *op.cit.*
13. Namgyal & Dolma, *op. cit.*, Vol. I, para. 139 & Vol. II, para. 28.
14. H.K. Kuloy (ed.) "Report on a visit to Sikkim and Tibetan Frontier in October, November and December, 1873" by J.M. Edgar, Manjushri Publishing House, New Delhi, 1967, p. 62.
15. Political Officer's Notification, No. 2328, August 25, 1906.
16. Sikkim State Revenue Administration Deptt. Notification No. 2753-3258/CF August, 1949.
17. Govt. of Sikkim, *Report of the Committee on Land Reforms*, 1975 Department of Land Revenue, 1975, p. 1.
18. Govt. of Sikkim: *The Survey Report on Sikkim Settlement, 1950-1958* (MS), Gangtok, 1958.
19. Report of the Committee on Land Reforms, *op. cit.*, p. 23.
20. Notification No. 138/LR dated Gangtok the 28th August 1975, and Notification No. 41/LR dated Gangtok the 15th June 1977.
21. Committee of the senior monks of a monastery.
22. 1 murri = 80 seers.
23. Report of the committee on Land Reforms, *op. cit.*, p. 29.
24. *Ibid.*, p. 13.
25. *Ibid.*, p. 30.
26. Notification No. 14/LL 78 dated Gangtok, the 2nd June, 1978. The Sikkim Agricultural Land Ceiling and Reform Act, 1977 (as amended) 1978.
27. Notification No. 138/LR, *op. cit.*

7

Realms of Spiritual Ecology in Sikkim

SECTION I

NATURE, RELIGION, SPIRITUALITY AND HUMAN ECOLOGY

Introduction

Religion involves a set of beliefs and practices. It is a social system through which people seek mental and physical harmony with the powers of the universe, through which we attempt to influence the forces of nature. It is therefore generally considered of life and death to be part of culture. As such, religion has been an essential attribute of culture, which cannot be left out from the realms of human ecology. (Jordan and Rowntree, 1990).[1] Durkheim (1964)[2] describes God as society divinized. The rule of religion thus are the rules of society. The object of worship is the society itself.

Some of the principal religious realms as described by Swanson (1960)[3] are:

(a) Monotheism is positively related to the presence of a hierarchy of three or more sovereign (decision-making) groups in a society.

(b) Polytheism (belief in multiple superior gods) is correlated with social classes.

(c) Belief in active ancestral spirits is correlated with importance of kinship groups.

(d) Belief in reincarnation is correlated with small and nomadic settlement patterns (inspite of its high frequency in India, a highly evolved group of societies with many large settlements).

(e) Belief in witchcraft is most common in societies with few or no other kinds of social controls.

(f) Supernatural sanctions for interpersonal relations are most frequent in societies with interpersonal differences in wealth.

Nature in Spiritual Traditions

Throughout the centuries humans have had a love-hate relationship with the natural environment. This inter-relationship generally corresponds to (Egri, 1999)[4]:

(a) We depend on nature for the air, water, food, clothing and shelter.

(b) From the natural environment we obtain the resources to be transformed to meet our material needs.

(c) The natural environment serves as the repository for our waste products.

(d) The aesthetic beauty of nature in all its forms is a source of spiritual and cultural inspiration as well as emotional sustenance.

(e) The powerful forces of nature are also the harbingers of destruction and death.

When nature wills, droughts, floods, fires, hurricanes, and earthquakes occur. Humanity is virtually powerless against the forces of nature. There are aspects of nature, living and non-living, with which contact is dangerous for humans. Nature reminds us in innumerable ways of our mortality, that individual lives are but preciously brief journies in time.

Humans depend on nature, for water, for air, for wood and all others essential which man has invented. It uses and misuses nature at will. Man's its fear of nature and its expectations from nature found its way into religion and spiritual realms in almost all human societies. Because human feared nature, it became an accepted necessity to appease the natural forces, some of which took the demonical form. Shamans and *jhakris* came into being. Nature in all its forms entered the passages within the religious texts. Religious prayers and hymns were composed and sung in reverence to nature. Alongside, however, the misuse of nature, and exploitation of all non-human resources on the planet earth continued. Biotic life and abiotic environment were both targetted for exploitation.

The primary concern of this chapter is on spiritual discourse (with special reference to Upper Rangit Basin of Sikkim) as a means of constructing and reconstructing humankinds' relationship with the natural environment. The ways in which spiritual communities, monasteries and clergy have worked for sustenance of environment is presented in succeeding sections of the chapter. How these lessons have been accessed by individuals and collectives to effect transformational change in ecological consciousness and action are given below:

Animism: The Nature Centred Spiritual Tradition

Different peoples of the world believed—and some still do—that behind the immediate physical reality of things lie spirits, that even seemingly dead objects, rocks or earth have a living force within them (Toffler, 1980)[5]. Nature-centred spiritualities have existed since before the advent of modern human civilizations. For over 20,000 years, animistic spiritual traditions have guided indigenous peoples throughout the world. In this holistic and integrative tradition, "spirituality is not a religion with a fixed set of dogmas, but rather, spirituality pervades and infuses all forms of existence—human, animate and inanimate" (Frost and Egri, 1994)[6]. It informs the view that all that exists in nature is living and sacred, therefore deserving of respect and care (Halifax, 1990)[7]. The original spiritual traditions of Limbus (Risley, 1894[8]; (Subba, 1999)[9] and Lepchas (Foning, 1987)[10] fall under this category. Even though these two tribal entities have embraced Hinduism and Buddhism during later periods between 17th to 20th centuries, they have maintained most of their original traditions.

Egri (1999)[11] describes three assumptions which underlie the animist belief system:

(a) The existence of numerous coexisting and interpenetrating worlds of experience.

(b) The need for holistic balance amongst these worlds.

(c) That change is a continuous transformational process.

The nature-centred spiritual traditions emphasize human beings' physical and spiritual connections with an animate and respect of all that exists in the natural environment, as well as the need for transformational change to regain holistic balance and harmony in the cosmos. This, in a nutshell, is also the concept of deep ecology.

Spirituality and Deep Ecological Consciousness: Buddhist and Hindu Philosophies on Interrelationship

"Deep Ecology" says Macy (1994)[12] is a term coined by Norwegian Philosopher Arne Naess to contrast with "shallow environmentalism", a Band-Aid approach applying piecemeal technological fixes for short-term goals. Deep Ecology teaches us that we humans are neither the rulers nor the centre of universe, but are embedded in a vast living matrix and subject to its laws of reciprocity. Deep Ecology represents basic shift in ways of seeing and valuing, a shift beyond anthropocentricism.

Macy further consider the Tibetan and Sikkimese 'wheel of life', depicts all the realms of being. This is basically a Tibetan and Sikkimese thought. At the centre of that wheel of suffering are three figures: the pig, the rooster, and the snake—they represent delusion, greed and hatred—and they just chase one another around and around. The linchpin of all the pain is the notion of ourself, the notion that we have to protect that self or conquer on its behalf—or do something with it. This point of Buddhism, Macy thinks, is Deep Ecology too, in that we do not need to be doomed to the prepetual rat race. The vicious circle can be broken through wisdom, meditation and morality.

Hindu and Mahayana Buddhist philosophies, followed within the study area, offer much to ponder on the spiritual and metaphysical connections between human and nature. The Hindu religion teaches that earth is the Universal Mother, with the rivers and earth being personified as goddesses and the winds and fire as male deities (Chapple, 1993)[13]. Nature is the spiritual guide and teacher in a religion, which has codified environmentally beneficial practices in its rituals, proverbs and stories (Gadgil and Guha, 1992)[14]. For example, respect and even reverence for other species is based on Hindu beliefs that the Supreme Being is incarnated in various species, and that human themselves can be reincarnated as animals and birds. In Hindu religion trees and plants are seen as possessing divine powers, and thus are to be protected from destruction.

Buddhism proposes that *'nirvana'* is a higher ultimate spiritual reality and truth which transcends all else. The 'Middle Way' of Buddhism teaches the importance of simplicity in living, that attachment and craving for material wealth and goods, stands in the way of liberation (Badiner 1990)[15]. The Buddhist principle of the truth of personal experience emphasizes the importance of experiential learning, practicing the 'art of mindfulness' (described further in section on chortens and monasteries) to resensitize oneself to abstract ideas of reality.

The Buddhist principle of reciprocity and interdependence is based on the belief that all events and beings are interdependent and interrelated in a universe which is 'a mutually causal web of relationship' (Kaza 1993)[16].

Buddhist relational ethics teach that moral actions are those, which are informed, sensitive to and respectful of all beings (sentient or not) within interdependent relationships. In both, Buddhism and Hinduism, violence to other beings within the biotic community is immoral, given the percept of interdependence and self-destructive. The principal of non-violence is also central to both traditions' concept of *Dharma*, which has been interpreted to mean 'moral duty', 'right action' and 'the truth about right living' (Bhatt 1989)[17].

The Buddhist and Hindu doctrine of *Karma* (fate or destiny) also teaches the importance of taking responsibility for moral action in all of one's relationships. Religious monastic orders have also served as models for radical environmentalist proposals for ecologically sustainable communities. In a spiritual extension of 'Deep Ecology' concept, Devall (1990)[18] proposes that Buddhists develop ecocentric *Sangha* communities within bioregions. The wildlife in such regions is not only protected, but also fed and groomed towards being a climax biotic community—both botanic and zoological life.

The Case of Upper Rangit Basin: Sikkim

As enumerated earlier, Hinduism and Buddhism, both interlaced with animist spiritualism are the main religious traditions in the Uppper Rangit Basin. Since the impact of popular urban culture has not been fully felt in the region, the old traditions and customs continue to dominate the life cycles of the inhabitants. There has been however a diffusion of cultural and religious rituals from within the inhabitants. The Bhutias who immigrated from Tibet, follow the Lamaist Mahayana Buddhism diffused with the Bon animist spiritualistic traits. The Lepchas embraced Buddhism on coming in contact with the Bhutias, but retained their animist *bon-thin* and *mun* traditions. The Kiratas (Limbu, Rai and Gurung) embraced Hinduism through continuous interrelationship with the other Hindu Nepali castes. The traditional spiritual elements of

Buddhism and animism can still be noticed amongst the Kirata communities. The other Nepali communities are mainly Hindus; Tamangs and Sherpas being Buddhists. The Tamang community generally follow the Mahayana Buddhist religion, but their cultural traditions are of the kind of Nepali Hindu style. Both the religious groups have borrowed from each other to such an extent, that sometimes it is not easy to distinguish one from the other.

Sikkim was under the rule of Chogyals till 1975. The state religion during the Chogyal period was Mahayana Lamaist Buddhism. Although the followers of Hindu faith were numerically larger, the culture had greater impact of Buddhism and monastic life. The state character was therefore mainly Buddhist, which is evident from the architecture, laws, education, and the power centres—the monasteries. The Lama's word has been taken as the law by the laymen. Almost every action and routine, including the rites during birth, marriage, death, agricultural harvest, and festival celebrations are carried out by the Lamas.

In the sections of this chapter, the spiritual aspects of the *gompas,* monasteries and *chortens* will be discussed with amplified emphasis on the aspects of human ecology, spiritual ecology and deep ecology.

SECTION II

ARCHITECTURE AND SPIRITUAL ECOLOGY OF MONASTERIES

Introduction

According to Risley (1891)[19] monasteries in Sikkim are of three kinds, namely:

(a) *Tak-phu (brag-phug)* or cave-hermitage.

(b) *Gompa,* literally 'a solitary place', or monastery proper.

(c) The smaller *gompas* without the educational infrastructure found in larger monasteries. The *gompas* as a rule, are merely temples *(hlakhang)* with one or more *lamas* engaged in ministering to the religious wants of the villagers.

The Upper Rangit Basin is unique for the fact, that it contains monasteries from the three major sects of Lamaist Buddhism viz. *Nyingma, Karma Kagyu* and *Gehug*. The Gelug monastery of the reformed school (of which the Dalai Lama is the functional head) is located on the

Eastern end of the basin at Ravangla in the Kunphenling Settlement of Tibetan refugee camp. Ralang, the oldest monastery of Karma Kagyu sect in Sikkim is located at a 13 km distance from Ravangla, in full view of the *Nyingma* sect monasteries of Pemayangtse and Tashiding. Dubdi, the oldest monastery of Sikkim is located on top of Eastern banks of Rathongchu near Yuksom. A monastery belonging to the Bon practitioners (the religion of Tibet during pre-Buddhist period) has also been constructed at a distance of 6 km from Ravangla on its western slopes, on road to Kewzing-Tashiding. Hindu temples also exist in all villages and towns. The Basin finds itself as a spiritual centre of Buddhism, Bon and Hinduism. It is probably the smallest geographical area housing monasteries from all sects making the place spiritually unique. Only Sakyapa do not live here.

Architecture of the Monasteries

The Buddhist *gompas'* and *monasteries* in the Basin are characteristic of building tradition which came from Tibet together with the religion. However, at least three factors (GRIT library Gangtok Wall display)[20] have given rise to alteration that determine a style typical of Sikkim:

(a) Sikkim, especially the Rangit Basin was up to recent times very sparsely populated and relatively poor. Large buildings were not affordable, and the building enterprises had to be adapted to the economy of the state. The monasteries were therefore initially more modest in size and decorations.

(b) Secondly, the differences in altitude and wet climatic conditions of Sikkim necessitated a change in the types of roofs. The flat roofs of Tibet were replaced by slant ones, originally thatched from split bamboo, and later from corrugated iron galvanized sheets.

(c) Lastly, the sect of Buddhism that gained the firmest foothold was Nyingma—that is the unreformed school within Tibetan Buddhism—and these gave rise to a type of monasteries that was radically different to that of Tibet, where the prevailing school was of the Gelugpa sect.

Site Selection Methodology for Monasteries

In the Basin, the monasteries usually consist of one or several '*gompas*' (hlakhangs) depending on their size. They are surrounded by other smaller houses for accommodation of the monks during short stays. Meditation halls, kitchen and store rooms are constructed separately. The Ralang monastery has a large central courtyard, and a large dining hall. The building site for such monasteries is selected with great care, with due considerations to auguries and omens. The courses of streams, the shape of mountains, the ground configuration and the colour of soil—all come into consideration and deep study prior to erection of the structures.

All preliminary investigations are carried out not only for reasons of rituals, but also take into account the centuries old experience of generations, so as to avoid areas prone to earthquakes, landslides, floods, avalanches and wind hazards. Simple geo-technical tests are also carried out, such as digging holes in the soil and refilling them. This test reveals the density of soil and ensures that monasteries are not constructed over ground containing hollow space beneath the top layers. Likewise, a hole in ground is filled with water. It is taken as a positively good sign if the water sinks slowly.

Construction and Design

Wall Designing. By laying in laid in courses of alternate thick and thin sizes. Outer walls of the *gompas* are constructed from rough hewn stones. The thick ones are called 'males' and the thin ones 'females' of human species. Cracks between the stones are filled with clay-mortar. In some *gompas* the entire wall surface way be plastered. The walls may be as much as one metre thick at the base, tapering as one reaches the top, the inner side being vertical all the while. All inner sides of the walls are plastered with clay.

Doors and Windows. The doors, windows, balconies and other similar wooden structures have a number of constructural details protruding from the facade. These are emphasized by painting relief carvings, giving the wood work an elevating effect, almost jolly, in contrast to the substantially slanting walls, which reflect an attitude of tranquility (SRIT staff interview, 2000).

Wall Painting. Colour of the masonery is pale greyish yellow, which may sometimes be white washed. All *gompas* have a broad horizontal band painted brick-red around the top of the walls, bounded on both sides by a plank painted with a carved motif of white pearls.

Roofs. The roofs are hipped with small triangular gables placed vertically just under the ridge this has been mentioned early. The overhang may project upto two or three metres, protecting the wall, and at the same time covering the prayer wheels, that usually circumference the temple at the base. As new roofing materials were introduced, the shape of the roofs (as in the case of remodeled Pemayangtse and Tashiding monasteries) has gradually changed. The chubby profile of the thatches became more rigid when it was replaced by corrugated iron, and it was possible to make concave upward—swinging roofs as witnessed in Burma, Japan and China with flanged galvanized sheet iron. Many of the old *gompa* buildings were, in a way, disfigured, taking away with it, the rusty but soothing ethnic look.

The Directional Aspects. The entrance to the *gompa (hlakhang)* faces East, and the altar is built up against the West wall. The *gompas* entrances thus receive the first rays of the rising sun. Access to the loft is from an outdoor stair case on the North side of the building, or via a ladder indoors.

The Interior. The larger *gompas* contain sizeable prayer halls down stairs, with four or six columns. Usually there is an entrance hall to the East. Some rooms are constructed in Northern and Southern directions for larger sized prayer wheel drums or for storage, and a stair case leading to the first floor. At the first floor again, the central hall has an altar at the Western end, and is generally arranged systematically. One of the side rooms on first floor is sometimes used for spiritual and *tantric* rites. The doors to the *tantric rites* are painted with demon heads.

First and Upper Floors. The wooden structures supporting the first or upper floors are rather complicated. The corbelled pillars support a beam, upon which rest, first smaller, then larger cross beams. Since new materials have replaced the older ones, beams and floors are now cast in concrete. However, the top floor at Pemayangtse supports woodwork however.

Gompa features in Other Buildings. The older government buildings and some living houses of the *Kazis* adopted many features from the monasteries. The embellishment on the doors and windows was often the same, and also the construction of the beams and pillars. This is more common with the Bhutia houses and houses of some richer Lepchas.

Economically less fortunate Lepchas however retained their original building traditions, usually simple huts made mainly from bamboo.

The Artisans

Some artisans are trained in the various skills of building. They must at the same time do other works besides this to support the family, usually farming. The more delicate decoration work in the temples is performed by specially trained monks.

Certain Designing Aspects

The sun and the moon designs mark the centre over the doors, windows or portals. These prevent evil from peneterating into the building.

The traditional carving and decoration of the cantilevered capitals, symbolize the seven items necessary for the lord of the universe.

DESIGNS OVER DOORS AND WINDOWS

The sun and moon design marks the centre over a door, window or a portal. It prevents evil from penetrating into the building. The row of white circles represents pearls.

Prayerwheels

One does not pray for one's own sake, but prays for all other beings as well. The prayerwheels and drums contain strips of paper or cloth with prayers written on them, all of which are said to be sent up with each rotation.

Prayerwheels may function through the force of water, and are placed at man-made or natural water falls, where foot tracks or roads cross a rivulet or a fast flowing stream. Their blessings reach out to the travellers. Some prayer wheels function on wind energy as well. One such set of prayerwheels, functioning on wind energy is placed at the entrance of the Tashiding monastery.

Prayerwheels inside the *gompas* and some houses work on the principle of heat waves provided through lighted lamps or electric bulbs. A low pressure is built inside the wheel covering, which rotates due to gush of air from outside.

Prayer Flags

The prayer flags are erected outside the monasteries during various religious ceremonies coloured prayer. These flags are also erected outside houses and at the outer boundaries of villages, towns, localities and even the government buildings. The flags are differentiated on the basis of their colour pattern. The colours represent various elements found in nature, which are the following types:

(a) Blue-Sky.

(b) White-Iron.

(c) Red-Fire.

(d) Yellow-Earth.

(e) Green-Wood (Tree or Forest).

When prayer flags are hoisted, it is done to bring good luck, harmony and to spread the holy messages. It is believed that the holy messages inscribed on these flags spread to distant places with the flow of wind, thereby purifying the whole environment. A single prayer flag can consist of all the colours or different flags of single colour can be erected. These colours are arranged in a pattern with blue being on top, followed by white, red, yellow and green at the bottom. Same pattern is followed from left to right if uni-coloured flags are erected.

Certain mythological figures are printed on the flags, which may be of following types.

(a) Divine horse *(Lungta)* symbolizing good luck.

(b) Buddha *(Gyantse-tsenmo)* design, mainly for bringing good luck to warriors. It also epitomizes law of the land.

(c) Guru Rinpoche *(Benza-Guru)* for curing ailments and for speedy recovery of health.

(d) Mani, which is a form of Lord Vishnu for washing away any sin, which might have been committed while performing duties.

(e) *Dolma,* which is form of Goddess Tara symbolizing good luck.

(f) *Dorjee-Choepa,* which is one of the forms of Lord Buddha.

The lama decided the type of flag to be hoisted. He takes into consideration the occasion for which the flag is being erected, and also in some cases the horoscope of the individuals.

Archaclogy-Symbolism-Nature' Interrelationship

Nature and animal world form an integral part of the *gompas,* including the symbols of prayers wheels and flags:

(a) The monastery gates are decorated with deer paintings at the top. The wheel of life compares human spirituality and actions through the actions of animal life.

(b) Monastery construction itself commences after all aspects of natural order, and building sustainability are taken into account.

(c) The natures power of wind and water energy find their uses in rotation of the prayer wheels.

(d) The prayer flags depict all elements of nature through the colour combinations.

Natural forces are given full reverence, respect due to them in all prayer rituals. It is for followers to understand, and apply these lessons into their daily routine, while interacting with the environment and the biotic life around them.

SECTION III

TASHIDING MONASTERY: ITS HISTORY, AND STRUCTURAL LAYOUT—A CASE STUDY

History and Location

Tashiding monastery is considered to be the holiest of all the monasteries in Sikkim. It stands on a helmet shaped feature atop the confluence of Rathong chu and Rangit chu. Tashiding can be reached by road from Legship along a 17 km gravel road after crossing the majestic hanging bridge two km upstream from the Rangit hydel project. Legship itself is a injunction of roads connecting it to Jorethang, Gyalshing and Ravangla. Though at a comparatively low altitude of about 4000 ft a.s.l, the feature stands like a majestic barge above the Rathong-Rangit confluence, which itself is marked by virtue of a serene *chorten* and a cave in vicinity.

The location itself is spiritual. There is the Dubdi monastery 25 kms to the north, the wishfulfilling Khecheopalri lake to the north-west, the Pemayangtse monastery to the west, the Legship Shiva temple to the south, the Mongbrue *gompa* and Ravangla Bon monastery to the south-east, the Ravangla Gelug monastery to the east and the Karma Kagyud Ralang monastery to the north-east, making Tashiding virtually the spiritual centre atop the base, wherefrom geographically the Upper Rangit Basin takes off towards the Kanchandzonga massif and the two water sheds of Singalila and Mainam-Tendong ranges. Barring Dubdi and Khecheopalri, all other features named above are visible from Tashiding.

Spiritual Beliefs

The site where the present monastery stands has several legends associated to it. Guru Rinpoche 'Padmasambhava' is believed to have stayed here for meditation. Legend has it that he shot an arrow, vowing to meditate at the place where it fell. It dropped on the place where the present monastery is located. It is also believed that the site at Tashiding was accepted as the most sacred in Sikkim by the first three monks following the observance of occurrence of the divine phenomenon. A bright streak of light issuing from the top of Mount Khangchendzonga is believed to have shone right upon a spot at Tashiding. Simultaneously a most delicious fragrance of incense and notes of melodious music filled the atmosphere. The monks accompanied by King Phuntshog Namgyal visited the spot, and built the *chorten* named 'Thongwa-Rang-Grol', the sight of which confers self-emancipation. (Namgyal and Dolma, 1908).[21]

The Ngadak Lama built the monastery of 'Tashi-ga-legs' and also a Maitreya Temple at the site. The Chogyal Lhakhang was built by Pema Wangmo, elder sister of king Chagdor Namgyal during first half of 18th century. In 1715 Jigme Pao and King Chagdor Namgyal constructed Guru Lhakhang, and also supervised the internal furnishing. Jigme Pao himself performed the consecration ceremony of all Lhakhangs and *chortens* at Tashiding. (Dhamala, 1993).[22]

Legend and Anecdotal Accounts

A study of literature at Sikkim Research Institute of Tibetology, Gangtok revealed the history, legends, and anecdotal accounts attached with the spirituality of Tashiding monastery. True or not, the messages emnating out of the accounts reveal the Sikkimese peoples high esteem and faith in spirituality, leading to *karma,* which is central to balance of nature or 'Deep Ecology'

A conversation with monks at Tashiding confirms this Beyul Demojong (Hidden Valley of Rice) had five great provinces and six hidden spots which protected all living beings. Guru Rinpoche concealed innumerable scriptures (Vhos), Wealth (Nor) and sacred objects (Wangten) in those holy places and performed many inexpressible benedictory prayers for the benefit of sentient beings, thereby entrusting all the treasures to the protectors and tutelary deities for their preservation. This is confirmed by Neyig (Guide Book to the Holy Places).

He blessed and consecrated this land as sacred as Urgyen Zangdogpalri and Kanchopalgiriwo, the realms of unlimited happiness and abode and assemblage of female divinities (Mamo Khandos) like clouds in space. Likewise the innumerable Buddhas and Bhodisattavas of ten directions also blessed the land.

It is believed that one who visits these sacred lands, the doors of hell would be closed for him, i.e., they become immortals. Tashiding which is one of the most sacred places of Sikkim has four holy caves in four different directions. They are Sharchog Bephug in the East, Khandozangphu in the South, Dechenphug in the West and Lhari Nyingphug in the North. The centre of the holy place is known as Dakkar Tashiding, which is also the main deity of Tashiding. During the first dissemination of Buddhism in Tibet in the 8th century A.D. the illustrious Guru Padmasambhava and twenty-five disciples (Je-bang nyer-nga) had blessed the land (Beyul Demojong). Thereafter, they tamed all malevolent spirits and evil forces which infested this country. They also erected a number of places of worship, such as monasteries and *chortens.* The land was thus transformed into a great sacred and holy place.

In course of this process of propagation of Buddhism into Sikkim two great Siddhas (Tertons-revealers of Tantra) Rinzin Godemchen (1340-1396) and Kathog U,o'd Yeshe Bumpa came to Sikkim and established monasteries and meditation centres at sacred places of 'Pawo Hungri' and Tashiding. The reincarnation of Rigzin Godemchen, Terton Ngari Ringin Chenpo Lagdendorjee discovered the sublime tantra called Khadoi Khalangma from the cave of Lhari Nyingpo.

Came to Sikkim in the seventeenth century. That way it was the turning point in the history of Sikkim as the first Chogyal Phuntshog Namgyal was enthroned at Yuksom by these holy men. Three great

Lamas of Tibet namely Lhatsun Namkha Jigme (the embodiment of compassion was known to be the incarnation of Indian Maha Pandita Vimalamitra and Tibetan omniscient Kunkhen Longchenpa Dema Hozer), Ngadag Sempachenpo Phuntshog Rigzin and Kathog Rigzin Chenpo.

Under the Patronage of King Phuntshog Namgyal, monasteries, hermitages for meditation and *chortens* were built. Chogyal Phuntshog Namgyal proclaimed Buddhism as the state religion. Through the revelation of Zogchen system of meditation and Sadhana, Sikkim became the main centre of Zogchen teaching. Its followers came to be called Denzong Zogchenpa. The two great scholars ' Ngadag Sempachenpo and Ngadag Rinchen Gon' established the holy shrine at Dakkar Tashiding gave Buddhism thus got two greatest religious places in Sikkim.

'Holy Water Vase' and Bum chu Origination

In what way the celebration of 'Holy Water Vase' festival originated is briefly narrated here. During the reign of the religious king Trisong Deutsen in Tibet, Guru Padmasambhava, bestowed the unparralel tantric system of tutelary deity Mahakarunika Avalokitesvara Sadhana and initiation on emancipation from the cycle of mundane existence to king Trisong Deutsen, prince Murub Tsenpo, Yeshe Tsogyal and Verotsana. He at the same time consecrated the same Holy Vase this is preserved in the Tashiding monastery till today.

According to the works of Zhigpo Lingpa, the Holy Vase is made of various kinds of sacred soil, water and five kinds of precious jewels (Rinchen Na-nga) collected from the holy places of India, Odiyana and Zahar by Guru Padmasambhava. It is said that the Vase is made by Damchen Gar-bgag, wrathful Dharmpala and consecrated by Guru Padmasambhava by conducting Sadhana of Yidam Chuchig Zhal (tutelary deity of eleven heads). When he performed the sadhana, the entire retinue of the deity and deity himself are said to have appeared in the sky and inseparably merged into the Holy Water contained in the Vase.

Thereupon the holy water overflowed and spread in all directions in the form of rays. That very moment, as a sign of good omen, there was earthquake, the four guardian deities (Gyalchen Dezhi/Cutur-Maharajika) of Dharma and the gods of thirty-three heavens (Sumchu Tsasumgyi Lhanam) showered flowers from the sky. This event was witnessed by the people assembled there. All the people were overjoyed at this spectacular event and Holy Water was distributed to the devotees from the Vase. Yet it was found that the holy water of the Vase never decreased. Inspired by this, the sinners became virtuous, the pious people realised the lofty divine qualities and all were spiritually benefited. Finally, Guru Padmasambhava concealed the 'Holy Water Vase' into the sublime hidden treasure. Since then, it is believed that deities are protecting the 'Holy Water Vase.'

In the later period, the great Terton (revealer of hidden treasures), Chokyi Gyalpo Garwang Rigzin Zhinpolingpa, the reincarnation of prince Murub Tsenpo of Tibet, unearthed the Vase of Holy Water for the sake of sentient beings. After the discovery of the Vase, Terton Zhipolingpa maintained it as his Thugdam Ten and in the later part of his life, he offered it to Terton Tagshamchen with special instruction Terton Tagshamchen then handed over the 'Holy Vase' to Ngadag Sempachenpo Phuntshog Rigzin to be kept and installed at Dakkar Tashiding, the holiest and most blessed hidden land of Guru Padmasambhava.

So, Terton Ngadag Sampachenpo brought the Vase to Tashiding and installed it in the Tshuglagkhang. He is known to have conducted special recitation of 1,300 million syllables 'OM MANI PADME HUM', 'Om Mani Padme Hum' through Thugjechenpo Khorwalegrol Sadhna under the royal patronage of the first Chogyal Phuntshog Namgyal. At that time many unprecedented and auspicious signs had appeared in the country. Bumchu celebration is one of the most important and holiest events in Sikkim and thousands of devotees from all over the state and its neighbouring countries come on pilgrimage and participate in the holy occasion. The Vase, containing holy water, was kept in a miniature mansion (cho-sham) under lock and seal of the Chogyal of Sikkim. Every year special recitation is conducted and the seal is checked by the high officials and Lamas before the Vase is taken out of the mansion. The Vase is opened on the night of the 14th day of the first month of the Tibetan Almanac. From the Vase three cups of the water is first taken out. The first cup is meant for the royal family, the second cup for the Lamas and the third is distributed among the devotees on the full moon day. Fresh water is brought from Rathong Chu, which is also considered as a blessed river, as replacement.

In some years the Holy Water in the Vase increases by 21 cups. When it increases, it was the sign of prosperity. Other times it decreases. When it decreases, it is an indication of bad year of drought and diseases. In some cases the water of the Vase remains at the same level but other times it is found dusty. These are believed to be the predictions of auspicious and inauspicious occurrences in the country. The dusty water indicated conflicts and unrest.

Summary

For Tashiding, one can say "Seeing is believing'. The monastery is historically illustrious, geographically well located, aesthetically beautiful, spiritually divine—a place where nature and spirituality dwell together, urging the human race to be ecologically upright.

SECTION IV

CHORTENS; ARCHITECTURE, SPIRITUAL AND ECOLOGICAL SIGNIFICANCE

Introduction

Life and death were always the greatest agents of religious ritual and speculation. These are the mysteries man has never been able to solve. Through the experience of death man becomes conscious of life. Thus, the cult of the dead stimulated primitive man to build the first great monuments (tumuli), while the other side of religious activity, which was concerned with the living and the mundane aspects of life, found expression in the simpler forms of tree and fire-worship. The tumuli originating from the burial mound, were massive structures of stone, taking the forms of hemispheres, cones, pyramids and similar plain stereometrical bodies, containing small cells which preserved the bodily remains and other relics of heroes, saints, kings and similar great personalities. In India, as in many other parts of Asia, the hemispheric form seems to have been the prevalent type of such monuments. According to the oldest tradition they were erected for great rulers and sages. (Govinda 1970).[23]

It became a tradition that while the tumuli and the cult of the dead had their place outside the village, the sanctuary of the life-giving and life-preserving forces (personified in the sun-god) had its place in the centre of the village. It consisted of a simple altar (a sanctified form of the domestic hearth, the fire of which was always regarded sacred as a symbol of family life) or a small shrine (an idealized form of the village hut) which stood in the shadow of the sacred tree (the Tree of Life) and was surrounded by a fence as a demarcation of the sacred place. The

Buddhist *stupa* combined the elements of the village sanctuary with the monumental dome of the ancient tumulus *(caitya),* thus uniting the two oldest traditions of humanity, as expressed in the lunar and solar cult, fusing them into one universal symbol which recognized formally for the first time that life and death are only two sides of the same reality, complementing and conditioning each other. To think of them as separate is illusion, and only as long as the veil of Maya has not been lifted, the worship of these two forces proceeds separately, sometimes even as two separate forms of religion. Only when it has been understood that there is no life without transformation, and that the power of transformation is the essence of life—then the great synthesis takes place and the foundation of a world-religion is established. (Yeshe and Zopa Rinpoche 1982).[24]

Harmika

The Buddhist *stupa* originally consisted of an almost hemispherical tumulus, an altar-like structure *(harmika)* on its top, surmounted by one or several superimposed honorific umbrellas. The flattened hemisphere was compared to an egg and therefore called *anda*, a terms which did not only allude to the shape (which was also compared to a water-bubble) but to its deeper significance as well, namely, as a symbol of latent creative power, while the quadrangular *harmika* on the summit of the cupola symbolized the sanctuary enthroned above the world *(anda* was also a synonym of the universe in the oldest Indian mythology) beyond death and rebirth.

A similar parallelism exists between the *harmika* in the shade of the sacred tree, because the Holy One, whose ashes were enshrined in the altar like sanctuary of the *harmika,* instead of sacrificing other beings, had sacrificed himself for the welfare of all living beings. According to the Buddha there is only one sacrifice which is of real value, the sacrifice of our own desires, our own self. The ultimate form of such a sacrifice is that of a Bodhisattva, who renounces even the ultimate peace of final *nirvana (Parinirvana)* until he has helped his fellow-being to find the path of liberation.

The Monorific Umbrella

It is an abstract representation of the shade-giving tree in this case representing the sacred Tree of Life—is one of the chief solar symbols, and in Buddhism that of Enlightenment *(samyak-sambodhi).* The importance of this symbol becomes clear from the Buddhist Scriptures, describing the struggle of the Buddha and Mara, the Evil One, for the place under the Bodhi Tree, the holiest spot in the world, later known as the Diamond Throne *(vajrasana, Tib. rDo-rje gdan).* According to the custom, the head of the community had his seat of honour under the sacred tree in the centre of the settlement where public meetings used to take place on religious and other important occasions. When the head of the community moved about or presided over similar functions in other places, he moved with an umbrella. It later became one of the insignia of royalty. In order to mark the distinctions in rank, the ceremonial umbrella was doubled or trebled, or increased by even greater number of umbrellas, which were fixed one above the other, thus transforming the umbrella back again to the original tree-shape with its numerous layers of branches spreading around the stem and gradually getting shorter towards the top. These layered umbrellas are the thirteen rings or wheels along the entire length of the cone placed on top of *harmika* and *pema.*

Historical Backdrop

In order to understand the transformation of the ancient customary tumulus into the universal conception of the *Caitya,* from which later the Tibetan *Chorten* developed, we must have a look at the earliest known Buddhist Stupa Sanchi. The great Sanchi Stupa was crowned by a threefold honorific umbrella and the altar-shrine on top of the hemispherical main structure was surrounded by a railing *(vedika),* exactly as in the case of the village sanctuary. Similar railings were repeated at the foot of the *stupa* and on the low circular-terrace upon which the flattened hemisphere rested. The lowest railing was provided with four gateways *(torana)* which opened towards the east, the south, the west and the north, emphasizing the universal character of Buddhism which is open to all the four quarters of the universe and invites all humankind with the call "Come and see!", and which exhorts its followers to open their hearts to all that lives, while radiating love, compassion, sympathetic joy and equanimity towards the whole world. The inner space between the stone railing and the *stupa,* as well as the circular terrace *(medhi)* at the base of the cupola were used as *pradaksina patha* for ritual circumambulation in the direction of the sun's course.

The orientation of the gates equally corresponds to the sun's course: to sunrise, zenith, sunset and nadir. Just as the sun illuminates the physical world, so does the Buddha, the Enlightened One, illuminate the spiritual world. The eastern gateway represents his birth, the southern (which was regarded as the most important and therefore built first) his enlightenment, the western his "setting in motion the Wheel of the Law" *(dharma cakra pravartana):* the proclamation of his doctrine, and the northern his final liberation *(pariniravana).* This universal attitude and orientation remained one of the characteristics of the *stupa,* especially in the northern countries of Buddhism, like Tibet, even after railings and gateways had disappeared. In the course of time all these details were fused into a quadrangular substructure, which finally took the form of four terraces.

The layers of superimposed umbrellas became more and more numerous. They were transformed into the more architectural shape of a solid cone with a corresponding number of horizontal notches, which finally amounted to thirteen. With this transformation the original idea of the Tree of Life and Enlightenment was visibly restored and steadily gained in importance. That the conical spire was no more regarded as a set of umbrellas, can be seen from the fact that later on an honorific umbrella was again fixed on top of the cone. The details are there in the section which follow.

The different strata of the cone (separated by horizontal notches) were now explained to correspond to certain psychic faculties or stages of consciousness on the way to enlightenment and to their respective world-planes. Thus, the spiritual rebirth of the world starts in the mind of man, and the Tree of Life grows out of his own heart, the centre of his world, and spreads into ever new infinities, into ever higher and purer realms, until it has turned into a Tree of Enlightenment.

Stupa and Individual Spirituality

Nepalese *stupas,* which in many respects have preserved archaic features, decorate the *harmika* (the cubic structure above the cupola) with painted human eyes, thus suggesting a human figure in the posture of meditation hidden in the *stupa* the crossed legs in the base, the body up to the shoulders in the hemisphere, the head in the *harmika.* This also corresponds to the psycho-physical doctrine of the centres of psychic force *(cakra)* which are located one above the other in the human body, and through which consciousness develops in an ascending order: from the experience of material sense-objects through that of the immaterial worlds of pure mental objects, up to the supramundane consciousness of enlightenment, which has its base in the crown-cakra of the head *(sahasrara).*

This *cakra* is symbolized by a dome-shaped or flame-like protuberance on the head of the Buddha, and by the cone-shaped Tree of Enlightenment which forms the spire of the *stupa* or the *Chorten,* or its various equivalents; like the *dogobas (dhatu-garbha)* of Sri Lanka or *pagodas* (a reversal of the word *dogoba)* in Burma, Thailand and Indo-China. It was one of the attributes of the sun-god, either in the form of a discus or in the form of the wheel, representing the rolling sun-chariot. This is in itself is a san symbol. The solar origin is testified by the description of the flaming and radiating wheel which appears in the sky with its thousand spokes (rays) when a virtuous ruler has established a reign of righteousness and has attained the spiritual power which entitles and enables him to extend the Good Law *(dharma)* over the whole world and to become a world-ruler *(cakravartin).* Similarly, the "turning of the Wheel of the Good Law" has become a synonym for the Buddha's first proclamation of his doctrine *(dharma-chakra-pravartana-sutra),* by which the thousand-spoked sun-wheel of the universal law was set in motion, radiating its light throughout the world. (Govinda 1960).[25]

Psychic Forces and Spirituality

The *cakras* as radiating centres of psychic force thus gave a new impetus to the interpretation of the human body as a cosmic manifestation. Not only is the spinal column compared to Mount Meru, the axis of the universe, and therefore called *rneni-danda* but the whole psycho-physical organism was explained in terms of solar and lunar forces, which through fine channels, the so-called veins or nadis, moved up and down between the seven *cakras,* which in their turn represented the elementary qualities of which the universe is built and of which the material elements are only the visible reflexes.

Unity of Spirituality and Nature Forces: Chorten and Human Ecology

A parallelism was established with respect to the psychic organism whose vital centres *(cakras)* were found to correspond to the elementary qualities of matter: the basic vital centre or "root support: *(muladhara-cakra),* situated in the perineum at the base of the spinal column, (which latter represents the Tree of Life) and corresponding to the element Earth, the solid state; the navel-centre *(manipura-cakra)* to the element Water, the fluid state; the heart-centre *(anahata-cakra)* to the element Fire, the heating, incandescent or radiating state; the throat-centre *(visuddha-cakra)* to the element Air, the gaseous state; and the centre on the crown of the head *(sahasrara-cakra)* to the element Ether (or in its passive aspect; Space), the state of vibration. Each of these elements is symbolized by a sound (bija-mantra, a mystic syllable of creative power), a colour and a basic form.

The latter two are of special interest to us, as they have been directly applied to the architecture of the *chorten.* Earth is represented by a yellow cube, Water by a white sphere or a white round pot, Fire by a triangular body of either round or square base; i.e. a cone or, less frequently, a pyramid. Air is represented two dimensionally as a semi-circular bow-shaped form of green colour, three-dimensionally as a hemisphere with the base upward, like a cup. Ether is graphically represented by a small-acuminated circle or blue dot *(bindu)* and appears in three-dimensional form as a multi-coloured flaming jewel, i.e., a small sphere.

If we put all these elements together in due order, namely, the sphere upon the cube, a cone or a pyramid upon the sphere, and upon the cone or pyramid a cup-like hemisphere which carries a flaming drop on its plane surface-then we get the ideal figure or the abstract stereometrical form which represents the basic principles of stupa-architecture, as preserved in the Tibetan *chorten* as well as in the Japanese *Sotoba* into a vase or pot-shaped vessel (Tib: *bum-pa).* which rests on a cubic substructure and is crowned by a tall cone, ending in a small upturned hemisphere, which carries on its plane surface a crescent, a sundisc and the 'flaming jewel', one upon the other (Dorjee 1996).[26] This represents all elements of universe and human body together, sanctifying the sum total—an idea wholly supporting the concept of 'Deep Ecology', the biocentric spiritual aspect of human ecology. Succeeding paragraph carry detailed account.

The colours of the 'great elements' *(mahabhuta)* are represented in the main parts of the Chorten: the cubical sub-structure yellow (Earth); the post-shaped central part white (Water), the conical spire red (Fired), while the fourth element (Air) which should show a green surface, is generally hidden under the honorific umbrella, a symbol which, especially in its Tibetan form, is closely connected with the concept of Air. Without taking into account its tree-origin and its natural relationship to sun, air and sky, it may be mentioned that according to the later Indian and Tibetan tradition honorific umbrellas were supposed to appear in the sky, when a saint had realized certain magic powers.

Between the umbrella and the flaming drop (Tib.: *thig-le),* the respective symbols of Air and Ether, there is a white crescent, in whose inner curve rests a red sun-disc. They repeat the colours of the two main elements of the *Chorten,* namely that of the moon-related, waterpot-shaped central part and that of the sun-related conical spire. The meaning of this repetition becomes evident if we remember the role of the lunar and solar forces moving through the main channels or *nadis* of the psycho-physical organism of man. The most important one runs through the spinal column and is called *susumna (dhu-ma-rtsa* in Tibetan), while *ida (*Tib.: *rkyang-ma rtsa)* and *pingala* (Tib.: *ro-ma-rtsa)* coil round the central channel in opposite directions, the pale white-coloured *ida* starting from the left (or, according to Tibetan tradition, controlling the left side of the human body), the red coloured *pingala* from the right (or controlling the right side). *Ida* is the conductor of the lunar or 'moon-like' *(candrasvarupa)* forces, which have the regenerative properties and the unity of undifferentiated subconscious life, as represented by the latent creativeness of seed, egg and semen, in which all chronic-telluric cults are centred.

Pingala is the vehicle of solar forces *(surya-svarupa)*, which have the properties of intellectual activity, representing the conscious, differentiated individualized life. Individualization, however, if separating itself, from its origin, is as death-spelling as knowledge severed from the sources of life. This is why wisdom and compassion *(prajna* and *karuna*) must be united for the attainment of liberation. And for the same reason *pingala,* the solar energy, without the regenerating influence of *ida,* the lunar energy, acts like a poison, while even the elixir of immortality *(amrita),* to which the regenerating lunar energy is compared, has no value without the light of knowledge. It is for this reason that only when the solar and lunar energies are united in the central channel, the *susumna,* and carried up from the root-centre *(muladhara-cakra)* through all the other centres of psychic power and consciousness until they reach the universal level in the Thousand-Petalled Lotus of the *sahasrar-cakra.*

The final integration of these two forces takes place and results in the ultimate state of illumination *(samyak-sambodhi)*. In the spherical and conical part of the *Chorten* the two currents of psychic energy are represented by their separate and elementary aspects; in the crescent and the sun-disc they are represented in their sublimated or spiritualized form as knowledge *(prajna)* and compassion *(karuna)*, from the union of which the dazzling flame-jewel of perfect enlightenment is born. This symbol of unity and ultimate reality has its latent counterpart in the form of a blue dot *(bindu;* Tib.: *thig-le)* or seed *(bija)*, the creative germ or spiritual potentiality, inherent in every sentient being as the potential consciousness of enlightenment *(budhicitta;* Tib.: *hyahng chub-sems)*.

The unfolding of this latent principle is the aim of the spiritual path, which is achieved when all our psychic faculties as embodied in the various centres are permeated by it. When the mystic union between the sun of knowledge and the moon of compassion has reached its zenith and consummation on the highest spiritual plane, the Thousand-Petalled Lotus, then it comes to pass that the dark seed, containing the essence of the universe and the ever-present reality of the *dharma-dhatu*. It breaks open and bursts forth into the dazzling flame of enlightenment this is the crowning symbol of the most universal type of the Tibetan Mahayana Chorten (Govinda 1970).[27]

Conclusion

Combination of universal elements and forces, uniting them with life system psychic powers and then placing them in the form of a *Chorten*, urges the living humans to understand and have *karuna* for all existance-biotic or abiotic. This is encompassed the following quotation from Chandogya Upanisad:

> *"The essence of all beings is earth,*
> *the essence of earth is water,*
> *the essence of water are the plants,*
> *the essence of the plants is man,*
> *the essence of man is speech,*
> *the essence of speech is the Rgveda,*
> *the essence of the Rgveda is the Samaveda,*
> *the essence of the Samaveda is the Udgita (which is OM),*

That Udgita is the best of all essences, the highest,
Deserving the highest place, the eighth."

(CHANDOGYA UPANISAD)

It is essentially 'knowledge of' and 'compassion for' all universal existence that leads to enlightenment. This message of *Karuna* and *gyan* is reflected in the *chortens.* This is human ecology in its deepest realms. This is the message of Buddha in the *chortens.*

SECTION V

CHORTENS OF TASHIDING

Introduction

The *chortens* seen in all parts of Sikkim follow Tibeto-Buddhist rituals and architecture. Mention of various types of chorten architecture is incomplete without making references to the eight *stupas* associated with the eight major events in the life of Lord Buddha as under:

(a) The first *stupa* was constructed in the Lumbini garden of Kapilavastu where the Buddha was born.

(b) The second *stupa* was on the banks of the Naranjana River in the kingdom of Magadha, where the Buddha had attained enlightenment.

(c) The third *stupa* was constructed in the Varanasi city of Kashi where he turned the great Dharmacakra.

(d) The fourth *stupa* was constructed in the Jetavana of Sravasti where he performed the great miracles.

(e) The fifth *stupa* was constructed in the Kanyakubja city of Sankasya where the Buddha descended from the Trayastrimsah (the palace of thirty-three gods).

(f) The sixth *stupa* was constructed at Rajagrha where he reconciled the schism in Sangha *(sarighabheda).*

(g) The seventh *stupa* was constructed in the city of Vaisali where he prolongated his life span *(ayuhpramana).*

(h) The eighth *stupa* was constructed in the city of Kusinagara where he entered Nirvana.

Early Indian Buddhist *stupa* had their pecular construction and design. Shapes and dimensions of the eight fundamental types of Tibeto-Buddhist *chortens* followed this pattern *stupas*. Despite this transformation, the Tibeto-Buddhist *chortens* have retained all architectural aspects and religious significance as well as spiritual values and symbolical meanings which originated in ancient Indian Buddhist culture, as described in previous section.

Types of Chortens

Chortens are of eight types. Structural distinctions amongst the eight types of *chortens*. These are explained below (Pema Dorjee 1996)[28]:—

(a) *Chorten of Enlightenment.* It has a flight of four perfect square steps, which are free from embellishments. There is a tradition of making all the upper edges of the steps bulge out by one-quarter part of their own height to have an attractive look.

(b) *Chorten of 'Heaped Lotuses.'* It is also called the *chorten* of "Auspicious Appearance" and "Appearance of Sugata". It comprises a flight of four circular steps adorned with heaped lotuses. There is also a tradition of making a maximum of seven steps to symbolize the seven paces that the Buddha took immediately after his birth in the Lumbini garden of Kepilavastu.

(c) *Chorten of 'Multiple Auspicious Doors'*. It is also called the *chorten* of 'Divine Wisdom'. It comprises a flight of four square steps, and each side's centre bulges out by one-third the size of their width. These *chortens* have 108 doors or niches at the maximum, 56 in the medium and 16 in the minimum. Symbolically, four doors on each side symbolize the four Noble-truths, eight doors on each side symbolize the eight doors of liberations, twelve doors on each side symbolize the twelve links of interdependent origination, and sixteen doors on each side symbolize the 16 types of emptiness.

(d) *Chorten of 'Great Miracle'*. This is also called *chorten* of "Conquest of Tirthikas'. This is identical to the preceding ones (having a flight of four square steps), although this does not have doors.

(e) *Chorten of 'Descent from Heaven'*. Alternatively it is called "Offered by Devas". The structural formation is similar to the preceding ones; it has three ladders in the centre of each side's projected area.

(f) *Chorten of 'Reconciliation'*. It comprises four octagonal steps formed by cutting off the four corners of the flight of four steps to form eight even sides. They are free from all embellishments. Occasionally, though rarely, there is a tradition of making all the upper edges of the steps projected out by one-third of their own height.

(g) *Chorten of 'Victory'*. It has three circular steps rather than four. Even the base often virtues and the vase-base are circular.

(h) *Chorten of 'Nirvana'*. It is rather unique type of a *chorten* because of its 'bell-shaped dome', in which mooth rests directly on the 'base of ten virtues' without any steps. [Structural Components of *Chortens.*]

The *Chortens* in all its styles comprises three main structural bodies:

(a) *The Lion Throne*. This consists of six symbolic structures from the ground plinth upto the frame.

(b) *The Intermediate Section.* This comprises six symbolical structures from the 'base of ten virtues' upto the *harmika.*

(c) *The Upper Section.* The upper section or 'upper extremity' consists of all structures from the 'lotus supporting umbrella' upto the spherical pinnacle, and surround the 'axle pole', which is the vertical at the centre of a *chorten.*

Symbolical Meanings of *Chorten* Components

The flight of four steps, vase-base, the Vase (dome) *harmika,* axle poles, thirteen wheels and the rain-cloak comprise the physical structure of the *chorten.* 'The accumulation' or 'essence' of *chorten* as explained by Angarika Govinda and Pema Dorjee is explained in succeeding paragraphs.

The Steps

The first step symbolizes the four close mindfulness *(catvari smrtyupasthana adhara vedi)* viz:

(a) The close mindfulness of body.

(b) The close mindfulness of feeling.

(c) The close mindfulness of mind.

(d) The close mindfulness of wisdom.

The second step symbolizes the four perfect abandonments viz:

(a) Efforts to abandon the non-virtues that have arisen.

(b) Efforts to prevents the non-virtues that have not yet arisen.

(c) Efforts to produce the virtues that have not yet arisen.

(d) Efforts to retain the virtues that have already arisen.

The third step symbolizes the four stages of miraculous powers *(catvari rddhipadas trtiya vedi)* viz:

(a) A miraculous power possessed of compositional factor renouncing an aspiration of meditative concentration or meditative concentration of desire.

(b) A miraculous power possessed of compositional factor renouncing a meditative concentration of mind.

(c) A miraculous power possessed of compositional factor renouncing a meditative concentration of effort.

(d) A miraculous power possessed of compositional factor renouncing a meditative concentration of analysis.

The fourth step symbolizes the five (moral) faculties viz:

(a) Moral faculty of faith.

(b) Moral faculty of effort.

(c) Moral faculty of mindfulness.

(d) Moral faculty of meditative concentration.

(e) Moral faculty of wisdom.

The Vase

The vase-base symbolizes the five (moral) powers viz:

(a) The moral power of faith.

(b) The moral power of effort.

(c) The moral power of mindfulness.

(d) The moral power of meditative concentration.

(e) The moral power of wisdom.

The vase dome of the chorten symbolizes the seven factors of enlightenment viz:

(a) The factor of enlightenment to the perfect mindfulness.
(b) The factor of enlightenment to the perfect dharma.
(c) The factor of enlightenment to the perfect joy.
(d) The factor of enlightenment to the perfect effort.
(e) The factor of enlightenment to the perfect suppleness.
(f) The factor of enlightenment to the perfect meditative concentration.
(g) The factor of enlightenment to the perfect equanimity.

The *harmika* symbolizes the Eightfold Noble paths viz:

(a) Right view.
(b) Right thought.
(c) Right speech.
(d) Right action.
(e) Right livelihood.
(f) Right endeavour.
(g) Right mindfulness.
(h) Right meditative concentration.

The axle-pole symbolizes the ten knowledge's viz:

(a) Knowledge of conventional phenomena.
(b) Knowledge of others' mind.
(c) Knowledge of dharma.
(d) Knowledge of realization of subsequent.
(e) Knowledge of sufferings.
(f) Knowledge of cessation.
(g) Knowledge of sources of origination.
(h) Knowledge of paths.
(j) Knowledge of exhaustion.
(k) Knowledge of non-productivity.

Symbolism of the wheels is as explained:

(a) The first bottom wheel symbolizes the power of understanding what is appropriate and inappropriate.

(b) The second wheel symbolizes the power of understanding that one is responsible for one's own deeds or action.

(c) The third wheel symbolizes the power of understanding, concentration, liberation, meditative stabilization and meditative absorption.

(d) The fourth wheel symbolizes the power of understanding the superior and inferior faculties.

(e) The fifth wheel symbolizes the power of understanding the various mental inclinations.

(f) The sixth wheel symbolizes the power of understanding various mental faculties/constitutions.

(g) The seventh wheel symbolizes the power of understanding the paths leading to all goals.

(h) The eighth wheel symbolizes the power of understanding the recollection of former existence.

(j) The ninth wheel symbolizes the power of understanding deaths and births.

(k) The tenth wheel symbolizes the power of understanding the exhaustion/cessation of contaminations.

(l) The eleventh wheel symbolizes the first peculiar close mindfulness (of the *Tathagata),* that by which, when the *Tathagata* teaches the dharma to his retinue, he does not get pleased when all his disciples listen with great respect.

(m) The twelfth wheel symbolizes the second peculiar close mindfulness, that by which, when, the *Tathagata* teaches the dharma to his retinue, he does not get angry when all his disciples do not listen with due respect.

(n) The thirteenth wheel symbolizes the third peculiar close mindfulness, that by which, when the *Tathagata* teaches the dharma to his retinue, he neither becomes joyful nor angry when part of his disciples listen with respect and part do not listen with respect.

The rain-cloak symbolizes the great compassion by which the *Tathagata* examines the mental disposition of his trainees who are mature, immature or maturing. For the benefit of universal people. The nature of the stupa indicate perfect apprehension of all the truth bodies *(dharmakaya)* at all the different occasions.

The umbrella represents the *Tathagata* a leader of all sentient beings, because the *Tathagata* became the supreme among the living beings without legs, among those having two legs, many legs, and among those who are corporeal and incorporeal.

The moon represents the brightness of the unsurpassed wisdom by which the *Tathagata* generates the eyes of the unsurpassed knowledges in the darkness of this world. Representation aspects of the sun and ether are given in previous section.

Chortens of Tashiding

There are a total of 41 *chortens* at Tashiding. They have been numbered for explanatory notes. Each number in plate V represents the location of the *chortens*. The *chortens* here are of three types:

(a) *Chorten of Enlightenment.* Numbers 1 to 4, 8 to 17, 19 to 32, 34 to 36 and 38 and 39. Total—33 *chortens.*

(b) *Chorten of Reconciliation.* Number 5 and 20.

(c) *Chorten of Great Miracle.* Numbers 7, 18 and 33.

Chortens mentioned below correspond to the *Tathagatas* and Gurus as mentioned below:

(a) **Dhudal Chorten.** 8. This is the protector deity of Tashiding Monastery.

(b) Lhabab *chorten* is at No. 24.

(c) Woe-Sung Ku-dhung, the oldest and largest *chorten* is at No. 25.

(d) Kagyu Lama *Chorten* is at No. 31.

(e) Lamyang Khentse Wongpo (Choe-ki-Lodoe form Tibet) is at No. 23.

(f) *Chorten* of Guru Rang Jong.

(g) Dhakar (White Rock) Tashiding, which is the key centre of main Tashiding pilgrimage is at No. 40.

(h) No. 41 is the location where Guru Rinpoche's arrow had contacted the ground, and where he sat in meditation.

Conclusion

We have reached the limit of what words can express. Beyond the words lies the practical relativity between the psychic, spiritual and natural forces, and this is exactly what the *chortens* of Tashiding, and other places in Himalayas and trans-Himalayas communicate to the living humans.

References

1. Jordan, T.G., and Rowntree, L., *The Human Mosaic: A Thematic Introduction to. Cultural Geography*, Harper Collin Publishers, New York, 1990.
2. Durkheim, E., The Dualism in Human Nature in *Essays on Sociology and Philosophy*, (ed). K.H. Wolff, New York, Harper Torch Books, 1964.
3. Swanson Guy. E., *The Birth of the Gods: The Origin of the Primitive Beliefs*, Ann Arbor, University of Michigan Press, 1960.
4. Egri, P.C., "Nature in Spiritual Traditions" in *Living with Nature* by Fischer, F., and Hajer, A., Oxford University Press, New York, 1999.
5. Toffler, A., *The Third Wave*, William Collins Sons & Co. Ltd., London, 1980.
6. Frost, P.J., and Egri, C.P., 'The Shamanic Perspective and Organizational Change and Development.' *Journal of Organizational Change Management*, 7(1):7-23, 1994.
7. Halifax, J., 'The Third Body: Buddhism, Shamanism and Deep Ecology,' in A.H. Badiner (ed), *Dharma Gaia: A Harvest of Essays in Buddhism and Ecology*, Calif: Parallax Press, Berkley, 1990.
8. Risley, H.H., (ed), *The Gazetteer of Sikkim*, Bengal Government Secretariat Calcutta, 1894.
9. Subba, T.B., *Politics of Culture*, Orient Longman Ltd, Chennai, 1999.
10. Foning, A.R., *Lepcha: My Vanishing Tribe*, Sterling Publishers Private Limited, New Delhi, 1987.
11. Egri, P.C., *ibid.*
12. Macy, J., 'Toward a Healing of Self and World', in *Ecology* (ed) Merchant, C, Rawat Publications, Jaipur, 1996.
13. Chappie, C.K., 'Hindu Environmentalism: Traditional and Contemporary Resources', in M.E, Tucker and J.A. Grim (eds) *World Views and Ecology*, Bucknell University Press, Lewisburg, 1993.
14. Gadgil, M. and Guha, R., *This Fissured Land: An Ecological History of India*, University of California, Berkley, 1992.

15. Badiner, A.H. (ed), *Dharma Gaia: A Harvest of Essays in Buddhism and Ecology.* Calif: Parallax Press, Berkley, 1990.

16. Kaza, S., 'Acting with Compassion: Buddism, Feminism and Environmental Crisis', in C.J. Adams (ed) *Ecofeminism and the Sacred.* Continuum, New York, 1993.

17. Bhatt, R., 'A Gandhian Perspective in the Himalayan Foothills', in J. Plant (ed) *Healing the Wounds*, New Society Publishers, Santa Cruz, 1989.

18. Devall, B., 'Ecocentric Sangha' in A.H. Badiner (ed) *Dharma Gaia: A Harvest of Essays in Buddhism and Ecology*, Parallax Press, Berkley, 1990.

19. Risley, H.H., *ibid.*

20. GRIT Library, Wall Display, Gangtok, 2000.

21. Namgyal, Thutob, and Dolma, Y., *History of Sikkim,* 1908.

22. Dhamala, R.R., *Monasteries of Sikkim*, Occasional Paper No. 8, University of North Bengal, Siliguri, 1993.

23. Govinda, Lama, Angarika., The Historical and symbolical Origin of Chorten, in *Bulletin of Tibetology*, SRIT. Gangtok, Vol. VII, No. 3, 1970.

24. Yeshe, L., and Rinpoche, Z., *Wisdom Energy: Basic Buddhist Teachings*, Wisdom Publications, 1976.

25. Govinda, Lama, Angarika, *Foundations of Tibetan Mysticism*, B.I. Publications, New Delhi, 1960.

26. Dorjee, Pema, *Stupa and its Technology*, IGNCA with Motilal Banarsidass Publishers, New Delhi, 1996.

27. Govinda, Lama, Angarika, *ibid.*

28. Dorjee, Pema, *Ibid.*

8

Tantric Buddhism[1]

There is one chief difficulty in achieving a just appreciation of the historical development of Buddhism and that is the geographic division of Buddhism as we see it at the present day. In the sixteenth and seventeenth centuries this division was causing the bewilderment among European travellers and missionaries, who were understandably slow in attributing the religions of Ceylon and Japan to a common source. In India itself Buddhism had been gradually sinking into oblivion since the destruction of the great monastic centres at the hands of the Moghuls. It was not until the first half of the last century that there appeared the two great pioneers of Indian Buddhism, Brian Hodgson, who was British resident in Kathmandu for twenty-five years, and Eugene Burnouf, who was his chief collaborator at the College de France. Now after a century of scholastic endeavour, it is possible to trace the history of this religion in the land of its origin.

Much uncertainty and obscurity remain, especially in the later period, but this does not excuse anyone who professes to write or speak of Buddhism from doing his best to take this whole period into account. For Buddhism is not just the word of one master, promulgated and fixed for all time. It was part of India's religious experience, changing, adapting, developing through the centuries, yet at the same time retaining a certain continuity and independence in its traditions. However far we go back in time, we can never discover such a things as pure Buddhism, for it inevitably shared its philosophical concepts, its moral and ascetic practices with the rest of the religious life of India. It adopted what came to be its characteristic dogma, *anatmata,* absence of self-nature, but this weakened neither its adherence to the generally accepted doctrine of rebirth nor its reliance upon the assistance of divine beings. Some monks, it is true, strove to 'be islands to themselves', but there were as many non-Buddhist ascetics who strove likewise, and as devotion developed towards the great Hindu gods, so it likewise developed towards those great beings, the bodhisattvas.

Historically, at least, one must conceive of Buddhism as an active living tradition, probably receiving its impetus from a great religious teacher round about the year 500 B.C. (who thought and taught, be it remembered, within the terms of his times) and continued to enrich and adapt itself on a give-and-take basis for 1,500 years and more. It spread to Ceylon, probably in the third century B.C., and although the connection with India certainly continued for several centuries, Buddhists there remained largely ignorant of subsequent developments in India and have remained so to the present day.

At about the beginning of the Christian era, it began to spread across central Asia to China and thence finally to Japan. From the eighth century onwards it become gradually became established throughout Tibet, but the forms in which it now appeared were very different from those which Ceylon had received a thousand years earlier. Tibet remained in contact with India to the last and today, in the first decade of the twenty first century, it is so. So it is the full inheritor of the Indian Buddhist tradition. Thus, the distance that separates Theravadin Buddhism from Tibetan Buddhism today provides some measure of the distance that separated Indian Buddhism of the third century B.C. from Indian Buddhism of the twelfth century A.D.

One sees, therefore how misleading it may be to speak of Northern and Southern Buddhism, for the difference between the Buddhism of Ceylon, Burma, Siam and Cambodia on the one hand and of China, Japan and Tibet on the other are not primarily geographical, but historical and temporal. The bond of their unity can still be traced, but only laboriously and with the help of texts and archaeological remains. These are scanty enough, if one relies upon Indian sources alone, for the climate is unsuitable for the preservation of manuscript material and the ancient sites were abandoned for centuries to the callousness of weather and of man. Some of the most important texts have been preserved in Nepal, but in order to gain any real impression of the immense growth of Indian Buddhist literature, we have to turn to the translations preserved in the languages of China, Japan and Tibet. In this labour of faith, the Tibetans were certainly the most successful, for they devised a more accurate and consistent means of translation than was possible in Chinese.

Also their proximity to Nepal and India rendered possible continuous cooperation between Indian and Nepalese and Tibetan masters, whereas the Chinese translator was often left to translate as he thought best. There will be occasion later to write of the Tibetan Canon in more detail, but it is important now to realize how much we rely upon it for an understanding of Buddhism even for the period preceding the introduction of the doctrine into Tibet itself. The Tibetans translated every Buddhist text they met with, texts which had originated at any time from the fifth century B.C. onwards.

The greater part of the texts they found were far later than this, usually from about the first century A.D. onwards. Moreover, we can be sure that whatever they did translate still formed part of the Indian Buddhist tradition in the eighth century and later. Therefore, the contents of their canon in themselves provide an accurate picture of later Indian Buddhism. So far as architectural and art forms are concerned, Nepal has preserved the most precious traces of what Buddhist India once was. The pagoda-type temple, which was already characteristic of the India of Yuan Chwang's times, but has now long since been replaced by other styles, was still being built in Nepal in the seventeenth century. Iconographic traditions continue even today and can be traced back directly to old Pala art of Bengal. An understanding of the last centuries of Buddhist India is essential for any just appreciation of Tibetan Buddhism. There are considerable means at our disposal for a reconstruction of the last centuries of Buddhist India.

The Texts

The basic meaning of both *sutras* and *tantras* is 'thread (of discourse)', but by and large they have come to be applied to different kinds of literary works. The texts to which we have chiefly to refer fall into two main categories, known as *sutras* and *tantras*. The *sutras* are mainly doctrinal in character. The earlier ones, such as those that appear in the Singhalese Canon, are historical or quasi-historical in character and represent the Sakya-Sage giving instruction to his followers at Rajgir or Benares or any other of their well-known places of sojourn in Magadha. The later ones present, with little serious attempt at historicity, a transcendent form of the sage, who gives instructions for the benefit of bodhisattvas in the new philosophical theories, commending the great career of the bodhisattva with its goal of buddhahood for all beings.

Although some of the philosophical ideas are abstruse, these texts are all reasonably straight-forward, if often monotonous to the extreme. They all, old and new alike, presuppose much the same sort of religious practice—namely, morality, concentration and wisdom—and they differ primarily in the end of their endeavour. The early disciples might hope to gain nirvana as the fruit of the striving of several lives. The bodhisattva looked forward to innumerable lives of effort and self-sacrifice throughout aeons of time. But all that was said in the previous chapter about the wheel of life applied to both equally, for there was no means of escaping the inevitable retribution for one's acts.

All being well, the early disciple would expect to continue to be reborn as a man with opportunities for practising the religious life until his course was run. The bodhisattva on the other hand possessed no such confidence. He must never lose hold of the thought of enlightenment, as expressed in his initial vow, and he was prepared to suffer in any of the spheres of existence for the welfare of all beings. The Mahayana is often represented as a way of faith and devotion, but it must not be thought to differ qualitatively from the earlier schools in this respect. The need for faith was stressed from the earliest times and there is no lack of evidence for quite fervid devotion towards the Master. The stupa and afterwards the buddha-image provided the focal-point of the cult. As has been emphasized above, these were not restricted to any one school.

The *tantras* are revealed by the Lord (*bhagavan,* about whose forms more will be said below) in a transcendent sphere of existence, and they differ from the *sutras,* old and new alike, by telling of an entirely different kind of practice, by means of which buddhahood can be gained in this very life. They contain magical spells, descriptions of divinities and sets of divinities arranged for meditational and ritual use, instructions in sacramental worship and in the bestowing of consecrations. These will all be discussed in detail, but their mere enumeration is sufficient to indicate that we are here presented with a very different form of religious practice.

These two types of text, *sutra* and *tantra,* are not entirely isolated from one another. Magical spells appear in several of the *sutras,* and at least two famous texts, which are known as *sutras* in the Sanskrit versions that are available to us, were firmly classed as *tantras* by the Tibetans.[2] There was inevitably a certain amount of mingling of the literary material. Some practices which would only gain their full effect as part of the ritual of the *tantras,* were also useful for straightforward devotional practices and so spells found their way into the *sutras.* Conversely, whenever the *tantras* appeal to philosophical considerations, the *sutras* provide their obvious source. Nevertheless as ways, they are quite distinct. A Buddhist often asks himself, I am following the *sutras* or *tantras.* In this they are repeating a question which was being asked in India 1,200 years ago. In the later days of Buddhism it was not *mahayana* and *hinayana* which presented themselves as alternatives, but *makayana* and *mantrayana,* that is to say, 'the way of spells', for it was by the use of spells that the ritual was characterized throughout. In these complicated rituals, far more than spells was involved, and so we must try to trace the various theories, beliefs and practices, which have come together in some form of coherent whole.

The Transcendent Buddha

More than one reference has been made to this continuity which exists throughout the whole historical development of Buddhism, and it was suggested that this continuity consisted primarily in the idea of a buddha, which has remained generally constant in content in spite of other changes in the doctrine. There is one particular conception of a buddha, which we may dismiss out of hand; namely, a buddha as a purely human teacher. This conception is a modern Western creation, and although it has been adopted by quite a number of Buddhists, whether from Ceylon or from Japan, who have come into contact with the West, it still remains no more than an attempted accommodation to present-day rationalist thinking.

Before a few Westerners began to suggest otherwise, no Buddhist, Singhalese, Japanese or Tibetan, conceived of a buddha other than as a transcendent being, and his canonical texts, in whatever language they were written, supported him in this view. It is indeed possible that there was a mere man, known as the Sage of the Sakyas, upon whom popular legends and cultural religious ideas centred themselves, but the point we must bear in mind is that it was belief in the supramundane being and not in a man, which accounts for the success of the doctrine in the first centuries throughout India and then later throughout the whole of the Far East. The most significant quality that attached to a buddha was royal dignity. His burial was to be that of a universal monarch and the symbol of his doctrine was the wheel of sovereignty. He was a Great

Man, repository of the thirty-two major marks and eighty minor marks of physical perfection. It is usually suggested that the idea of universal dominion entered India from the Middle East with the increase in communications which was one of the more beneficial results of the conquests of Alexander the Great. It is difficult to track down with certainty the traffic in ideas, for who can claim finally to separate the indigenous from the foreign? In India kings were never regarded as divine beings, but the theory would not have been unfamiliar, and it was certainly applicable to those who possessed power of another kind, namely, hermits who by their psychic power were thought to be able to coerce the gods. The Sakya-Sage was famed as a wonder-worker as well as a teacher, and with success and fame going hand in hand, he fulfilled all the beliefs and expectations of those times. This inevitably expressed itself in the texts. This process had already begun before his teaching established itself in Ceylon, but in India it continued to far greater lengths.

One has to look at the image of the preaching buddha, which appears so frequently at Ajanta, Nasik and elsewhere, and try to figure out the connection between these two some connection between these and the appearance of many texts. The early mahayana-sutras, of which *The Lotus of the Good Law* is the best known, are preached by the Sakya-Sage, who now appears as the Lord who shines transcendent at the centre of existence. As transcendent Lord, he turns the wheel of the doctrine. Iconographically this is represented by the thumbs and fingers of the two hands joined in front of the chest, and this is precisely the gesture of the buddhas of Ajanta and Nasik. At Nasik these buddhas are seated in what may be called the European posture, and this is also the posture in which the Kushan kings were carved. It is possible that we have here another suggestion of royalty.

Manjusri-mula-kapala

In the *Manjusri-mula-kalpa,* a voluminous text which represents the transitional: stage from *sutra* to *tantra* there is a description of the sovereign-buddha: 'He has the colour of saffron and is like the rising-sun. He holds a great wheel which is turning. He is like a great king with his crown and his decorations, a great being who is crowned and adorned with all adornments. His lower garment is of fine cloth and his upper garment of cloth of various colours. He is bewreathed and handsome, adorned with strands and garlands. He smells a wreath of flowers held in the right hand. He smiles just slightly. He is strong and mighty. Fair he is and handsome, neither young nor old. In his left hand he holds the wheel, wreathed in blazing light, which he is turning.' In this text generally, as in the *Lotus of the Good Law,* it is the Lord Sakyamuni, who occupies the central position, but it is a Sakya-Sage who has little to do with a wandering ascetic.[3]

It is not surprising therefore that in the texts that follow, the central figure, although still the Resplendent Lord, no longer goes by the name of Sakyamuni, but by that of Vairocana, which just means resplendent. The continuity is indicated by the preaching gesture, for from now on this pertains to Vairocana. One of the first texts in which Vairocana appears is the tantra *Symposium of Truth of all the Tathagatas (Sarva-tathagata—tattva-samgraba)* where before commencing his teaching, he manifests himself as representing the unity of all buddhas.[4] If we may revert once more to the previous chapter, it will be remembered that reference was made to the change of world-view which took place in the doctrine. Existence no longer proceeded along a temporal plane, but operated idealistically. Buddhas were therefore no longer conceived as following one another in time, but as manifesting themselves spontaneously from an undifferentiated absolute.

Centripetal Arrangement

There appears in the *Lotus of the Good Law* a centripetal arrangement of buddhas with two at each of the cardinal points and intermediate points of the compass. The emanative idealistic conception of buddhahood characterizes the whole of the *mahayana.* The set of five buddhas which is characteristic of the tantras merely conventionalizes this world-view in a form that accords with the several other sets of five. Just as personality consists of five components, so buddhahood is represented by five buddhas, and in accordance with the doctrine of the non-substantiality of everything whatsoever, both personality and buddhahood are equally void of subjective and objective content. This epitomizes the identity of samsara and nirvana, the realization of which is the prime object of the tantras.

As five-fold Lord the Lord (Vairocana) is no longer transcendent, for he becomes the symbol of the identity of samsara and nirvana. Thus, in the texts he appears as one when he instructs and as 'fivefold in the ritual.' This mingling of immanence and transcendence forms an essential part of the religious practice of Hinduism and the later Buddhism. One often finds the term pantheistic used of Indian religions, but its use merely reveals unawareness of the subtleties of these doctrines. The Lord, whether known successively as Sakyamuni, Vairocana or Vajradhara, remains preeminent, throughout the whole development of Indian Buddhism. The continuity of the doctrine consists in the notion of buddhahood. Although he may become manifest in any accepted form, he must always be recognized as the same in essence.

Other Buddhas and Bodhisattvas

Most of the names of the sixteen buddhas of the *Lotus of the Good Law* have the appearance of being pure invention. Names such as Lion-roar, Lion Banner of Victory, Space-abiding, Eternally Extinguished, can be nothing more than buddha-epithets. They serve no other purpose beyond the perfunctory supplying of the requisite number of names. But there are two among them, placed to the west and east respectively, who became important in the later developments. These are Amitayus (Boundless Life) and Akshobhya (Imperturbable). It is not unlikely that the cause of their enduring success is partly the mere succinctness of their names, but rather special associations are also involved.

The Imperturbable

The Buddha *Imperturbable* recalls the moment of enlightenment and the defeat of Mara, who retreats discomfited, leaving the victor unperturbed. When the buddhas came to be distinguished iconographically, his gesture was that of touching the earth with the right hand (earth-witness), thus clearly identifying this particular association. *Boundless Life* on the other hand suggests rather a general attribute of buddhahood, for one may remember that the early texts often speak of nirvana as the immortal or deathless state. It is typified iconographically by the gesture of blissful concentration, the hands together in the lap resting palm on palm. But there is another association, for this buddha was recognized as identical with Amitabha (Boundless Light).

The Iranian Influence

It has been often suggested that the whole idea of buddhahood as light is of Iranian origin, and this is quite plausible, for in the early centuries A.D. when the idea of buddhahood was open to new and developed interpretations, the empire of the Kushan kings bestrode both north-west India and Persia. But when one suggests influence of this kind, it is important at the same time to realize its limitations.

According to Iranian ideas, light and good stood in firm contrast to darkness and evil, but it is this very notion of duality, which the Buddhism of this period is most concerned to refute.

> 'There is no difference at all between nirvana and samsara,
> There is no difference at all between samsara and nirvana.
> What makes the limit of nirvana is also the limit of samsara.
> Between the two we cannot find the slightest shade of difference.'[5]

So influence there may well be, but no idea essentially foreign to the doctrine has found its way in. It would be wrong to think of a god of light entering buddhism in the name of Amitabha. Like the many other epithets, *Boundless Light* was adopted just as an attribute of buddhahood. At the same time, it is probably true that the enormous popularity of this particular buddha-name throughout Central Asia, China and Japan may be attributed largely to the importance of light in Iranian religion. No such exaggerated development seems to have taken place in India itself, where the buddhas remain not only doctrinally, but also in practice non-substantial, receiving conceptual form only in so far as they are united in the central idea of buddhahood and the person of the Lord. This will become clearer later on when we consider in some detail the fivefold set of buddhas and the interpretations placed upon it.

The Gentle-Voiced

Whereas in the early sutras the Sakya-Sage had addressed his disciples and hearers, in the later ones the audience consists of a vast concourse of bodhisattvas, *pratyeka-buddhas* and disciples, rendered the more impressive by interminable lists of names.[6] These names, like the names of the buddhas referred to above, are for the most part pure invention. Nevertheless there are one or two which are important for later developments. Maitreya, the next buddha-to-be, was the first to be named and is the only one known in the Singhalese Canon. His popularity has proved more widespread and more constant than that of any other bodhisattva.[16] The next is Manjusri, who is the foremost of mahayana bodhisattvas. He appears in the *Lotus of the Good Law,* fully conversant with the teachings which the Lord Sakyamuni is about to pronounce (whereas Maitreya is not), and throughout the *Manjusri-mula-kalpa* he is often represented as sovereign-lord. His full name is *Pancasikba*

Manjughosba, meaning Five-fold Crest and Gentle Voice. It is likely that the first was the original name and the second just an epithet.

As Gentle-Voiced, he became associated with the preaching buddha, appearing first as his lieutenant and then afterwards securing recognition as bodhisattva of Wisdom. He became generally known as Manjusri.—Glorious Gentle One—and *pancasikba* now appeared as the epithet. It caused difficulty and the explanations given betray the arbitrariness for which the Buddhists themselves were responsible. In the *Manjusri-mula-kalpa* it is understood as a gesture of the hand, representing the power of the bodhisattva. Later when his cult reached China, it was understood as *Manjusri* of the Five Peaks, and so it was assumed that he must have originally come from the China of the Five Sacred Mountains. This legend even reached India, and so still later we find Indians setting out on the long journey across Central Asia to China on pilgrimage to the abode of *Manjusri.*

The two next important bodhisattvas, *Avalokitesvara* (the Lord who directs his gaze downwards) and *Vajrapani* (thunderbolt in hand) seem to first rise to importance in the *Manjusri-Mula-kalp,* where they appear to the right and to the left of Sakyamuni, the one as foremost of the gods and the other as foremost of demon-magicians *(viyadhara).*[7] Manjusri is placed at the centre below Sakyamuni. This arrangement represents the beginning of the idea of sacred lineage which was later to play its part in the general fivefold arrangement. The lineage with which Avalokitesvara becomes associated is known as that of the *lotus,* presumably because the lotus was a commonly accepted emblem of the gods. The lineage which is represented by Vajrapani was known as the family of the *vajra* (thunderbolt), for this signified the power of powerful beings.

The central lineage was known simply as that of the *tathagata.* These three groups represent the three kinds of divine beings (only one of which was properly Buddhist) which were from now on accepted into the Buddhist fold. Their inclusion was justified by the belief that a bodhisattva might be born in any sphere of existence if it were but for the good of those beings. 'These are they who adopt any variety of *body* and act in accordance with any kind of practice, who do whatever is suitable for converting the minds of living beings and associate themselves with any suitable category. They understand the doctrine of the king of mantras and are perfected in the *dharma.* They appear in the lineage of the *tathagatas,* of the *lotus,* of the *vajra,* in any lineage on earth or in heaven. Without transgressing their vow, they devote themselves to the giving of instruction. They act without breaking from the family of the Three Jewels.'[8]

Lokeswara

It is interesting to speculate why Avalokitesvara should have appeared as head of the lotus-family. When he is first mentioned in the *Manjusri-mula-kalpa,* he appears quite insignificantly as one of a list of bodhisattvas: '. . . Dharmesvara, Abhavesvara, Sammatesvara, Lokesvara, Avalokitesvara, Sulokitesvara, Vilokitesvara, etc." Throughout the whole text the verbal form *avalokya = 'looking'* is used frequently of the Lord Sakyamuni before the discourse commences, and simply he-cause it indicated a well-marked buddha-gesture, this name may have lent itself readily to invocation. Having thus been hypostatized, he would very easily have become the peer of Lokesvara—'Lord of the World', viz. Siva. The Buddhists would not have invoked Lokesvara in the first place, for this would have been tantamount to recognizing a Hindu divinity, but having lighted on their own Great Being, they would willingly accord him overlordship of the world. They entrust to the powerful Vajrapani the task of dealing with Siva, who is forced into submission and only permitted to live on condition that he will acknowledge the supremacy of Three Jewels, thus becoming the first of those who bound themselves to be defenders of the doctrine.[9] Thus Buddhism developed, part fortuitous, part premeditated, like most human affairs.

Lord of the Yakshas

Vajrapani (thunderbolt-in-hand) is a more obvious choice of leader, where fierce divinities are concerned. He is also addressed as Lord of the Yakshas, thus implying a connection with still earlier Indian mythology, but he seems to be a completely Buddhist creation. There are several other bodhisattvas with analogous names: Supani (Good Hands), Anantapani (Limitless Hands), Kshitipani (World-in-Hand), Alokapani (Lamp-in-Hand), Ratnapani (Jewel-in-Hand). The last one in this list also became important later, but only because the jewel was an important religious symbol. Most of those who achieved any particular importance possess names of the kind that would clearly serve as buddha-epithets in invocations: Mahasthamaprapa (Possessed of Great Strength), Sarvanivaraviauvishkambin (Removing all Obstacles), Samantabhadra

(Entirely Good). This last name came to be applied later even to the supreme lord (Vairocana/Vajradhara).

The Five Buddhas

Though the development of a whole pantheon of buddhas, bodhisattvas and other divinities was largely haphazard, the arrangement of some of these into the sets, was the deliberate expression of the centripetal conception of existence. This we find in the tantras. Reference to this has been made above. Moreover far from pandering to popular taste, as they have sometimes been represented, the tantras were essentially secret rituals, which were on no account to be revealed to the uninitiated. 'Reveal nothing to those who have not seen the great circle of divinities *(mandala),* or the bond will certainly be broken!' Such is the admonition given to the pupil before his consecration into *The Symposium of Truth of all the Tathagatas.*

In the *Hevajra-tantra* one is warned that 'should anyone see the book or painting (of Hevajra), one will fail to gain perfection either in this world or the next. To one of our tradition it may be shown at any time, but on a journey the text should be hidden in the hair or under the arm'. This secret which is on no account to be revealed concerns in the first place the mandala itself with its fivefold set of divinities. Although some of the later tantras diverge from it with more elaborate arrangements, the fivefold set remains fundamental to them all, for it represents the simplest expression of the emanative nature of existence and the essential identity of samsara and nirvana. It is this that the pupil has to realize within himself by means of the ritual quoted below. The enactment of the rite must be preceded by normal instruction in the symbolism of the mandala with the object of producing understanding of a dialectical kind.

The ritual is intended to confirm this understanding in the form of absolute knowledge. The identity of samsara and nirvana is expressed by the equation of the simple sets of five, which are listed overleaf. Of these several sets only that of personality stems from the earliest period of Buddhism, but it was not then conceived of in the present centrifugal pattern. It is this personality which is resolved by purification into the condition of buddhahood, which by analogy also assumes a fivefold form. Likewise, the three basic evils of existence, desire, wrath and stupidity are extended to five by the addition of malignity and envy. In their condition of purification, these become the fivefold buddha-wisdom, Mirror-like Wisdom and the rest.

How the original threefold pattern, as typified by the three basic evils, persists behind the fivefold scheme it is interesting to study and observe. As has been shown above, the buddha-families were originally three, tathagata, lotus and vajra, and were devised in the first place as a means of finding place for non-Buddhist divinities within the Buddhist fold. These are also extended to five and by their equation with the five basic evils, it becomes logical to assign to such and such a family those living beings who show a preponderance in their personality of such and such an evil. Nevertheless the old set of three families is remembered in the set of Three Family Protectors, Manjusri, Avalokitesvara and Vajrapani, who are still commonly invoked in Nepal and Tibet.[10]

Likewise of the five buddhas, those who head the same three families, namely Vairocana, Amitabha and Akshobhya occupy a position of acknowledged preeminence. The three aspects of buddhahood, which come to the fore are sovereignty, light and power, which are the primary qualities of these three buddha-families. Although Vairocana is inseparable from the notion of sovereignty, his name actually means brilliance. It is thus significant that in the set of five buddhas of the *vajra-dhatu-mandala* which is found in the *Symposium of Truth.* Lokesvararaja (King of the Lords of the World) occupies the position, which is later unquestionably that of Amitabha. The two later families add no new definition to the nature of buddhahood, for the Jewel-Family of Ratnasambhava duplicates the aspect of sovereignty and the Karma-Family of Amoghasiddhi duplicates the aspect of power. The families are simply made up to five in order to accord with the requirements of the mandala.

The Five Buddhas and Their Equations

Direction	*Colour*	*Family*	*Family Symbol*	*Family Head*
Centre	White	Tathagata	wheel	Brilliant Vairocana
East	Blue	Vajra	vajra	Imperturbable *Akshobhya*
South	Yellow	Jewel	jewel	Jewel-Born *Ratnasambhava*

West	Red	Lotus	lotus	Boundless Light *Amitabha*
North	Green	Karma	sword	Infallible Success *Amoghasiddhi*

The Divinities of the Mandala

The divinities of a mandala always consist of the Lord and his entourage *(gtso-'khor)*. Thus, the *vajra-dhatu-mandala,* which represents a basic type, consists of Vairocana as central Lord with the other four buddhas as his four aspects at the main points of the compass, each of whom is accompanied by attendant bodhisattvas. The act of worship itself is symbolized by eight goddesses, who likewise may be associated two by two with the four directional buddhas. Their names are:

Vajra-Gaity	Vajra-Flower
Vajra-Garland	Vajra-Incense
Vajra-Song	Vajra-Lamp
Vajra-Dance	Vajra-Perfume

The Five Buddhas and Their Equations

Buddha Gesture	*Types of Wisdom*	*Type of Evil*	*Components of Personality*
Preaching	Pure Absolute	Stupidity	Form
Earth-witness	Mirror-Like	Wrath	Consciousness
Giving	Discriminating	Desire	Feelings
Meditation	Sameness	Malignity	Perception
Dauntlessness	Active	Envy	Impulses

Inconsistency in Numbers and Names

The number and the names of the attendant bodhisattvas are not consistent, for there may be two or four in each of the directions, and since the layout becomes purely schematic, few of them remain faithful to their original families. Thus, whereas Avalokitesvara remains firmly in the Lotus-Family, Vijrapani may be found in attendance on Amoghasiddhi. Vairocana as Lord has no need of a special bodhisattva, in that the whole circle forms his entourage. Thus, Manjusri moves to Amitabha's family. On the other hand Ratnapani (Jewel-in-Hand), conditioned by his very name, remains faithful to the jewel-family of

Ratnasambhava. Since these sets are inconstant, it will clarify nothing to list them here.[11]

The Circle

The circle is protected in each of the four directions by a fierce divinity, usually characterized by a hook, a noose, a fetter and a crossed-thunderbolt. They are known as:

Vajra-Hook *(Vajrankusa)*	—	East
Vajra-Noose *(Vajrapasy)*	—	South
Vajra-Burst *(Vajrasphota)*	—	West
Vajra-Fury *(Vajravesa)*	—	North

Furthermore each of the families of the four directions is represented vocally by a special spell *(mantra)* and corporeally by a special hand-gesture *(mudra)*. Since in the following ritual the pupil is consecrated as Vajrasattva *(Vajra-Being)*, the spell and gesture of the vajra-family will be in use. These spells are not constant, but in the case of the *Symposium of Truth*, from which the extract is taken, they are:

Sattva-vajri for Akshobhya
Ratna-vajri for Ratnasambhava
Dharma-vajri for Lokesvararaja
Karma-vajri for Amoghasidhi.

The ritual is essentially a combination of gesture *(mudra)*, spell *(mantra)* and concentrated thought *(dhyana)*, which corresponds with the common threefold formula of personality, namely Body, Speech and Mind, all of which must play a correlated part in the rite.

The Rite of Consecration

Attention has been drawn to the notion of universal sovereignty which was always associated with buddhahood, and now we come to the logical and practical development of this idea. Just as a man may be consecrated to kingship, so a would-be buddha must be consecrated to buddhahood, and the rite, if properly performed, will be infallibly efficacious. In the sections of the *Manjusri-mula-kalpa*, which describe this rite, there are constant references to ordinary regal consecration, and it is reasonable to assume that we have here the beginnings of such a ceremony in Buddhist circles. The consecration is performed by means of eight ritual jars, which are first dedicated to Sakyamuni, all buddhas, pratyekabuddhas and early disciples, great bodhisattvas, Manjusri, all divinities, all spirits, all living beings. Afterwards they are placed by the master against the pupil's head. Another important part of the ceremony is the possession by the pupil of the appropriate spell *(mantra).*

The Symposium of Truth

This is revealed by his being blind-folded and throwing a flower into the circle where the buddhas, bodhisattvas and so on are depicted. 'Wherever the flower falls, he should be given the *mantra* of the (being) there. This *mantra* must be revealed to him as his own. It is connected with him throughout his birth-series, It is the virtuous friend *(kalyanamitra)* who will bring him to enlightenment and so act as to perfect completely the all-knowing wisdom of the great bodhisattvas.'[12] At this period, possibly the fifth century A.D., the fivefold scheme had not yet been elaborated. *The Symposium of Truth* represents a considerable development. There are no longer direct references to brahmanical ritual, for the whole practice has been completely coordinated into a buddhist setting. The naive arrangement of the three families (viz. Sakyamuni and Manjusri at the centre with Avalokitesvara and Vajrapani to either side) is replaced by the centripetal arrangement with a buddha at each point of the compass. Moreover the circle of idealized existence *(mandala)* is now represented in its most elaborate form: a temple-palace with gates to the four quarters, an abode more fit perhaps for a universal sovereign than for the body of all the buddhas. Such symbolism leaves no doubt of the intended nature of buddhahood.

The Mandala

With a good new thread, well-woven and of the proper length, the mandala should be measured out by a man well-skilled who tries his best. It must be four-sided with four gates and adorned with four portals, hung with four cords and bewreathed with garlands and flowers. Then one should mark the outer circle of the mandala, adorning it with *vajras* and jewels, thus filling the interstices between the four corners and the limits of the gates. Then coming inside this outer ring, one should encircle it with a ring of *vajras* like a wheel. It is equipped with eight pillars and on the inside of these vajra-pillars it is adorned with five lunar discs. At the centre of the central disc one should place the buddha-image. Then in the centre of the discs of the buddha-directions one should place the four supreme guarantees. Approaching those four discs with a vajra-tread, one should place there all the four buddhas, Akshobhya and the rest.

> In Akshobhya's circle one must place Vajrapani and the rest,
>
> In Ratnasambhava's circle Vajragarbha and the rest,
>
> In Amitayus' circle Vajralocana *(rdo-rje-spyan)* and the rest,
>
> In Amoghasiddhi's circle Visvavajra *(rdo-rje-rgya-gram)* and the rest,
>
> On the outer corners of the mandala one should place (the goddesses of) the buddha-offerings.
>
> At the four gates one should place the four guardians.
>
> On the outer edge of the mandala one should place Great Beings *(mahasattva).'*

Now first the pupil should make four obeisances to all the tathagatas.[13] Bending his whole body in the vajra-salutation, he makes obeisance and pronounces this *mantra;*

> OM I OFFER MYSELF AS THE PLACE OF WORSHIP FOR ALL THE TATHAGATAS.
>
> MAY VAJRASATTVA, ALL THE TATHAGATAS, EMPOWER ME.

Then returning to his former position, he makes the vajra-salutation in front of his breast, and then touching the ground with his forehead in obeisance, he pronounces this *mantra:*

> OM I OFFER MYSELF FOR CONSECRATION IN THE WORSHIP OF ALL THE TATHAGATAS.
>
> MAY VAJRA DHARMA, ALL THE TATHAGATAS, PROMOTE ME.

Returning to his former position, he makes the vajra-salutation on the top of his head; then making obeisance flat on his face, he pronounces this *mantra:*

> OM I OFFER MYSELF FOR THE PROMOTION OF THE WORSHIP OF ALL THE TATHAGATAS.
>
> MAY VAJRARAKARMA, ALL THE TATHAGATAS, CONSECRATE ME

The Ritual

Then returning to his former position, he brings his hands down from the top of his head, and placing them before his breast, he touches the ground with his forehead in salutation and pronounces this *mantra:*

> OM I OFFER MYSELF FOR THE ACT OF WORSHIP OF ALL THE TILL-TATHAGATAS.
>
> MAY VAJRARATNA, ALL THE TATHAGATAS, ACT UPON ME

Then he should put on a red upper garment and one should wind a red cloth over his face. Making the hand-gesture which is called *sattvavajri'*, one should recite this *mantra: SAMAYA HUM*. Then one should make him hold the garland of flowers between his two middle fingers, and leading him forward, one again says: *SAMAYA HUM*. Then as soon as one has brought him to the mandala, one should instruct him in this wise: "Today you are entering the family of all the tathagatas, and so if I cause you to obtain that knowledge by which all the tathagatas are perfected, what need be said of other perfections?

Since vajra-knowledge of this kind will arise in you, say nothing to those who have not seen the great circle of the divinities, or the bond will certainly be broken." Then the vajra-master, making the Sattvavajri-gesture, which he shows from the inside and the out, places it upon the vajra-pupil's head and says: "This is your vajra-bond. If you tell anyone, your skull will burst apart." Then having empowered (the sacrificial water) with the bond-gesture and with the special *mantra* for the water of the oath, he should get the pupil to drink it. This is the *mantra* of the oath: "To-day Vajrasattva himself has entered into your heart. If you speak of the process, you will split open and burst. *OM VAJRA-VAJRA-WATER* THAN vajra-vajra-water than."

Then he should instruct the pupil in this way: "Since from to-day onwards, as far as you are concerned, I am Vajradhara, you must do whatever I order you to do. You must not speak ill of me. If you fail to avoid evil, you will certainly fall into hell when you die." Then he commands the pupil to say: "May all the tathagatas bless me and may Vajrasattva descend to me." Then the master quickly makes the *sattvavajri*-gesture and gets the pupil to say: "This is the vajra-bond, which is proclaimed as Vajrasattva, Even to-day may the supreme vajra-knowledge descend. OM VIJRA-DESCENT A."

The Perfection

Then he makes the wrathful gesture and forming the *sattvavajri*-gesture, he draws forth its power. He then gets the pupil to recite whatever vajra-verse he pleases that pertains to knowledge of the Great Way. Then (the power) descends, and as soon as it descends, divine knowledge manifests itself, and by means of that knowledge he will know the thoughts of others. He will know all that must come about in the past, in the future and in the present. His mind will be confirmed in all the teachings of the tathagatas. All his suffering will be at an end. He will be freed of all fears and nothing will harm him. He will be blessed by all great beings and by all tathagatas. All perfections will become manifest in him. Joy and gladness and gleeful happiness such as he has never known before without special cause will arise in him. At the manifestation of these joys, some will experience profound calm, some will bring all spells to fruition, some all their hopes, and some will arrive at the perfection of all the tathagatas.

The Practices

Then making the gesture, he should release it in front of his heart and pronounce this *mantra: "O VAJRA STAY, BE FIRM FOR ME, BE ETERNAL FOR ME. EMPOWE MY HEART AND GRANT ME ALL PERFECTION. HUM -HA HA-HA HA HO."* Then he should throw the garland of flowers into the mandala and say: *"RECEIVE, O VAJRA, HO."* Then wherever it falls, he performs that (particular spell). Taking up the garland, he makes the (appropriate) gesture over his (pupil's) head with that spell, making him say: *"OM RECEIVE ME, O THOU BEING OF CREAT STRENGTH* strength" One makes the appropriate gesture and that great being makes (the practiser) his own, and so it is quickly done. At the descent (of the divinity), the cloth round the face is removed and the pupil should be made to pronounce this spell:

"OM VAJRASATTVA . . .

HE OF ALL EYES, THE VAJRA-EYED, MAKES MANIFEST,
SEE SUBLIMITY, HEVAJRA!"

The Blessings

Then he is shown the great circle in due order. As soon as he sees the great circle, he receives the blessing of all the tathagatas. Moreover Vajrasattva dwells in his heart. Because he is blessed by all the tathagatas, he will see circles of light-rays of different colours and so on, and phantom shapes and forms, and the great lord Vajradhara himself or the person of one of the tathagatas will become manifest. Thereafter he will succeed in all things, from whatever needful things he wants to the realization of the nature of Vajradhara or the tathagatas.

Then after having seen the great mandala he should be consecrated with the sacrificial water of the Vajra-blessed jar and with this mantra: "OM VAJRA—I CONSECRATE."

Then making the appropriate gesture, one should mark his sign on his hand and say: "To-day the tathagatas bestow upon you the vajra-consecration. Take this vajra for the sake of the perfection of all the buddhas. OM I CONSECRATE YOU LORD OF THE VAJRA. BE FIRM O VAJRA-BOND HUM."

Then with this mantra one gives the name-consecration: "OM—I CONSECRATE THEE VJRASATTVA AND BY THIS CONSECRATION YOUR VAJRA-NAME IS...HEVAJRA!"

The Translation of Rymns

The translation of this passage is very much a *tour de force,* but it should suffice as an example of the style and nature of the tantras. The Tibetans, conscious of the mysterious power of the spells, left these untranslated, for the potency was felt to reside in the sound rather than in the sense. Thus, for those who are unskilled in Sanskrit (and nowadays most Tibetan monks know nothing of it) these spells are nothing more than a string of meaningless syllables. But at least the Tibetan script lends itself to the transliterating of Sanskrit. The Chinese translators also left these spells untranslated, representing them syllable by syllable with Chinese characters of approximate sound. It is indeed doubtful whether a complete translation of any tantra from such a medium. Can be attempted.

Magical power Vajrasattva is represented by the *vajra,* and is all important in the tantras. It is inevitably the symbolism of the vajra-family that comes to the fore. Thus the buddha, who was placed to the centre of the mandala, although properly Vairocana is here known as Vajradhara (Holder of the Vajra). The pupil is entering the family of all the tathagatas but the symbolic gesture employed is called *sattvavajri* and he becomes identifiable with Vajrasattva, the bodhisattva who is associated with Akshobhya. Thus, in the later tantras Akshobhya is placed at the centre, Vairocana taking Akshobhya's place in the east.[14]

Vajradhara/Vajrasattva becomes then a sixth and supreme buddha, and all continuity seems to be lost in the line of development: Sakyamuni, sovereign-buddha, Vairocana, to which we referred above. In reality, however, the continuity, although unmarked, is still there. At every stage there is only one essential buddha, and perhaps nothing can make this more clear than the directions (already quoted) for laying out the *vajra-dhatu-mandala:* at the centre one places the buddha and in the four directions the guarantees of unity with him *(samaya).*

It is imagined that the pupil has a special affinity with one of these guarantees, because of a predominance of wrath or ignorance or passion or envy or malignity in his nature. Thus:

> Akshobhya's *vajra*-family is also called the family of wrath,
> Vairocana's *tathagata*-family is called the family of stupidity,
> Amitayus/Amitabha's *lotus*-family is called the family of passion,
> Ratnasambhava's *jewel*-family is called the family of envy,
> Amoghasiddhi's *karma*-family is called the family of malignity.

Irasian Beliefs and Buddhist Mahayana

In the mere listing of these equations one is made immediately aware of the fundamental difference between Iranian beliefs in general and the whole Buddhist Mahayana. Wrath and the other evils merely represent the nature of *samsara* (phenomenal existence), and since *samstara* and *nirvana* are essentially identical, these five evils are indentifiable with the five buddhas. Good does not overcome evil. Evil is transmuted into good. Buddhahood is but the experimental knowledge of their identity.

One must observe, however, that the law of *karma* still applies, for evil will always bear its fruits in hell and good will earn the delights of heaven, for ultimately unreal as both may be, they are real enough to the unenlightened who experience them. Buddhism moves quite logically from a moral to an entirely amoral viewpoint. The early schools preached morality as part of the necessary means towards nirvana. One must exercise such personal control that the non-virtuous elements *(akusaladharma)* cease to manifest themselves.

The Mahayana still preached morality, but they also taught its complete relativity. Charity, righteousness and fore-bearance are great perfections, but useless for the gaining of buddhahood unless they are permeated with the perfection of wisdom, which is the doctrine of the essential emptiness of all concepts. Moreover the one thing necessary for ultimate buddhahood is the thought of enlightenment *(bodbicitta)*. Only he will be saved from the consequences of all his deeds, who clings to this.

The Vajrayana in its extreme form brutally rejected the practising of virtue as a means to an end, for if the end is realizable here and now, why concern oneself with relative truths? 'In the matter of introducing the pupil to the mandala one should make no distinction between who is suitable and who is unsuitable. And should you ask why, it is because beings, even though they have committed great evil, if they but enter into this great *vajra-dhatu-mandala* and see it, they will be freed from all types of wretched rebirth. Even those beings who cling to wealth and food and drink and desirable things, who take no pleasure in the vow and are not proficient in the preliminaries and so on, even they, by acting in accordance with their understanding and entering the mandala, will bring to perfection what they have in mind.'[15]

The mandala is the sphere of the divinity with whom the practiser identifies himself, thus exercising the power which pertains to the divinity. The acquisition of buddhahood was merely a special application of a general magical practice, for there were mandalas of all sorts and sizes. The tantras refer to rites of all kinds: petrifying, subduing, exorcizing, causing hatred amongst one's enemies, mesmerizing, slaying, propitiating, causing prosperity, bringing rain, winning a woman, finding a thing which was lost and so on.

After the higher type of *mantra*-practice, which was illustrated above, it may be useful to have before us examples of a lower kind.

The Ritual for Goddess Vajra

In order to petrify someone 'one should mentally produce the goddess Vajra, who becoming manifest from the syllable AM is white in colour. She treads upon a corpse and holds a knife, a skull and the gruesome wand.[16] One should worship her as prescribed, repeating the spell: OM HUM SVAHA one hundred thousand times. Then one should write in chalk the syllable MAM on a dish of unbaked clay. In the middle of it one should place the spell: OM HUM MAKE SUCH AND SUCH A ONE STAY HUM SVAHA. Then one must fill it with ashes from a funeral pyre, place another unbaked dish on top to serve as a cover, and on top of this draw the square mandala of the god Mahendra. Then place it on the ground, put you foot on it and repeat the "staying-still" spell one hundred and eight or one thousand times: OM HUM MAKE SUCH A ONE STAY HUM SVAHA. Then he will be made to stay.'

In order to cause hatred 'one should meditate on the goddess Vajrayogini with the syllable U and one should imagine the syllable **JRIM** dark blue in colour on a solar disc at the heart. One should worship her as prescribed, repeating the spell: OM JRIM SVAHA one hundred thousand times. Then one should imagine the two against whom the rite is to be practised as mounted on a horse and a buffalo and as fighting together. One repeats the spell: OM JRIM VAJRADAKINI CAUSE SO AND SO TO HATE SO AND SO JRIM HUM HUM HUM PHAT and it will certainly cause them to hate one another.'[17]

The Rites

Of these many rites four were singled out and endowed with some symbolic significance as special powers of buddhahood, namely pacifying, prospering, empowerment and destroying. The rest were never more than simple magic and it might seem that they set the tone of the tantras generally, consecration ceremonies included. Certainly the means employed are identical. One conjures forth the divinity, identifies oneself with him by means of his mystic spell and so appropriates his powers. The five buddhas and their attendant divinities in the mandala each possess their mystic spell. By the throwing of the flower the pupil discovers with which of them he personally has affinity and consequently to which buddha-family he belongs. In his practice he must concentrate upon his own divinity, so that he like the divinity may be consubstantiated in final buddahood.

The Family of Wrath

It is easy to forget that Buddhists and Hindus were one and the same people. They practised their religions in the same cultural *milieu,* and so it would be strange indeed if their beliefs were not analogous and even sometimes identical. Divine beings appeared in Buddhism just because Buddhists themselves believed in them. At first they were called bodhisattvas and given Buddhist-sounding names, but afterwards no one bothered with these artificial distinctions. Sarasvati, the spouse of Brahma, was accepted as the spouse of Manjusri, the Buddhist counterpart of Brahma. Avalokitesvara was recognized as Lokesvara, and so long as his identity with Siva was ignored, Nartesvara (Lord of the Dance) was equally welcome. So too were Halahala, Lokanath, Nilakantha, who were all accepted as forms of Lokesvara. Then came Jambhala, god of wealth, and his spouse, Vasudhara, the powerful goddess Kurukulla and the saviouress Tara. Equally welcome were the fierce divinities, Bhairava (the Terrible), Canda-roshana (Fierce and Wrathful), Samvara, Heruka and Hayagriva (the horse-necked God). All these except the last were assigned to the vajra-family, the family of wrath, where they might appear as fierce forms of Akshobhya, implicitly receiving buddha-rank. If it is asked with surprise how such brutish forms should have found so high a place in the Buddhist pantheon, the only proper answer is that Buddhists believed in them, and so a place for them was found. Tibetans will tell one nowadays that they are defenders of the doctrine and so the nature of their duties makes them fierce. But this is only part of the truth. Indians have never conceived of existence as fundamentally good. They have been aware rather of its cruelty and its voraciousness and so they conceived many of their gods accordingly.

Dual Appearancis

Nevertheless these fierce beings could only be properly absorbed into a Buddhist tradition in so far as it was possible to bring them into relationship with other members of the pantheon. There thus developed the theory of gentle and fierce aspects of the same divinity and this was quite in accordance with the fundamental teaching of the relativity of good and evil, of samsara and nirvana. Since the final truth will reveal the essential sameness of these pairs of concepts, so the devotee must know the single nature in the dual appearances. Thus, the five buddhas came to be paralleled by a fivefold manifestation of the fearful Heruka:

Vairocana	Buddha-Heruka[18] (pl. 9)
Akshobhya	Vajra-Heruka
Ratnasambhava	Ratna-Heruka
Amitabha	Padma-Heruka
Amoghasiddhi	Karma-Heruka.

Fundamental Pattern

It is interesting to observe that however great may be the divergence between the Buddhism of the early schools and the stage we have now reached, nothing new has been adopted without first ensuring that it should accord with the doctrinal position. The doctrine itself still remained consciously Buddhist and what is more remarkable still continued to do so, even when feminine partners were introduced into the system. One should note also that Hindu divinities of first rank, Mahadeva (Siva), Vishnu, the Goddess Kali, Mahakala (the Great Black One), Rahula (god of the eclipse), were permitted entry only in the capacity of defenders of the doctrine. So long as these were kept in their place, it seems that almost any name might find a place in the higher Buddhist circles. Hence, there has developed an enormous variety of mandalas to the bewilderment of anyone who attempts to gain a full acquaintance with the gods of Tibetan Buddhism. Nevertheless the fundamental pattern and mental process remain the same.

The central requirement is an appropriate divinity. For normal magical rites this should be the god or goddess who is especially associated with the task in hand. For the attaining of spiritual powers and eventually buddhahood, it must be one of the divinities who is associated with the five buddhas in the mandala. Therefore, the pupil casts the flower so that he may know with which divinity he is personally associated. In practice, however, a monk often just accepts as his chosen divinity the one who is representative of his order or his monastery. This divinity becomes his guarantor (Tibetan: *yi-dam)* and he enters into a condition of union with him by a process of continual meditation.

The Consecration

'Imagine that from the seed in your own heart you send forth a ray, and by means of this ray which is shining black in colour and has the form of a hook, you should draw in the buddhas who are stationed throughout the triple world, and having worshipped them in company with the eight attendant goddesses, you should beseech them saying: OM MAY ALL THE BUDDHAS CONSECRATE ME. Then you will be consecrated by those buddhas, all of whom assume the form of Heruka, with the five jars which symbolize the five tathagatas and contain the five ambrosias. . . . When you have been thus consecrated the Lord of your Family will appear above your head and Heruka is manifest in you. Performing morning, noon and night this meditation which bestows such power, when you arise, you should remain at all times consubstantiated with the divinity.'[19]

It is by constant practice of this kind that the pupil must realize in himself the truth, which was first revealed to him by his master in the mandala. In theory even the initial consecration must accord with the character of the pupil. Thus, the *Symposium of Truth,* from which we extracted the description of the *vajra-dhatu-mandala* quoted above, also contains fivc-buddha mandalas suitable for the lotus and jewel families, in which naturally the symbols of lotus and jewel predominate. But in any studies of the tantras, one must not permit oneself to be bewildered by the mere appearance of diversity.

Feminine Partners

In India, as in many other countries, the gods were often so anthropomorphized as to be represented as marrying and begetting offspring. At least from the times of the epics this was so. But this had no influence upon Indian conceptions of transcendent being, whether conceived as *nirvana* or *brahman.* Nor was it to be expected that ascetics who abandoned their homes for a homeless state, whether Buddhist or Jain or orthodox brahmans, would conceive of a divine being as male and female in character. Their goal in any case was an impersonal absolute, in which all human distinctions and all human passions were annulled. Yet feminine divinities were not unknown even in Vedic times, where they appear as the personification of natural phenomena: Prthvi, the earth, Ushas, the dawn, Sarasvati, the goddess of knowledge. Most important of all was *Vac,* the word. It was through her that Prajapati, the Lord of all creatures, produced this creation. Later Sarasvati, possibly because of her fertilizing powers, was identified with Vac and came to be regarded as the partner of Brahma. She was then regarded by Buddhists at a later stage as the partner of the peculiarly brahmanical bodhisattva, Manjusri. There is no need for us to follow the development of these different goddesses, for they all tended eventually to accord with one basic form, that of the Great Mother Goddess, in whom they all more or less lost their separate identities. Moreover it is in the type of Mother Goddess that we can so clearly distinguish the Buddhist from the Hindu tantras.

Mother Goddess

We have referred frequently to the general tendency of all accretions to adapt themselves to the already existent tradition, and we observe the same tendency at work now that the Buddhist pantheon is swelled by numerous feminine forms. Whereas in the Hindu tantras the Mother

Goddess was typified in the spouse of Siva and known as Parvati, Kali or Durga, the active blood-demanding partner of a lord who would without her have remained in the deep sleep of the undifferentiating absolute, in the Buddhist tantras the feminine partner is in every case a form of Prajnaparamita, the Perfection of Wisdom, the tranquil Void. The roles are in fact the very opposite of those found in the Hindu tantras. Hence the term *sakti,* 'energy', which is applied to Siva's partner, is completely inapplicable in the Buddhist tantras.[20] Here, she is known usually just as *prajna,* 'wisdom', or as Mother, Yogini or Symbol (mudra). It is the male partner who represents the energetic element, for he embodies the compassionate activity and skill in means which are the essential characteristics of the bodhisattva. Thus, it comes about that all buddhas and bodhisattvas may be represented either as single or as dual. If present their partners partake of the nature of the individual buddha-families. Thus:

Locana belongs to Akshobhya's vajra-family and is blue;
Mamaki belongs to Ratnasambhava's jewel-family and is yellow;
Panduravasini belongs to Amitabha's lotus-family and is red;
Tara belongs to Amoghasiddhi's karma-family and is green.[21]

Position in the Mandala

Their normal position in the mandala of the five buddhas is at the intermediate points of the compass and in the general process of equating samsara and nirvana, they symbolize the four gross elements, earth, water, fire and air. This position presumably precedes their actual partnership with the buddhas themselves and at this later stage it becomes necessary to provide a partner for Vairocana at the centre. This central goddess is with rare exception a complete abstraction, bearing the title of Lady of the Sphere of Space *(Akasadhatvisvari)* or Lady of the Adamantine Sphere *(Vajradhatvisvari)* or She who takes the Lead *(Nayika)* or just Absence of Self-Nature *(Nairatmya).*[22]

Likewise the partner of the fierce Buddha-Heruka is just named Lady of Wrath *(Krodhesvari)* and she is particularized in the different directions merely by prefixing to this name vajra-, lotus- or whatever it may be. The great goddesses of Hinduism, Kali and Ekajata, are accepted in a purely subservient role as defenders of the doctrine and are never permitted to intrude within the mandala.

Thus, when sexual symbolism establishes itself in Buddhism, it is immediately identified with the traditional philosophical and doctrinal concepts of the Mahayana. Final enlightenment was the realization of the essential unity of an apparent duality, which might be expressed from several different viewpoints:

samsara	compassion	subject	consonants
nirvana	wisdom	object	vowels

Existence

Existence is the diversity of *samsara* and *nirvana* and enlightenment is their unity. The career of the bodhisattva is the practice of compassion and wisdom in equal measures and the consummation of his career is their final unity. Subject and object are the two supports of phenomenal existence and their final merging is the end of existence. The mystic syllables and spells consist of consonants and vowels and their proper combination effects the intention of the practiser. A new term becomes current in the sense of final perfection, namely 'two-in-one' (Sanskrit: *yuganaddha,* Tibetan: *zung-jug*), just because the fundamental pattern of existence was conceived as unity in apparent duality.

Compassion/Wisdom

The pair compassion/wisdom subsumes all the perfections of the earlier Mahayana and so its praises are constantly being sung by the tantric yogins.[23] It represents the essential nature of the inmost buddha Vajrasattva and of the triple buddha-body. This pair is sometimes known as Wisdom and Compassion and sometimes as Wisdom and Means. Compassion and Means are practically synonomous. 'Because one is passionately devoted to all beings who have failed to extricate themselves from a whole flood of suffering, this passionate devotion of which their suffering is the cause is known as Compassion. In that one thereby brings a man to the desired end by a combination of appropriate measures, it is also called the Means.'[24] Hence, Wisdom and Means or Compassion represent the foremost significance with which the coupled figures are endowed. 'Twofold is the Innate, for Wisdom is the woman and Means is the man.'[25]

Lotus and Vajra

More subtle symbolism was also used. The lotus represents wisdom and the vajra represents means. The reader will remember that in the

Manjusri-mulakalpa the families of lotus and vajra were placed on either side of the Lord, thus suggesting the general notion of two as manifest from one. These two terms came later to be endowed with a sexual significance, so that the expression 'union of vajra and lotus' could refer as much to the ritual union of the yogin and the yogini as to the consummation of the bodhisattva's career. For the followers of the tantras, these were in any case essentially the same thing. It is the practice of using terms capable of different kinds of interpretation, which render the tantras seemingly difficult to understand. When one has grasped the essential idea however, one ceases to wonder whether one interpretation is to be preferred to another, although in translation it may be necessary to choose one at the expense of the others.

It is not to be pretended of course that the female partners were introduced for the sake of mere symbolism and no more. In some circles they were used for the ritual enactment of the Wisdom/Means union. Indeed it is often assumed that late Indian Buddhism was corrupted precisely by the introduction of sexual ritual. This, however, is quite untrue, for Buddhism seems finally to have remained faithful to its traditions, even when it met with these practices. They had their origin in circles which were neither properly Hindu nor Buddhist and it would be impossible to say how long they had previously continued. The crudity of the beliefs is revealed in the actual texts of the later Buddhist tantras. Thus, in the *Hevajra-tantra* we read: 'A man who has been hanged, a warrior killed on the field of battle and one who has been born seven times as a brahmin, of the flesh of these one should partake.[26]

In the company where this verse originated it was no doubt believed that by eating his flesh one could appropriate to oneself the lost years of one whose life had been cut short or the innate power of one so virtuous that throughout seven rebirths he had always been born as a brahmin. What is important to observe, however, is that the very earliest commentators were already interpreting these injunctions in a completely Buddhist sense. It means no more, they say, than the consuming of the notion of a self. Instances of this kind could be multiplied. It seems therefore that the texts themselves reveal a class of yogins who really performed all the rituals referred to and who were at the same time imbued with certain fundamental Buddhist notions, which they were not concerned to distinguish from non-Buddhist formulations. Thus, the supreme knowledge is described as 'pure and void like the sky, the essence of existence and non-existence, a mingling of Wisdom and Means', but it is also equated with 'all other things that there are: the universal consciousness, the primaeval man, the Lord, the self *(atman)*. the soul *(jiva)*, essence, time, the person.[27]

Free Wandering Yogins

Their experiences, justified as they could only be—by success, were taken note of in the monasteries, where the texts were finally written down and commentaries, always Buddhist in intention, were prepared. It would be quite erroneous to assume that the literal contents of these tantras describe the type of life led by the monks of the great monasteries of Vajrasana, Vikramasila and Nalanda. The references are all to yogins who wander free from all ties, coming together with their fellows only for the seasons and at the places of pilgrimage. Such fellows are still characteristic of the Indian scene.[28] Both Buddhist and Shaivite tradition preserve the memory of eighty-four great yogins or perfected ones *(siddha)*. Their biographies are to be found in the Tibetan canon, and although the tales related of them are of no direct historical worth, they portray well enough the general religious setting, in which the actual tantric texts originated. These eighty-four Great Perfect Ones are still revered by the Buddhists of Tibet, for whom they represent the first transmitters of the occult doctrines (pls. 10 and 11). Their central divinity is the Holder of the Vajra (Vajradhara) who was already, as has been shown above, the central buddha of the earlier class of tantras, and thus appearance of continuity is maintained. The period to which these great yogins are to be assigned seems to reach from about the seventh to the eleventh centuries.[29] They form several lines of succession, for since the doctrines were secret, they could only be transmitted from master to pupil. Altogether they represent a strange collection of people, brahmins, kings, scribes, huntsmen, weavers, etc., who abandoning their rank and caste, acquire from their chosen master super-human powers, do good in the world and conduct living beings to heaven.

Goal of Perfection

In these popular accounts the goal of perfection seems to be immortality in the form of eternal youth. In fact it was as always the all-resolving trance. This becomes quite clear from the mystical verses of several of these yogins which have been preserved in translation in the Tibetan canon and a few of them even in the proto-Bengali in which they were originally composed.[30] Some of them were monks and even abbots and at the last stage of Buddhism in India one may conceive of the relationship of monks and yogins to be much as it has continued to this day in Tibet. The monasteries are primarily seats of learning and places of worship, whose inmates follow the safe but slow way of the sutras, namely, the practice of conventional morality, the reciting of texts, performing of ceremonies and immersion into bouts of meditation. There have always been certain natures who remain dissatisfied with such methods and aspire to experience here and now the conviction of permanent release. India and Tibet have always counted amongst the great variety of those who practice religion in one form or another some who are held to have finally reached their goal.

Conventional Morality

Success of this kind is achieved at the price of complete renunciation and such men have lived apart from society, even monastic society, and often in complete revolt against it. Hence, one will find sometimes a deliberate denial of the value of the conventional religious practices:

'Will one gain release, abiding in meditation?'
What's the use of lamps?
What's the use of offerings?
What's to be done by reliance on mantras?'
'Mantras and tantras, meditation and concentration.'
They are all a cause of self-deception'.

Only one way can lead to complete realization of the truth and that is contact with one who already knows.

'If the word of one's master but enter the heart, '
It is like a treasure in the palm of one's hand'.[31]

Weakening of Scholastic Tradition

One easily tends to regard late Buddhism as debased just because from the seventh century there was a marked weakening of the scholastic tradition. But it would be just as plausible to point to a new flowering of religious genius as a result of the new impulse of life which was received from the non-scholastic yogins. In any case we have firm evidence of both trends entering Tibet. On the one hand we have the typical scholar, the Great Translator Rin-chen S'ang-po, about whom more will be said in a later chapter, and on the other the supreme type of yogin, Mila Rapa, who draws his experience direct from the circle of Indian yogins.[32] Both aspects of a religion are necessary if it is to be a vital force, and both were certainly present in India at the time when the religion was transferred to Tibet, where they have persisted to the present day. No one would pretend of course that Tibetan monks are all models of virtue; it matters merely that some are. Nor would one insist that the Indian yogin or the Tibetan nal-jor-pa always possess the knowledge and the powers attributed to them; it matters only that some do bear witness to an extraordinary perfection of spiritual equilibrium through the writings they have left us. Probably Saraha on the Indian and Mila Rapa on the Tibetan side present the finest examples.

The Internal Mandala

It is of course extremely difficult to write of experiences and modes of training, which were intended to be secret and which in any case could not be committed explicitly to writing. The basic texts were certainly the tantras, whose unattractive features can easily perturb the modern scholar. But then one must remember that they were not interpreted verbally. The union of the yogin and the yogini is an internal psycho-physical process, the whole symbolism of which is sexual. Just as in the mundane sphere the union of man and woman produces a consummation of bliss, so the reintegration of the severed personality produces the full awareness of its transcendent unity and concurrently of its unlimited potentiality. As the desired condition is the realization of the essential identity of microcosm and macrocosm, so the whole symbolism is transferred within the body of the yogin. We have referred above to the external mandala as representing the essential identity of buddhahood, personality and phenomenal existence.

Unity of Wisdom and Means

The body of the yogin is now conceived as representing the unity of Wisdom and Means or in other terms of yogin and yogini. It becomes the active repository of the process of the realization of the 'two-in-one'. Thus, its main arteries are three: the one to the left is known as *Lalana* and like Wisdom is feminine; the one to the right is known as *Rasana* and like Means is masculine; the one in the centre is known generally as *Avadhuti*, sometimes as *Candali* or just as the *Yogini*. The two outside arteries join the central one at its base. The yogin by controlling and stilling his breath through the left and right nostrils induces the psychic energy, which flows in the two arteries to unite at the base of the central one. This union corresponds with sexual union, and the psychic energy in the arteries is indeed conceived as blood and semen. Their mingling is the birth of the Thought of Enlightenment, which, in the more conventional Mahayana practice, represented the beginning of the bodhisattva's career. Here, the act is endowed with a quasi-physical significance. In the yogin's body there are four psychic centres, envisaged as lotuses, transpierced by. the central vein and level with the navel, the heart, the throat and the top of the head. The Thought of Enlightenment must be consciously raised up the central vein, passing the four psychic centres and pervading the body with bliss as it goes up. These four stages are related to various other sets of four, which characterize other meditative and ritualistic practices. Thus, they are equated with four grades of consecration, of the kind we have considered above; also with four moments and four joys, which in the tantras mark the different stages of the sexual ritual.

Buddha-Bodies

Perhaps most important of all, they are also equated with the buddha-bodies: at the heart is the *Dharma-kaya,* at the throat the *Sambhoga-kaya* at the navel the *Nirmana-kaya* and at the top of the head the Self-Existent Body, which absorbs the other three.[33] The texts can be most bewildering when they write of these equations, for everything and anything must be located within the body without regard for apparent contradictions. Also the notion of two-in-one can be envisaged in different manners, for although the chief representation is that of the veins to left and right, the base and head of the body serve the same symbolism. Thus, the union of the psychic energies at the base of the Central vein brings Candali or the Yogini blazing into life. She rises, finally uniting with her Lord in the head. Thus, the mind (represented by the head) is male and the physical (represented by the lower regions) is female, and here we find a scheme which accords properly with the Hindu tantras, but not with the Buddhist. Sometimes the raising of the Thought of Enlightenment suggests the actual passing up the body of the male fluid, as though it were transmuted from its coarse condition into the Self-Existent Buddha-Body. These are just different modes of expressing the same experience.

'There is bliss when Candali-blazes in the body.

There is bliss when the veins Lalana and Rasana enter Avadhuti.

There is bliss when the flow of the Thought of Enlightenment descends from above.

There is bliss when the translucent male fluid pervades from below.

There is bliss from their loving when the white (masculine) and the red (feminine) come together at the centre.

There is bliss from contentment when the body is purified.

Sixfold is the bliss of the experience of yoga.'[34]

When the Tibetans set about systematizing the tantras, they placed in the highest class, namely that of the Supreme Yoga Tantras *(anuttarayogatantra)* those very texts, which seem to prove the most disconcerting to the western reader. Thus, two of the most revered, the Guhyasamajatantra and the *Hevajratantra,* refer explicitly to the meetings of yogins and yoginis, to the sexual ritual, to the eating of unpleasant sacramental food. But as the commentaries make clear, they were placed in the highest class, because they were interpreted and practised simply as internal yoga. There remains the interesting problem of how such texts came to be put to a use, which seems to be more successful in achieving results than modern psychology. Perhaps the eighty-four Great Perfect Ones are more deserving of our esteem than their biographies would allow.

NOTES

1. The term *tantric,* popularized in European and modern Indian works, has no basis in any Sanskrit adjectival form. This form of Buddhism is known either as *mantrayana,* the Way of Spells, or *vajrayana,* the Adamantine Way. Nevertheless the term is apt, for it characterizes that whole development which is based on the class of texts known as *tantras*. It could be adequately glossed by *ritualistic* and it should certainly not be pervaded by the sense of opprobrium which some writers have attached to it.
2. The *Suvarnaprabhbasottama-sutra* and the *Manjusri-mula-kalpa.*
3. *muni* sage; Tib. *sba-kya-tbub-pa.*
4. The Tibetan Text is in *Nr. Kj. rgyud,* Vol. vii. Of the Sanskrit the opening verses will be found in Indrabhuti's *Jnanasiddhi, GOS,* xliv, p. 81. See also p. 63 fn.
5. See Stcherbatsky, *Nirvana,* p. 77 (Nagarjuna's *Madhyamakakarika,* XXV 19-20.)
6. A *pratyeka-buddha* is the solitary sage of Indian religious life. The

Buddhists were willing to include these solitary practisers in their ranks, accounting them as the followers of another Way *(yana)*. The followers of the Mahayana classed them with the Disciples *(sravakas)* as followers of an interior way *(Binayana)*.

7. See J. Przyluski, 'Les Vidyaraja,' *BEFEO*, 1923, p. 301ff.
8. *MMK*, p. 9, line 12 ff.
9. This event is recorded in *STTS*, Part 4 *(Nr. Kj.rgyud* vii, folio 291*b*, ff.). A fragment of Sanskrit text, found by G. Tucci, has been edited and translated by him in *Ind-Tib.*, Vol. I, p. 135 ff.
10. See p. 116.
11. For examples refer to the arrangement at Tabo, p.184, and to the mandala of the Tranquil Divinities, p. 231.
12. *MMK*, p. 49, l. 19ff.
13. The names given to the four tathagatas in these mantras accord with their individual spells as given above on p. 68. They are each addressed as representing all the tathagatas and at the same time one particular aspect of buddhahood. It is impossible to bring this out fully in the translation. Vajrasattva (Akshobhya) is associated with the place (literally: establishing) viz. the vajra'throne *(vajrasana)* upon which every buddha symbolically (in the earlier conception—literally) establishes himself. Vajraratna (Ratnasambhava) represents the consummation of buddhahood, conceived as a consecration in a regal sense. Vajradharma (Lokesvararaja/Amitayus) represents the promoting (literally: causing to turn) of (the wheel of) the *dharma*. Vajrakarma (Amoghasiddhi) represents the effectiveness of the *dharma* in its tantric form.
14. See *Buddhist Texts*, p. 247.
15. *STTS*, folio 252a.
16. This is the *khatvanga*, a rod upon which three human heads are transfixed, one freshly severed, one decomposed and one already a skull. The rod is topped by a trident. See pi. 23 where it is being held by Padmasambhava.
17. *Yogaratnamala* (commentary to *Hevajra-tantra)*, Part I, ch. 2. 77.
18. See p. 205.
19. *Hevajra-tantra*, Patt I, ch. 4.
20. I quote a general observation of Prof. Bourda, which although applied by him to another argument, would fit the present one juts as well. 'Rien n'est.
21. See also pp. 114-15.
22. An exception is Vajravarahl (p. 210 fn.).
23. see *Buddbist Texts*, p. 240 ff.
24. *Ibid.*, p. 241.
25. *Hevajra-Tantra*, Part I, ch. 8.
26. *Ibid.*, Part I, ch. 7.

27. *Ibid.*, Part I, ch. 10.
28. See G. W. Briggs, *Gorakhnatb and the Kanpbata Yogis.*
29. See Sankrtyayana, 'Recherches Bouddhiques: L'Origine du Vajrayana et les 84 siddhas'.JA, 225, 1934, pp. 218-30; also Tucci, *TPS*, I, p. 226 ff.
30. See 'Saraha's Treasury of Songs', *Buddhist Texts, p.* 224 ff.
31. *op. cit.*, pp. 226 and 227.
32. See W. Y. Evans-Wentz, *Tibet's Great Yogi Milarepa,* O.U.P.(London) 1928.
33. The technical terms relating to this internal mandala are fully discussed in my Introduction to the *Hevajra-Tantra.*
34. B. Laufer, *Aus den Gestbithen and Litdern des Milaraspa,* p. 20.

Index

M

N

T

U

V

W

Y

Z